Churches in Struggle

Churches in Struggle

Liberation Theologies and Social Change in North America

edited by William K. Tabb

**Monthly Review Press
New York**

Library of Congress Cataloging in Publication Data

Churches in Struggle

1. Sociology, Christian—North America.
2. Liberation theology.   3. Christianity and politics.
4. Communism and Christianity.   I. Tabb, William K.
BT738.C54   1986   261.8   86-5285

ISBN 0-85345-692-5
ISBN 0-85345-693-3 (pbk.)

Monthly Review Press
122 West 27th Street
New York, NY 10001

Manufactured in the United States of America

10   9   8   7   6   5   4   3   2

To the millions of "theologians"
who are creating theologies of liberation
and transforming the world

To Sergio Torres and Virginia Fabella,
and the other "reverse missionaries"
whom the United States has needed for so long

To Paul Sweezy and Harry Magdoff,
who know that rigor in their science means
that nothing human is alien to them

Contents

Part II
Reclaiming the Christian Message
for the North American Churches

Part III
Marxism and Religion

Part IV
Theology Rooted in the Community

Part V
Political Activism
and the Mission of the Church

Acknowledgments

A number of people helped in the making of this book. They include Bobbye Ortiz and Karen Judd at Monthly Review Press; those many contributors who were also active in the planning stages; and a number of individuals who were of assistance at different points in the process: Ruth Harris, Paul Surlis, Nora Quiroga Boots, Joe Holland, William Sloan Coffin, Pablo Richard, William Wipfler, Balfour Brickner, Dieter Hessel, Terry Cambias, John Eagleson, Pat Hines, Shirley Cloyes, Liz Bounds, Marty Zimmerman, Rob Kogol, Rosalinda Ramirez, Jean Woo, Robert Goldberg, Hal Recinos, Franklin Woo, David Kalke, John Collins, Virginia Fabella, and Sergio Torres. Thanks most of all to Susan Lowes at Monthly Review Press, who has skillfully, with humor and insight, played a major role in shaping this book.

Introduction: Transformative Theologies and the Commandment to Do Justice

William K. Tabb

In the spring of 1984, Paul Sweezy and Harry Magdoff, the editors of *Monthly Review,* were urged by Bobbye Ortiz to do a special summer issue on "Religion and the Left." Over lunch one day, as I was suggesting people who might be asked to write essays, Harry asked me how I knew about this subject and why I had not told him before about this thing called Liberation Theology. Without rehearsing my many attempts on previous occasions to explain to Marxists that there are huge numbers of committed Christians who in their practice challenge injustice, it is perhaps useful to say something about my own involvement. It is only because of a unique and perhaps accidental set of circumstances that I was privileged to be a participant in events that were not accessible to other nonchurch socialists.

In 1973, after the coup in Chile that overthrew Salvador Allende, Father Sergio Torres, a Chilean priest active in the Liberation Theology movement, came to the United States and decided to facilitate the process of introducing Liberation Theology to North Americans by building an interracial, interreligious community of progressive church people in the United States, similar in inspiration to those that have developed in Latin America. I am an economist and happened to be in the office of the Union for Radical Political Economics when Father Torres called for help. I soon found myself at the headquarters of the Maryknoll Fathers, a Catholic order involved in missionary work, acting as an economics consultant at a planning session out of which came an exciting project called Theology in the Americas. TIA is unique in its effort to bring together all those who work in communities of struggle for social justice and to build a unity that both respects diversity of group identity and reflects faith commitment in actions in the world.

I have been back to Maryknoll many times since then, and have been significantly influenced by individual Maryknoll sisters and fathers, lay missionaries, and the people at the Maryknoll publishing house, Orbis Books. The commitment to doing justice in the spirit of love and humility, rarely seen in secular circles, draws me back to be refreshed and strengthened again and again.

The essays in this book, while written by individuals, are in a real sense the reflection of the creativity of social movements and religious groups that are committed to the struggle for economic and social justice and see the biblical message as a profoundly radical one: that God is active in history, siding with the oppressed in their struggle for liberation. The theology of such groups is shaped by their praxis. Responding to their God's desire that they do justice, they act and reflect on their actions in the light of their reading of the Bible. In the United States, many of those inspired by such an understanding of their religion have been influenced by third world theologies—in particular, but not solely, by the movement known as Liberation Theology that has developed in Latin America. Because Liberation Theology is historically specific to Latin America, I would have preferred to adopt an entirely different term—transformative theologies—to describe those new theologies that are developing both in the third world and in the United States, and that are described and discussed in this book. But the term "liberation theology" has become so accepted that it seems unnecessary to create linguistic confusion by insisting on a new term. Thus in this book the plural, liberation theologies, will be used to encompass all those theologies that have in common a commitment to do justice and transform social reality as a fulfillment of the biblical message.

All the "new" theological interpretations are seeking to revitalize the Christian religion by going back to the Bible, re-reading it through the eyes of the poor and oppressed, the people to whom Jesus first preached his good news. In one way, then, they are not new at all. But they seem so, because the biblical message has long been a captive of the principalities and powers of the world, which have sought to domesticate those radical impulses that are at the center of all religions at their birth. New religions—from Judaism to Christianity to the many other religions of the world—are created when an articulation of what is wrong with the current order coincides with a statement of an alternative vision so powerful that it compels large numbers of people to accept its truth. Yet over time this all-encompassing coherence becomes lost, as institution-building takes precedence over belief and the new church gains a vested interest in the material trappings of power and influence. The descendants of those who were touched by the spirit of the original power of the faith only know the ritual; they have moved far from the central beliefs of the original commitment. The Old Testament tells this story in terms of Israel, which, forsaking its convenant with God, becomes an imperialist power, its kings then called to task by the prophets. In a sense, then, what Christians today call Liberation Theology is not really a new idea for those Jews who claim a continous heritage of—in the words of the prophet Micah—knowing God by doing justice. Indeed, once the battle for acceptance of the legitimacy of Liberation Theology is over, continuity will develop as an important moment in this theological process.

But the essays in this book deal less with the continuities of the Judeo-Christian tradition and more with the task of reconnecting with these earlier understandings in a different historical context, a context of suffering and oppression in the third world. Out of this situation has come a new way of doing theology, from the vantage point of the poor, the sufferers. In each nation, each area, a new theology has arisen, one that melds the different experiences of national culture, regional church, and denominational community into a unique theological reflection. And the good news has traveled from the exploited outer regions of the third world to the exploiting metropolitan centers in that center of the first world, the United States, until the affluent churches of suburban North America echo with feelings, words, and concerns of those who will no longer collaborate in the oppression of their brothers and sisters, either in their own country or abroad.

The rejection of possessive individualism, of national chauvinism, and of the implicit racism that characterizes the American notion of patriotism is both a return to the ethical beliefs of an earlier Christianity and a challenge to the secular religion of America, which celebrates getting rich and being important as reflections of God's favor. For the theologies of liberation, the central message of the Bible is that to know God is to do justice, and that women, men, and nations are to be judged by how they treat the most vulnerable members of the human family, rather than by the rituals they observe or their private experiences of conversion, which leave the individual's social role unchanged.

Yet in the United States today it is commonly believed that religion is a personal matter, and that conversion involves the acceptance of Christ as a personal savior. Such an individualistic religious stance is often wed to a conservative political outlook in which the United States stands for the good, while the Soviet Union stands for the evil empire, the devil incarnate, and in which freedom is to be ensured by military virility and wise all-knowing authority figures, who—like God himself—are powerful, white, and male. We see ourselves as God's chosen people, in our virture fit to lead the "Free World," which is composed of lesser peoples infected by socialism, full of poorer nations that can accomplish much if they would only follow our lead.

Although this picture of the religious community in the United States is extreme, even liberal Protestantism is, in some of its versions, a more sophisticated celebration of America's chosenness, with a similar implicit acceptance of our elect status as the leader of other nations. Versions of liberal Protestantism that are more imbued with social gospel thinking do challenge such elitist notions of the rightness of the class, race, and gender hierarchies that exist today, but until very recently they have had privileged access to the nation's decision-makers and have accepted the position of advisors to the powerful, rather than a role as their adversaries. Thus religion, for most Americans, has offered comfort, not a challenge, to our world view and way of life.

This book was planned with the goal of introducing the religious left to the secular left, and one of its aims is to overcome the suspicion and even hostility that exists between two groups of people who should be allies and who have much to learn from each other. Just as Christians who are new to a serious consideration of the possible relevance of socialism can be confused by the fifty-seven varieties of Marxist, Marxist-Leninist, socialist humanist, Trotskyist, Maoist, and other labels competing for attention, so secular leftists confronting their need to rethink the possible progressive content of religious movements and church dogma face a bewildering array of viewpoints and practice.

To many secular leftists, even the stances taken by the progressive churches are full of contradictions. Thus progressive churches seem more aware of the suffering of black South Africans than of the role the United States plays in aiding South Africa's destabilization of Angola, more sympathetic in their understanding of the feminization of poverty than willing to come to terms with the class basis of that poverty. To secular leftists, then, the antipathy to the concept of class struggle, the emphasis on reconciliation, the belief in the possibility of convincing the powerful to change their ways and become more sensitive to the needs of the poor disqualifies even the progressive church from serious consideration as a source of transformation.

Yet perhaps this view is the result of misunderstanding—or partial understanding. For it can be argued that the strands of the emerging theologies of liberation that are represented in this book show a religious understanding that does have a revolutionary potential, one that is having a ripple effect in the progressive mainstream churches in North America. This is an exceedingly important development, and secular leftists need not embrace "religion," or uncritically accept that all progressive church people share with them a common understanding of either social reality or analytic method, to recognize that there are common interests and overlapping values. The hostility to religion that exists on the left will continue as long as the appeal of religion seems to be based on superstition, otherworldliness, a blind faith in authority and dogma, and a willingness to attribute to the supernatural that which is the creation of flesh-and-blood men and women.

But criticism of this type of religion—of religion that denies the creative intervention of ordinary human beings, that refuses to allow them to reflect on their own reality and to act upon it to bring about justice—is in fact part of the critique of mainstream religion mounted by liberation theologians. For these are truly *transformative theologies* which call upon people to act to create a just world. That the inspiration for such a praxis is religious need not be a barrier to cooperation between secular and religious activists.

The similarities between Marxism and liberation theologies come in an implicit and explicit class analysis, in giving economic institutions and their core social relations a central place in the analysis, and in seeing unequal power and participation in our society as the result of unequal control over the means of production. That human beings make their own history within the constraints of existing power relations, that they can be united around common interests and oppressions, and that they can understand the forces that oppress them and envision an alternative social order—all these are points of shared belief for both liberation theologians and Marxists.

By reclaiming the Christian message of liberation, people of faith are offering a profound challenge to institutions of injustice and to the pillars of our economic system, whether they know it or not. To those who equate any challenge to the status quo, no matter how motivated, with Communism, the struggle to reclaim the biblical understanding of justice is called Communist. And the fact that liberation theologies are in many respects consistent with much Marxist analysis—although not with Soviet state practices or other self-serving interpretations of Marx—makes it easier for critics of liberation theologies to label their opponents Communist. But there are *not* two choices, Soviet Communism or U.S. capitalism, as the powers that be would have us believe. That is one of the secrets of liberation theologies. For them, there is at least one other choice, and that derives from the biblically based notion of social justice, which has little in common with either Soviet-style communism or U.S. capitalism. There is no need to choose the lesser of two evils— and *that* is what scares the guardians of the system under which we live.

Ironically, in our so-called free society there cannot at this point in time be an open discussion of Marxism without the charge of "Communist" coming to the fore. Perhaps this is because the defenders of the system know that although Soviet Communism as it is presented to the populace here is not attractive to North Americans, there may be much in Marxism that would be if Marx were studied and understood. But whether this is true or not, it is marginal to what liberation theologies are about. A language that rings as authentically indigenous to North American culture is being forged in the progressive churches. This too is of historic significance. The idiom of liberation theology, the methodology of personal reflection, the social activism and political organization discussed in the essays that follow—all these come from a belief system that is based on an original vision of Christianity. This, not Communism, is the spector that now haunts the principalities and powers of the world.

At a time in U.S. history when the religious right speaks effectively to people's insecurities and to their easily aroused fears, liberation theologies offer an alternative religious discourse that appeals to the best in the collective consciousness. Because liberation theologies respect both individual needs and identities built in community, they are tolerant of other belief systems. They therefore stand in stark opposition to uniformity-demanding visions of a "Christian America." They judge people by their fidelity to love and justice commandments, and not to whether they believe in rituals or personalistic saviors and elect salvation by a faith divorced from how one lives in society.

These are exciting times. The emergence of liberation theologies among peoples and communities marginalized by the powers of this world is an important political fact of our time. A new church is emerging out of a reflection on the original texts in the light of the realities of human suffering today. The inspiration that the more affluent mainstream churches of North America have received from their sisters and brothers to the south has profoundly shaken the comfortable and challenged them to a new understanding of faith. It is important for both the secular community and for church and synagogue goers to understand the theologies and transformative impulses that are revitalizing the religious life of millions of fellow believers. This volume is an introduction, a start in this process of mutual acquaintance.

Part I

Theologies of Liberation

The essays in this section discuss the new theologies of liberation that are developing outside the Euro-American white male religious mainstream and are influencing the church both in the third world and, increasingly, in North America as well. These theologies proclaim that the central meaning of the Bible lies in the stories of struggle, liberation, and redemption in which God takes the side of the oppressed. Thus Exodus is the exemplary story of God seeing injustice, taking the side of the afflicted, and helping the people to bring about their own liberation. "I know their sufferings," God tells Moses, "and I have come down to deliver them out of the land of the Egyptians, and to bring them up out of that land to a good and broad land" (Exodus 3:7–8). Similarly in the New Testament: here the central event is described in Luke 4:18–19, where Jesus proclaims what can only be seen as a revolutionary message, the likes of which humankind had never heard before. He announces that God has sent him to bring the good news to the poor, to release the captives, to recover sight to the blind, to set at liberty those who are oppressed, and to proclaim the acceptable year of the Lord—the jubilee year when debts will be forgiven, liberty granted to all inhabitants, and land redistributed so that all can share in the collective fruits of God's gifts and of human labor (Leviticus 25:1–24). Such social relations are "acceptable" to the Lord. The basic theme, then, is that those who do not do justice do not know God.

Liberation theologies with these basic themes are developing in many parts of the world—in Latin America, in Asia, in Africa, each with its own language, each reflecting its particular cultural and historical setting, but all reflecting on oppression and asking how God would have us act. In Korea, for instance, Minjung theology, or "people's theology"—a poor translation for a very complex idea—is mounting a profound challenge to accommodationist views of the message of the Bible. It sees the Christian task as the creation of the just society God wills, and of a theology built from the bottom up by the little people, who are God's children.

All such theologies are a leaven for societal transformation, and, while not directly political, necessarily have profound political impact if their mission is carried out. And all such theologies are theologies of liberation, but it is what has come to be known as Liberation Theology, which has developed in Latin America, that has had the most profound influence on the North American context. Within the Protestant churches in the United States, but particularly among Catholics, Liberation Theology presents an ecclesiastic challenge to the church hierarchy, a challenge not only to take sides, but to *change* sides.

In Latin America, in part because there was no other refuge from the oppressive tyranny of the police, the army, and the landowners, the church became a center of resistance and a place to reflect on social reality. In countries where to criticize injustice is to court death but where religious belief is officially venerated, reading the Bible with other people became a powerful way of expressing solidarity. What happens when people read together and share their understanding of those biblical passages that bring good news to the captives? In such a context, how do these "communities of the base" (as they have come to be called) understand the following biblical passages?

• Learn to do good; seek justice, correct oppression . . . (Isaiah 1:17)

• Is not this the fast that I choose: to loose the bonds of wickedness, to undo the thongs of the yoke, to let the oppressed go free, and to break every yoke? (Isaiah 58:6)

• But let justice roll down like waters, and righteousness like an ever-flowing stream. (Amos 5:24)

• And what does the Lord require of you but to do justice, and to love kindness, and to walk humbly with your God? (Micah 6:8)

• He has filled the hungry with good things, and the rich he has sent empty away. (Luke 1:53)

These are not isolated passages. To Liberation Theologians they, along with the biblical stories of God's intervention, provide a radical message, one that if taken seriously has enormous political consequences. For the oppressed, and for those who stand in solidarity with them, to accept the message of liberation as the will of God is to follow the way of the cross, and such a path cannot be chosen without acknowledging the risks. As Oscar Romero, El Salvador's beloved bishop who was murdered by death squads even as he officiated in his cathedral, said, "One who is committed to the poor must run the same fate as the poor. And in El Salvador we know what the fate of the poor signifies: to disappear, to be tortured, to be captive—and to be found dead."

It is perhaps understandable that the oppressed, the marginalized, and the scorned read such texts as the message of God's partisanship—as proclaiming what theologians today call the "preferential option for the poor"—but the comfortable, those who receive the benefits from the system of exploitation, are more likely to spiritualize the message, or to call these quaint Bible stories, or to say that God was around in the world in biblical times but is not now. The first two essays in this section, by Robert McAfee Brown and Rosemary Ruether, focus on the disjuncture between the way that affluent communities and those who understand the Bible from the perspective of the preferential option for the poor can read the same texts and find very different meanings in them.

While it is certainly true that the sharpness of the Latin American struggle, occurring as it has on a continent with strong religious institutions and commitments, has provided fertile soil for the flowering of the mustard seed of Liberation Theology, the initial claim to an almost total uniqueness on the part of some of its exponents has, as a result of contact with the theology of other oppressed groups, given way to an awareness of a universal thread that connects the experiences and theological reflections of all peoples in struggle. Thus the situation of North American blacks, as James Cone demonstrates in his essay, encourages a reading of the gospel message that is similar to that of Latin American Liberation Theologians. Yet it is not that Black Theology derives from Liberation Theology—indeed, as Cone argues, Black Theology antedates the published work of the Latin American Liberation Theologians—but rather that the experience of oppression provides a perspective out of which all theologies of liberation emerge. Blacks in the United States, reflecting on their own history as strangers in a strange land, have also come to recognize this as a new way of doing theology. Martin Luther King, Jr., in one of his last speeches, preached an understanding that parallels that of Oscar Romero:

> On the one hand, we are called to play the Good Samaritan on life's roadside; but that will be only an initial act. One day we must come to

see that the whole Jericho road must be transformed so that men and women will not constantly be beaten and robbed as they make their journey on life's highway. True compassion is more than flinging a coin to a beggar; it is not haphazard and superficial. It comes to see that an edifice which produces beggars needs restructuring.

In an interview in 1982, Jose Miguez-Bonino of Argentina, a leading Protestant Liberation Theologian, discussed the evolution of third world theology:

> An important evolution in Third World theology is the recognition the participants from the different continents have of the need to adjust themselves to a wider understanding of theology. Take Africa, for example. Countries there have become independent only recently. They are still struggling for their cultural and religious identity. They have been colonized, not only politically but also culturally. So liberation for them means liberation from foreign culture; it means finding their traditional identity in the African context of traditional religions and African anthropology. The Asians, as I mentioned before, have to face other problems, such as the strong cultural and religious influence of the ancient religions of the Orient—Buddhism and Hinduism.
>
> So today we all recognize that we need one other and that Liberation Theology in Latin America is but a part. We still have to work to find the common elements of this Third World theology. I think that in the beginning we were naive in saying that Liberation Theology is equivalent to Third World theology. Africa and Asia have something very important to contribute to this dialogue. We Latin Americans have learned a lot from our brothers and sisters of Africa and Asia.[1]

A third theology of liberation has been developed by feminists, as Elizabeth Schüssler Fiorenza's essay demonstrates. Feminists trace the ban against women's equality within the church through the Apostolic constitutions of the third and fourth centuries, the precursors of the current ban on women being ordained or giving the sacrament by the Catholic church. They have traced the long and disappointing misogynous history of the exclusion of women from equal participation in God's community as interpreted by patriarchy. Although feminist theology is now a recognized alternative theology—in large part because so many women have been engaged in this struggle in our times—most of its proponents do not see it as attempting to win a place as the single "correct" theology (as Euro-American male theology has been). As Rosemary Ruether has written:

> Theology should overcome patterns of thought within it that vilify or exclude persons by gender, race, or religion. But this does not mean that we seek a theology that is universalistic in the sense of encompass-

ing all cultures and religions. Such universalism is, in fact, cultural imperialism—an attempt by one religious culture to monopolize not only theology but salvation, to claim that it alone has authentic access to the divine. Christian patriarchal theology has typically been imperialistic, claiming that white male Christian experience is equivalent to universal humanity.[2]

Feminist theologians are instead restating the norms and methods of theology in the light of their critique, "acting as constructive theologians for a contemporary community of faith." Such a critique is attempting to create a "contemporary understanding of church which seeks to live its faith as repentance of sexism, exodus from patriarchy, and entrance into a new humanity."[3]

Marc Ellis, a synagogue-attending Jew who works on the staff of the Maryknoll Fathers, is the final contributor to this section. Like the liberation, black, and feminist theologies of today (and like earlier Christianity), Judaism originated as part of a radical challenge to the society in which it was born. Ellis argues that Judaism, again like Christianity, is in need of getting back in touch with its roots, in this case the prophetic tradition that nurtured the faith of an oppressed people. Jews today must therefore reassess their place in the world in the light of a rereading of their history from the Old Testament, and, importantly, in the light of a self-definition that has been profoundly—and often contradictorily—reshaped by the experience of the Holocaust, the defining experience for many (perhaps most) contemporary Jews.[4]

There seems little doubt that we have entered a period in our nation's history which, rather than being one in which religion will wither away as modernism and science progress, is one in which dislocation, suffering, and injustice have created a climate where restorative movements can flourish. Many of these are conservative and backward-looking, and are in fact—albeit unwittingly—fostering the development of the very forces that create suffering in the first place. But others—those that develop a practice that reflects on injustice in the light of biblical faith—are developing a theology that inspires those who would be part of the project of the liberation of the oppressed and the transformation of our societal institutions.

Notes

1. "Signs of the Kingdom Are Many in Latin America," *A New Way of Being Church* (Lima: Latin American Press, 1984), p. 38.

2. Rosemary Ruether, "Feminist Theology in the Academy," *Christianity and Crisis,* 4 March 1985, p. 57. She cites I Timothy 2:12 to illustrate that the attempt to exclude women as subjects of theology begins at least within the New Testament: "I permit no women to teach or to have authority over men; she is to keep silent."
3. Ibid., p. 60.
4. Readers are encouraged to read the important critiques of this paper that appeared in the first issue of *Doing Theology in the United States* (Spring/Summer 1985), a publication of Theology in the Americas. Ellis's interlocutors were from the Pacific/Asian American, black, Hispanic, Christian, and traditional indigenous, women's, and alternative (Euro-American) theology projects, and they raised a number of useful questions in a fruitful dialogue. *DTUS* is available from TIA, Room 1244AA, 475 Riverside Drive, New York, NY 10115. It promises to be an important vehicle for the exchange of ideas concerning transformative theologies in North America.

The "Preferential Option for the Poor" and the Renewal of Faith

Robert McAfee Brown

Most North American church members, pastors, and theologians are rendered uncomfortable by the phrase "preferential option for the poor." This is because most North American church members, pastors, and theologians are not poor; their nervousness is heightened by the hunch that if the church is called to make a "preferential option for the poor" that excludes them, and that if *God* is making a "preferential option for the poor," they are in even deeper trouble.

The phrase, when it arrived on the theological scene, was not initially threatening because it originated in the Latin American church and could be safely confined, it was assumed, within churches to the south of the Río Grande, a slogan for "down there" that need not be taken seriously "up here." Implicit in the documents of the Roman Catholic bishops at Medellín, Colombia, in 1968, the theme became explicit in their report at Puebla, Mexico, in 1979.[1]

But it is no longer possible to view the "preferential option for the poor" as an exotic cultural expression of folks unlike ourselves, for the United States Catholic Bishops, in the first draft of their letter on the economy, adopted the phrase and fleshed it out in relation to the North American scene.[2] In subsequent discussions of the draft much attention centered on the phrase, and we can be sure that Roman Catholic conservatives will try to get it excised from later drafts. I believe that it should not only be retained but strengthened, so as to provide a centerpiece for the document as a whole. It contains not only a key to the task of the Latin American church, but the North American church as well.

1

It is important, first of all, to be clear about the phrase itself. To speak of a "preferential option for the poor" is not to speak about an "exclusive" option for the poor, as though God loved only the poor and did not love anybody else, especially the rich. What is being claimed is that in responding to the long-range concern God has for *all* people, and (to employ a familiar phrase) for "liberty and justice *for all*," one starts with an immediate concern for, and involvement with, the poor. To the degree that the cries of the poor are given priority over the complaints of the rich, there can be movement toward a society that is more, rather than less, just. The bishops themselves adopt this perspective: *"Our fundamental norm is this: will the decision or policy help the poor and deprived members of the human community and enable them to become more active participants in economic life?"*[3]

This claim would seem unexceptionable in terms of any Christian theology and ethics derived from the Old Testament prophets and the teachings of Jesus (especially in the gospel of Luke), but there are many who continue to feel that it is the wrong way to go about social change; the writers of a counter-letter on the economy, many of them wealthy Catholic businessmen, argue in effect that there should be a preferential option for the rich, and that by some mysterious trickle-down theory of private charity the poor will finally benefit. The bishops' letter, however, and the Latin American perspectives that helped inspire it, insist that Christian concern comes from the bottom up, not from the top down, and that it is out of empowerment of the poor themselves, and their ability to articulate their needs, that the struggle for justice will be advanced.

Another thing to be noted about the phrase is that in the Puebla documents the well-quoted section on the preferential option for the poor is followed by another section that has been virtually ignored, entitled "A Preferential Option for Young People."[4] The bishops are saying that in terms of moving from injustice toward justice, the needs of both the poor and of young people must be given priority, and that whatever is working to their advantage will ultimately work to the advantage of all. It is not hard to discern how intimately the two are related, for in situations of extreme poverty those most affected are the young, whether by hunger, malnutrition, starvation, or the creation of situations so desperate that children are caught in the midst of violent upheavals that can both terrorize and destroy them.

2

With these observations in mind, we can move on to consider what it would mean for a "renewal of faith" if the preferential option for the poor were taken seriously. Fortunately, we need not answer in speculative terms, for there is a wealth of experience in the Latin American church that illustrates the transformative character of such a conviction, that shows how new insights and dynamics enter the life of the church when traditional themes are reconceived out of a preferential option for the poor.

The very way of *doing theology,* for example, has been turned upside down. Theologians have usually been well-educated, elite males inhabiting comfortable surroundings. Out of their study of tradition and Scripture they have created systems of thought through which the various components of the faith could be articulated. Theology thus conceived was a set of timeless truths, eternally valid, that could, when occasion demanded, be "applied" to problems in society.

But a preferential option for the poor calls this elitist way of thinking into question. Latin American Liberation Theology has been a "theology of the people," meaning (in most instances) poor people, who out of their situations of poverty and oppression struggle to work out a faith that springs from, and is related to, the "underside" of history, history as seen from below.[5] Hugo Assmann, a Brazilian theologian, has referred (in a mouth-filling phrase) to the "epistemological privilege of the struggling poor." He and others point out that the main written repository of the faith, the Bible, is for the most part the work of oppressed peoples living in oppressive situations, writing to oppressed peoples elsewhere about how oppression can be overcome, how there can be "liberation," and how God is involved in the process. If this premise is accepted, it means that those who are in a similar situation of oppression today are likely to understand the heart of the Bible's radical message of justice better than those who approach the same texts from a position of privilege and have a vested interest in "taming" the otherwise challenging biblical stories of upheaval and change.[6]

We are likely to miss how deeply ingrained this notion of a "peoples' theology" is when we refer too exclusively to well-known Latin American theologians such as Gustavo Gutiérrez, Leonardo

Boff, José Porfirio Miranda, Elsa Tamez, and others, as though they had individually or collectively gone to the library stacks and said, "Go to, now; let us create a theology for the masses." The actual process has been nearly the reverse: the "masses" have reflected, worked, studied, and acted together, and people—including the above-named scholars—have, so to speak, taken notes on what was happening and reported to the rest of us. As Gutiérrez put it: "All liberation theology originates among the world's anonymous, whoever may write the books or the declarations articulating it."[7]

The poor, the "world's anonymous," are being heard on their own terms, and the emphases are different from traditional emphases, as a brief examination of certain items of content will show.

3

Classical conceptions of *God*, for example, depict Him (classical conceptions of God are always male) as all-powerful, all-knowing, and far removed from earth—"transcendent" is the term usually used. There is much speculation in classical theology about who God is "in Himself," His eternal unchangeableness, and so forth.

By contrast, or at least by way of supplement, the God of those committed to a preferential option for the poor is a God unalterably committed to the cause of the poor, taking sides with the poor, in the name of justice, which appears to be God's middle name. In a classic self-definition preceding the ten commandments, God presents a *curriculum vita* not by referring to timeless attributes or remoteness, but by saying, "I am the Lord your God, who brought you out of the land of Egypt, out of the house of bondage" (Exodus 20:2). This is a God who intervenes to overcome bondage, to ensure that the oppressive power of the Egyptian pharaoh can no longer be exercised, a God who liberates those who have been victims, seeing to it that they get a fresh start. This is a God, in other words, whose activity embodies a preferential option for the poor, thereby providing the reason why those who believe in such a God must do likewise.

Classical Christian faith asserts that God is not only transcendent but also immanent, i.e., not only in eternity but in the midst of human history as well, in the particular human life of one *Jesus* of Nazareth. But this daring and unique claim has frequently been swallowed up in new rounds of speculation about how "true God" and "true humanity" are related in this one life. The emphasis has usually been on a heavenly creature, now safely returned to the "right hand of God," who sojourned briefly on earth and then departed.

Those committed to a preferential option for the poor, while not denying that there is a decisive and unique manifestation of God in Jesus of Nazareth, put a great deal of stress on the human side of the equation. It is not enough to affirm, for example, that in Jesus of Nazareth God became "human." One has to ask, "What kind of human was he?" And the answer is that Jesus was a human who was a worker, a lower class peasant who lived on the "underside" of history. Rather than stressing a crowned deity reigning in heaven, Liberation Theologians picture Jesus as a very human being, sharing utterly in the lot of the poor and oppressed, dwelling in their midst, helping them fashion the tools for overcoming their poverty and oppression. So if they are asked, "Where is God to be found?" they will answer, "Look among the poor, look at where the oppressed are struggling for their liberation, identify with the victims as they refuse to accept their victimization any longer. There you may find that the contemporary counterpart of the God who brought the Israelites out of bondage is helping to bring contemporary people out of bondage, and you may discover that God is in human form in the person of Jesus of Nazareth, the son of a carpenter, who spent his life in the midst of just such people."

Such talk almost imperceptibly moves toward describing the Christian God as the *Holy Spirit,* a place where classical and Liberation Theology can potentially come closer together. For on any reading the notion of God as Spirit has been a way of speaking about the *power* of God at work today. Images of wind and fire abound: wind that batters down what does not deserve to stand, fire that burns away what is an offense to justice. That God is a God of power is claimed by all; the difference lies in varied claims about where that power is discerned.

The issue is clearly joined in the recent controversy between Friar Leonardo Boff, a Brazilian Franciscan, and the Sacred Congregation of the Doctrine of the Faith in Rome. Boff has written supportively about the power of the Spirit at work in what are called the "base communities" *(comunidades de base),* small groups of lay people who gather for liturgy, Bible study, and social action. Rome, on the other hand, is fearful that such groups will deflect the allegiance of their members away from the hierarchical church, centered in the bishops and the pope, traditionally seen as the locus of God's power. Those in the base communities do not see any conflict, however and engage in their activities as committed Roman Catholics; but those within the hierarchy are increasingly perturbed by the notion that God's power could be manifested outside of institutionally appointed channels. It is clear that those who make a preferential option for the poor find the base communities an important resource of God's power.

Within the Catholic faith, the figure of *Mary* always occupies a central place, both in theology and in private devotion. The classical images of Mary have her dressed in beautiful blue cloth, rings on her fingers, a crown on her head, standing in the curve of the moon. Such a figure seems remote from the life and concerns of the disadvantaged, and those who make a preferential option for the poor have rediscovered quite another Mary, a Mary based on the "Magnificat," a song placed on Mary's lips by the author of Luke's gospel, sung when she learns that she is to be the mother of Jesus. This Mary is a radical, even a revolutionary, one who says such wild things as that "God has scattered the proud in the imagination of their hearts, God has put down the mighty from their thrones, and exalted those of low degree; God has filled the hungry with good things, and the rich God has sent empty away" (Luke 1:51–53). Mary is here identified as a leader in the struggle for justice rather than a mild, acquiescing woman whose sole purpose is to bring children into the world.

In almost no other part of the theology that has flourished in Catholic cultures has there been a more significant reworking of traditional imagery, a reworking that Liberation Theologians insist is not some "new" or Marxist wrinkle, but simply a recovery of the original biblical understanding of Mary which was quickly smothered by conventional and unthreatening images imposed by a male-oriented hierarchy that wanted no challenge to the status quo.

In our discussion of the Spirit we have already seen how changes in the understanding of the *church* are developing. Without denying that institutions need structural form, and that bishops, priests, and deacons are a part of church structure, those committed to a preferential option for the poor insist that such structures must be characterized by the quality of servanthood rather than domination, and that they exist for the sake of helping people rather than for their own self-perpetuation.

That the base communities have produced people of tremendous empowerment is beyond dispute, and that the Spirit of God has been at work within them is likewise apparent to all but the most jaundiced observers. The base communities are locations where the poor have assumed places of leadership and carved out roles that have vast implications for the future of the church. So widespread is the impact of the base communities—there are over 100,000 in Latin America; 80,000 in Brazil alone—that it is cause for amazement that the *New York Times Magazine* could publish a long article purporting to be a description of Liberation Theology in Latin America and make no reference to this central phenomenon.

The other reality of a church that makes a preferential option for the poor is, of course, that it takes sides, and taking sides means being political. Wealthy Latin Americans object to this, insisting that the church is supposed to be above such matters, to remain impartial. To such criticism it must be responded that the church has always taken sides, usually the side of the rich, and that the rich did not object when that was the case. What has happened recently, in relation to a preferential option for the poor, is not that the church has taken sides for the first time, but that it has *changed* sides. There is no such thing as neutrality in such matters.

There has also been a new appraisal of the role of the *Bible*. In response to the charge that those making a preferential option for the poor have launched a new and dangerous kind of ecclesiastical dilettantism, it is argued that what is new in Liberation Theology is really old, in the sense that its roots are biblical. From this perspective, Liberation Theology can be seen as a reclaiming of the dynamism of the biblical story over against the abstract speculative kind of thinking that has dominated the church for centuries. As we have seen, the message of the Bible is preeminently the message of a God taking sides, a God concerned for justice, a God found in the midst of the here and now—all of this contained in a text which is not the product of the *literati*, the elite, or the university-trained, but of the common people, the impoverished, the victims. The Old Testament is a product of the ongoing trials and anguish of the Jews, always on the "underside" of history, always victimized by their more powerful neighbors, frequently taken off into captivity. The very dialect of the New Testament, *koiné* Greek, is the dialect not of the classical literature of Greek epics and tragedies but of the ordinary marketplace, the dialect of the untutored. So the Scriptures themselves exemplify the use of the undistinguished as the vehicle for acquainting the world with God.

It is a sign of the immense ingenuity of the human race (what theologians might cite as a capital instance of "original sin") that it has been possible for people to take these very radical documents, centering on justice and revolution and the rights of widows and orphans (the most oppressed and powerless members of the ancient world), and "tame" them into documents that not only demand no change, but that offer a divine blessing to the status quo no matter how unjust it may be. And it is an equally powerful sign of another side of the human spirit that there continues to be resistance to such cooptation, so that in our day, among those who make a preferential option for the poor, there has burst forth a new way of reading these ancient documents, so that they offer a radical vision of what humankind can become when "justice roll[s] down like waters, and righteousness like an ever-flowing stream" (Amos 5:24).

Something similar happens in the church that is making a preferential option for the poor when the community gathers for *worship*. Worship has often been a soporific that deadens any implicit concern for justice, offering consolation rather than challenge. But in the new situation dynamic and unexpected things happen. As we have seen, the decision to act in the face of injustice often grows out of the exposure of the base communities to biblical stories of similar acts of commitment in past times.

But other dynamisms are also created, particularly in relation to the central act of Catholic worship, the eucharist—the celebration of thanksgiving and sharing of bread and wine. This has often been the point at which inner-directed mysticism and social quiescence went hand in hand. But as Christians have rediscovered, the actions centering around bread and wine grow out of the Jewish celebration of the Passover, the meal at which Jesus for the last time broke bread and shared wine with his followers. The Passover meal recalls that very political/economic event in Jewish history—the liberation story *par excellence*—and to celebrate Passover is to offer thanks to the liberating God who had sided with the oppressed and delivered them in a mighty act of justice from the oppressive power of the pharaoh. Such a celebration should occasion a new commitment to contemporary struggles for justice, and yet for generations the church "tamed" this celebration into a time exclusively for inner reflection and meditation. And it is one of the great contributions of those committed to a preferential option for the poor that they have recovered this initial understanding of what the liturgy was all about. By its celebration, those who are committed to liberation struggles receive courage and empowerment to believe that God, too, is working toward those same ends.

The nature of the vehicles employed at the eucharist has similar political and economic implications. In asserting that in the breaking of the bread and the pouring of the cup Christ is present in a unique way, the church is also asserting that the fullness of God's presence does not come in prayer or meditation or silence, but only through the use of the most mundane of vehicles, food and drink, and that believers signify their appropriation of that presence by the equally mundane acts of chewing and swallowing. The actions proclaim loudly that God is not found apart from, but rather in the very midst of, the mundane. This invests the mundane with ultimate significance as the chosen arena of God's activity, the place where God is at work—which means that whatever happens within it is of concern to all believers. If things are happening within the mundane that are contrary to God's will, such as the spread of injustice and oppression and terror, it is the duty of those energized at this eucharistic meal to do battle with oppression and injustice and terror, confident that in so doing they are furthering, rather than working against, the will of the God they worship. So a commitment to break bread at Christ's table must also be a commitment to see that there is bread on all other tables. If food is available for some, that means that its recipients cannot rest until sufficient food is available for all.

4

So far we have been noting resources from within the Christian tradition that are highlighted, and reconceived, from the vantage point of the preferential option for the poor. But those in the church who are sharing in the liberation struggle draw on another kind of resource for understanding their world and their faith, the resource of *social analysis*. Theology does not provide tidy plans for action; nor does the Bible provide all the tools needed for understanding the contemporary world. And so another component in the renewal of faith is a clear-headed attempt to understand the world in which faith struggles to bring about change. One needs, for example, to know where power resides in a society that is unjust; one needs to discover who really makes the decisions, whatever outward circumstances may suggest; one needs to understand the motivations that lie behind the rhetoric of those who use power for their own ends. Some of the insights for this descriptive analysis come from Marxism, and the point needs to be addressed—especially in North America, where the very mention of Marx is likely to end any attempt at genuine understanding.

While not many Latin Americans would accept the designation of "Christian Marxists," some would surely describe themselves as "Marxist Christians": which word is the adjective and which the noun makes a difference. In other words, they see themselves as basically Christians, but as Christians whose understanding of the world is partly informed by certain insights drawn from Marx. They raise questions about the unbridled possession of private property, and they have discovered that in seeking to understand how society works, Marx's theory of class struggle makes good descriptive sense. There *are* classes—notably the tiny oligarchy and the masses—and they *are* struggling, since the former seek to abuse and dominate the latter. Marx, they would say, did not invent class struggle, but he noticed it and wrote about it in such a way that others have to notice it as well. And Marxism is not only a useful descriptive tool; it also provides a basis for action: if one is committed to the struggle of the poor to achieve liberation, one must be against those who seek to keep them enslaved. This means that there will be conflict in society, and no amount of Christian wishful thinking will dissipate it.

In the light of such an analysis—that there is a class struggle going on and that conflict is a part of the social structure—the task, in the light of commitment to the concerns of the God of justice, is to discover how justice can become more truly embodied in society and injustice rooted out. So social analysis is an important ingredient in attempts to embody the liberating message of God.

5

In the lives of their practitioners these are not theoretical issues, but are matters, quite literally, of life and death. The story of the emergence of a church that makes a preferential option for the poor has not been told until we realize that it is the story of a martyr-church, a church in which people who risk offending the status quo regularly end up dead. For every Archbishop Romero, whose name we know, and for every group of sisters tortured and raped and killed, whose names we likewise know, there are tens of thousands of nameless who have likewise been terrorized, tortured, and killed. They have taken risks because they believe that their faith speaks to the immediate situation of injustice with which they must do combat, and having discerned to their satisfaction on which side of that struggle God is to be found, they have no choice but to be there too. If the cost is great, they reflect that God also paid a great price—a truth for which the suffering and dying of Jesus on the cross is their sustaining image. And if the hope is great, that is because they believe that the God with whom they struggle will not be destroyed by the powers of evil but will end up victorious over them—a truth for which the Easter message of resurrection is their sustaining image. All over Nicaragua one sees signs that say, "Sandino vive" (Sandino lives). Sandino, the folk hero of the revolution, dead fifty years, is still alive in the hearts of the people. In the same way, Christians can say "Jesús vive," meaning by that many things, but meaning at least that Jesus lives in the hearts of *his* people, and that the things for which he lived and died continue to live and will never die.

Notes

1. See John Eagleson and Philip Scharper, eds., *Puebla and Beyond* (Mary-knoll, N.Y.: Orbis Books, 1979), especially paras. 1134–65.
2. National Conference of Catholic Bishops, *Pastoral Letter on Catholic Social Teaching and the Economy* (Washington, D.C., 1984).
3. *Pastoral Letter,* para. 21.; italics in the original.
4. Eagleson and Scharper, *Puebla and Beyond,* paras. 1166–1205.
5. On these themes, see Gustavo Gutiérrez, *The Power of the Poor in History* (Maryknoll, N.Y.: Orbis, 1983), esp. pp. 169–221.
6. An excellent example of how this works can be found in Ernesto Cardenal's four volumes, *The Gospel in Solentiname* (Maryknoll, N.Y.: Orbis Books, 1976–82), in which untutored members of a fishing village reflect each week on the meaning of each day's liturgical lessons for their own situation.
7. Quoted in Sergio Torres and Virginia Fabella, eds., *The Emergent Gospel: Theology from the Underside of History* (Maryknoll, N.Y.: Orbis Books, 1978), p. 250.

The Conflict of Political Theologies in the Churches: Does God Take Sides in Class Struggle?

Rosemary Ruether

Many North American Christians have been confused in recent years by conflicts within the Roman Catholic church, particularly over Liberation Theology. They hear this theology condemned as subordinating theological or spiritual goals to political concerns, and as being a "Marxist" theology. Since most North Americans know very little of Marxism, either in its various schools of theory or its many different lines of practical application, and since the word "Marxism" functions as the American national heresy and bogeyman, simply to apply this label to Liberation Theology is automatically to evoke a negative reaction. In this essay I would like to analyze the connections between theology and politics in Christian history as a context for revealing the real battle lines over Liberation Theology in Latin America and in the global Roman Catholic church today. I will then discuss what Latin American Liberation Theology means by the incorporation of class analysis into theology and by the use of the concept of "God's preferential option for the poor."

The first myth that must be exploded is that theology and Christian faith have been normatively and traditionally apolitical. The notion that theology and the Christian faith have to do only with the spiritual, with the private or personal self in relation to God, and therefore that it is a deformation of theology and the Christian message to relate it to politics, is frequently evoked against Liberation Theology. This assumption has little basis either in biblical or Christian history. It would be more accurate to say that theology has always been political, either overtly or covertly. The conflict over

Liberation Theology today is simply the latest expression of two different political theologies, both of which have roots in the Bible and both of which have been in continual conflict throughout Christian history. One of these political theologies is biased on the side of the political status quo. It regards the existing social hierarchies as divinely ordained and thus regards the existing ruling classes as agents of God's will in ruling the social universe. Those who dissent from, and seek to topple, the existing rulers are regarded as rebels against God. The Marxist critique of religion was shaped in the nineteenth century as a criticism of this kind of theology on the side of the ruling classes.

A second theology, by contrast, evaluates the present rulers as apostate from God. They see the existing social hierarchies of power, not as divinely ordained, but rather as expressions of human sin and injustice which have distorted and turned to its opposite God's true mandate for creation. They see God, through the prophets, denouncing the evils of these systems and their ruling classes, and they envision God intervening in history to lead the saints to overthrow these evil systems of power and to bring in a new order of history where peace and justice will prevail.

Biblical Roots of Royal Versus Prophetic Theologies

Although both of these perspectives are found in the Hebrew Scriptures and the New Testament, it is the second or prophetic theology which predominates. Royal theologies were, of course, found among the imperial peoples that surrounded ancient Israel. The ancient Near Eastern states regarded the king as an elect of God, and Egyptians saw the pharoah as God incarnate. Royal theology was taken into ancient Israel with the Davidic monarchy, despite the negativity of the prophetic tradition toward the institution of kingship. The Davidic king was seen as an elect Son of God and as the corporate representative of Israel before God. Divine promises of victory over his enemies and for prosperity were claimed for him.

But Hebrew prophetic tradition did not allow simply for the sacralization of kingly power. The promises of victory and prosperity to the king were contingent upon the king's justice and righteousness. Kings, as well as other powerful rulers in society, were called to account for their treatment of the poor and the weak. When the powerful oppressed the poor and defrauded the widow and the orphan, God's judgment was called down upon them. The prophets also denounced the religious authorities when they made religious fidelity solely cultic or legalistic and ignored the authentic demands of justice and mercy. This denunciation of social injustice by the powerful of Israelite society and its sanctification by the leaders of the temple cult was denounced in ringing phrases by the Prophet Jeremiah:

> Thus says the Lord of hosts, the God of Israel,
> Amend your ways and your doings, and I
> will let you dwell in this place.
> Do not trust in these deceptive words: "This
> is the temple of the Lord, the temple of
> the Lord, the temple of the Lord."
>
> For if you truly amend your ways and your doings,
> if you truly execute justice with one another,
> if you do not oppress the alien, the fatherless,
> or the widow, or shed innocent blood in this place,
> and if you do not go after other gods to your own hurt,
> then I will let you dwell in this place, in
> the land which I gave of old to your fathers for
> ever.
>
> Behold, you trust in deceptive words to no avail.
> Will you steal, murder, commit adultery, swear falsely,
> burn incense to Ba'al, and go after other gods
> that you have not known, and then come and stand before me
> in this house, which is called by my name, and say,
> "We are delivered!"—only to go on doing all these
> abominations? Has this house, which is called by my name,
> become a den of robbers in your eyes? Behold,
> I myself have seen it, says the Lord. [Jer. 7, 3–11]

Prophetic faith transforms the relationship between religion and politics. It allows neither the sacralization of existing power structures nor a private otherworldly escape from history and society. Rather, the prophets take the idea of a just and righteous king, and the peace and prosperity promised under his sway, and turn it into a critical ideal by which the present rulers and their religious associates are judged. The people, especially the powerful among the people, are called to repent of their hypocritical and oppressive ways. The promise of a righteous king and a reign of peace and justice is projected upon an ideal future. It becomes the content of a messianic future that will be brought in by God when the people have repented.

This prophetic tradition was renewed and deepened in the ministry of Jesus of Nazareth. According to the Gospel of Luke, Jesus defined the essence of his ministry in the words of the ancient prophetic text from Isaiah 61, declaring that he has come to "preach good news to the poor, to proclaim release to the captives, recovering of sight to the blind, to set at liberty those who are oppressed." Jesus' announcement of good news to the poor was directed particularly at marginalized classes and groups within Israel and among the ethnic groups, such as the Samaritans dwelling alongside of the Jews. He directed his denunciations particularly at the Jewish ruling classes, at the local rulers, the landowners, and particularly at the religious authorities. It was the religious authorities who, through their law and class-based system of religion, excluded the little ones, the despised people of the land, from hope of salvation.

The gospels present us with a drama in which these poor and despised peoples—the widow, the Samaritan woman, the Syro-Phoenician woman, the tax collector, the leper, the woman with the flow of blood (making her ritually impure), the blind, the lame, and the demon-possessed—are able to hear and respond with faith to the message of God's prophet, while reigning religious and political authorities, blinded by their systems of power and privilege, refuse to hear the prophet and plot to eliminate him. In the gospel story, then, divine approbation is withdrawn from the ruling classes of society. God's favor is extended to the victims of these systems of unjust privilege, not in the sense of excluding the power but in the sense of calling them to repent of their unjust systems of power as their path to entrance into God's kingdom. In the words of the Gospel of Matthew, "The Scribes and the Pharisees will enter the kingdom of God after the prostitutes and the tax collectors." The authorities place themselves under divine judgment by rejecting this path of salvation and seeking to destroy the Messenger. The resurrection represents God's vindication of his prophet against the religious and political authorities and the extension of the message of good news to the poor through the church.

This denunciation of religious and political authorities is polarized in the apocalyptic tradition in inter-testamental Judaism and in the New Testament. Here the focus is on the great systems of oppressive power of the ancient Near Eastern empires of Babylonia, Persia, Greece, and Rome, rather than on local Jewish authorities. These imperial powers are linked with the cosmic power of fallen angels or evil spirits, who are seen as having rebelled against the sovereignty of God. Human history is seen as having fallen under the power of these negative forces, these Princes of this World, manifest in the great world empires. God's people, Israel or the church, are seen as suffering victims under the power of these rulers. But soon God will intervene through His Messiah to overthrow these demonic powers and their human minions and to bring in a new cosmic order of justice and peace.

The language of the Book of Revelation for this final world revolution is graphically political and socioeconomic. The kings of this earth, the merchants and shipmasters, are all called upon to weep in consternation as they see all this wealth and power, in which they have put their trust, go up in smoke. Apocalyptic political theology lends itself to a paranoid world view which denounces abstract cosmic systems of evil outside one's own group, as distinct from prophetic language which uses the more concrete self-critical language of struggle for justice within local communities.

The Transformation of Political Theology in Christendom

Although Christianity originated as a movement of small powerless people in the eastern provinces of the Roman Empire, using a language of apocalyptic world revolution against the emperor and his imperial power, this gradually changed as Christianity integrated itself into the social systems of the empire in the second and third centuries. In the first quarter of the fourth century, when the Emperor Constantine declared Christianity to be the new imperial religion, prophetic and apocalyptic judgment against a reigning power was converted into a new version of royal theology. For Eusebius of Caesarea, the leading theologian of Constantinian Christendom, Constantine represented the fulfillment of the ancient messianic hopes for a righteous king through whom God's reign could be established on earth. Constantine was seen as the political expression of the Lordship of Christ over the universe. Constantine's defeat of his political enemies was the equivalent of God's defeat of the demonic powers, and the Constantinian Christian version of the Pax Romana was the fulfillment of the ancient dream of the coming of the Kingdom of Peace on earth.

The great Latin theologian Augustine was more skeptical of the claim that the empire could become converted to Christianity and thus be viewed as a fulfillment of messianic hopes. For Augustine, the destinies of the church and the empire could never converge within history; there would be no messianic reign on earth, but only the period of the mission of the church which would culminate in the end of history and the creation of a transcendent heavenly world beyond history, where the redeemed would enjoy eternal blessedness. Yet the empire, particularly when exercised by

Christian rulers, might become an instrument of God's negative or judgmental power on earth through which the godless are restrained.

Medieval and Reformation Christianity inherited a combination of these Eusebian and Augustinian traditions. It was assumed by the dominant theological schools that the Powers and Principalities, the systems of political and social power, had now come under the sway of Christ within Christian society. Thus it could be assumed that the existing hierarchies of power were founded by God and expressed the rule of God on earth. The claimants to the throne of the Christian Roman emperor in Constantinople, Russia, and Germany, as well as the kings of the rising European nations, claimed to be kings by divine right, representing the fatherhood of God and the Lordship of Christ on earth. The church sought to modify these political theologies of Christian emperors and kings by putting royal power under the judgment of ecclesiastical power. But the church was equally sure that its own ecclesiastical hierarchy was founded by Christ to govern the church directly and the political world indirectly. The other social hierarchies—feudal lord over serf, master over slave or servant, husband over wife—were likewise believed to be a part of the created order of nature, mandated by God.

These traditions of political theology were modified, but not greatly changed, in the mainstream of the Reformation, which basically followed the Augustinian tradition. Luther sought to curb the temporal power of the church by putting the temporal governance of the church under the state; this greatly increased the power of the Christian princes and kings over the church. Like Augustine, Luther did not believe that the state could ever become an expression of God's redemptive reign on earth, but it did manifest God's negative power of restraint of evil. Even evil government was mandated by God for this purpose, and thus Lutheranism practically ruled out rebellion against constituted authorities. Calvinism, by contrast, suggested that both the state and the church in the hands of the godless, of which they counted both Catholics and Anglicans, could be rebelled against. Calvinism was thus at the forefront of the civil wars in France, England, and the Netherlands which sought to replace Catholic and Anglican governments with churches and social systems reformed by Calvinist principles. But once the godly—that is, the Puritans—were in power, Calvinism saw the power systems as having come under the sway of Christ. To resist constituted authorities in the hands of the godly was to sin and rebel against God. The hierarchies of husband, master, and father over wife, servant, and children was, for Calvinism, the order of creation. The subordinate people in the patriarchal family should accept their place as divinely given. The social contract, by which the people entered into a covenant to set up a new reformed society according to divine law, which so influenced U.S. constitutional theory, would have been applied by Calvinists, as it was by the American Founding Fathers, only to male heads of families, not to women or to males in a status of servitude.

The Reappearance of Prophetic Theology

The dissident apocalyptic traditions of the Bible and early Christianity by no means disappeared with the triumph of these new versions of royal theology. From the twelfth century on, medieval and left-wing Protestant sectarian movements continually revived and reapplied the notion that the dominant power systems of the state, and even of the church, were expressions of demonic power rather than the order of creation and the will of God. The followers of Joachim of Fiore in the fourteenth century declared the advent of a Third Age, the Reign of the Spirit, which would supersede the clerical church. The sectarians saw themselves as a new spiritual elite who were presently being persecuted by evil power but would soon be vindicated by God, who would intervene in history to end the present reign of Babylon and bring in a redeemed era of church and world history. This radical apocalyptic or millennialist tradition was carried on by the left-wing sectarians of the Reformation, such as the Anabaptists in the sixteenth-century Continental Reformation, and the Baptists, Seekers, Levellers, and Fifth Monarchy men of left-wing Puritanism in the seventeenth-century English Civil War.

Seventeenth-century left-wing English Puritanism presents the beginning of a transition from earlier religious apocalyptic sectarianism to the increasingly secular expression of future historical hope that came to characterize European ideologies in the eighteenth and nineteenth centuries. The Enlightenment secularized the Joachite language about the Third Age of the Spirit by looking forward to a new age of the triumph of reason and education that would overcome the dark era of religious superstition and clerical power. Militant deist or atheistic liberalism in eighteenth-century France declared religion to be a tool of the ruling class to make the oppressed classes submit to the unjust power of the rulers, an idea that would be taken over into Marxism. Socialism would lift up the proletariat, the impoverished working classes of early industrialization, as the elect of God or history, through which a new age of just sharing of wealth in a classless society would be brought in after the overthrow of the present oppressive capitalist owners.

These eighteenth- and nineteenth-century secular traditions were militantly antireligious, based on their identification of religion with the political theology of the status quo. They believed that a secular scientific method could create both objective truth and a just society of equal sharing of knowledge, wealth, and power. But by the mid-nineteenth century various groups of Christian socialists began to reclaim these secular traditions of social reform and revolution for Christian faith. They recognized that beneath the apparent atheism and secularism was an attack on oppressive religion, on the side of unjust power, and a vision of moral transformation of society that had its root in biblical prophetic faith. They sought both to reintegrate Christianity into these modern traditions of social change and also to ground these social hopes in the deeper foundations of religious hope. Twentieth-century Liberation Theology is basically a third world rediscovery of this same project.

The Rediscovery of Prophetic Theology in Latin American Christianity

Latin American Christianity was planted by Spanish and Portuguese Counter-Reformation Catholicism and thus had a pervasive theology of royal power as the agent of Christ on earth. Hispanic Christendom saw itself as mandated to combat the Protestant heretic and to spread true Christianity among the heathen. Although a few prophetic voices, such as Bartolomé de Las Casas in the sixteenth century, spoke up against the enslavement of the Indian, Latin American Catholicism basically legitimated the hierarchical power of the ruling classes over exploited slaves and serfs. In the 1820s these colonial regimes, with their ruling classes of *penisulares,* were overthrown, but there was little change in the fundamental socioeconomic structures put in place by colonialism. The creoles, or locally born Spanish and Portuguese, moved into the places of power vacated by the colonial elites. The vast tracts of land which had been given to the settlers continued, reducing the Indian to serfdom or to marginal land on the hills. England, and then the United States, took the place of Spain and Portugal as controllers of the world market for Latin American sugar, coffee, tobacco, and other export crops. Economic dependency continued and was deepened by neocolonial aid and by development plans which were aimed primarily at using cheap labor and resources to make high profits on minerals, agricultural products, and later manufactured goods exported to the affluent overseas market.

In the nineteenth century secular democratic movements, influenced by the French Enlightenment, sought to modernize Latin American cultural and political systems. These nineteenth-century liberals were militantly anticlerical and sought to disestablish the church. Catholicism was seen as a key factor in legitimating the old ruling classes. These liberals were followed by populist movements between 1910 and 1930 which, on the model of the Mexican Revolution, sought to overcome the historic impoverishment of the Indian through land reform. In the 1950s the new answer to Latin American poverty was developmentalism. Latin America was seen as an "underdeveloped" region that needed to industrialize. Foreign aid coming from governments and businesses in the industrialized countries was seen as vital to this process of industrial development.

By the early 1960s Latin American economists were criticizing the fallacies of a concept of development that saw it as a unilineal process in which Western Europe and North America were regarded as being at an advanced state, while Latin America was seen as being at the beginning stages, but needing to follow the same path. They saw this as an unhistoric notion that failed to recognize the legacy of colonialism and the present reality of neocolonialism in Latin America. In reality Latin America was not in some primitive "underdeveloped" state, just beginning to emulate the Western world, but was the victim of four hundred and fifty years of distorted 'misdevelopment. For more than four centuries its gold and silver, oil and copper, rich soil, mild climate, and impoverished populations had been used to extract the vast wealth upon which European capitalism had been built. Latin American poverty was the underside of North American and Western European wealth.

These critical sociologists and economists spoke, not of development, but of liberation. What they meant by liberation was the national reappropriation of the land and subterranean wealth of their countries from foreign-owned and controlled companies, such as United Fruit in Central America. Liberation also meant the reorganization of the ownership and organization of production. Redistribution of land from the vast *latifundias* and foreign-owned plantations to the landless peasants, either in family farms or peasant cooperatives, and a popularly based development of diversified products aimed at the needs of local consumers, rather than a global market of the elite, would create a development from the bottom up, one that would meet the basic needs of the masses of the people.

This concept of liberation entailed a socialist, rather than a capitalist, path of development. By socialism, Latin Americans did not mean a slavish imitation of socialist systems found in Eastern Europe or China, and certainly not the replacement of a Western European or North American imperialist presence by a Russian one. What they meant most of all was political and economic independence and self-determination. Capitalism in Latin America meant a foreign-owned and controlled capitalism, an international system of dependency. The real question was how to shake off that dependency, with its powerful control of international capital through the World Bank and other lending agencies. North America proved more than willing not only to use all these international sanctions against any Latin American country seeking to move out of its orbit of control, but also to topple such new governments, whether they came into power through revolutionary or electoral means and flew the banners of populism, democratic reform, or socialism. The ultimate sanction was armed military invasion, a tool that was used repeatedly in Central America and the Caribbean in the first half of the twentieth century to prevent independence movements from succeeding. In the 1930s the funding of local military governments favorable to U.S. interests took the place of the landing of the marines, but today the failure of these U.S.-backed militias to control popular revolutions is again suggesting the need for so-called U.S. "advisors" and perhaps ground troops as well. The present administration has clearly learned nothing from the failures of such efforts in Indochina in the 1960s and 1970s.

In the 1960s the Second Vatican Council helped spark a revival of prophetic Christianity in Latin America. Theologians such as Gustavo Gutiérrez began to create a "theology of liberation." They meant by this the theological reflection upon the project of the liberation of the Latin American people from poverty and from military oppression by national security states. Liberation Theology linked this contemporary project of liberation with the biblical traditions of prophetic criticism of oppressive elites and God's good news to the poor. Good news to the poor meant that the authentic message of biblical faith was God's denunciation of oppression and His liberating work in history to bring about a new humanity and community, where the fruits of the earth could be shared justly. The redemptive work of Christ had to be understood essentially as that of liberator, as the one who renews the prophetic denunciation of injustice and the annunciation of hope for an alternative society of justice.

Liberation, as the essential theme of biblical faith, means that the church itself must be converted from its historic role as sanctifier of the power of the wealthy elites. The church itself must be converted to God's work of liberation of the poor and only in so doing is it authentically the church of Christ. The church of Christendom, the church that sided with and sanctified oppressive power, was apostate. Its god was not the true God of biblical faith, but an idol, an apotheosis of the Powers and Principalities of fallen history. Liberation Theologians unpacked the atheism of Marxism and the anticlericalism of the Enlightenment tradition. They recognized in it the essential prophetic message of denunciation of religion, as a tool to justify oppression and to divert piety into an individualistic and otherworldly form that mandated passive acceptance of injustice on earth.

For Liberation Theologians, the theological issue behind the conflict between dominant systems of religious power on the side of the rich and the modern attack on religion is the conflict between idolatry and biblical faith. Although the U.S. government might have embraced secularism in the nineteenth century as part of its own emancipation from European colonialism, capitalist societies have increasingly appropriated a right-wing Christianity as a tool to legitimate their power over dependent economies. The U.S. president grows ever more pious as he seeks to justify intervention in third world popular revolutions. His geopolitical conflict with the rival Russian world power takes on the language of the angels of light against the forces of darkness.

Liberation Theology thus sees the critique of religion as an essential part of biblical faith. Essential to the work of the prophet is the unmasking of idolatrous counterfeits of biblical faith. Religious systems that claim to speak for Christ, but who use the name of Christ to mandate systems of oppressive power, whether that be the old elites of Latin American Christendom or North American global hegemony, worship idols. Their gods are the Powers and Principalities of apostate history, and not the God of Exodus, of the prophets, and of Jesus Christ.

The key to biblical faith, therefore, for Latin American liberation is the preferential option for the poor. This is not simply the message the church must preach. It is, first and foremost, the praxis or life ethic that Christians must live. To be converted to Christ is to be converted to Christ's preferential option for the poor. God's option for the poor is not based on the personal holiness or righteousness of the poor. God opts for the poor, not because they are saints, but because they are poor. The poverty of the poor reveals the structures of systemic sin or evil in history. God opts for the poor because human sinful power has chosen to oppress the poor in order to make itself wealthy and powerful. God's option for the poor is thus a revelation and denunciation of these systems of evil and a call to conversion.

Conversion is both personal and systemic. It means that Christian leadership classes, particularly the priests and teachers of Christian faith, must abandon their false religiosity of sacralized power and side with the most impoverished in concrete ways. It means that such priests and teachers must locate their ministry in the barrios and pueblos where the poorest live and teach the gospel in a way that can emancipate their spirits from apathy and dependence and inspire them in the tasks of collective organization for change. The priests are not to take over these movements of the people, which would be a new form of clericalism, but rather to empower the people through the gospel to construct their own grassroots movements for liberation. Further, conversion means the revolutionary conversion of the social structure, the dismantling of the systems of land ownership and modes of production that create vast wealth for the few and grinding poverty and repression for the masses, and construct a new society where the people's basic needs for food, shelter, education, health, and above all for dignity and self-determination, are met.

It is not surprising that this project of Liberation Theology, which lays claim to the hope for social liberation in the Christian gospel, quickly fell into conflict with the guardians of both the old order of Latin American elites and the international systems of church and of global power, represented particularly by the U.S. government and the Vatican. The reintegration of social hope and prophetic faith in Liberation Theology has generated a peculiar new collaboration of conservative political and religious power that seeks to repress and discredit it. A National Security Council report in the 1960s advised the U.S. president that radical priests and nuns had become one of the greatest dangers to U.S. power in Latin America. More recently, there was a congressional investigation of Liberation Theology.

As a result of the renewal of elements of social gospel in the Second Vatican Council, sectors in the Vatican, as well as in the hierarchy of the Latin American church, were open to Liberation Theology. It was approved in a moderate form in the Declaration of the Latin American Bishops' Conference at Medellín in 1968. In the 1970s, however, conservative bishops and Christian elites mobilized to combat it. The election of the conservative Pope John Paul II, who brought an anticommunism that had been shaped in Polish national conflict with Russia to bear on third world movements, gave these conservatives a more sympathetic ear in Rome. Increasingly, the speeches of the Pope not only condemned violence and class conflict, long a staple of papal rhetoric, but began to condemn any focus on social rather than personal sin. The Pope constantly invites the impoverished of the world to focus on secularism as the great danger and the sacraments of the church as the means of spiritual nourishment, rather than on that merely material bread that feeds the body.

Yet despite this hostility from Rome, Liberation Theology, and the Christian base communities which form its ecclesiastical foundation, were reaffirmed in the Third Latin American Bishops' Conference in Puebla, Mexico, in 1979. Recent efforts by the Vatican, spearheaded by the German conservative Joseph Cardinal Ratzinger, head of the Congregation of the Doctrine of the Faith (formerly the Inquisition), to condemn such Liberation Theologians as Gustavo Gutiérrez and Leonardo Boff have resulted in something of a debacle. The Brazilian bishops in particular were indisposed to such intervention from Rome, and attempted to head off the condemnation of Boff by arriving in force as his defenders. But the attack was soon renewed. The Ratzinger document criticizing Liberation Theology focused on a condemnation of Marxism, especially Marxist ideas such as class struggle, as being contrary to the gospel. But since its account of Marxism was the abstract and dogmatic Marxism of the Eastern European Communist parties, which has little currency in Latin America—particularly among Liberation Theologians—it was easily dismissed by Gustavo Gutiérrez and other theologians as irrelevant to their work.

For Gutiérrez, the primary inspiration for Liberation Theology is the Bible, not Marx. Marxism is at best a strictly subsidiary tool of critical sociological analysis that helps reveal the economic structures of dependency and cultural ideology. But Marxism did not invent class struggle or ideology. It merely recognized these realities of social oppression and taught people to name them. Latin Americans therefore do not need Marxism to know about class hierarchy and social propaganda. They know about such things from their own experience and can name them quite well in their own words. Thus Liberation Theology in recent years has tended to use fewer and fewer of the catchwords of European Marxism in favor of a critical language drawn from the prophetic tradition of the Bible and from Latin America's own historical experience.

Thus the hostility of both the Vatican and the U.S. government to Liberation Theology is neither a contest between the Bible and secular humanism, as the U.S. religious right would like to style it, nor a contest between spirituality and merely political projects, as the Vatican would like to see it. Rather, it is a contest between two different visions of social order, and between their religious expressions, a contest that is as old as the Bible itself. One vision regards the existing systems of social hierarchy as divinely ordained and teaches people to accept these systems as necessary, to turn inward to a private spirituality which will save their souls after death. The other vision sees these social hierarchies as evil and apostate from God. It sees the gospel as dispelling the false mythologies that sacralize these systems and mandating a new society of justice. This second understanding of biblical faith is no more popular with the contemporary Caesars and High Priests than it was when the prophet went forth from the villages of Galilee to the city of Jerusalem in the first century of the Common Era.

Black Theology: Its Origin, Method, and Relation to Third World Theologies

James H. Cone

The term Black Theology refers to a theological movement that emerged among North American black people during the second half of the 1960s. Although its impact has spread since then, in this essay I will limit my analysis to the origin and meaning of North American Black Theology, with special reference to its methodology, as defined by its dialogue with the third world theologies of Africa, Asia, and Latin America.[1]

The Origin of Black Theology

The origin of Black Theology has three contexts: (1) the civil rights movement of the 1950s and 1960s, largely associated with Martin Luther King, Jr.; (2) the publication of Joseph Washington's book *Black Religion* (1964); and (3) the rise of the black power movement, strongly influenced by Malcolm X's philosophy of black nationalism.

1. *The civil rights movement.* All those involved in the rise of Black Theology were also deeply involved in the civil rights movement, and participated in the protest demonstrations led by Martin Luther King. Unlike most contemporary theological movements in Europe and North America, therefore, Black Theology's origin was not in the seminary or the university. In fact, most of its early interpreters did not even hold advanced academic degrees. Black Theology came into being in the context of black people's struggle for racial justice, which was initiated in the black churches but was chiefly identified with such protest organizations as the Southern

Christian Leadership Conference (SCLC), the National Conference of Black Churchmen (NCBC), the Interreligious Foundation for Community Organization (IFCO), and many black caucuses in white churches.

From its beginnings Black Theology was understood by its creators as a Christian theological reflection upon the black struggle for justice and liberation, largely defined in the life and thought of Martin Luther King. And when Martin Luther King and other black church people began to relate the Christian gospel to the struggle for justice in U.S. society, the great majority of white churches and their theologians denied that such a relationship existed. Conservative white Christians claimed that religion and politics did not mix. Liberal white Christians, with few exceptions (this was during the 1950s and early 1960s), remained silent on the theme or advocated a form of gradualism that denounced boycotts, sit-ins, and freedom rides.

Contrary to popular opinion, Martin Luther King was not well received by the white U.S. church establishment when he inaugurated the civil rights movement with the Montgomery bus boycott in 1955.[2] Because black people received no theological support from white churches and their theologians (who were occupied with Barth, Bultmann, and the death of God controversy!), black people had to search deeply into their own history in order to find a theological basis for their prior political commitment to set the black poor free. They found support in Richard Allen (the founder of the African Methodist Episcopal [AME] church in 1816), Henry Highland Garnet (a nineteenth-century Presbyterian preacher who urged the slaves to resist slavery), Nat Turner (a slave Baptist preacher who led an insurrection that killed sixty whites), Henry McNeal Turner (an AME Bishop who claimed in 1898 that "God is a Negro"), and others.[3] When blacks began to investigate their religious history, they found that their struggle for political freedom had not begun in the 1950s and 1960s but had roots stretching back many years. They also discovered that black people's struggle for political justice in North America had always been located in their churches. Whether it is the independent Northern churches (AME, AMEZ, Baptists, etc.), the so-called invisible institution among slaves in the South (which emerged with the independent black churches after the Civil War), or blacks in white denominations, black Christians have always known that the God of Moses and of Jesus did not create them to be slaves or second-class citizens in North America. In order to make a theological witness of this religious knowledge, black preachers and civil rights activists of the

1960s developed a Black Theology that rejected racism and affirmed the black struggle for liberation as consistent with the gospel of Jesus.

2. *Joseph Washington's black religion.* When black preachers and lay activist Christians began the search for the radical side of their black church history, they also began to ask about the distinctive religious and theological contributions of black people. It was generally assumed—by most whites and by many blacks—that black people's culture had made no unique contribution either to Christianity in particular or to humanity in general. Indeed, white liberal Christians understood integration to mean assimilation, and that meant blacks rejecting their cultural past, adopting European cultural values, and becoming like whites. The assumption behind the white definition of integration was the belief that African values among North American blacks had been completely destroyed during slavery. Therefore, if blacks were to develop a cultural knowledge of themselves, they had to find it in their identification with white American values.

Joseph Washington, a black scholar, wrote his book during the hegemony of the ideology of integration in black-white relations in America. Contrary to the dominant view, Washington contended that there is a unique black culture, a distinctive black religion that can be placed alongside of Protestantism, Catholicism, Judaism, and secularism. This black religion is not identical with white Protestantism or any other expression of Euro-American Christianity.

But Washington was not pleased with the continued existence of black religion, and he placed the blame squarely on white Christians. He contended that black religion exists only because black people have been excluded from the genuine Christianity of the white churches. Because blacks have been excluded from the faith of white churches, black churches are not genuine Christian churches. And if there are no genuine Christian churches, there can be no Christian theology. Blacks have only folk religion and folk theology. In Washington's own words: "Negro congregations are not churches but religious societies—religion can choose to worship whatever gods are pleasing. But a church without a theology, the interpretation of a response of the will of God for the faithful, is a contradiction in terms."[4]

Although *Black Religion* was received with enthusiasm in the white community, it was strongly denounced in the black church community. Indeed, Black Theology was, in part, created in order to refute Washington's thesis. Black preachers wanted to correct two misconceptions: (1) that black religion is not Christian and thus has no Christian theology; and (2) that the Christian gospel has nothing to do with the struggle for justice in society.

3. *The black power movement.* After the march on Washington in August 1963, the integration theme in the black community began to lose ground to the black nationalist philosophy of Malcolm X.[5] The riots in the ghettoes across the United States were shocking evidence that many blacks agreed with Malcolm X's contention that America was not a dream but a nightmare.

However, it was not until the summer of 1966, after Malcolm X's assassination (1965), that the term black power began to usurp the term integration among many civil rights activists. The occasion was the continuation of the James Meredith "march against fear" (in Mississippi) by Martin Luther King, Jr., Stokely Carmichael, and other civil rights activists. Carmichael seized this occasion to sound the black power slogan, and it was heard loud and clear throughout the United States.[6]

The rise of black power had a profound affect upon Black Theology. When Carmichael and other radical activists separated themselves from Martin Luther King's absolute commitment to nonviolence by proclaiming black power, white church people, especially clergymen, called upon their black brothers and sisters in the gospel to denounce black power as un-Christian. To the surprise of white Christians, black ministers refused to follow their advice and instead wrote a "Black Power" statement that was published in the *New York Times* (31 July 1966).[7]

The publication of the "Black Power" statement may be regarded as the beginning of the conscious development of Black Theology. Black ministers consciously separated their understanding of the gospel of Jesus from white Christianity and identified it with the struggles of the black poor for justice. Radical black clergy created an ecumenical organization called the National Conference of Black Churchmen (NCBC), as well as black caucuses in the National Council of Churches and almost all white churches. Black clergy denounced white racism as the antichrist, and were unrelenting in their attack on its demonic presence in white denominations. It was in this context that the term Black Theology emerged.

Black Theology as Liberation Theology

It is one thing to proclaim Black Theology and quite another to give it theological substance. Many white Christians and almost all white theologians dismissed Black Theology as nothing but rhetoric. Since white theologians controlled the seminaries and university departments of religion, they made many blacks feel that only Europeans and those who think like them can define what theology is. In order to challenge the white monopoly on the definition of theology, many young black scholars realized that they had to carry the fight to the seminaries and universities where theology was being written.

The first book on Black Theology was written by me and called *Black Theology and Black Power* (1969). The central theme of that book was the identification of the liberating elements in black power with the Christian gospel. A year later I wrote a second book, *A Black Theology of Liberation* (1970), which made liberation the organizing center of my theological perspective. I wrote: "Christian theology is a theology of liberation. It is a rational study of the being of God in the world in the light of the existential situation of an oppressed community, relating the forces of liberation to the essence of the gospel, which is Jesus Christ."[8]

After these two books appeared, other black theologians joined me, both supporting my theological project and in challenging what they regarded as my excesses. In his *Liberation and Reconciliation: A Black Theology* (1971), J. Deotis Roberts, while supporting my emphasis on liberation, claimed that I had overlooked reconciliation as central to the gospel and to black-white relations in general. A similar position was advocated by Major Jones in *Black Awareness: A Theology of Hope* (1971). Other Black Theologians claimed that I was too dependent upon white theology and thus was not sufficiently aware of the African origins of black religion. This position is taken by my brother, Cecil, in his *Identity Crisis in Black Theology* (1975), and it is also found in Gayraud Wilmore's *Black Religion and Black Radicalism* (1972).

While my perspective on Black Theology was challenged by some black scholars, they all supported my claim that liberation was the central core of the gospel as found in the scriptures and the religious history of black Americans. For Black Theologians the *political* meaning of liberation was best illustrated in the Exodus and its *eschatological* meaning was found in the life, death, and resurrection of Jesus. The Exodus was interpreted as being analogous to Nat Turner's slave insurrection and Harriet Tubman's liberation of an estimated three hundred slaves. Slave songs (often called "Negro spirituals"), sermons, and prayers expressed the in-the-future character of liberation found in the resurrection of Jesus.

Because many black male theologians were reluctant to take up the subject of sexism and because others were openly hostile when black women raised the issue as a critical theological problem, a black feminist theology is emerging in open challenge to the patriarchal nature of the current perspectives of Black Theology. Jacquelyn Grant and Pauli Murray are prominent examples.[9] While they accept the liberation theme of Black Theology, black feminist theologians reject the narrow limitations of that theme to racism, as if sexism is not an important problem in the black community. Because of the urgency of the problem of sexism, black women have begun to insist on doing theology out of their experience. Black feminist theology is both a challenge to the sexist orientation of Black Theology and a deepening of the black struggle against racism.

Black Theology's Method and Relation to Third World Theologies

During the early 1970s Black Theologians from North America began to have some contact with other forms of liberation theology in Africa, Latin America, and Asia.[10] Black Theology in South Africa was a natural ally. Black and Latin theologies became co-partners in their identification of the gospel with the liberation of the poor, although one emphasized racism and the other classism. A similar partnership occurred with black, African, and Asian theologies regarding the importance of culture in defining theology.

In the dialogue between black and third world theologians, the striking difference between the theologies of the poor and the theologies of the rich became very clear to blacks. As long as our dialogue was confined to North American whites who oppressed blacks, and to European theologians whom our oppressors venerated, our understanding of the theological task was determined too much by our reactions to white racism in the United States. African, Asian, and Latin American theologians enlarged our vision by challenging us to do theology from a global perspective of oppression. Third world theologians urged us to analyze racism in relation to international capitalism, imperialism, colonialism, world poverty, classism, and sexism. For the first time, Black Theologians began to seriously consider socialism as an alternative to capitalism. We began to see the connections between the black ghettoes in the United States and poverty in Asia, Africa, and Latin America, between the rising unemployment among blacks and other poor people in the United States and the exploitation of the labor of third world peoples, and between the racist practices of white churches of North America and Europe and the activities of their missionaries in the third world. These discoveries deeply affected our political and theological vision, and we began to see clearly that we could not do theology in isolation from our struggling brothers and sisters in the third world. As oppressors band themselves together in order to keep the poor of the world in poverty, so the world's poor must enter into political and theological solidarity if they expect to create a movement of liberation that is capable of breaking the chains of oppression.

Early in the dialogue, black and third world theologians realized the importance of building a common theological movement of liberation. Although we have experienced several differences among ourselves (especially with Latins during the early stages of our dialogue regarding race and class analyses), our mutual commitment to doing theology in solidarity with the poor has held us together. We have too much in common to allow our differences to separate us. Furthermore, it became increasingly clear that our differences were largely due to a difference in context and to our mutual internalization of the lies that our oppressors had told us about each other. And after nearly seven years of dialogue under the auspices of the Ecumenical Association of Third World Theologians (EATWOT), including five major conferences, our differences have diminished considerably, while our similarities have increased to the extent that we are now engaged in the exciting task of creating a third world theology of liberation that we all can support.[11]

When the question is asked, "How do we do theology?" black and third world theologians agree that theology is not the first act but the second. Although our Latin American brothers and sisters, with the aid of Marxist class analysis, were the first to explicate this methodological point,[12] it was already present—and has now been reaffirmed—in all our theologies.[13] The first act is both a religio-cultural affirmation and a political commitment on behalf of the liberation of the poor and voiceless people of our continents. Our cultural identity and political commitment are worth more than a thousand theology textbooks. Our first concern is with the quality of the commitment that each of us has made, and will continue to make, for those about whom and with whom we claim to do theology. We contend that we know what people believe by what they do and not by what they say in their creeds, conference statements, or theological textbooks.

Praxis (i.e., a reflective political action that includes cultural identity) comes before theology in any formal sense. Therefore the initial motivation that compels us to do theology is not our desire to place books in university and seminary libraries for professors and their graduate students. On the contrary, our reason for making theology arises from our experience in the ghettoes, villages, and churches of the poor in our countries. We do not believe that it is necessary for our people to remain poor. Something must be done about their misery. Doing and saying are therefore bound together, so that the meaning of what one says can only be validated by what one does. Theology for us is critical reflection upon a prior religio-cultural affirmation and political commitment to be in solidarity with the victims of our continents.

Because the starting point of black and third world theologies is defined by this prior cultural affirmation and political commitment, our theologies bear the names that reflect our affirmations and commitments. We call our theologies, Black, African, Hispanic-American, Asian, Red, Latin American, Minjung, black feminist, and a host of other names that still sound strange to persons whose theological knowledge has been confined to European and white North American theologies. The identity of each of our theologies is determined by the human and divine dimensions of the reality to which we are attempting to bear witness. We do not begin our theology with a reflection on divine revelation, as if the God of our faith is separate from the suffering of our people. We do not believe that revelation is a deposit of fixed doctrines or an objective Word of God that is then applied to the human situation. On the contrary, we contend that there is no truth outside of, or beyond, the concrete historical events in which people are engaged as agents. Truth is found in the histories, cultures, and religions of our peoples. Our focus on social and religio-cultural analyses separates our theological enterprise from that of the progressive and abstract theologies of Europe and North America. It also illuminates the reasons why *orthopraxis,* in contrast to orthodoxy, has become for many of us the criterion of theology.[14]

Although black and third world theologians have been accused by many European and North American critics of reducing theology to ideology, that criticism is misplaced because it camouflages the human character of all theologies, particularly the ideological option for the rich that our critics have endorsed. Unlike our critics, we do not claim to be neutral in our theology, because the enormity of the suffering of our people demands that we choose *for* their liberation and *against* the structures of oppression. We cannot let the people who support the structures of oppression define what theology is. On this point, Black Theologians identify with Malcolm X: "Don't let anybody who is oppressing us ever lay the ground rules. Don't go by their game, don't play by their rules. Let them know that this is a new game, and we've got new rules."[15] The dominant theologians of Europe and North America want the old theological rules because they made them, and because their rules will help keep the world as it is—whites controlling blacks, men dominating women, and the rich nations keeping the poor nations dependent. But what most European and North American whites find difficult to understand is that we are living in a new world situation, and that this requires a new way of making theology. Again, I like the way Malcolm put it:

> The time that we're living in . . . and . . . are facing now is not an era where one who is oppressed is looking toward the oppressor to give him some system or form of logic or reason. What is logical to the oppressor isn't logical to the oppressed. And what is reason to the oppressor isn't reason to the oppressed. The black people in this country are beginning to realize that what sounds reasonable to those who exploit us doesn't sound reasonable to us. There just has to be a new system of reason and logic devised by us who are at the bottom, if we want to get some results in this struggle that is called "the Negro revolution."[16]

In EATWOT and other forums, black and third world theologians have been attempting to develop a new way of making theology. In contrast to the dominant theologies of Europe and North America, which are largely defined by their responses to the European Enlightenment and the problem of the unbeliever that arose from it, our theological enterprise focuses on the European and North American invasion of the continents of Africa, Asia, and Latin America, inaugurating the slave trade, colonization, and neo-colonialism. Our primary theological problem is not how we can believe in God in view of the modern, Western confidence in reason, science, and technology, which seem to exclude the necessity for faith in God; our theological problem, which arises from our encounter of God in the experience of the misery of the poor, is how to speak about Jesus' death on the cross without first speaking about the death of people. How can the poor of our countries achieve worth as human beings in a world that has attempted to destroy our cultures and religions? The chief contradiction, out of which our theologies achieve their distinctiveness, is the problem of the nonperson. That is why our most important conversational partners are not metaphysicians and other socially disinterested intellectuals in the university, but social scientists and political activists who are engaged in the liberation of the poor.

These concerns force black and third world theologians to establish links with the communities of the poor, and we have experienced in their ecclesial life something more than a routine gathering of like-minded people. In their worship life poor people reveal a knowledge of themselves that cannot be destroyed by the structures that oppress them. The liberating character of their spirituality can be seen in the way their faith in God evolves out of their cultural and political aspirations. It can be seen in the Christian base communities of Latin America, the black and Hispanic churches of North America, the indigenous churches and traditional religions of Africa, and in the religious life of Asia. In their worship, the God of grace and judgment meets the poor, transforms their personhood from nobody to somebody, and bestows upon them the power and courage to struggle for justice. Worship, therefore, is not primarily an expression of the individual's private relationship with God. It is rather a community happening, an eschatological invasion of God into the gathered community of victims, empowering them with "the divine Spirit from on high" "to keep on keeping on," even though the odds appear to be against them. In the collective presence of the poor at worship, God recreates them as a liberated community that must bring freedom to the oppressed of the land. Black and third world theologies are being created out of poor people's ecclesial and religious life, and they seek to interpret the God encountered in their religio-cultural and political struggle to overcome Euro-American domination.

It has been within the context of the churches and the religions of the poor that black and third world theologies have begun to reread the Bible. In this rereading many of us have begun to speak of the "hermeneutical privilege of the poor" and of "God's bias toward the poor." Although Latin theologians have done the most exegetical work to demonstrate the biblical option for the poor,[17] a similar concern is shared by most third world theologians. Suh Nam-Dong, an interpreter of the Minjung theology of South Korea, may be quoted as an example:

> Theological activities do not end with the exposition of biblical texts on salvation or liberation of people by God. In the Bible, the Exodus, the activities of the prophets, and the event of the Cross offer new insights, but these texts ought to be rediscovered and reinterpreted in the context of the human struggle for historical and political liberation today.[18]

While acknowledging that the distinctiveness of black and third world theologies is primarily defined by their particular contexts, the method of making theology may nevertheless be summarized as follows:

(1) Black and third world theologians make theology in complex religio-cultural contexts and with the political commitment to liberate poor people from oppression. Theology, then, is reflection upon the meaning of God in solidarity with the poor people who are struggling to overcome cultural and political domination. The acid test of any theological truth is whether it aids the victims in their struggle to overcome their victimization. There are no abstract, objective truths that are applicable for all times and situations. Truth is concrete, and it is inseparable from the oppressed who are struggling for freedom.

(2) Because the liberation of our people is the central factor motivating us to engage in the theological enterprise, the second element of our method is social analysis. Social analysis is bringing to light that which is hidden. It is unmasking untruth so that truth can be seen in a clear light. Black and third world theologians do not believe that the work of theology can be done unless the truth is known about the systems of domination. Racism, sexism, colonialism, capitalism, and militarism must be comprehensively analyzed so that these demons can be destroyed. We agree with Karl Marx's eleventh thesis on Feuerbach: "The philosophers have only *interpreted* the world, in various ways; the point, however, is to *change* it." In our use of the critical tools of the social sciences, as well as religio-cultural analyses, black and third world theologians have been attempting to make theologies of liberation rather than theologies of domestication.

(3) Through a political commitment that is informed by social and cultural analyses, a new hermeneutical situation is created. The Bible is no longer a mere ancient document whose meaning can only be uncovered by the historical criticism of biblical experts. Political commitment, informed by social analysis, provides an angle of vision that enables us to reinterpret the scripture and thus bring to light the message that European and North American biblical exegetes have covered up.

When the Bible is read in the community of the poor, it is not understood by them as a deposit of doctrines or of revealed truths about God. Rather it becomes a living book that tells the story of God's dealings with God's people. Its importance for black and third world theologians as a source for creating theology cannot be overstated. Even feminist and South African theologians, who question its authority (largely because of its sexist and racist misuses), do not ignore the Bible.[19] They wrestle with it, refusing all the time to allow an abstract biblical authority, written by men and interpreted by whites, to negate the authority of their own experience. God, they insist, cannot be less than the human experience of liberation from oppression. We must not allow an abstract Word of God to usurp God's Word as Spirit that empowers people to be who they are—fully human in search of the highest beauty, love, and joy.

(4) The meaning of the gospel that is derived from our rereading of the Bible cannot be communicated with old European and white North American theological concepts. The truth derived from our people's struggles must be communicated through the histories and cultures of our people. Truth is embedded in the stories, songs, dances, sermons, paintings, and sayings of our people. Since many of us have learned how to do theology in European and North American universities and seminaries, we have had to be converted to a radically new way of doing theology. We have had to ask ourselves how to make theology using the history and culture of our people, and what method is appropriate for these sources. The answer to these questions is not clear to many of us, and we are still working on it.

Because black and third world theologians have been doing theology for so short a time, and doing it together for an even shorter time, we do not have a fully developed method for making theology. These points represent my attempt to listen to what we have been saying to each other in our search to build a third world theology that is derived from the religio-cultural and political struggles of our people to overcome Euro-American domination.

Notes

1. This is a slightly revised version of an essay that was written for the Ecumenical Association of Third World Theologians' Conference on "Doing Theology in a Divided World: A Dialogue Between First and Third World Theologians" held in Geneva, Switzerland, 5–13 January 1983.
2. For an account of this bus boycott, see Martin Luther King, Jr., *Stride Toward Freedom* (New York: Harper, 1958).
3. The best general history of the black church is Gayraud S. Wilmore, *Black Religion and Black Radicalism* (Maryknoll, N.Y.: Orbis Books, 1983). See also Vincent Harding, *There Is a River: The Black Struggle of Freedom in America* (New York: Harcourt Brace, 1981).
4. *Black Religion* (Boston: Beacon, 1964), pp. 142–43.
5. The best source for an introduction to Malcolm X's nationalist views is his *Autobiography* (1964).

6. The best analysis of black power is Stokely Carmichael and Charles V. Hamilton, *Black Power: The Politics of Liberation in America* (New York: Random House, 1967).

7. This statement is found in Gayraud S. Wilmore and James H. Cone, eds., *Black Theology: A Documentary History, 1966–1979* (Maryknoll, N.Y.: Orbis Books, 1979). This is the most informative single volume on black theology.

8. *A Black Theology of Liberation* (Philadelphia: Lippincott, 1970), p. 17.

9. See especially Jacquelyn Grant, "Black Theology and Black Women," and Pauli Murray, "Black Theology and Feminist Theology: A Comparative View," in Wilmore and Cone, eds., *Black Theology*, pp. 418–33 and 398–417. See also the important essay by Theressa Hoover, "Black Women and the Black Churches: Triple Jeopardy" in the same volume, pp. 377–88.

10. An important account of Black Theology's contact with third world theologies is found in ibid., pp. 445–608. Black theologians have been involved in the Ecumenical Association of Third World Theologians dialogues since its organizing meeting in Tanzania (1976). Since Tanzania, dialogues have been held in Ghana (1977), Sri Lanka (1979), Brazil (1980), and India (1981). Accounts of these meetings have been published by Orbis Books: Sergio Torres and Virginia Fabella, eds., *The Emergent Gospel* (1978); Kofi Appiah-Kubi and Sergio Torres, eds., *African Theology en Route* (1979); Virginia Fabella, ed., *Asia's Struggle for Full Humanity* (1980); Sergio Torres and John Eagleson, eds., *The Challenge of Basic Christian Communities* (1981); Virginia Fabella and Sergio Torres, eds., *Irruption of the Third World* (1983). For an interpretation of Black Theology's dialogue with African, Asian, and Latin theologies, see my "A Black American Perspective on the Future of African Theology," *African Theology en Route;* "A Black American Perspective on the Asian Search for a Full Humanity," in *Asia's Struggle for a Full Humanity;* "From Geneva to São Paulo: A Dialogue Between Black Theology and Latin American Liberation Theology," in *The Challenge of Basic Christian Communities;* "Reflections from the Perspectives of U.S. Blacks," in *Irruption of the Third World.*

11. Our first efforts to transcend the particularities of our respective continents and to create a third world theology of liberation occurred at the New Delhi, India, conference (1981). See especially Fabella and Torres, eds., *Irruption of the Third World.*

12. The classic description of this methodological point is found in Gustavo Gutiérrez: "Theology is reflection, a critical attitude. Theology *follows;* it is a second step. . . . The pastoral activity of the Church does not flow as a conclusion from theological premises. Theology does not produce pastoral activity; rather it reflects upon it." (*A Theology of Liberation,* trans. Sister Caridad Inda and John Eagleson [Maryknoll, N.Y.: Orbis Books, 1973], p. 11.)

13. Black Theology emerged as a reflection upon the civil rights and black power movements. African theology's origin can be located as early as the 1950s and was inseparable from the movement toward nationhood

on that continent. A similar happening occurred earlier on the continent of Asia. An analogous comment can be made about feminist and other forms of liberation theology as well. The distinctiveness of Latin theology is its careful formulation of this methodogical point with the use of Marx's philosophy.

14. Again Latin Americans have been the most articulate in the formulation of this point regarding orthopraxis. See Gutiérrez, *A Theology of Liberation*, p. 10.

15. Malcom X, *By Any Means Necessary*, ed. George Breitman (New York: Pathfinder Press, 1970), p. 155.

16. Archie Epps, ed., *The Speeches of Malcolm X at Harvard* (New York: Morrow, 1968), p. 133.

17. See especially José Miranda, *Marx and the Bible: A Critique of the Philosophy of Oppression*, trans. John Eagleson (Maryknoll, N.Y.: Orbis Books, 1974) and his *Being and the Messiah: The Message of St. John*, trans. John Eagleson (Maryknoll, N.Y.: Orbis Books, 1977); Elsa Tamez, *Bible of the Oppressed* (Maryknoll, N.Y.: Orbis Books, 1982).

18. "Towards a Theology of Han" in Kim Yong Bock, ed., *Minjung Theology: People as the Subjects of History* (Singapore: Commission on Theological Concerns of the Christian Conference of Asia, 1981), pp. 53–54. A further explication of this point is made by Cyris Hee Suk Moon, "An Old Testament Understanding of Mingjung," and Ahn Byung Mu, "Jesus and the Minjung in the Gospel of Mark," in ibid. For Black Theology's use of the Bible, see my *God of the Oppressed* (New York: Seabury Press, 1975), especially chapters 4–7. For African theologians' view of the Bible, see Kwesi Dickson and Paul Ellingworth, eds., *Biblical Revelation and African Beliefs* (Maryknoll, N.Y.: Orbis Books, 1969).

19. The questioning of the authority of the Bible was sharply expressed by several South African and feminist theologians at EATWOT's Geneva conference (January 1983). While the attitude of many feminist theologians is well known, the biblical questioning of South African theologians was new to me. Some North American feminists reject the Bible and Christianity as incurably sexist. For a variety of perspectives on white North American feminist theology, see Carol P. Christ and Judith Plaskow, eds., *Womanspirit Rising: A Feminist Reader in Religion* (New York: Harper & Row, 1979).

It is important to note that many third world women theologians in Asia, Africa, and Latin America do not like the term "feminist" as a description of their theological work. They view it as Western and thus not fully accountable to their cultural and political aspirations. They do, however, affirm the importance of women's experience in making theology. See especially Amba Oduyoye, "Reflections from a Third World Woman's Perspective: Women's Experience and Liberation Theologies," in Fabella and Torres, eds., *Irruption of the Third World*, pp. 193–200. While black North American women do not reject the term feminist, they are not as negative in their attitude toward the Bible and Jesus as are many white feminists.

Feminist Theology as a Critical Theology of Liberation

Elisabeth Schüssler Fiorenza

Writing an article on feminist theology for an established theological journal is as dangerous as navigating between Scylla and Charybdis. Radical feminists might consider such an endeavor as cooperation with the "enemy," or at best as "tokenism." Professional theologians might refuse to take the issue seriously or might emotionally react against it. Even though the women's movement has been with us almost a decade, it is still surrounded by confusion, derision, and outright refusal to listen to its arguments. Yet since I consider myself a feminist as well as a Christian theologian, I am vitally interested in a mediation between feminism and theology. And good theology always was a risky enterprise.

In the first part of the article I intend to circumscribe the concrete situation in which feminist theology is situated, insofar as I summarize some of the main tenets of the feminist critique of culture and religion and its reception by churchmen and theologians. The second part will present feminist theology as a critical theology. First, I will attempt to point out the feminist critique of the practice of theology by professional theologians and institutions. Then I intend to show how in the tradition, androcentric theology functions to justify the discriminatory praxis of the church toward women. A final part will deal critically with myths and images of women. Even though the Mary-myth has emancipatory elements, it was not used to promote the liberation of women. Therefore it has to be balanced and replaced by a new myth and images which evolve from a feminist Christian consciousness and praxis. The article concludes with such an example of the feminist search for new liberating myths and images. [. . .]

Feminist Critique of Culture and Religion

Whereas the suffrage movement did not so much attempt to change society as mainly to integrate women into it, in the conviction that women would humanize politics and work by virtue of their feminine qualities,[1] the new feminist movement radically criticizes the myth and structures of a society and culture which keep women down. The women's liberation movement demands a restructuring of societal institutions and a redefinition of cultural images and roles of women *and* men, if women are to become autonomous human persons and achieve economic and political equality.

The feminist critique of culture has pointed out that nature and biology are not the "destiny" of women, but rather the result of sexist culture and its socialization. Women are denied the full range of human potentiality; we are socialized to view ourselves as dependent, less intelligent, and derivative from men. From earliest childhood we learn our roles as subservient beings and value ourselves through the eyes of a male culture.[2] We are the "other," socialized into helpmates of men or sex objects for their desire. Journals, advertisements, television, and movies represent us either as dependent little girls (e.g., to address "baby"), as sexy and seductive women, or as self-sacrificing wives and mothers. Teachers, psychologists, philosophers, writers, and preachers define us as derivative, inferior, and subordinate beings who lack the intelligence, courage, and genius of men.

Women in our culture are either denigrated and infantilized or idealized and put on a pedestal, but they are not allowed to be independent and free human persons. They do not live their own lives, but are taught to live vicariously through those of husband and children. They do not exercise their own power, but manipulate men's power. They usually are not supposed to express their own opinion, but to be silent or to voice only that of their fathers, husbands, bosses, or sons. Not only men but women themselves have interiorized this image and understanding of women as inferior and derivative. Often they themselves most strongly believe and defend the "feminine mystique."[3] Since women have learned to feel inferior and to despise themselves, they do not respect, in fact they even hate, other women. Thus women evidence the typical personality traits of oppressed people who have internalized the images and notions of the oppressor.

In the face of this cultural image and self-understanding of women, feminism first maintains that women are human persons, and it therefore demands free development of full personhood for all, women and men. Secondly, feminism maintains that human rights and talents or weaknesses are not divided by sex. Feminism has pointed out that it is necessary for women to become indepen- dent economically and socially in order to be able to understand and value themselves as free, autonomous, and responsible subjects of their lives. If women's role in society is to change, then women's and men's perceptions and attitudes toward women have to change at the same time.

Feminism has therefore vigorously criticized all institutions which exploit women, stereotype them, and keep them in inferior positions. In this context, feminist analysis points out that Chris- tianity not only had a major influence in the making of Western culture and sexist ideology,[4] but also that the Christian churches and theologies still perpetuate the "feminine mystique" and women's inferiority through their institutional inequalities and theological justifications of women's innate difference from men. Christian ethics has intensified the internalization of the feminine, passive attitudes, e.g., meekness, humility, submission, self-sacri- fice, self-denying love, which impede the development of self- assertion and autonomy by women. "The alleged 'voluntarism' of the imposed submission in Christian patriarchy has turned women against themselves more deeply than ever, disguising and reinforc- ing the internalization process."[5] [. . .]

Feminist Theology as a Critical Theology

Historical studies and hermeneutical discussions have amply demonstrated that theology is a culturally and historically con- ditioned endeavor. Moreover, historical-critical studies and her- meneutical-theological reflection have shown that not only the- ology but also the revelation of God in Scripture is expressed in human language and shares culturally conditioned concepts and problems. Revelation and theology are so intertwined that they no longer can be adequately distinguished. This hermeneutical insight is far-reaching when we consider that Scripture as well as theology is rooted in a patriarchal-sexist culture and shares its biases and prejudices. Scripture and theology express truth in sexist language and images and participate in the myth of their patriarchal-sexist society and culture.

The feminist critique of theology and tradition is best sum- marized by the statement of Simone Weil: "History, therefore, is nothing but a compilation of the depositions made by assassins with respect to their victims and themselves."[6] The hermeneutical dis- cussion has underlined that a value-free, objectivistic historiogra- phy is a scholarly fiction. All interpretations of texts depend upon the presuppositions, intellectual concepts, politics, or prejudices of the interpreter and historian. Feminist scholars, therefore, rightly point out that for all too long the Christian tradition was recorded and studied by theologians who consciously or unconsciously understood them from a patriarchal perspective of male dominance. Since this androcentric cultural perspective has determined all writing of theology and of history, their endeavor is correctly called his-story. If women, therefore, want to get in touch with their own roots and tradition, they have to rewrite the Christian tradition and theology in such a way that it becomes not only his-story but as well her-story recorded and analyzed from a feminist point of view.

Yet a hermeneutical revision of Christian theology and tradition is only a partial solution to the problem. Radical Christian feminists, therefore, point out that the Christian past and present, and not only its records, victimized women. A hermeneutics which merely attempts to *understand* the Christian tradition and texts in their historical settings, or a Christian theology which defines itself as "the actualizing continuation of the Christian history of interpretation," does not suffice,[7] since it does not sufficiently take into account that tradition is a source not only of truth but also of untruth, repression, and domination. Critical theory as developed in the Frankfurt school provides a key for a hermeneutic understanding which is not just directed toward an actualizing continuation and a perceptive understanding of history but toward a criticism of history and tradition to the extent that it participates in the repression and domination which are experienced as alienation.[8] Analogously (in order to liberate Christian theologies, symbols, and institutions), critical theology uncovers and criticizes Christian traditions and theologies which stimulated and perpetuated violence, alienation, and oppression. Critical theology thus has as its methodological presupposition the Christian community's constant need for renewal. Christian faith and life are caught in the middle of history and are therefore in constant need of prophetic criticism in order not to lose sight of their eschatological vision. The Christian community finds itself on the way to a greater and more perfect freedom which was initiated in Jesus Christ. Christian theology as a scholarly discipline has to serve and support the Christian community on its way to such eschatological freedom and love.

Toward a Liberated and Liberating Theology

Feminist theology presupposes as well as has for its goal an emancipatory ecclesial and theological praxis. Hence feminists today no longer demand only admission and marginal integration into the traditionally male-dominated hierarchical institutions of the churches and theology; they demand a radical change of these institutions and structures. They do this not only for the sake of "equal rights" within the churches, but because they are convinced that theology and church have to be liberated and humanized if they are to serve people and not to oppress them.

Although we find numerous critical analyses of hierarchical church structures,[9] we do not find many critical evaluations of the theological profession as such. Most recently, however, liberation theologians have pointed out that theology in an American and European context is "white" theology and as such, shares in the cultural imperialism of Europe and America.[10] Theology as a discipline is the domain of white clerics and academicians and thus excludes, because of its constituency, many different theological problems and styles within the Christian communities. Whereas in the Middle Ages theology had its home in cloisters and was thus combined with an ascetic life style, today its place is in seminaries, colleges, and universities. This *Sitz im Leben* decisively determines the style and content of theology. Since theology is mainly done in an academic context, its questions and investigations reflect that of the white, middle-class academic community. Competition, prestige, promotion, quantity of publications, and acceptance in professional societies are often primary motivations for the members of the theological guild.

Feminist theology maintains that this analysis of the life-setting of theology does not probe far enough. Christian theology is not only white-middle-class but white-middle-class-male, and shares as such in cultural sexism and patriachalism. The "maleness" and "sexism" of theology are much more pervasive than the race and class issue. The writers of the Old Testament lived in Palestine, and Augustine in North Africa, but their theology is no less male than Barth's or Rahner's. Today established theologians often feel free to tackle the social, class, and race issue, precisely because they belong as males to the "old boys club," and they themselves are neither poor nor oppressed. They generally do not, however, discuss the challenges of feminist theology, precisely because they refuse to begin "at home" and to analyze their own praxis as men in a sexist profession and culture. Therefore the much-invoked unity between theory and praxis has to remain an ideology.

Since the New Testament beginnings and the subsequent history of Christianity were immersed in cultural and ecclesial patriarchy, women—whether white or black or brown, whether rich or poor—never could play a significant rather than marginal role in Christian theology. When women today enter the theological profession, they function mostly as "tokens" who do not disturb the male consciousness and structures, or they are often relegated to "junior colleagues" dependent on the authority of their teachers, to research assistants and secretaries, to mother figures and erotic or sex partners; but they are very rarely taken as theological authorities in their own right. If they demand to be treated as equals, they are often labeled "aggressive," "crazy," or "unscholarly."

How women feel in a sexist profession is vividly illustrated in an experiment which Professor Nelle Morton devised. In a lecture "On Preaching the Word,"[11] she asked her audience to imagine how they would feel and understand themselves and theology if the male-female roles were reversed. Imagine Harvard Divinity School, she proposed, as a school with a long female theological tradition. All the professors except one are women, most of the students are women, and all of the secretaries are men. All language in such an institution has a distinctly feminine character. "Womankind" means all humanity: "women" as generic word includes men (Jesus came to save all women). If a professor announces a course on "the doctrine of women" or speaks about the "motherhood of God," she of course does not want to exclude men. In her course on Christian anthropology, Professor Ann maintains that the Creator herself made the male organs external and exposed, so that men would demand sheltering and protection in the home, whereas she made the female reproductive organs compact and internal so that woman is biologically capable of taking her leadership position in the public domain of womankind.

> Once in a while a man gets nerve enough to protest the use of Mother God, saying that it does something to his sense of dignity and integrity. Professor Martha hastens to explain that no one really believes that God is female in a sexual sense. She makes it quite clear that in a matriarchal society the wording of Scripture, of liturgy and theology, could only come out in matriarchal imagery.[12]

This experiment in imagination can be extended to all theological schools or professional societies. Imagine that you are one of the few men at a theological convention, where the female bishop praises the scholarly accomplishments of all the women theologians without noticing that there are some men on the boards of this theological society. Or imagine that one of the Roman Catholic seminarians tells you, who cannot be ordained because you are a man, that (after her ordination) she will be essentially different from you. If your consciousness is raised and you complain that you are not considered a full human being in your church, then a liberal colleague might answer you that you yourself should protest, since after all it is not her problem but yours. And all this is done to you in the name of Christian sisterhood!

Such an experiment in imagination can demonstrate better than any abstract analysis how damaging the masculine language and patterns of theology are to women. Therefore feminist theology correctly maintains that it is not enough to include some token women in the male-dominated theological and ecclesial structures. What is necessary is the humanization of these structures themselves. In order to move towards a "whole theology," women and men, black and white, privileged and exploited persons, as well as people from all nations and countries, have to be actively involved in the formulation of this new theology, as well as in the institutions devoted to such a "catholic" theologizing.

What, then, could feminists contribute to such a new understanding and doing of theology? Naturally, no definite answer can be given, since feminist theology is an ongoing process which has just begun.[13] I do not think that women will contribute specifically feminine modes to the process of theology.[14] However, I do think that feminist theologians can contribute to the development of a humanized theology, insofar as they can insist that the so-called feminine values,[15] e.g., concreteness, compassion, sensitivity, love, relating to others, and nurturing or community, are human and especially central Christian values which have to define the whole of Christian existence and the practice of the Christian churches. Feminist theology thus can integrate the traditionally separated so-called male-female areas, the intellectual-public and the personal-emotional. Insofar as it understands the personal plight of women in a sexist society and church through an analysis of cultural, societal, and ecclesial stereotypes and structures, its scope is personal and political at the same time.

Against the so-called objectivity and neutrality of academic theology, feminist theology maintains that theology always serves certain interests and therefore has to reflect and critically evaluate its primary motives and allegiance. Consequently, theology has to abandon its so-called objectivity and become partisan. Only when theology is on the side of the outcast and oppressed, as was Jesus, can it become incarnational and Christian. Christian theology, therefore, has to be rooted in emancipatory praxis and solidarity. The means by which feminist theology grounds its theologizing in emancipatory praxis is consciousness-raising and sisterhood. Consciousness-raising makes theologians aware of their own oppression and the oppression of others. Sisterhood provides a community of emancipatory solidarity of those who are oppressed and on the way to liberation. Consciousness-raising not only makes women and men aware of their own situation in a sexist society and church, but also leads them to a new praxis insofar as it reveals to us our possibilities and resources. Expressed in traditional theological language: feminist theology is rooted in conversion and a new vision; it names the realities of sin and grace and it leads to a new mission and community.[16]

As theology rooted in community, feminist theology finds its expression in celebration and liturgy.[17] Feminist theologians maintain that theology has to again become communal and holistic. Feminist theology expresses itself not only in abstract analysis and intellectual discussion, but it employs the whole range of human expression, e.g., ritual, symbol, drama, music, movement, and pictures. Thus feminist celebrations do not separate the sacral and the profane, the religious and daily life. On the contrary, the stuff of feminist liturgies is women's experience and women's life. In such liturgies women express their anger, their frustrations, and their experience of oppression, but also their new vision, their hopes for the coming of a "new heaven and earth," and their possibilities for the creation of new persons and new structures.

In conclusion: since feminist theology deals with theological, ecclesial, and cultural criticism and concerns itself with theological analysis of the myths, mechanisms, systems, and institutions which keep women down, it shares in the concerns of and expands critical theology. Insofar as it positively brings to word the new freedom of women and men, insofar as it promotes new symbols, myths and life styles, insofar as it raises new questions and opens up different horizons, feminist theology shares in the concerns and goals of Liberation Theology.[18] But because Christian symbols and thought are deeply embedded in patriarchal traditions and sexist structures, and because women belong to all races, classes, and cultures, its scope is more radical and universal than that of critical and Liberation Theology. Feminist theology derives its legitimization from the eschatological vision of freedom and salvation, and its radicalism from the realization that the Christian church is not identical with the kingdom of God.

Tension Between Christian Vision and Praxis

Christian feminism is fascinated by the vision of equality, wholeness, and freedom expressed in Gal. 3:27 ff.: in Christ Jesus "there is neither Jew nor Greek, there is neither slave nor free, there is neither male nor female." This Magna Carta of Christian feminism was officially affirmed by Vatican II in the Constitution of the Church (no. 32): "Hence there is in Christ and in the Church no inequality of the basis of race and nationality, social condition or sex, because there is neither Jew nor Greek. . . ." (Gal. 3:28) Yet this vision was never completely realized by the Christian church throughout its history. The context of the conciliar statement reflects this discriminatory praxis of the church, insofar as it maintains the equality for all Christians only with respect to salvation, hope, and charity, but not with respect to church structures and ecclesial office. The failure of the church to realize the vision of Gal. 3:28–29 in its own institutions and praxis had as consequence a long sexist theology of the church which attempted to justify the ecclesial praxis of inequality and to suppress the Christian vision and call of freedom and equality within the church.

A feminist history of the first centuries could demonstrate how difficult it was for the ecclesial establishment to suppress the call and spirit of freedom among Christian women.[19] Against a widespread theological apologetics which argues that the church could not liberate women because of the culturally inferior position of women in antiquity, it has to be pointed out that the cultural and societal emancipation of women had gained considerable ground in the Greco-Roman world. Paul, the post-Paul tradition, and the Church Fathers, therefore, not only attempted to limit or to eliminate the consequences of the actions of Jesus and of the Spirit expressed in Gal. 3:28, but also reversed the emancipatory processes of their society.[20] They achieved the elimination of women from ecclesial leadership and theology through women's domestication under male authority in the home or in the monasteries. Those women who did not comply but were active and leading in various Christian movements were eliminated from mainstream Christianity. Hand in hand wihth the repression and elimination of the emancipatory elements within the church went a theological justification for such an oppression of women. The androcentric statements of the fathers and later church theologians are not so much due to a faulty anthropology as they are an ideological justification for the inequality of women in the Christian community. Due to feminist analysis, the androcentric traits of patristic and Scholastic theology are by now well known.[21]

Less known, however, is how strong the women's movement for emancipation was in the various Christian groups. For instance, in Marcionism, Montanism, Gnosticism, Manicheism, Donatism, Priscillianism, Messalianism, and Pelagianism, women had authority and leading positions. They were found among the bishops and priests of the Quintillians (cf. Epiphanius, *Haer.* 49, 2, 3, 5) and were partners in the theological discourses of some church theologians. In the Middle Ages women had considerable powers as abbesses, and they ruled monasteries and church districts that included both men and women.[22] Women flocked to the medieval reform movements and were leading among the Waldenses, the Anabaptists, the Brethren of the Free Spirit, and especially the Beguines. The threat of these movements to the church establishment is mirrored in a statement of an East German bishop, who "complained that these women [the Beguines] were idle, gossiping vagabonds who refused obedience to men under the pretext that God was best served in freedom."[23] Such an emancipatory herstory is surfacing in the story of the mystics of the twelfth to fourteenth centuries,[24] or in that of the witches; in figures like Catherine of Siena, Elizabeth I of England, Teresa of Avila; in groups like the Sisters of the Visitation or the "English Ladies" of Mary Ward, in Quakerism or Christian Scientism.

Feminist theology as critical theology is driven by the impetus to make the vision of Gal. 3:28 real within the Christian community. It is based on the conviction that Christian theology and Christian faith are capable of transcending their own ideological sexist forms. Christian feminists still hope against hope that the church will become an all-inclusive, truly catholic community. A critical analysis of the Christian tradition and history, however, indicates that this hope can only be realized if women are granted not only spiritual but also ecclesial quality. Twelve years ago, in my book on the ministries of women in the church, I maintained that women have to demand ordination as bishops,[25] and only after they have attained it can they afford to be ordained deacons and priests. Today I would add that the very character of the hierarchical-patriarchal church structure has to be changed if women are to attain their place and full authority within the church and theology. The Christian churches will only overcome their patriarchal and oppressive past traditions and present theologies if the very base and functions of these traditions and theologies are changed.[26] If there is no longer a need to suppress the Spirit who moves Christian women to fully participate in theology and the church, then Christian theology and community can become fully liberated and liberating. Church fathers and theologians who do not respect this Spirit of liberty and freedom deny the Christian community its full catholicity and wholeness. Feminist theologians and Christian feminists will obey this call of the Spirit, be it within or outside established church structures. They do it because of their vision of a Christian and human community where all oppression and sin is overcome by the grace and love of God.

Christian feminists are well aware that this vision cannot be embodied in the "old wineskins" but has to be realized in new theological and ecclesial structures. If change should occur, a circular move is necessary.[27] Efforts concentrated on bringing women's experience and presence into the church and theology, into theological language and imagery, will not succeed unless the ecclesial and theological institutions are changed to support and reinforce the new feminist theological understanding and imagery. On the other hand, efforts to change the ecclesial and theological institutions cannot be far-reaching enough if theological language, imagery, and myth serve to maintain women's status as a derivative being in church and theology. Structural change and the evolution of a feminist theology, and nonsexist language, imagery, and myth, have to go hand in hand.

Toward New Symbols, Images, and Myths

Whereas theology appeals to our rational faculties and intellectual understanding, images and myths provide a world view and give meaning to our lives. They do not uphold abstract ideals and doctrines but rather provide a vision of the basic structure of reality and present a model or prototype to be imitated. They encourage particular forms of behavior and implicitly embody goals and value judgments. Insofar as a myth is a story which provides a common vision, feminists have to find new myths and stories in order to embody their goals and value judgments. In this search for new feminist myths integrating the personal and political, the societal and religious, women are rediscovering the myth of the mother goddess,[28] which was partially absorbed by the Christian myth of Mary, the mother of God.

Yet feminist theologians are aware that myths have also a stabilizing, retarding function insofar as they sanction the existing social order and justify its power structure by providing communal identity and a rationale for societal and ecclesial institutions. Therefore, exactly because feminist theologians value myths and images, they have first to analyze and the "demythologize" the myths of the sexist society and patriarchal religion in order to liberate them.

Feminist Critique of the Mary-Myth

Since the "myth of Mary" is still today a living myth and functions as such in the personal and communal life of many Christian women and men,[29] it is possible to critically analyze its psychological and ecclesial functions. From the outset it can be questioned whether the myth can give to women a new vision of equality and wholeness, since the myth almost never functioned as symbol or justification of women's equality and leadership in church and society, even though the myth contains elements which could have done so. As the "queen of heaven" and the "mother of God," Mary clearly resembles and integrates aspects of the ancient goddess mythologies, e.g., of Isis or the Magna Mater.[30] Therefore the myth has the tendency to portray Mary as divine and to place her on an equal level with God and Christ. For instance, Epiphanius, Bishop of Salamis, demonstrates this tendency in the sect of the Collyridians, which consisted mostly of women and flourished in Thracia and upper Scythia: "Certain women adorn a chair or a square throne, spread a linen cloth over it, and on a certain day of the year place bread on it and offer it in the name of Mary, and all partake of this bread."[31] Epiphanius refutes this practice on the ground that no women can exercise priestly functions and makes a very clear distinction between the worship of God and Christ and the veneration of Mary. Through the centuries church teachers maintained this distinction, but popular piety did not quite understand it. The countless legends and devotions to Mary prove that people preferred to go to her instead of going to a majestic-authoritarian God.

Yet although this powerful aspect of the Mary-myth affected the souls and lives of the people, it never had any influence upon the structures and power relationships in the church. That the Mary-myth could be used to support the leadership function of women in the church is shown by the example of Bridget of Sweden,[32] who was the foundress of the Order of the Most Holy Savior, a monastery which consisted of nuns and monks. She justifies the leadership and ruling power of the abbess over women and men with reference to Acts 2, where Mary is portrayed in the midst of the apostles. This instance of a woman shaping the Mary-myth for the sake of the leadership and authority of women is, however, the exception in the history of Mariology.

On the whole, the Mary-myth has its roots and development in a male, clerical, and ascetic culture and theology. It has very little to do with the historical woman Mary of Nazareth. Even though the New Testament writings say very little about Mary and even appear to be critical of her praise as the natural mother of Jesus (Mark 3:31–35),[33] the story of Mary was developed and mythologized very early in the Christian tradition. Even though some aspects of this myth, e.g., the doctrine of her immaculate conception or her bodily assumption into heaven, were only slowly accepted by parts of the Christian church, we find one tenor in the image of Mary throughout the centuries: Mary is the *virginal* mother. She is seen as the humble "handmaiden" of God who, because of her sub- missive obedience and her unquestioning acceptance of the will of God, became the "mother of God."[34] In contrast to Eve, she was, and remained, the "pure virgin" who was conceived free from original sin and remained all her life free from sin. She remained virgin before, during, and after the birth of Jesus. This myth of Mary sanctions a double dichotomy in the self-understanding of Catholic women.

First, the myth of the virginal mother justifies the body-soul dualism of the Christian tradition. Whereas man in this tradition is defined by his mind and reason, woman is defined by her "nature," i.e., by her physical capacity to bear children. Motherhood, there- fore, is the vocation of every woman regardless of whether or not she is a natural mother.[35] However, since in the ascetic Christian tradition nature and body have to be subordinated to the mind and the spirit, woman because of her nature has to be subordinated to man.[36] This subordination is, in addition, sanctioned with refer- ence to Scripture. The body-spirit dualism of the Christian tradi- tion is thus projected on women and men and contributes to the man-woman dualism of polarity which in modern times was sup- ported not only by theology but also by philosophy and psychol- ogy.[37] Moreover, the official stance of the Roman Catholic church on birth control and abortion demonstrates that woman in distinc- tion from man has to remain dependent on her nature and is not allowed to be in control of her biological processes.[38] According to the present church "fathers," as long as woman enjoys the sexual pleasures of Eve, she has to bear the consequences. Finally, all the psychological qualities which are associated with mothering, e.g., love, nurture, intuition, compassion, patience, sensitivity, emo- tionality, etc., are now regarded as "feminine" qualities and, as such, privatized. This stereotyping of these *human* qualities led not only to their elimination from public life but also to a privatization of Christian values,[39] which are, according to the New Testament, concentrated and climaxed in the command to love.

Second, the myth of the virginal mother functions to separate the women within the Roman Catholic community from one an- other. Since historically woman cannot be both virgin and mother, she has either to fulfill her nature in motherhood or to transcend her nature in virginity. Consequently, Roman Catholic traditional theology has a place for women only as mother or nun. The Mary-myth thus sanctions a deep psychological and institutional split between Catholic women. Since the genuine Christian and human vocation is to transcend one's nature and biology, the true Christian ideal is represented by the actual biological virgin who lives in concrete ecclesial obedience. Only among those who represent the humble handmaiden and ever virgin Mary is true Christian sisterhood possible. Distinct from women who are still bound to earthly desires and earthly dependencies, the biological virgins in the church, bound to ecclesial authority, are the true "religious women." As the reform discussions and conflicts of women congregations with Rome indicate, dependency on ecclesial authority is as important as biological virginity.

The most pressing issue within the Catholic church is, therefore, to create a "new sisterhood" which is not based on sexual stratification. Such a new sisterhood is the *sine qua non* of the movement for ordination within the Roman Catholic community.[40] Otherwise the ordination of some women, who are biological virgins and evidence a great dependency on church authority, not only will lead to a further clericalization and hierarchization of the church, but also to an unbridgeable metaphysical split between woman and woman.[41]

Traditional Mariology thus demonstrates that the myth of a woman preached to women by men can serve to deter women from becoming fully independent and whole human persons. This observation has consequences for our present attempts to emphasize feminine imagery and myth in feminist theology. As long as we do not know the relationship between the myth and its societal functions, we cannot expect, for example, that the myth of the mother goddess in itself will be liberating for women. The myth of the "Mother God"[42] could define, as the myth of the "mother of God" did, woman primarily in her capacity for motherhood and thus reduce woman's possibilities to her biological capacity for motherhood. We have to remain aware that the new evolving myths and images of feminist theology necessarily share the cultural presuppositions and stereotypes of our sexist society and tradition, into which women as much as men are socialized. The absolute precondition of new liberating Christian myths and images is not only the change of individual consciousness but that of societal, ecclesial, and theological structures as well.

Yet at the same time feminist theologians have to search for new images[43] and myths which could incarnate the new vision of Christian women and function as prototypes to be imitated. Such a search ought not to single out and absolutize one image and myth but rather put forward a variety of images and stories,[44] which should be critical and liberating at the same time. If I propose in the following to contemplate the image of Mary Magdalene, I do not want to exclude that of Mary of Nazareth, but I intend to open up new traditions and images for Christian women. At the same time, the following meditation on Mary Magdalene might elucidate the task of feminist theology as a critical theology of liberation.

Image of Mary Magdalene, Apostle to the Apostles

Mary of Magdala was indeed a liberated woman. Her encounter with Jesus freed her from a sevenfold bondage to destructive powers (Luke 8:3). It transformed her life radically. She followed Jesus.

According to all four Gospels, Mary Magdalene is the primary witness for the fundamental data of the early Christian faith: she witnessed the life and death of Jesus, his burial and his resurrection. She was sent to the disciples to proclaim the Easter kerygma. Therefore Bernard of Clairvaux correctly calls her "apostle to the apostles."[45] Christian faith is based upon the witness and proclamation of women. As Mary Magdalene was sent to the disciples to proclaim the basic events of Christian faith, so women today may rediscover by contemplating her image the important function and role which they have for the Christian faith and community.

Yet when we think of Mary Magdalene, we do not think of her first as a Christian apostle and evangelist; rather we have before our eyes the image of Mary as the sinner and the penitent woman. Modern novelists and theological interpreters picture her as having abandoned sexual pleasure and whoring for the pure and romantic love of Jesus the man. This distortion of her image signals deep distortion in the self-understanding of Christian women. If as women we should not have to reject the Christian faith and tradition, we have to reclaim women's contribution and role in it. We must free the image of Mary Magdalene from all distortions and recover her role as apostle.

In her book *A Different Heaven and Earth,* Sheila Collins likens this exorcising of traditions to the process of psychoanalysis. "Just as the neurotic who has internalized the oppressive parent within himself (herself) must go back to the origin of the trouble in his (her) childhood, so the oppressed group, if it is to move from a condition of oppression to one of liberation, or from self-contempt to self-actualization, must go back to its origins in order to free itself from its psychic chain."[46] Just as black people search history for models of identification that indicate the contributions of blacks to culture and history,[47] just as they strive to eliminate racist interpretations of history and culture, so too women and men in the church must attempt to rewrite Christian history and theology in order to recover aspects that have been neglected or distorted by patriarchal historians and theologians.

A close examination of the gospel traditions discloses already in the beginning of the tradition a tendency to play down the role of Mary Magdalene and the other women as witnesses and proclaimers of the Easter faith. This tendency is apparent in the Markan tradition, which stresses that the women "said nothing to any one, for they were afraid" (16:8). It is also evident in the comment of Luke that the words of the women seemed to the Eleven and those with them "an idle tale and they did not believe them" but instead checked them out (24:11). It is, moreover, reflected in the Lukan confessional statement "The Lord has risen indeed, and has appeared to Simon" (24:34). This Lukan confession corresponds to the pre-Pauline credal tradition quoted in 1 Cor. 15:3 ff., which mentions Cephas and the Eleven as the principal Resurrection witnesses, but does not refer to any of the women. This tendency to play down the witness of Mary Magdalene is also apparent in the redaction of the fourth gospel that takes pains to ensure that the Beloved Disciple, but not Mary Magdalene, is the first believer in the Resurrection (John 20:1–18).

The apocryphal traditions acknowledge the spiritual authority of Mary Magdalene, but can express her superiority only in analogy to men. They have Jesus saying: "I will make her male that she too may become a living spirit resembling you males. For every woman who makes herself male will enter the kingdom of heaven."[48]

The liturgy and the legend of the Western church have identified Mary Magdalene with both the sinner in the house of Simon and the woman who annointed Jesus' feet before his death. Modern piety stresses the intimacy and love of the woman Mary for the man Jesus.

In looking at these various interpretations of Mary Magdalene, we find our own situation in the church mirrored in her distorted image. Women still do not speak up "because they are afraid"; women still are not accepted in theology and the church in positions of authority but only in junior ranks and special ministries because they are women. The measure of humanity and Christianity is still man even when we stress that the term is generic, for only those women can "make it" who play the male game. Love and service are still mainly the tasks of women.

Looking at this distorted image of Mary Magdalene and of ourselves, we are discouraged and in danger of trying to avoid suffering. Thus we tend to fall back into the bondage of the "seven evil spirits" of our culture. Let us therefore recall the statement of Bernard: Mary and the other women were chosen to be the "apostles to the apostles." The first witness of women to the Resurrection—to the new life—is, according to all exegetical criteria of authenticity, a historical fact, for it could not have been derived from Judaism nor invented by the primitive church. Christian faith and community has its foundation in the messsage of the "new life" proclaimed first by women.[49]

Notes

This article first appeared in *Theological Studies* (1975), and is reprinted by permission. Part of the first section, which discusses the theological response to the feminist critique, has been condensed for reasons of space.

1. Beverly Wildung Harrison, "Sexism in the Contemporary Church: When Evasion Becomes Complicity," in A. L. Hageman, ed., *Sexist Religion and Women in the Church* (New York, 1974), pp. 195–216, makes the very helpful distinction between "radical" or "hard" feminism and "soft" feminism. See also her article "The Early Feminists and the Clergy: A Case Study in the Dynamics of Secularization," *Review and Expositor* 72 (1975): 41–52.
2. This is elucidated from a linguistic point of view by Robin Lakoff, *Language and Woman's Place* (New York, 1975).
3. See the now classic analysis of Betty Friedan, *The Feminine Mystique* (Baltimore, 1965).
4. Simon de Beauvoir's analysis is still paradigmatic: *The Second Sex* (New York, 1961); see also the discussion of her position by Mary Daly, *The Church and the Second Sex* (London, 1968), pp. 11–31.
5. Mary Daly, *Beyond God the Father: Toward a Philosophy of Women's Liberation* (Boston, 1973), pp. 140 and 98–106. See also G. Kennedy Neville, "Religious Socialization of Women within U.S. Subcultures," in Hageman, *Sexist Religion*, pp. 77–91. N. van Vuuren, *The Subversion of Women as Practiced by Churches, Witch-Hunters, and Other Sexists* (Philadelphia, 1973) deals with the "traits due to victimization" from a historical perspective.
6. Simone Weil, *The Need for Roots* (New York, 1971), p. 225.
7. Against E. Schillebeeckx, *The Understanding of Faith* (New York, 1974).
8. Jurgen Habermas, "Der Universalitätsanspruch der Hermeneutik 1970," in *Kultur und Kritik* (Frankfurt, 1973), pp. 264–301; "Stichworte zu einer Theorie der Sozialisation 1968," ibid., pp. 118–94. For a discussion of Habermas and the critical theory, see the Spring–Summer 1970 issue of *Continuum,* which was prepared by Francis P.

Fiorenza. See also A. Wellmer, *Critical Theory of Society* (New York, 1974), esp. pp. 41–51.

9. See, e.g., E. C. Hewitt and S. R. Hiatt, *Women Priests: Yes or No?* (New York, 1973); C. H. Donnelly, "Women-Priests: Does Philadelphia Have a Message for Rome?," *Commonweal* 102 (1975): 206–10; C. M. Henning, "Canon Law and the Battle of Sexes," in R. Radford Ruether, *Religion and Sexism: Images of Woman in the Jewish and Christian Traditions* (New York, 1974), pp. 267–91; L. M. Russell, "Women and Ministry," in Hageman, *Sexist Religion*, pp. 47–62; cf. the various contributions on ministry in C. Benedicks Fischer, B. Brenneman, and A. McGrew Bennett, *Women in a Strange Land* (Philadelphia, 1975), and the NAWR publication *Women in Ministry* (Chicago, 1972). I find most helpful the collection of articles by R. J. Heyer, *Women and Orders* (New York, 1974).

10. See F. Herzog, "Liberation Theology Begins at Home," *Christianity and Crisis*, 13 May 1974, and "Liberation Hermeneutics as Ideology Critique?" *Interpretation* 28 (1974): 387–403.

11. N. Morton, "Preaching the Word," in Hageman, *Sexist Religion*, pp. 29–46, and "The Rising Women Consciousness in a Male Language Structure," in *Women and the Word: Toward a Whole Theology* (Berkeley, 1972), pp. 43–52.

12. Morton, "Preaching the Word," p. 30.

13. See P. A. Way, "An Authority of Possibility for Women in the Church," in Doely, *Women's Liberation*, pp. 77–94; also M. A. Doherty and M. Earley, "Women Theologize: Notes from a June 7–18, 1971 Conference," in *Women in Ministry*, pp. 135–59. For a comprehensive statement of what Christian feminist theology is all about, see the working paper of N. Morton, "Toward a Whole Theology," which she gave at the Consultation of the World Council of Churches on "Sexism," 15–22 May 1974, in Berlin.

14. Here I clearly distance myself from those Christian feminists and authors leaning in the direction of Jungian psychology. The "equal or better but different" slogan is too easily misused to keep women in their traditional place. Nevertheless I appreciate the attempt to arrive at a distinct self-identity and contribution of women based on female experience. For such an attempt, see Sheila D. Collins, *A Different Heaven and Earth* (Valley Forge, 1974).

15. For philosophical analyses of how these "feminine" values contribute to women's oppression, see J. Farr Tormey, "Exploitation, Oppression, and Self-Sacrifice," *Philosophical Forum* 5 (1975): 206–21, and L. Blum, M. Homiak, J. Housman, and N. Sheman, "Altruism and Women's Oppression," ibid., pp. 222–47.

16. See *Women Exploring Theology at Grailville*, a packet prepared by Church Women United, 1972, and S. Bentley and C. Randall, "The Spirit Moving: A New Approach to Theologizing," *Christianity and Crisis*, 4 February 1974, pp. 3–7.

17. See the excellent collection of feminist liturgies by A. Swidler, *Sister-*

celebrations: Nine Worship Experiences (Philadelphia, 1974), and S. Neufer Emswiler and T. Neufer Emswiler, *Women & Worship: A Guide to Non-Sexist Hymns, Prayers, and Liturgies* (New York, 1974).

18. L. M. Russell, *Human Liberation in a Feminist Perspective: A Theology* (Philadelphia, 1974); J. O'Connor, "Liberation Theologies and the Women's Movement: Points of Comparison and Contrast," *Horizons* 2 (1975): 103–13.
19. See my "The Role of Women in the Early Christian Movement," *Concilium* 7 (January 1976).
20. See the excellent article by K. Thraede, "Frau," in *Reallexikon für Antike und Christentum* (Stuttgart) 8 (1973): 197–269, with extensive bibliographical refererences. See also C. Schneider, *Kulturgeschichte des Hellenismus* (Munich) 1 (1967): 87–117, and W. A. Meeks, "The Image of the Androgyne: Some Uses of a Symbol in Earliest Christianity," *History of Religion* 13 (1974): 167–80, who also point out that the emancipation of women in Hellenism provoked in some groups misogynist reactions.
21. Representative is the work of Rosemary Radford Ruether; see especially her article "Misogynism and Virginal Feminism in the Fathers of the Church," in *Religion and Sexism,* pp. 150–83.
22. See my book *Der vergessene Partner: Grundlagen, Tatsachen und Möglichkeiten der beruflichen Mitarbeit der Frau in der Heilssorge der Kirche* (Düsseldorf, 1964), pp. 87–91; and J. Morris, *The Lady Was a Bishop: The Hidden History of Women Within Clerical Ordination and the Jurisdiction of Bishops* (New York, 1973).
23. N. Cohn, *The Pursuit of the Millennium* (Essential Books, 1957), p. 167.
24. E. L. McLaughlin, "The Christian Past: Does It Hold a Future for Women?" *Anglican Theological Review* 57 (1975): 36–56.
25. Schüssler, *Der vergessene Partner,* pp. 93–97.
26. This is not sufficiently perceived or adequately stressed by G. H. Tavard, *Women in Christian Tradition* (Notre Dame, 1973). See also his statement in his article "Women in the Church: A Theological Problem?" in G. Baum, ed., *Ecumenical Theology No. 2* (New York, 1967), p. 39: "Once a Christian woman knows—not only in her intellect, but in her heart and in her life—that in her mankind is fulfilled, it makes no more difference to her that, in the present circumstances, she cannot be ordained. . . ."
27. This is also pointed out by Sherry B. Ortner, "Is Female to Male as Nature Is to Culture?" in Michelle Zimbalist Rosaldo and Louise Lamphere, *Woman, Culture, and Society* (Stanford, 1974), pp. 67–87.
28. See, e.g., B. Bruteau, "The Image of the Virgin Mother," in Plaskow and Romero, *Women and Religion,* pp. 93–104; Collins, *A Different Heaven,* pp. 97–136.
29. A. M. Greeley, "Hail Mary," *New York Times Magazine,* 15 December 1974, p. 14, 98–100, 104, 108.
30. For a wealth of historical material, see H. Graef, *Mary: A History of*

Doctrine and Devotion, 2 vols. (London, 1963), and C. Miegge, *The Virgin Mary* (Philadelphia, 1955).

31. Epiphanius, *Panarion* 79. See F. J. Dölger, "Die eigenartige Marien-verehrung," *Antike und Christentum* 1 (1929): 107–42.

32. Schüssler, *Der vergessene Partner,* p. 91.

33. The interpretation which points out that the fourth gospel conceives of Mary as the prototype of a disciple overlooks the fact that the scene under the cross defines her as "mother" in relationship to the "Beloved Disciple."

34. This image of Mary led in Roman Catholic thought to the ideologization of womanhood and to the myth of the "eternal woman." See G. von le Fort, *The Eternal Woman* (Milwaukee, 1954), and my critique in *Der vegessene Partner,* pp. 79–83; see also Teilhard de Chardin, "L'Eternel féminin," in *Ecrits du temps de la guerre (1916–1919)* (Paris, 1965), pp. 253–62; H. de Lubac, *L'Eternel féminin: Etude sur un texte du Père Teilhard de Chardin* (Paris, 1968).

35. G. H. Tavard, *Woman,* p. 136: "Pope Paul clearly asserts one basic notion about woman: all her tasks, all her achievements, all her virtues, all her dreams are derived from her call to motherhood. Everything that woman can do is affected by this fundamental orientation of her being and can best be expressed in terms of, and in relation to, motherhood."

36. V. L. Bullough, *The Subordinate Sex: A History of Attitudes Toward Women* (Baltimore, 1974), pp. 97–120.

37. Numerous analyses of the treatment of women in psychoanalysis and psychotherapy exist; see, e.g., Phyllis Chesler, *Women and Madness* (New York, 1972).

38. Cf. the analyses of phallic morality by Mary Daly, *Beyond God,* pp. 106–31; J. Raymond, "Beyond Male Morality," in Plaskow and Romero, *Women and Religion,* pp. 115–25; J. MacRae, "A Feminist View of Abortion," ibid., pp. 139–49.

39. E. Hambrick-Stove, "Liberation: The Gifts and the Fruits of the Spirit," in *Women Exploring Theology at Grailville.*

40. The issue is correctly perceived by G. Moran, "The Future of Brotherhood in the Catholic Church," *National Catholic Reporter,* 5 July 1974, p. 7, and G. B. Kelly, "Brothers Won't Be Priests Because Priests Won't Be Brothers," ibid., 18 July 1975, pp. 9 and 14.

41. For an exegetical and theological discussion of the notion of priesthood in early Christianity, see my book *Priester für Gott* (Münster, 1972), pp. 4–60.

42. This does not mean that we ought not to revise our sexist terminology and imagery in our language about God. It is absolutely necessary, in my opinion, that in a time of transition our vision and understanding of God be expressed in female categories and images. However, I do think we have to be careful not to *equate* God with female imagery, in order that Christian women remain free to transcend the "feminine"

images and roles of our culture and church and be able to move to full personhood.

43. On the relationship of the image to the self, see E. Janeway, "Images of Women," *Women and the Arts: Arts in Society* 2 (1974): 9–18.

44. A creative and brilliant retelling of the biblical aitiological story of the origin of sin is given by J. Plaskow Goldenberg, "The Coming of Lilith," in Ruether, *Religion and Sexism*, pp. 341–43.

45. *Sermones in Cantica, Serm.* 75, 8 (*PL* 183, 1148).

46. Collins, *A Different Heaven and Earth*, p. 93.

47. For the justification of such a comparison, see H. Mayer Hacker, "Women as a Minority Group," in Roszak, *Masculine/Feminine*, pp. 130–48, especially the comparative chart on pp. 140ff.

48. *The Gospel of Thomas*, Logion 114. See also the apocryphal writings *Pistis Sophia, The Gospel of Mary* [Magdalene], and *The Great Questions of Mary* [Magdalene] in Hennecke–Schneemelcher, *New Testament Apocrypha* 1 (Philadelphia, 1963), pp. 256 ff., 339, and 342 f.

49. This meditation was first published in the *Union Theological Seminary Journal* (April 1975): 22 f. It formed part of a liturgy which was led by women of Union Theological Seminary. I am grateful to the women at Union for the experience of sisterhood. They and the Feminist Scholars in Religion of the New York area helped me to sharpen my thinking on some issues of feminist theology.

Notes Toward a Jewish Theology of Liberation

Marc H. Ellis

The history of the Jewish people is one filled with anguish and struggle. More often than not, the defining motif of Jewish life has been exile, forced wandering, and lament. And yet through this travail the Jewish community has bequeathed much to the world: a developed monotheism, a prophetic social critique, an awareness of God's presence in history, as well as the foundation of two world religions, Christianity and Islam, to cite but a few of its major contributions. Perhaps as important for us, the paradigm of liberation that forms the heart of the Jewish experience, the dynamic of bondage confronted by the call to freedom, has been appropriated by struggling peoples throughout the ages. The songs of African slaves in nineteenth-century America, calling on God for freedom, echoed the lamentations of the Jews in Egypt. The Exodus tradition again emerges within the struggle of Latin Americans for justice, articulated in the writings of Latin American Liberation Theologians.

To cite these contributions is to pose a fundamental contradiction of world history, one that has been posed often and answered weakly. Why is it that a people that has contributed so much to the world has received such treatment in return? Why is it that to be a Jew today is to claim not the status of honor but that of victim and survivor? And why is it that such a status, born of suffering, is doubted and dismissed, as if a long and difficult history has no place in our concern or affirmation? And finally, with the concern for empowerment shown by the secular and religious left, why is it that a small and suffering people just emerging from the ovens of

Nazi Germany is ostracized and often condemned for its difficult attempts to empower itself in the state of Israel?

To a progressive Jew who has tried to understand the rebirth of a prophetic Christianity and affirm the genuine humanist-community of our day, these contradictions are haunting. For historical reasons, for a Jew to frequent Christian circles is to court suspicion of betrayal in the Jewish community; at the same time, to be a Jew among Christians is to become invisible, a relic of past suffering. Further, to be a progressive Jew who is religiously oriented is to be out of step with the secular left, Jewish and otherwise. Their claim to universality in concern for the suffering is here challenged by a similar concern, coupled with an energetic Jewish particularity. Finally, Jewish particularity challenges Christians to reflect critically on their own history so as not to engage in still another triumphalism, even if this time in the service of liberation. At the same time, a Jewish particularity which seeks to serve the world challenges the Jewish community, a community becoming increasingly conservative in its social and political stances.

Without overstating its significance, I believe that the recovery of genuine Jewish particularity challenges the secular and religious communities, including the Jewish community to be self-critical and to rethink many of its basic presuppositions.

Though we await a more specific definition, some main outlines of a contemporary Jewish theology of liberation can be posited now. First, it must be poised in the dynamic of particularity and universality, as a self-critical voice that comes from the depths of Jewish tradition and seeks to serve the world. Second, it must be distinctly Jewish in category and speech, thus carrying the Jewish people forward, yet generous toward other religious and humanist communities. Finally, a Jewish theology of liberation posits that genuine affirmation comes only through critical discourse and responsible activity in light of historical events. It seeks to be present in history rather than pretending to isolation or transcendence.

1

One cannot understand the Jewish community today without a sense of the past, for it was born in struggle and hope. The birth of the Jewish community obviously lies in ancient Egypt as recalled in the Hebrew Scriptures in the Book of Exodus. However, the experience of slavery and liberation has been repeated time and again in Jewish history, and for the last two thousand years the theme has been one of exile rather than liberation. To be in the throes of suffering repeatedly and still retain the promise of freedom is necessarily to take seriously the origins of both contemporary history and community. Interpretation of events becomes crucial, even consuming: at the heart of Jewish life is the dialectic of slavery and liberation, a paradox to be thought through and sorted out in each generation.

For contemporary Jews, the overwhelming experience of suffering is the Jewish Holocaust, the death of 6 million Jews and the attempted annihilation of an entire people. Interpretation of the event is omnipresent, though insights are diverse and often controversial. There are essentially four basic positions on the meaning of this event for the Jewish community, represented by four major Jewish thinkers: Elie Wiesel, writer and survivor of the Holocaust; Richard Rubenstein, a professor of religious studies at Florida State University; Emil Fackenheim, a professor of philosophy at the University of Toronto; and Irving Greenberg, a rabbi and director of the National Jewish Conference Center in New York City. One point at least is agreed upon: fidelity to the Jewish people in the present lies in grappling with this experience of destruction and death.

Elie Wiesel is a survivor of the Holocaust. Fundamental to his struggle to be faithful is the recounting of the story itself. Through fiction, essays, and public talks, Wiesel has tried to put into words the undescribable and to articulate the unimaginable as fidelity to the experience of the victims. From the first he knew that his role was to testify as a survivor; what eluded him was how to fulfill that role:

> I knew that the role of the survivor was to testify. Only I did not know how. I lacked experience, I lacked a framework. I mistrusted the tools, the procedure . . . . how can one be sure that the words, once uttered, will not betray, distort the message they bear? So heavy was my anguish that I made a vow not to speak, not to touch upon the essential for at least ten years. Long enough to see clearly. Long enough to learn to listen to the voices crying inside my own. Long enough to regain possession of my memory. Long enough to unite the language of man with the silence of the dead.[1]

Yet Wiesel's task is to find a voice for the voiceless and to keep alive a memory that is always on the verge of extinction. The task of remembering is in a sense more important than an answer to the question of the meaning of their suffering, because there is no answer. It is more important than prayer because, after Auschwitz, there is no prayer save that memory articulated in solemn silence.

Wiesel's mission is simply put: "Anyone who does not actively, constantly engage in remembering is an accomplice of the enemy. Conversely, whoever opposes the enemy must take the side of his victims and communicate their tales, tales of solitude and despair, tales of silence and defiance."[2]

For Richard Rubenstein, professor of religious studies at Florida State University, the stories of the dead coalesce in a different way. The challenge of Auschwitz is not simply to remember but to investigate its meaning in its religious and historical dimensions. The religious dimension is complex, relating to a belief in a God of history, the tradition within which Jews placed themselves, and the leadership of the Jewish community. Rubenstein sees all three aspects as having contributed to the death of 6 million and thus having been negated by the Holocaust event. The omnipotent benevolent God of history is shown to be a farce in the face of systematic death of the innocent. This God is culpable in that belief in God's omnipotence and benevolence contributed to the feeling among Jews that they would be preserved by God as a tribute to their chosenness. The tradition which posited suffering as an integral part of this special relationship with God is blamed because it encouraged passivity in the face of annihilation. Jewish leadership embodied this form of belief in God and compliance with those authorities who sought their annihilation. Thus the Jewish councils in Europe presided over the ghettos, provided all basic services to the people (including the policing of the ghetto), and fulfilled the orders of the Nazis even to the point of organizing the evacuation of Jews to the death camps.

For Rubenstein, the failure of God, tradition, and leadership signal the end of Jewish life as we know it, and to believe in its continuance is to indulge a fantasy which portends a repetition of the Holocaust event. And this failure moves beyond the Jewish community, the Jewish Holocaust represents the severing of the relationship between God and human beings, God and community, God and culture. The lesson of the Holocaust is that humanity is alone and that there is no meaning in life outside of human solidarity.

Yet the possibility of human solidarity itself is thrown into question by the Jewish Holocaust because it introduces systematic mass death as a permanent possibility of increasingly powerful states. Secular society is characterized by a form of rationality and systemic life that renders entire populations superfluous at a time when population itself increases exponentially. Thus a tragic impasse is reached: the religious world collapses of its own inadequacy and the modern world devours its own children.

Rubenstein's understanding therefore differs from Wiesel's in significant ways. Wiesel's overall sensibility is in story, recounting the horror and yet willing to remain in the tension of belief, though silent and unnamed. The way to prevent another holocaust is to preserve the memory of the first. For Rubenstein, the tension of belief is broken and holocaust continues unabated. The need now is to create a political sensibility both within the Jewish community and outside of it which responds to the social, economic, and political crises of modern life. If Wiesel's fidelity is found in the memory of the suffering, Rubenstein's is defined by a refusal to accept indiscriminate evil as an attribute of divinity, as well as the embracing of human solidarity as necessary in a desacralized world.[3]

The thought of Emil Fackenheim is best described as finding a middle ground between Wiesel and Rubenstein. Fackenheim is a professor of philosophy at the University of Toronto. For him the Holocaust is a challenge to both the faith and secularism found in a Jewish context. The midrashic framework of interpretation, which sees the present experience as continuous with the past and there-fore counterposes the two to lend depth to interpretation and mystery, breaks down in the cataclysmic event of the Holocaust. Root experiences such as the Exodus are challenged and over-shadowed as the clarity of faith is diminished. However, the secular option is also challenged, for in the final analysis the secular Jew was also singled out for annihilation. Even in claiming one's status as a born Jew, the secularist gives testimony to the survival of the Jewish people:

> A Jew at Auschwitz was not a specimen of the class "victim of preju-dice" or even "victim of genocide." He was singled out by a demonic power which sought his death absolutely, i.e., as an end in itself. For a Jew today merely to affirm his Jewish existence is to accept his sin-gled-out condition; it is to oppose the demons of Auschwitz; and it is to oppose them in the only way in which they can be opposed—with an absolute opposition. Moreover, it is to stake on that absolute opposition nothing less than his life and the lives of his children and the lives of his children's children.[4]

For Fackenheim, Auschwitz has a voice and a command: "Jews are forbidden to hand Hitler posthumous victories." The Jew after Auschwitz who claims affiliation with the Jewish people is a witness to endurance because Jewish survival is a dangerous and holy duty.

In another sense, this identification as a Jew after the Holocaust is an offering to humanity about the possibility of survival and testimony in an age on the verge of extinction. Thus Fackenheim rules out two possibilities as authentic responses to the Holocaust: abandoning Jewish identification with the poor and persecuted, and abusing identification with universal causes by fleeing from Jewish destiny. Still, if the option becomes one of either/or, the Jew must identify with the Jewish people. This identification is the essence of the commanding voice of Auschwitz.

Fackenheim's fidelity to the experience of the Holocaust places him midway between Wiesel and Rubenstein. Like Wiesel, he remains in the dialectic of faith, but he moves beyond story to the recognition that the Jewish present, in its diversity, is the locus of fidelity. A new midrashic framework has emerged that counterbalances annihilation and survival. This framework is chastened by the Holocaust and must be articulated lest the people perish through cynicism and attrition. The present Jewish community thus becomes a witness of survival and perseverance, and it is in this activity that the story of evil is remembered.

On the other hand, Fackenheim refuses Rubenstein's secular option because even secular Jews are within and testify to Jewish survival. The Jewish community is neither split nor irretrievably broken; Jewish life continues in an altered, though more urgent, form. The option that Rubenstein offers (seeing the Jewish Holocaust as a broader experience of the twentieth century) is neither denied nor affirmed. Fackenheim is propelled by the singularity of the Jewish experience both in slaughter and survival.[5]

In an important way, Irving Greenberg encompasses the previous interpretations of the Jewish Holocaust and moves beyond them. A rabbi and director of the National Jewish Conference Center in New York City, Greenberg perceives the Jewish Holocaust both as an indictment of modernity, because of its false universalism and the evil perpetrated under its aegis, and also as a critique of the Jewish and Christian religions, because they have contributed to powerlessness and hatred. Both modernity and religion have essentially passed over the critical challenge of the Holocaust in silence. The message of the victims to halt the carnage and to reevaluate the dynamics of social and religious life has fallen on deaf ears.

The recovery of the story and meaning of the Holocaust, then, is essential to the redirection of modern life. However, this redirection can only occur if the brokenness is affirmed and taken seriously. For the past two centuries a transference of allegiance from the "Lord of History and Revelation" to the "Lord of Science and Humanism" has occurred, but the experience of the death camps asks whether this transfer is worthy of ultimate loyalty. The record of secular culture does not justify its claim to authority: it provided the setting for massive death. According to Greenberg, above all else the victims ask that we not "allow the creation of another matrix of values that might sustain another attempt at genocide." The experience of the past and the possibility of the future urge resistance to the "absolutization of the secular."

This refusal does not, however, allow an escape into the religious sphere. After Auschwitz we can only speak of "moment faiths," moments when a vision of redemption is present, interspersed with the "flames and smoke of the burning children" where faith is absent. Greenberg describes these "moment faiths" as the end of the easy dichotomy of atheism/theism and the confusion of faith with doctrine:

> It makes clear that faith is a life response of the whole person to the Presence in life and history. Like life, this response ebbs and flows. The difference between the skeptic and the believer is frequency of faith, and not certitude of position. The rejection of the unbeliever by the believer is literally the denial or attempted suppression of what is within oneself. The ability to live with moment faith is the ability to live with pluralism and without the self-flattering, ethnocentric solutions which warp religion, or make it a source of hatred for the other.[6]

The dialectic of faith is illustrated in contemporary Jewish experience by the establishment of the state of Israel, which, like the Holocaust, takes on an aspect of a formative experience as well. "The whole Jewish people is caught between immersion in nihilism and immersion in redemption," Greenberg suggests, and fidelity in the present is remaining in the dialectic of Auschwitz (the experience of nothingness) and Jerusalem (the empowerment of a suffering community). It is Greenberg's understanding that the victims of history are now called to refuse victimhood as fidelity to the dead, and he adds the proviso that remembering the suffering compels the community to refuse to create other victims.[7]

In the Jewish experience, then, fidelity to the Other Kingdom revolves around the themes of remembrance, critique, and affirmation, all three of which are to be sought within a broken world. Complexity and diversity are recognized within these themes, and though urgency calls for clarity, the questions are not easily resolved. The emergence of the state of Israel is an example of this difficulty. From the vantage point of holocaust, empowerment of the Jewish community cannot be denied as an essential form of fidelity to the dead, but empowerment, particularly in the form of a state, places the community in an obvious dilemma: the desire to nurture life and community is often frustrated by the demands of security and material well-being in a hostile environment. We are also beginning to learn that entry into history as a powerful community can lead to faithfulness to or abuse of the formative event that is the justification for its existence.

Having emerged from the prospect of annihilation, the Jewish community has thus entered a present which offers possibility and danger. The formative event of the Holocaust can serve as a legitimator or a critique of power and so will determine how the desire to be faithful works itself out in concrete history. It is not too much to say that the road taken will be the ultimate judgment of fidelity itself, for if the struggle to be faithful is open to the future, it is constrained by the memory of the suffering.

For the Christian, the Jewish Holocaust is no less challenging. Whether in Nazi Germany or Poland or dozens of other countries, the persecutors were often identified as Christians. Though it is inappropriate to label any of these movements authentically Christian, the symbolic formation and reservoir of hatred which allowed Jews to be isolated and finally destroyed owes much to a millenium of Christian anti-Semitism. If this was not enough, at the great moment of crisis the institutional church sought self-preservation rather than the commitment necessary to mend a history covered with blood. It is the fact that there were Christians willing to place their lives in jeopardy to provide refuge from evil that allows the question of Christian fidelity to remain before us today.

Unfortunately, few Christians have contemplated the haunting difficulty raised by the Jewish Holocaust: What does it mean to be a Christian when Christian understandings and activity issued in the death camps of Nazi Germany? The first response of those who have authentically confronted this evil is to ask forgiveness of the Jewish people and seek repentance from the Jewish Christ whose essential message of love was betrayed. The second response is to remain in dialogue with the experience of the Holocaust as a formative event for Christians as well. Recognizing the reality of the death camps and the Christian complicity involved renders Christian faith and activity doubtful. Only by entering into the nothingness of the Other Kingdom can a Christian way of life become authentic in the present. This is what Johannes Metz, the German Catholic theologian, means when he writes, "We Christians can never go back behind Auschwitz; to go beyond Auschwitz is impossible for us by ourselves. It is possible only together with the victims of Auschwitz."[8]

What of those born Jewish or Christian whose faith has been torn away within and in response to the Other Kingdom? Whether consciously affirmed or not, the experience of dislocation and death has caused a great crisis in belief, to the point where the language of transcendence seems irrelevant to many. The result is usually either a passion to transform the world so as to prevent injustice and indiscriminate torture or more often a numbness and passivity that results in cynicism and paralysis. Is it not correct to say that just as the Jewish and Christian sensibilities were found wanting in the Kingdom of Death so, too, was the humanist tradition which carried the secular hope of the twentieth century? As noted earlier, it was the very advances of modern life which contributed to the construction and operation of the death camps. Like Judaism and Christianity, the humanist tradition became immersed in a formative event which challenged its interpretation of life. While some are able to remain in the framework of faith and human concern, vast numbers of people are now unable to continue in the dialectic and are either passively accepting their fate or else actively, through cynicism and power, causing others to suffer. For those divorced from religious sensibilities, can the Other Kingdom become an event which helps form an active and reflective orientation toward the world in which we live?

These are difficult questions which await further clarification. Jewish thinkers are courageous in their ability to face the unknown, though in a sense they have no choice but to face the darkness. Whatever their conclusions, it is the grappling with the horrific which signals the desire to be faithful to the experience of the Jewish people. As a whole, Christians and humanists have not honestly addressed the terror of systematic annihilation and what it means for their faith and their world view. For many the experience of the Jews is too bothersome to contemplate or is relegated to the dustbin of history, as if an enterprise 1900 years in the making, which issued in its most horrific form only forty years ago, is already archaic.

Difficulties glibly addressed or passed over in silence do not of course disappear but instead await rediscovery and interpretation. In the meantime we travel a path of ignorance toward an unknown destination which as often as not is recognizable in the form of nightmare.

2

Immersion into the Kingdom of Death represents a critique of twentieth-century religion and humanism in the theoretical and practical realm; it demands a rethinking of where we have come from and where we are going. In one sense, the Holocaust is a Christian and Western inheritance and the victims cry out for an answer. Yet in another sense the Jewish community carries forth this memory and therefore has a special task to be faithful.

The Jewish writers analyzed earlier pose the question of fidelity in stark terms: memory, survival, empowerment. However, the price now seems prohibitive. The rise of the neoconservative movement in North America, with its visible and articulate Jewish component, and the ascendancy to power in Israel of religious and secular expansionists (with the inevitable collaboration between the two), begin to cloud the horizon. Innocence is confronted by the marginalized of the North American continent: blacks, Hispanics, Native Americans. The necessity of empowerment in Israel is critiqued by the existence of an ever growing displaced Palestinian people. The desire to remain a victim for its moral capacity is evidence of disease; to become a conqueror after having been a victim is the recipe for moral suicide. It is not too much to claim that the acquired values of the Jewish people, discovered and hammered out over a history of suffering and struggle, are in danger of dissipation. In our liberation, the dialectic of slavery is in danger of being lost, allowing us to forget what it means to be oppressed. To forget one's own oppression is to open the possibility of becoming the oppressor.

In an imaginative and controversial book, *Jews Without Mercy,* Earl Shorris illustrates this drift by describing positions on social issues that are increasingly held by the American Jewish community:

> Blacks betrayed the Jews, the very people who helped them up out of racism and poverty into their current situation. Blacks are anti-Semitic. Jews should not help Blacks anymore, nor should they help other minorities, such as Hispanics, because they will only turn on the Jews as the Blacks did. . . . The poor of America are wretches without dignity. They constitute an underclass that it is best to neglect, for only through the rigors of necessity can they achieve dignity in the last decades of the twentieth century as the Jews did in the first decades of this century. . . .
>
> The State of Israel can do no wrong. The Palestinian people have no right to exist as a state, nor do Palestinian territorial claims have

any validity. The killing of an Israeli civilian by a Palestinian is an act of terrorism.

The killing of a Palestinian civilian by an Israeli is a justifiable act of self-defense. Any political position taken by an American Jew is justified if it can be associated with the survival of Israel.[9]

Shorris' descriptions are well stated and lead to important questions which he does not shirk: Are not those who take these neoconservative positions fundamentally changing the definition of what it means to be Jewish? Are those who adhere to these positions on social issues really justified in claiming to be Jewish? Or are they searching out a new religion which is something other than Judaism?

From the perspective of the Holocaust and the radical critique it offers to the religious and secular powers of our day, there can be little doubt. An empowerment which oppresses loses its claim of fidelity; hence, in the instant case, the claim to be Jewish cannot be sustained. Perhaps, then, a continuing and paradoxical feature of a contemporary Jewish theology of liberation is its existence on the periphery of sociopolitical and religious consciousness, not only vis-à-vis the contemporary world, but increasingly within the Jewish community itself. This position on the edge is reluctantly taken as fidelity to the victims of the Jewish Holocaust and to those everywhere who are suffering under the dominant economic and political systems of our time.

Our critique does not mean that the community should be abandoned. Rather, it is the call to recover the values of our tradition and to consciously choose them as the orienting focus of our life: to affirm life in a world of dislocation and death. Unfortunately, such a course cannot help but place one in conflict with the very community one loves because recognizing the conflict which exists means seeking to articulate it for the sake of the Jewish community and the world.

At least four movements of renewal are alive in the Jewish community today that are worthy of exploration on this point. They consider seriously the formative events of our time—the Holocaust and the birth of the state of Israel—and pose critical questions as to the direction of Jewish life.

The first is a neo-orthodox movement sparked by the charismatic Arthur Waskow. Waskow's journey is not unfamiliar to many Jews on the left. For years a secular social activist, in the 1970s he returned to Judaism to search out a rootedness and community previously neglected. The journey was far from easy, for recovery of his Jewishness necessitated a rigorous study of the tradition's sources, the Torah and Talmud. As Waskow describes it, the sojourn was akin to a conversion in that it was a radical change of perspective that reoriented his life and thought. From this point on, his social theory and activity proceed from wrestling with the tradition and the need to articulate its significance for modern life. Biblical images such as exile, idolatry, and covenant are ever present in Waskow's work, and for him the renewal of sociopolitical reality and the path toward justice lie in ancient biblical commands, like that to redistribute wealth every fifty years:

> The Jubilee traditions say . . . there is no way to achieve equality unless you accept that no human really owns the wealth, not even the proletariat, not even the people as a whole. It says, There is no way to achieve spiritual transcendence, no way to renounce material values, unless you know that everyone needs and must share the wealth. Moreover, the Jubilee speaks about a cycle of change. It does not imagine that the land can be shared and justice achieved once and for all. . . . The Jubilee says that in every year the poor must be allowed to glean in the corners of the field, that in every seventh year loans must be forgiven and the poor lifted from the desperation of debt, but that once in every generation there must be a great transformation—and that each generation must know it will have to be done again, in the next generation.[10]

Waskow's hope is for a renewal of Judaism that will release the Jewish community from wandering in alien concepts and struggles and allow it to become fully itself. "Wrestling" with the tradition provides insight into the modern world which contemporary life, by its very nature, lacks.

Waskow's sensibilities are fascinating and complex, and justice can hardly be done them here. What is crucial for our understanding, though, is the neo-orthodox strain Waskow displays: a relevant prophetic tradition is available to us if we take our own tradition seriously. Conversely, a renewal of body and soul leading to wholeness is unavailable to a people set loose from their past. Wholeness, as in the biblical Shalom, is impossible without justice.[11]

In the 1980s another movement arose which seeks to address the specific social and political realities that Jews face in the present rather than the spiritual roots of the tradition. Calling themselves the New Jewish Agenda, this movement hopes to bring progressive religious and secular Jews into a community of concern and activity to counteract the neoconservative drift. In so doing, they also seek to reaffirm the agenda of the Jewish community as being in solidarity with those who struggle for justice everywhere. The national platform they adopted in November 1982 includes progressive positions on feminism, lesbian and gay rights, economic justice, militarism, and the nuclear arms race. Following are excerpts from "Jewish Communal Life in the United States" and "Relations Between Israel and North American Jewry" which provide a flavor of the movement itself:

> We call for the full empowerment of all Jews. Our communal institutions must involve those whose needs have been consistently disregarded: our elders, Jews with disabilities, the poor, Lesbians and Gay men, Jews not living in nuclear families, Jews of color, Jews by choice, those of mixed marriages, and recent immigrants. All aspects of Jewish life, including leadership, must be shared equally by women and men. Leadership should not be based on financial status. Such a practice is contrary to Jewish values and excludes creative individuals. . . . We call for the reassertion of spirituality as the central component of our community's religious life, rather than the sterile institutionality that often predominates. We join with Israelis and others in calling for: Renunciation by all parties of all violence, including terrorism, as means to achieve their aims; recognition by the Arab states and the P.L.O. of the right of the State of Israel to exist within secure and recognized borders; recognition by Israel of the right of Palestinians to national self-determination, including the right to the establishment, if they so choose, of an independent and viable Palestinian state in the West Bank and Gaza, existing at peace with Israel; cessation of further Israeli settlement on the West Bank and Gaza, and an end to the repression of the Palestinians; direct negotiations between Israel and legitimate representatives of the Palestinian people, including the P.L.O., on the basis of mutual recognition and a commitment to peaceful co-existence.[12]

A third movement, Oz VeShalom—Religious Zionists for Strength and Peace—comes from within Israel itself. Founded in 1975 as a reaction to the misinterpretation of biblical texts and distortions of religious Zionism, particularly in the promotion of Jewish settlements in the occupied territories, Oz VeShalom has waged a political and educational campaign aimed at viewing these territories within a broader moral framework. As Torah-committed Israelis, they have taken up the political challenge of calling Jewish citizens back from the path of ethnocentricity and chauvinism. Moshe Unna, a founder of the Religious Kibbutz Movement, and Uriel Simon, professor of bible at Bar Illan University, are quoted in "The Cry of Religious Conscience," Oz VeShalom's first publication in English:

Our approach sees in Zionism a constructive movement which is based on positive ethical and social principles. The ties to religious and traditional foundations are vitally important in providing a value content to our national aspirations. These principles have prevented us in the past, and should prevent us in the future, from being drawn into blind nationalism, militarism, and the ignoring of fundamental humanitarian values. When we were weak, we had faith in the strength of morality and in the power of justice. This belief gave us strength. Today, when we are many times more powerful than in our near or distant past, we educate our young to a nearly all-encompassing faith in military strength. In the religious community an additional belief is fostered—that God must intervene on our side. This reversal happened to many revolutionary movements after they assumed power. It is the first sign of deterioration.[13]

A final movement within contemporary Jewish life is the burgeoning feminist consciousness. Feminism is active within all three branches of Judaism—Orthodox, Conservative, and Reform—and is extremely strong among secular Jewish women. Citing the patriarchal quality of Judaism, past and present, as the fundamental issue, proponents call for dealing directly with this most basic injustice. Many positions are encompassed within this critique, from a call for changes in leadership patterns to substantive criticism of a tradition formed for and around men. Dr. Paula Hyman, dean of the College of Jewish Studies of the Jewish Theological Seminary, believes that the very survival of Judaism is at stake:

I think that we have to be willing to bring our message continually to the Jewish community; that is, not only to issue a list of demands, but to point out the negative impact on the Jewish community of doing nothing and of the loss of women to that community. We feminists have not been completely successful in communicating that this is a fundamental and basic *moral* issue. If the subordination of women is at the core of Judaism, then Judaism doesn't deserve to survive. As a feminist, I am not willing to accept my subordination and the subordination of my daughters and my sisters as the price for the survival of Jewish tradition. We are, in a sense, calling Judaism morally to account—Judaism is on trial in some ways for us. It must be able to contend with this moral issue—and resolve it.[14]

These four movements represent a small but growing minority which seeks a redirection of Jewish life. To a remarkable degree they pose a similar question: what does it mean to be faithful to the Jewish community and the world? Though answers vary, a commonality is seen in their thrust for inclusivity (e.g., religious and secular Jews, men and women), their search for a renewal of community life in the midst of Holocaust and empowerment, and their refusal to be silent despite the pressure from political and religious neoconservatives for a moratorium on critique of the Jewish community. Thus a third area of a Jewish theology of liberation emerges: the movement toward inclusivity and renewal and the refusal to remain silent.

3

The dialectic of empire and community has surfaced in every age. "Empire" goes beyond the attempt to dominate, control, or manipulate others for one's own survival and affluence; it represents the organization of this impulse and the creation of structures that ensure a pattern of dominance and control. The impulse toward community is to choose another direction. Equality, cooperation, and mutuality in decision-making become the goal, and structures are created that call forth the nurturance of life rather than death. It is rare that either empire or community is perfectly realized, for much of both impulses remains to be recovered. In eras of domination, those who seek community become the way of the future; in eras of community, the will to dominate remains.

In a small but nonetheless intense way, we can see how this dialectic of empire and community is being played out in Jewish life at the close of the twentieth century. The will to community present in the Exodus was deepened through a history of suffering. Though there are many reasons for the survival of the Jews in desperate circumstances, it seems that this will to community is preeminent among them. The post-Holocaust world, however, is a different place with different demands for survival. There are many who fear that the Jewish people cannot survive without empire. Over against this view, there are those who reassert that the values of Jewish life are the essential witness to the world and that without that witness, Judaism ceases to be Judaism. A Jewish theology of liberation, then, has no choice but to balance the survival of the Jewish people with the preservation of its essential message of community. It asserts that the survival and preservation of its essential message are ultimately one and the same thing: there is no survival in any meaningful sense without a deepening of the witness its values offer to the world.

The witness of the Jewish people through the ages has been one of negation and affirmation: a *no* to unjust political, social, economic, cultural, and religious power and a *yes* to the struggle for freedom and justice. In every age the Jew has said no and yes while paying the price for both. Traditionally this negation and affirmation have been tied to the rejection of idolatry, the refusal to worship false Gods. Seen more broadly, this rejection of idolatry is the refusal to place systems of domination over the human quest for compassion and solidarity. The Jewish community and the early Christians maintained the essence of this witness against idolatry by refusing homage to the Roman emperor as a god. At the same time, they were refusing to bow before the empire as the defining and organizing force of community life.

As we know from history, the early Christians soon became aligned with the state and hence part of the empire. It was at this critical juncture that the radical message of Christianity began to lose its edge, and Christian peoples became the oppressor rather than the persecuted. The original impulse against idolatry lost itself in the construction of Christendom, which came to fruition in the death camps of Nazi Germany sixteen hundred years later. The rebirth of Christianity after the Holocaust lies precisely in its attempt to claim its own sin of idolatry and its refusal to be or serve the oppressor.

It is not too much to claim that idolatry, in its worship of power and materialism, is the major sin of the modern world. More than ever, modernity needs a witness against idolatry which will serve as the bridge to a new way of life. May we not say that the Jewish people, immersed in the dialectic of holocaust and empowerment, is unmatched in its ability to refute idolatry if only it will address its own recently acquired idols of capitalism, nationalism, and survival at any cost? Perhaps this witness can also serve as a bridge between religious and secular Jews among whom the question shifts from belief in God to the values of a good and just life that we mutually affirm. It may be a bridge among religious communities, for the focus need no longer be what God we worship, but the path of life we can travel together. Finally, it may provide the nexus between the progressive religious and humanist community because it avoids the question of theism in the concerted effort to focus on the human. Thus a Jewish theology of liberation requires a recovery of Jewish witness against idolatry as testimony to life in its private and public dimensions, as the essential bond of Jews everywhere, and as the fundamental link to religious and humanist communities of good will around the globe.

Witness against idolatry means, among other things, a rigorous analysis of our own empowerment and the need, difficult as it might seem after the holocaust, to break with that empowerment if the marginalization of others is the persistent cost. Israeli militarism and expansionist Zionism must be critiqued. However, the difficult question for North American Jews lies much closer to home: the neoconservative service of unjust power and the acquiescence of the community to American and global capitalism. The focus on Israel, as important as it is, has allowed American Jewry to neglect its own economic and political responsibilities. It continues to speak in a vague, liberal dialogue, though addressed to the powerful rather than the poor and oppressed. We now take pride in being more liberal and compassionate than conservatives and racists, as if being better than the worst is somehow worthy of celebration. The United States is still viewed as the land of freedom and opportunity for Jews, yet a prophetic critique would also name it as an empire which may imprison our will and values as the cost for our affluence and power. The ultimate price of empire is death, even when it pretends to life.

Thus in America, witness against idolatry means the revival of a theme which runs through Jewish history—the exile. The dynamic of slavery and liberation is upon us once again and the bondage of the death camps, partially relieved in Israel and America, arises within our empowerment. It is not so much a geographical exile, nor forced wandering; it is a new form of exile, rather, within those lands we legimately call our own.

The exile has always been a call to conversion, that is, a radical clarification of values, and to commitment, the willingness to bond oneself out of love. It is a gesture of solidarity—the movement of the heart, mind, and body toward those who are suffering—lived out amid conflict, doubt, and even martyrdom. Ultimately, a Jewish theology of liberation is a call to conversion, commitment, and solidarity in all its pain and possibility. To preserve our own heritage, to be faithful, we have no other choice but to walk this path.

Notes

This article originally appeared as part of an inter-ethnic/indigenous dialogue in *Doing Theology in the United States* 1, no. 1 (Spring/Summer 1985). Responses to it from different racial ethnic perspectives are available from the publisher, Theology in the Americas, 475 Riverside Drive, Room 1244AA, New York, NY 10115. It is reprinted by permission.

1. Elie Wiesel, *A Jew Today* (New York: Random House, 1978), p. 18.
2. Elie Wiesel, *Dimensions of the Holocaust* (Evanston, Ill.: Northwestern University Press, 1977), p. 16.

3. See Richard Rubenstein, *After Auschwitz* (Indianapolis: Bobbs-Merrill, 1966); *The Cunning of History* (New York: Harper, 1975); *The Age of Triage* (Boston: Beacon, 1982).

4. Emil Fackenheim, *God's Presence in History* (New York: New York University Press, 1970), p. 81.

5. See also Emil Fackenheim, *To Mend the World: Foundations of Future Jewish Thought* (New York: Schocken, 1982).

6. Irving Greenberg, "Cloud of Smoke, Pillar of Fire: Judaism, Christianity, and Modernity after the Holocaust," in *Auschwitz: Beginning of a New Era?* ed. Eva Fleischner (New York: KTAV, 1977), p. 27.

7. Ibid., pp. 7–55.

8. Johannes Baptist Metz, *The Emergent Church: The Future of Christianity in a Postbourgeois World* (New York: Crossroad, 1981), p. 19.

9. Earl Shorris, *Jews Without Mercy: A Lament* (Garden City, NY: Doubleday, 1982), pp. 12–16.

10. Arthur Waskow, *Godwrestling* (New York: Schocken, 1978), p. 116.

11. See also Waskow, *These Holy Sparks: The Rebirth of the Jewish People* (New York: Harper, 1983).

12. "New Jewish Agenda National Platform," 28 November 1982, pp. 1–6.

13. "The Cry of Religious Conscience," *Oz VeShalom English Bulletin*, no. 1 (March 1982): 1.

14. "Evaluating a Decade of Jewish Feminism: An Interview with Paula Hyman and Arlene Agus," *Lilith* 11 (Fall/Winter 1983/5744):24.

Part II

Reclaiming the Christian Message for the North American Churches

How have progressives in the North American churches heard the voices of the new theologians, both those in the third world and those in their midst? How have progressive theologians and church leaders responded? How would a different theology be done by the prosperous and comfortable? These are some of the questions that are addressed by the authors of the essays in this section.

On the occasion of her presidential address to the Society of Christian Ethics, Beverly Harrison, professor of theology at Union Theological Seminary, spoke of the need to adopt the tenets of liberation theology:

> You are well aware of the thesis of liberation theology that structures of power and privilege thwart and dehumanize not merely individuals, but groups of persons who as a result must live out their lives without the degree of self-direction appropriate to the human person, and without the necessary participation in the human community which would make it possible for "community" to be understood as genuinely encompassing them.[1]

In the first essay in this section, Harrison offers an agenda for a new theological ethic consistent with her belief in the necessity for a theology of liberation. This agenda provides a context for, and a challenge to, the essays that follow.

In the second essay, the Reverend Charles W. Rawlings presents a perspective on the difficulty that the Protestant church has in grappling with the issue of economic justice. Rawlings writes from the perspective of his own work, in Youngstown, Ohio, which involved the building of a church-labor-community coalition to

stop plant closings, and the unwillingness of the institutional Protestant church to deal with these issues. His essay is followed by one
by the Reverend Charles Yerkes, who ministers to an "inner-city"
church in New York City, and writes of his struggle to come to
terms with his role as a white male in the church, and the role of
that church in the struggle for justice. Both Rawlings and Yerkes
write as white male Protestants, and discuss the efforts of the
church to come to terms with the demands of the oppressed.
Rawlings talks about how the predominantly white male Protestant
church, which has had a privileged access to power, has interpreted
its mission as one of offering guidance and counseling and now
must hear the voices from the periphery (in this case, from Appalachia and the mid-West) and lead the church to take a more
confrontational stance. Yerkes discusses some of the same issues,
but with a focus on language. He argues that white male Protestant
perceptions of reality are embedded in the language of the church,
and that the time has come for the new understandings and perceptions developed by liberation theologians to be heard and internalized by the mainstream.

The theme of commitment and contradiction also occupies center stage in Gregory Baum's discussion of the Catholic church.
Baum, a Canadian Catholic theologian and editor of *The Ecumenist*,
argues that because the Catholic church sees itself as a worldwide
institution, its hierarchy must both coordinate and control national
churches, local tendencies, and individuals, all of whom, by moving
too fast and too far in any one direction, run the danger of disrupt-
ing the unity and tradition that is at the heart of Catholicism.
Nevertheless, the present Pope is attempting to bring about a
reorientation of the church, but one that at the same time deflects
the more radical challenges of Liberation Theology. This involves
the church in a "contradictory stance," for although it is influenced
by new currents, it cannot be a prophetic institution.

There is much to argue with here. The Vatican has silenced, or
attempted to silence, the strongest voices among the Liberation
Theologians and given encouragement to the voices of reaction,
already too powerful in Latin America. And the Vatican, despite its
voiced concern for the poor, sides with their oppressors and encourages the local hierarchy to do likewise, instructing them to
discipline radical priests and theologians. This debate is complex,
however. Some Liberation Theologians say to the Vatican: the
criticism you make of some aspects of Liberation Theology is certainly correct, and we accept your guidance in these areas, but *we*
do not believe the things you tell us we believe, and so your

criticism cannot be addressed to *us*. Since for strict Catholics there is no acceptable religious life outside the church, the decision to leave is made at great spiritual cost and is to be avoided if at all possible—instead, every effort is made to negotiate disputes. This is not so true for the Protestant world, where institutional schism is an accepted result of the individual's direct relation to God. The different givens assumed by Baum and Rawlings in their essays reflect these theological and ecclesiastical differences.

The last essay in this section, by Norman Gottwald, also a Protestant theologian and an Old Testament scholar, offers a case study of how a commitment to Liberation Theology can influence the approach to scholarship. In Gottwald's case, his adoption of a Liberation Theology perspective, combined with a keenly developed historical materialist methodology, has allowed him to develop revolutionary new interpretations of just who the biblical Jews actually were. Some of the fruits of his investigation are used in the essay included here to make telling points about the function of official religion in our own time.[2]

What unites all the essays in this section is a common commitment to understanding the core message of the Bible as being one of liberation. Harrison's essay points the way to a Christian ethics grounded in this approach. Yerkes offers a personal reflection and a theological understanding drawn from this perspective. Rawlings and Baum reflect on their Protestant and Catholic traditions in the light of the challenge to liberation theology. And finally, Gottwald offers an example of biblical scholarship and reflection on the parallels that can legitimately be drawn from the Bible, one key historical moment in the life of Israel and our own times. They all show us some of the ways in which Liberation Theology has spread into the centers of liberal religious thought and practice in North America.

Notes

1. Beverly Wildung Harrison, "The Dream of a Common Language: Toward a Normative Theory of Justice in Christian Ethics," *The Annual of the Society of Christian Ethics* (1983): 3–4.
2. *The Tribes of Yahweh: A Sociology of the Religion of Liberated Israel, 1250–1050 B.C.E.* (Maryknoll, NY: Orbis Books, 1979).

Agendas for a
New Theological Ethic

Beverly Wildung Harrison

Establishing Radical Justice
as the Theological and Moral Norm

To this point, the panoply of liberation theologies generated by communities of struggle and resistance have focused chiefly in two directions. The first aims to engage and sharpen the challenge that each theological movement addresses to mainstream and dominant Christian theologies. Reigning traditionalist theologies purport to speak, not from the "underside of history," but from the presumed "center" of Christian life and culture. The thesis of liberation theologies is that this "center" is, in fact, strongly shaped "from above"—from the voice of those who presume they can speak for all. Over against this "universal voice," the various liberation theologies have attempted to clarify the profound methodological shift involved in their perspectives. A mode of theological discourse that takes praxis, and more particularly a praxis of resistance to concrete and particular modes of historical suffering, as the appropriate locus of theological annunciation, must also challenge existing forms of theological discourse shaped, however inadvertently, by specific structures of domination in which Christianity has participated.[1] Liberation theologians have identified ways in which economic imperialism and class, white supremacy, Western/ Christian cultural and religious imperialism, or male supremacy and compulsory heterosexism have become imbedded in Christian teaching.[2] Participation in major historical contradictions results in far-reaching, even glacial, distortion in the purported "seamless garment" of truth claims made by Euro-centered "orthodox" Christianity.

Even so, it would be a half-truth to claim that the "hermeneutic of suspicion" opened up by various liberation struggles converges to yield either similar critiques of dominant Christianity or a harmonious reenvisagement of Christian truth. Tension, not convergence, is the order of the day among Christian liberation theologies. This tension is sustained in part by the neoconservative ethos of the dominant culture. Its religious acolytes feed a "divide and conquer" strategy toward progressive groups. However, liberation theological communities, no less than dominant theological groups, also internalize social contradictions that fall outside of their critical awareness. None of us easily sheds blindness to our/their historical privilege over others even more marginated than our/themselves. The underside of history, we are discovering, is no more a seamless garment than the overside, and the critical sensibility that unmasks theological legitimations of political-economic imperialism can re-annunciate hope in a "good news" of a gospel of liberation as adamantly white or male or Euro–North American supremacist as traditional Christianity has been. Conversely, black liberation theology or white feminist liberation theology can perpetuate political-economic imperialism or racial or male chauvinism as familiar to the ears of its victims as the cadences of those theologies produced by trafficking with Kings, Sovereigns, and Bourgeoise Magistrates. There is much that invites liberation theologians to avoid "making the connections" between the full spectrum of historic structures of domination and to trim the contours of their own "hermeneutic of suspicion" to placate the anxieties of those who mint the coinage of theological approval from the overside of history.[3]

Nevertheless, the cutting edge of theological critique among liberation theologians does converge sufficiently to enable an explicit shift in the criterion used to measure an adequate theological understanding of divine-human relationship.[4] The basic theological hermeneutic, or principle of interpretation, of liberation theologies places justice, as communal right-relationship, at the center of a proper understanding of spirituality. On this reading, theological utterance evokes our *shared* passion for justice.[5] Our common longing for a world "where there are no excluded ones" is literally the form divine presence takes among us.[6] A correlate of this insight is that the extinction of a concrete, embodied longing for justice is, literally, an experience of practical atheism, the repudiation of our shared, relational power—genuinely sacred power—to together create a world where mutual well-being conditions genuine personal well-being and fulfillment.

This shift to a hermeneutic of radical justice is a precondition for the reformulation of a Christian theological ethic that does not legitimate oppression either explicitly or covertly. Recent dominant Christian theological ethics has been characterized on the one hand by epistemological idealism and an abstract and overly personalized "love" ethic formulated by theological liberalism, or, on the other, by a Divine Command ethics that modern neo-orthodoxy reintroduced over against theological liberalism. The neo-orthodox ethic reaffirmed a radical disjuncture between divine agency and human action as a means of breaking theological liberalism's too uncritical liaison with dominant political groups. Liberalism's "love ethic" did indeed mesh too readily with bourgeois individualism and the public-private split endemic to liberal political theory, leaving Christians without a critical paradigm for political engagement. But the neo-orthodox corrective also mislocated the problem. It extended the liberal dualism in which the "spiritual" or "theological" was conceived as autonomous from the "political." Politics, on the liberal model, is always perceived as an *optional* engagement in "civil society"; the "spiritual" is perceived as the arena of *inter*personal, *not* of intercommunal, relations. The neo-orthodox theological-ethical paradigm perpetuated this liberal split. Purporting to "reobjectify" divine action, it located the "mighty acts of God" vaguely in the collective historical realm, but maintained continuity with liberalism by presuming that the really relevant nexus of divine-human relations is in the interpersonal realm. Neither theological ethic recovered a dialectical understanding of God and the world because they did not posit a direct relationship between human *social* justice and *personal* well-being.[7]

The diverse historical roots of the many Christian liberation theologies make it inevitable that varying types of resistance will be encountered between a theological hermeneutic of radical justice and existing traditionalist conceptions of Christian truth and ethical responsibility. For example, liberation theologies in a Roman Catholic context tend to converge with traditional Roman Catholic moral theology's insistence upon the priority of norms of social justice and communal well-being over against individualistic conceptions of happiness or well-being that have primacy in Protestant and/or secular cultures. Roman Catholic traditionalist moral theology also affirms, at least in principle, the capacity of human reason to grapple with moral dilemmas in ways that Protestant versions of Divine Command ethics do not. In spite of this convergence with traditionalist Catholic ethics, however, liberation theologians in a Roman Catholic context must contend with the intractable institutionalization of Christian theological truth-claims within a hierarchical structure that affirms the papal perogative to determine what theological claims are legitimate. The continuous threat of being declared "outside the pale" of Catholic truth that this structure delimits is obvious in the current Vatican witch-hunts against Latin American Liberation Theologians and against any who support women's liberation in a Catholic context.

Conversely, liberation theologies in mainstream Reformation contexts, or in left-wing Protestant settings, gain a positive hearing insofar as they appeal to the continuity between a radical justice hermeneutic and biblical or scriptural warrants central to Protestant traditionalist theological methods. However, liberation theologies in Protestant settings remain susceptible to charges of heresy, albeit of a different sort, whenever they press claims of justice in a way that threatens bourgeois notions of love, or when their proponents employ sources for theological ethics not derived from scripture. Any views that collide with a largely unconscious bourgeois scriptural hermeneutic, one suffused with the capitalist world view that has shaped mainstream Protestant (and, more recently, Roman Catholic) exegesis of scripture, is suspect. For example, when Liberation Theologians insist upon the pre-givenness of violence through institutional racism, class structure, or male gender privilege and *encourage* resistance to these oppressions, they are constantly accused of endorsing violence or rupturing the presumed "loving unity" of "universal" Christian community. The catch-22 nature of these charges is particularly acute for Protestant-rooted forms of Liberation Theology because mainstream Protestant Reformational theologies are identified with radical theories of human evil, i.e., those that are said to rule out confidence in our capacity to create more just and humane societies.

Achieving Historical Concreteness in Theological-Ethical Method

This array of accusations becomes even more acute when liberation theologies, whether in Catholic or Protestant settings, move to engage the second direction of the work of liberation theology alluded to at the outset. Traditionalist theological methods assume that Christian truth, whether embedded in scripture and/or tradition, is to be "applied" to historical situations. Such application—or causuistry—is presumed to follow upon clarification of theological truth claims arrived at apart from concrete historical analysis. By contrast, liberation theologies presume that analysis of historical contradiction is *the* starting point of the theological process itself. A consequence of the shift to a praxis-based theological method is such that historical analysis is *the* generative source of the critical theological-hermeneutical circle. Liberation theologies further contend that reinterpretation of scripture and formulation of discrete theological discourse is the *second,* not the first, step in a properly theological process.[8] Since the first step is shared resistance to oppression and engagement in concrete sociopolitical struggle, liberation communities must analyze carefully the historical roots of the oppression they resist.

Such analysis requires a conscious and specific integration of social theory into one's theological paradigm, whereas "established" theologies tend, on the whole, to represent largely unconscious integrations of the social theory of earlier dominant groups. For example, the traditionalist theologies of Roman Catholicism have been resistant to a historical mode of analysis precisely because premodern organicist and hierarchical conceptions of society still predominate over Enlightenment ones.[9] Protestant theologies, by contrast, are wed to conceptions of society derived from liberal political theory, embedding the main contours of capitalist social theory unawares. The organic and hierarchical metaphors of Catholic traditionalism were supplanted by the mixture of naturalistic and historical assumptions of the bourgeois era. Family and so-called economic activity were perceived as shaped by the order of "nature," while politics is perceived as that "sphere" of activity governed by human law and social contract. Mainstream Protestants have internalized an appreciation for the limited state and for constitutionally derived norms of politics, including a concern for historical methodology in understanding political process. But proponents of this liberal theory had no interest in integrating a historical understanding of family and kinship institutions or economic institutions into its historical paradigm.

Since the post-World War II era, mainstream Catholic thought in Europe and the United States has joined mainline Protestant social ethics in embracing the need for a historical method in social ethics. Ironically, Catholic theologians and ethicists have often appropriated the same streams of liberal social theory as Protestants had earlier. While historical method is embraced in principle, the bourgeois conception of the social world prevails. Politics, conceived as legislative and regulatory, is interpreted historically, but economic life and ethnic and kinship relations remain outside of the focus of the historical method employed.

Without exception, liberation theologies have had to break explicitly with the largely tacit assumptions of this liberal social theory. Contemporary liberation struggles provide living laboratories that expose the actual ahistorical perspective that limits the analytic value of bourgeois theories of social relations. The search for methods that cast genuinely critical historical light on social contradictions has led each genre of liberation theology to reengage Marxian social theory, albeit a "people's Marxism" rather than abstract academic-based neo-positivist Marxist theories such as structuralism.[10] This reengagement with Marxian social theory has hardly been uncritical. For example, movements aimed at resisting white supremacy rightly have challenged the lack of attention Marxian theory gives to the contradiction of racism as a precapitalist form of social oppression.[11] Feminist social theorists also have protested the failure of Marxian theory to clarify adequately the ways in which precapitalist modes of gender control and social reproduction condition property relations underlying the capitalist organization of social production.[12] Nevertheless, this liaison between liberation theologies and Marxian social theory—a liaison, it cannot be too strongly stressed, that is born of the more inclusively historical approach of radical social theory by comparison with bourgeois theory—has accelerated the suspicion of dominant theological groups toward liberation theologies.

There are many tensions between the newer liberation theological ethics that explicitly integrate radical social theory and the reigning liberal and neo-orthodox forms of Christian theological ethics that are at best quasi-historical. Insofar as neo-orthodox theologies deny the role of social theory in theological ethics altogether, liberation theologies are caricatured as "mere sociology." However, even the more sophisticated liberal modes of theological ethics, those that explicitly employ modern social theory, tend to disdain radical theory as "ideological." This state of affairs is exacerbated by both liberal and neo-orthodox caricatures of what Marxian social theory is about. Prevailing characterizations of radical social theory by dominant theologians include a broad range of erroneous claims. For example, it is often presumed that Marxism is *a theory of economic determinism that denies the relevance of politics to social change.*[13] Marx's metatheory of dialectical materialism is frequently confused with his concrete historical hypotheses about the development of capitalist social relations. Since Marx was a metaphysical materialist, it is assumed that he also meant to claim that economic activity always causally controls all historical development. Furthermore, it is presumed that a Marxian philosophy of social science is inherently positivist, that is, that Marxists believe that scientific knowledge is a noncontingent, predictive form of knowledge that aims at technological control of social process. While there are indeed forms of neo-Marxism, such as structuralism, that reinterpret the Marxian tradition in a scientific positivist mode, Marx himself inveighed against such theories of social science, insisting that positivist theories of political economy were themselves products of bourgeois mystification. He stressed the distinction between *positive* and *critical* knowledge and insisted that political economy yields critical knowledge, that is, knowledge that demystifies social appearances so that historical processes may be more effectually impacted by human agency.

Nor do liberal and neo-orthodox theological critics of Marxian social theory have a substantive understanding of the basic contours of Marx's critique of capitalist political economy. His attack on the naturalistic reductionism of rising bourgeois theories of political economy is ignored completely. Marx's debates with his contemporaries regarding their ahistorical presentation of the "market" are ignored. His challenge to the notion that economic rationality consists only of maximizing utility is discounted and his conviction that work is a necessary form of creative human self-expression is neglected. His insistence that *sensuous human labor,* not buying and selling, is the fundamental human economic activity—a claim that resonates with the economic world view of the Prophets of Israel—also is completely ignored. In the present neoconservative climate, polemics against the use of neo-Marxian social theory by liberation theologians are on the increase. However, if my analysis is correct, neither neo-orthodox nor liberal theological ethics can develop a serious socio-ethical alternative to liberation theology and ethics. Neither can illumine the range of social crises we now face in a historically concrete manner or find alternative strategic options for the social and cultural malaise we face. In fact, developments within Christian theological ethics confirm the thesis that in crisis "the center cannot hold."[14] Practitioners of Christian ethics are forced either toward neoconservative stances or toward more radical ones. (One popular neoconservative trend involves regression to moralizing about "lost" traditional values, a tepid form of neoconservative nostalgia.) A major symptom of the limits of liberal social theory in mainstream theological ethics is the inability of these theologies to analyze and illumine the contemporary dynamics of the U.S. political economy that daily shape the lives of people in this society. The absence of a serious economic ethic bespeaks a pervasive suppression of economic reality, which remains all but invisible in both neo-orthodox and liberal Christian social ethics.[15]

Both of these types of Christian social ethics leave unchallenged the basic paradigm of neoclassical economics, unaware that a Marxian understanding of economic reality challenges this paradigm in terms of what economic reality is. Even deeply committed liberals who strongly support liberal welfare policies tend to portray our public policy options as necessary trade-offs between support for capital formation and the dangers of economic stagnation. Liberal theories of justice characterize social justice as a desirable goal, but one beset by inevitable trade-offs between more equitable distribution and threats to personal liberty. The "justice imaginable" within liberalism does not address at all the issues of economic power and control.[16] Economic ethical concerns are expressed only as a question of income distribution, the division of resources already produced. All challenges to capitalist modes of production are heard, within the liberal paradigm, as calls for state-centralized economic planning. In fact, dominant Christian theological ethics defines socialism as capitalist ideologists define it—as state capitalism. The historical roots of socialist or communist social theory are not understood; nor is the history of debate among progressive theorists appreciated. The basic thesis of all early anticapitalist social theory—that political democracy cannot survive in the absence of economic democracy—is in no way grasped.

The ambiguities of liberal and neo-orthodox social ethics on economic questions are reflected even in the best of mainstream Christian theological ethics. For example, the first draft of the National Council of Bishops' Pastoral Letter on Catholic Social Teaching and the Economy, for all its moral concern, reflects the absence of a historical perspective on economic development, most particularly in the ambivalence of policy prescriptions it embraces.[17] Failure to challenge basic patterns of economic control, or to identify how neoclassical political economy marginalizes questions of human well-being in relation to economic policy, weakens the incisiveness of this otherwise morally sensitive analysis.

A central challenge for a liberation theological ethical agenda, then, is to restore the centrality of economic well-being to a Christian theological-moral vision. We must insist that economic well-being is not merely a matter of income distribution, but requires a conjoining of sensuous human labor with human dignity and self-direction, and involves participation in decisions about the use of socially produced wealth. We must also challenge the commoditization of all human activity and all social relations which is the consequence of capitalist hegemony over all aspects of life. And we must demonstrate, in the face of growing ideological mystification of dominant groups, that our own society—like the wider global community—is undergoing increased class stratification, racial oppression, and gender injustice.

To make clear why advanced capitalist political economies are unwilling to substantively address the issues of domestic justice, and are even less capable of facing the global scope of these same injustices, requires a massive reorientation of our political sensibilities and our collective understanding of our own national history. In spite of the theological pretensions of mainstream theologians who claim to challenge prevailing cultural myths, Christian theological ethics has not yet achieved a genuinely critical stance toward reigning economic interests. The theological ethic of liberation theologies must aim, finally, to place economic justice squarely at the center of the agenda of Christian moral imagination.

Notes

1. On the meaning of "annunciation" see Gustavo Gutierrez. *A Theology of Liberation* (Maryknoll, New York: Orbis, 1973), pp. 265–272.
2. Economic imperialism and class are, of course, the primary contradictions stressed in Latin American Liberation Theology. On *white supremacy*, see especially Cecil Cone, *Identity Crisis in Black Theology*; James Cone, *God of the Oppressed* (New York: Seabury Press, 1975) and *For My People: Black Theology and the Black Church* (Maryknoll, NY: Orbis Books, 1984), Cornel West, *Prophesy Deliverance: An Afro-American Revolutionary Christianity* (Philadelphia: Westminster Press, 1982). On *Western/Christian cultural and religious imperialism*, see Rosemary Radford Ruether, *Faith and Fratricide: The Theological Roots of Anti-Semitism* (New York: Seabury Press, 1974); Kosuke Koyama, *Three Mile an Hour God* (Maryknoll, NY: Orbis Books, 1979); C. S. Song, *Tell Us Our Names: Story Theology from an Asian Perspective* (Maryknoll, NY: Orbis Books, 1984). On *male supremacy*, see Mary Daly, *Beyond God the Father: Toward a Philosophy of Women's Liberation* (Boston: Beacon, 1973) and *Gyn/Ecology: The Metaethics of Radical Feminism* (Boston: Beacon, 1978); Carter Heyward, *The Redemption of God: A Theology of Mutual Relation* (Washington, DC: University Press of America, 1982); Rosemary Radford Ruether, *Sexism and God-Talk: Toward a Feminist Theology* (Boston: Beacon, 1983); Starhawk, *Dreaming the Dark: Magic, Sex, and Politics* (Boston: Beacon, 1982). And on *compulsory heterosexism*, see Carter

Heyward, *Our Passion for Justice: Images of Power, Sexuality, and Liberation* (New York: Pilgrim Press, 1984).

3. On "making the connections," see Beverly Harrison and Carol Robb, *Making the Connections: Essays in Feminist Social Ethics* (Boston: Beacon, 1985).

4. See Beverly Harrison, "The Dream of a Common Language" in the *Annual of the Society of Christian Ethics* (1983).

5. See Heyward, *Our Passion for Justice.*

6. Jules Girardi, "Class Struggle and the Excluded Ones," trans. and distrib. by New York Circus; from *Amor Cristiano y Lucha de Classes* (Salamanca, Spain: Ediciones Sigueme, 1975).

7. See Beverly Harrison, "Human Sexuality and Mutuality" in Judith L. Weidman, ed., *Christian Feminism: Visions of a New Humanity* (San Francisco: Harper and Row, 1984).

8. Gustavo Gutiérrez, *A Theology of Liberation* (Maryknoll, NY: Orbis Books, 1973).

9. Ibid.

10. Ibid. This distinction originated with Latin American Liberation Theology.

11. See West, *Prophesy Deliverance.*

12. Nancy Hartsock, *Money, Sex, and Power: Toward a Feminist Historical Materialism* (New York: Longmans, 1983).

13. For a more detailed analysis of Christian theological misinterpretations of Marxism, see Beverly Harrison and Carol Robb, *Making the Connections* (Boston: Beacon, 1985), especially pp. 54–80.

14. See Marvin Mahan Ellison, *The Center Cannot Hold: The Search for a Global Economy of Justice* (Washington, DC: University Press of America, 1983). Ellisons's work is invaluable for clarifying the ideological dimensions of the debate on economic development in social theory, ecclesiastical discussion, and theological ethics.

15. See Harrison, *Making the Connections,* chap. 4. See also Eugene Jones, "The Justice Imaginable: The Conceptions of Action and the Possibilities of Justice Delimited in Neo-classical and Marxian Value and Distribution Theories," Ph.D. diss., Union Theological Seminary, New York, pending.

16. On "justice imaginable," see Jones, ibid.

17. See Beverly Harrison, "Social Justice and Economic Orthodoxy," and Gregory Baum, "A Canadian Perspective on the US Pastoral," *Christianity and Crisis* 44, no. 22 (21 January 1985).

A Late Awakening
in the Churches

Charles W. Rawlings

The church's story after World War II is about the struggle to come to terms with the intractable arrangements of power rooted in economic domination and the mask of legitimacy that makes it palatable to most people. The future of the witness for peace and justice in the Judaeo-Christian community depends on the clarity with which we sort out this puzzle of modern culture that combines the ideals of freedom and equality with the submission expected of us all with respect to market forces. During the war Karl Polanyi characterized us as a society that had become an "accessory to the economic system."[1] In the forty years since then most of the commonplace religious and ideological formulas used in more liberal churches and among politically progressive people have failed to come to grips with the complexity of a culture that measures freedom by possessions and finds equality largely in passivity and dependency.

While it is tempting to believe that these problems have been shaped by sinister and powerful forces exploiting the potential of mass media propaganda, the failure of both secular and sacred formulas to mobilize a strong movement for economic justice in the face of catastrophic social crises suggests that we do not yet understand how we have come to hold such blunt spears.

The matter requires urgent examination because we now live in a period of immense economic upheaval on a global scale. With capital shifting to worldwide investments, with the traditional manufacturing sectors of Western Europe and the United States drastically and permanently retracted, with millions of skilled people walking the streets with the pieces of their broken vocations in their hands, it is staggering to discover that no new social movement has yet been formed from the worst economic crisis in fifty years. Growing economic concentration and its effect in declining democratic institutions suggest that the absence of a new justice movement is a road to generations of darkness in human society.

In hundreds of communities across the United States where the economic lifeblood has been cut off by deindustrialization and where the stability of families and local institutions has been destroyed, a ghastly suicide pact has emerged. For the sake of their identity with the ideals of freedom and individualism, people pledge themselves to the very systems of power that have stripped them of their dignity. Their hope is that loyalty will bring its reward. On countless shop floors where shut-down notices have gone up workers scramble and struggle with one another for seniority positions and benefits, they cajole and "work" the outplacement counselors the large corporations bring in to provide job search assistance, but they do not, except in rare cases, join together to plan and execute a common strategy aimed at the power of others to disempower themselves.

In the present crisis, economic chaos and disarray may have shaken confidence in the rhetoric of freedom and opportunity, but the patriotic slogans and popular cliches represent a symbolism upon which people have become dependent. The result is a humiliating and tragic surrender of basic dignity. "My job," said one personnel manager, "is to terminate everyone on the workforce by Chrismas and last of all to terminate myself." He was talking about the fate of twenty-five hundred people. The plant closed without a protest.

Both the religious and progressive secular communities must take a measure of responsibility for this tragedy. Its pathos and scope document the failure of our own voices and not a few of our ideas.

Our soul-searching should lead us to at least two strategic reflections: one on the church's relations with power and wealth—especially since World War II—and the other on the ultimately antisocial ideal of individualism. If we are to discover a fresh language of human vision and hope, a relational and communitarian sense of social justice must be found and expressed that will help people to a new understanding of their own dignity.

The Churches in the Age of Affluence

There is a striking discontinuity in the American experience before and after World War II. The nation had been in a ten-year depression when the war abruptly created full employment. Afterward the socialist organizing efforts that had flourished in the 1930s were resumed but foundered, not only because of anticommunist purges but also because good times were increasingly prevalent. The mood had changed from dark pessimism to great optimism.

While the United States had emerged from the war the preeminent world power, the war also seemed to transcend and resolve the contradictions and inequalities of economic life. Good had overcome evil. National solidarity was made sacred and tangible by the patriotic sacrifices of the dead. The new optimism grew well in soil made fertile by the mythic history of the westward frontier movement and the sense of American destiny. Postwar U.S. imperialism and prosperity seemed not only the appropriate reward for those who had sacrificially vanquished evil in the name of virtue, but formed a new civil religion that could rationalize inequality. This same mood change pressured the churches to confirm and support the new national optimism. One might say it captured the churches by giving them a more comfortable role in a culture that established everyone's identity in relation to domination.

In the first half of the century the churches had often been involved in struggles for industrial democracy and advocacy for socialism. At the turn of the century Walter Rauschenbusch's social gospel was only one aspect of a widespread socialist sentiment among many clergy. Although this sentiment waned after the Bolsheviks joined the Germans in 1918, other clergy emerged in the 1920s and 1930s who crossed swords with industrialists over specific issues of industrial injustice.

Reinhold Niebuhr, who moved from a prophetic pulpit in Detroit's labor battles to teach at Union Theological Seminary in New York, was perhaps the outstanding example. Before World War II he had been an explicit socialist and frequent critic of management. His most famous early book, *Moral Man and Immoral Society,* saw the vision of perfect justice as a "sublime madness" necessary to do battle against malignant power and wickedness in high places.[2] But Niebuhr did not like the perfectionist stance of the Communists and by the 1940s he had much less to say about his socialist affinities and spoke more often of Christian realism. By 1948 the publishing giant, Henry Luce, had put Niebuhr on the cover of *Time* magazine, making him a symbol of a sort of "third way" (between capitalism and socialism), in the form of harmony between the church and business.[3] Its secular version was a more subtle change in which labor in its anti-communist form became the partner of business instead of its adversary.

This sharp discontinuity with ethical questions and the restless and militant spirit of struggles for workplace democracy in the 1930s led to the uncritical era of postwar affluence in the churches. With Niebuhr as their symbol, most clergy measured their personal success in terms of their partnership with the postwar generation of prosperous and worldly business leaders (who were all too ready to agree with the theologians that ethics and virtue always remained proximate and somewhat ambiguous). It is not fair to Niebuhr to characterize him as the cause of all this coziness. Whatever his own relationship to the reactionary and anti-communist mood of the 1950s, the churches themselves were prosperously involved with programs of church growth and suburban construction. This meant that their former affinities for the struggles of working-class people in the decades before the war were increasingly embalmed in the status-conscious rise of middle-class suburban America. New management classes living in communities outside the central city created a separation of consciousness that made the old clashes between mill owners and mill workers in the same community impossible. Not only did the church's commitment to workers diminish, but workers themselves knew the new Jerusalem was in suburbia instead of in the old causes. Many abandoned old identities of solidarity in union struggles for Little League coaching assignments. As a seasoned AFL-CIO field representative told this writer while lamenting the lack of solidarity among workers, "The trouble is, we taught our children not to be like us."

As the churches left the cities and as southern in-migrations began to fill them with poor blacks and whites, some in the churches began to reconsider their role as the economic contradictions reasserted themselves. By the 1950s new, seminal movements began to re-claim the cities and the poor as the only genuine place for a church with justice perspectives to be. National denominations organized large urban church departments to support this renewed emphasis on the people of the city. But this new generation of clergy and lay leaders, influenced by the Niebuhrian pattern, saw corporate business as a potential partner in the reconstruction of the life of the city and its people. The labor struggles of an earlier era seemed remote in an age of labor laws and protected collective bargaining rights. The return of the church to the city had a certain simplistic and evangelical zeal that assumed all people of good will (regardless of distinct class boundaries) could be won to the cause of social justice.

Nothing in the experience of this new generation of clergy and lay leaders prepared them for the powerful reaction and rejection that exploded over their heads when the civil rights movement came north and the stability of urban communities created by the industrial age was shattered by social and racial conflict. It was only then that clarity returned about who owned the city. A whole generation of talented church leaders committed to the city was shattered by the reaction of business leaders, which abruptly altered the terms of the Niebuhrian peace. As many of these clergy were driven from their pulpits, they asked themselves what had happened that led both their mentors as well as themselves to be without comprehension of the vital distinctions they encountered when the owners and managers of capital claimed the prerogative to define justice.

It was not that clergy and lay leaders did not know about capitalism or the class-divided society. Many of them were at least liberals, if not vague closet socialists. But they did not conceive that irreconcilable forces were in place. If they had read Marx—and many clergy have had at least some exposure—they assumed that a modern and progressive transition was gradually underway. In the Niebuhrian age they had been led to the proposition that business leaders were increasingly accessible if tough-minded people not essentially hostile to the ends of economic justice.

In the 1960s the churches ran head-on into the self-legitimating pretenses of power in modern culture. The general trend to the political right since then demonstrates the charisma of this formula. It is this claim of power's legitimacy that must be sorted out if the suicide compacts between local communities and capital are to be overcome with a new politics. Moreover, the doctrinaire belief on the left that holds these forces to be purely expressions of monopoly capitalism cannot adequately account for the moral respect commanded by power. A new politics of communitarian justice cannot emerge until we see the complex forces that underly power's modern respectability.

Sorting out this problem involves an appreciation that both the religious community and the secular left have been complicit with some of the ideas that undergird power's claim to truth.

The root of our problem lies in the extent of the separation of the age of individualism from the social covenant between individuals. The holistic, communal, and hierarchical order of traditional societies, including the Middle Ages, was radically abandoned in the West in a movement increasingly intoxicated and optimistic about individual potential.

Roots of Individualism

The Renaissance and Reformation were both essentially movements that turned aside the traditional order of society by enlarging upon the significance and dignity of the individual person. The Renaissance uncovered a rational and courageous human dignity in its revival of Greek culture and the ethics of private virtue of the Roman Stoics. The Reformation encouraged the growth of the responsible individual who must deal with the question of his salvation alone and without the protection of a clerical order. The formerly unapproachable power of medieval crown and church was translated into new authoritative claims of the Protestant religious movements, remarkable among other things for their unique, iconoclastic, individualist, even anarchistic ways. A hundred years of warfare on religious grounds had helped the new and increasingly secular nation-state emerge from the seventeenth century. The humanist and scientific trends of the Renaissance also fed this secular culture, increasingly challenging the arbitrary, if prophetic, religious voices about their authoritative (and therefore authoritarian) claims. The liberated intellect quickly perceived that authority was a game anyone could play. Ultimately the very religious movement that had played a fundamental role in confirming the new authority of individual dignity was gradually discredited by its increasing alliances with the desacralized modern states of Europe and its unconvincing moral authority in an age that estimated truth both by science and by its relation to power and wealth.

While the eighteenth-century French Enlightenment of Rousseau, Diderot, and Voltaire despised the pretenses of the church on both the Protestant and Roman Catholic sides and claimed moral authority for the autonomous and self-reliant individual, the earlier English philosophers of the Enlightenment, such as John Locke, had already developed the notion of "possessive individualism," making it possible to measure dignity according to one's wealth. (English culture and economic life had long prepared the way for this with the early action of manor lords who cut off the peasants from the commons for the sake of their profits in wool.) Neither religious rigor nor the courage and ethicality of the philosophers averted the rise of autonomous self-legitimating power and wealth.

In its idealistic form the modern development created the man or woman of many parts—the Renaissance man—much admired in the United States in the figures of Benjamin Franklin and Thomas Jefferson. But the new humanistic culture concealed much of its underlying generative force which lay in the burgeoning commercial, industrial, and technical opportunities.

The very value the churches had placed on the individual, together with the humanist optimism of the age, when joined to private opportunism became a rampant individualism cut off from all notions of commitment to community or responsibility for justice. The point is that secularism and its sciences, and religion with its freedom, played mutually destructive moral roles in the age of individualism. They shared the common root of an abandonment of a moral order that, whatever its vices, viewed individual claims to moral authority as preposterous.

In the famous discussions of Max Weber and R. H. Tawney on the role of a so-called Protestant ethic,[4] it was observed that Calvinism's emphasis on the solitary plight of the individual before God made it imperative to see the rewards of wealth as a sign of election and salvation. Such conscientious rationalizations are not unusual in history. But a more important feature of these writers is their identification of the emergence of two seperate moral realms. "When the Reformation begins," says Tawney,

> economics is still a branch of ethics, and ethics of theology. . . . The secularization of political thought which was to be the work of the next two centuries . . . converted religion from the keystone which holds the social edifice together. . . . Thus the conflict between religion and those natural economic ambitions which the thought of an earlier age had viewed with suspicion is suspended by a truce. . . . The former takes as its province the individual soul, the latter the intercourse of man with his fellows in his activities of business and the affairs of society. Provided each keeps to its own territory, peace is assured. They cannot collide because they can never meet.[5]

With this division of realms in place, Western culture set itself on the track to full-scale moral disability. At liberty in the economic whirl of modern commercial and industrial development, men and women exercised and measured their individual prowess in accumulation, an activity that did not take long to find translation into political power.

In Steven Ealy's recent discussion of liberty in the American revolutionary period he describes James Madison's perspective in *The Federalist Papers:* Madison called for a political variation of Adam Smith's "invisible hand," asserting that the "protection of liberty had to be entrusted to something more certain than religious or moral principles; namely individual ambition and self-love." Madison argued that "a coalition of the whole society could seldom take place on any other principles than those of justice and the general good."[6]

But the general good became, in Ealy's words, "whatever is able to make it through the system of checks and balances and coalition formation." With the franchise in the new United States still limited to property owners, a political economy that wedded wealth to power was in place and on terms universally recognized as morally acceptable. In the second half of the nineteenth century the explosion of industrialization and technology further confirmed a moral code that found legitimacy in the successful and profitable exercise of self-interest. While liberalism attempted to use democratic institutions and an expanding franchise to modify and curtail the worst excesses, the recourse to ethical concern was "more honored in the breach than in the observance."[7]

We come, then, to the present period of our own late twentieth century with virtually every aspect of intellectual and cultural life affected by what amounts to an age of individualism. Bolstered by science and rationalism, truth is an object over which all can contend. Both the Marxist who trusts his/her power of analysis and objectivity and the capitalist who trusts the virtue of production are equally in the debt of the liberty granted in the sixteenth century when Renaissance and Reformation replaced the authority of church and state with the authoritative character of self-interest.

But this has not proved to be a route to either a high sense of human dignity or to peaceable and just communities and civilization. Self-expression, as a means of personal aggrandizement, clearly has turned all means into ends, so that society, community, family are all put to the service of the individual. It is a culture without transcendence that may still traffic in the rhetoric of the common good and justice, but which cannot really order its priorities for the sake of such values. To do so would be to destroy the absolute authority and autonomy of the self, that most preposterous of all the gods.

The result is an era of "winner individualism" whose cultic sacrifices form popular civil religion today. If one does not win in the competition of the marketplace where self-interest is both exercised and satisfied, the sole responsibility and guilt fall to the losers who must be willing to accept their own destruction, if necessary, to maintain confidence in the reality of a world where it is possible for someone to win.

Searching for a Language for Justice and Community

The difficulties of overcoming this cultural framework are demonstrated in the very widespread dislocations of the economy, with tragic consequences for millions of people who nevertheless remain largely locked in apathy and passivity. In spite of many vigorous community organizers and activist groups across the country, they seem to have the relatively limited response of people as their common denominator. The search further upstream for the cause of this apathy has been undertaken in this discussion with no hope of definitive analysis or prescription, but with a sense that there is no more important agenda for people concerned with issues of justice and community. Themes now arising from statements of religious groups ranging from the Ecumenical Great Lakes/Appalachian Project, the Canadian and Roman Catholic Bishops, and other groups now suggest that "justice is participation," that justice must be defined in the context of community.[8] Whether such statements capture the desperately needed new language and symbols of communitarian justice, they suggest the need to examine ancient biblical roots abandoned in the euphoria of the modern age.

The Hebrew scriptures are filled with the quite existential sense of justice and peace arising from right relations between people. This convenantal theme is an extremely radical one for the modern age because our relations with one another, the justice and wholeness we give each other, is an ancient biblical faith, of a different order of importance than our private liberty or personal self-interest. Moreover, such relationships in search of justice are not reducible to a social calculus. Biblical scholars today find ancient Israel's sense of tribal unity and identity emerging from its battle against the alienation power of idols and totems. As Israel grasped the idea of righteousness in relation to neighbor, it gained the power to overcome the domination and alienation of the Canaanite gods. Conversely, as it drifted toward monarchy in later years the king became justice in abstraction, destroying the relational and holistic meaning of a covenantal relation between people in favor of yet another idolatrous form of authority. The prophetic tradition emerges as a reaction against the destruction of covenant and community:

> For the Lord of hosts has a day against all that is proud and lofty, against all that is lifted up high. . . . The Lord enters into judgment with the elders and princes of his people: "It is you who have devoured the vineyard, the spoil of the poor is in your houses. What do you mean by crushing my people, by grinding the face of the poor?" (Isaiah 2:12; 3:13–15)

Basic to this prophetic sense of injustice is Israel's monotheism, extracted in its spiritual and physical struggle with the idolatries of the age, that has its roots in a profound sense of the real nature of human dignity, a dignity understood to express the very image of God. Such dignity cannot endure if there are to be other gods, other powers, other values than those that are rooted in the human purpose itself.

But those purposes are to be found in justice and community, not in power and possessions. The ethics of biblical tradition require the rejection of every pretense to the contrary.

Unfortunately, the problem of reviving this ethic in the culture of the late twentieth century is formidable because of the way in which both political reality and popular language have been subsumed in the ideology of individualism.

Perhaps the only way to make a new beginning toward the language and programs we need for a just society is to tackle the question at the practical levels that are now at hand. In the Great Lakes and Appalachian region an ecumenical coalition began by laying out principles for community and just economic life. They said:

- Community is primary, profit secondary. Profit is a means of building community, not an end in itself.

- The goal of economic policies should be to provide the basis for meaningful and sustaining work for all in stable communities.

- All persons, whether in or out of the job market, deserve the dignity of those economic resources needed to be full participants in the community.

- Communities and workers must participate meaningfully in economic decisions that shape the character of work and the quality of life of the community.

- Churches and synagogues must give priority to empowering workers and the poor so their voices are heard and their interests fully represented.

- The right to organize must be affirmed. Union ability to facilitate worker participation needs to be strengthened.

- The quality of life for families and communities must have priority over the interests of investments and corporate management.

- Worker- and community-controlled enterprises should be encouraged.

- Economic policies should be judged by long-term, not short-term, effects.[9]

Such lists still look like too radical an agenda to many people. This fact alone is a sure measure that American culture remains in the hold of its system of loyalty to individual ambition and opportunism. The fact that some voices in the churches have come to an awakening about the nature of forces of domination in the modern world is a sign that a historic corner may have been turned. But this does not mean that social transformation is necessarily at hand. Quite the contrary situation may be happening. Having finally begun to part with what is sometimes called the Constantinian establishment of the church, faithfulness to biblical principles of justice in community may bring the church not only a diminished role but a new age of persecution. If the churches leave the comfortable blandishments of accommodation with power and wealth, they will have become its enemy.

As progressive forces consider their own faithfulness to the vision of a just society, they can be chastened by the church's and their own complicated and common connection with a longer historical odyssey in the West. Whatever the hazards of the future, it is a strong and fresh beginning to see that we carry among us not just the worst of the human condition but the parables and metaphors of community.

Notes

1. Karl Polanyi, *The Great Transformation* (1943; Boston: Beacon Press, 1957). Polanyi identified the utopian claims of the modern state as being based in capitalism, and therefore used as the basis for claiming loyalty from all.
2. Reinhold Niebuhr, *Moral Man and Immoral Society* (New York: Charles Scribner & Sons), 1932.
3. *Time*, 8 March 1948.
4. Max Weber, *The Protestant Ethic and the Spirit of Capitalism* (1905; New York: Charles Scribner & Sons, 1930).
5. R. H. Tawney, *Religion and the Rise of Capitalism: An Historical Study* (New York: Harcourt Brace & Co., 1926).
6. In *Christianity and Crisis*, 25 September 1985.
7. Shakespeare, *Hamlet*, Act I, Scene 3.
8. *Doing Theology in the Economic Crisis: A Statement on Ethical and Moral Perspectives on the Economic Crisis in the Great Lakes/Appalachian Region*, prepared by the Task Force on Theology and Economic Justice of the Ecumenical Great Lakes/Appalachian Project on the Economic Crisis, Cleveland, Ohio, December, 1984; *Pastoral Letter on Catholic Social Teaching and the Economy*, first and second drafts, November 1984, October 1985.
9. *Doing Theology in the Economic Crisis*.

White Men Talk About Struggle? Take a Lesson from Doubting Thomas

Charles Yerkes

Liberation Theology has undertaken for a generation now to deal with the communication of oppression, in order to end it in faith and practice. As a white male Christian ethicist, I want to reflect on the socially conditioned thinking of fellow white religionists. In what follows, I shall say something about the role of language in insinuating society's problems into us, about the special role of religious language in this, and about what theologians—most of whom are, like me, white men—may have to do to remedy the situation. My point of view is that, far from being a spurious alternative to the material world we live and act in, our language is part of it: it is the physical medium through which that world comes to act in us. The theological discourse of white people is therefore necessarily bound up in the signal-systems of oppression; it needs to be extricated from these so that we too can speak and act our part in the age-old struggle for justice: the reign of God.

1

Society lives in us through language. You and I were socialized as we learned to talk, so that society came to live with us in speech and thought at the same time that we learned to live with others. This is not to say that society takes up occupancy in the brain either honestly or straightforwardly through language. On the contrary, it lies a lot, it covers itself up; it has us thinking that we do not really see what we see out there, so that the time comes when, in truth, we do not see or feel certain realities at all. Society's language has us thinking and communicating in this phony, masked fashion, i.e., in "ideology"; and it has us doing so in the interests of one faction or another in society. That faction is usually the dominant or ruling one—logically so, since, as Marx pointed out, the ruling class rules here too, over the means of education and communication, both public and personal.

The main thing that ideological language distorts and hides is conflict: that is, forces making for change through strife at many levels, from the most universal to the interior and intimate. But struggle is a pervasive fact of life. Its facets refract each other all the way from confrontations between world social and economic blocs down to contagious gentrification in the neighborhood where I live, and even to the hopes and fears I have, and the deeds I do, in response to these arguments from outside.

In U.S. society all aspects of struggle are interconnected through the measures capital is taking to extend and defend itself. The business of ideological talk, however, is first of all to keep us from seeing events with clarity and, second, to obscure the connections among them—to prevent us from understanding the struggle as it is and as a whole. Thinking and listening in ideology, we are disposed to act to the advantage of whoever has power. Our position in ideology is one of "up" or "down" relative to those with whom we work and live, and regardless of deeper truths about our trajectory through the reign of God. But ideology would not succeed at that job if its discourse were merely that of other people, say, newspaper columnists or TV characters. For it to work, we have to think it; more exactly, it has to tell us what to think before we do. Ideology tells us by means of words and their combinations, and the changes of attitude they ring in us, attitudes we have absorbed in connection with language, growing up. That is where the falsification begins.

2

A theologian works in religious language. That is the language which, to use Reinhold Niebuhr's image, acts as a vertical axis through the secular plane. Its resonances suggest the heights and depths of human experience. Religious language keeps alive the notion that there is a logic at work in your and my affairs that exists outside—and comes from beyond the limits of—what "this age" says it knows and has agreed to talk about. Since the Latin word for "this age" is *saeculum*, the rest of the world's discourse, we say, is "secular"; ours is not. Our way of speaking, meditating, praying, and singing opens out, we like to claim, on the past and future and on places beyond the given, the here and now.

As does every other kind of language, however, the religious variety also works ideologically: in the interests of dominant groups, it masks and falsifies. Above all, it harmonizes the sides in struggle and silences the conflict; and it does this to the advantage of those who have come to rule in a society and its churches. If I had written "in its churches and synagogues, temples, mosques, and meeting halls," that remark would have been less ideological than it is.

Today the language of the Christian religions in the United States tends to function among the North American majority—white people—so as to perpetuate an image of domination. But the image was never a true or just one, although it has been able to prevail. White, male, Christian ideology suppressed in the language of faith all hues of nonwhiteness and most degrees of poverty and exploitation. It did this at the same time that it repressed a good many sides of the human being as such, and nothing so much as our passions for one another. Such was the ideological movement that, beginning in the fifteenth and sixteenth centuries, paralleled the growth of empire and swept onward from Calvinism and Puritanism to its zenith during Queen Victoria's reign in Britain. It persists in a number of both "classical" and "liberal" versions to this day.

This suppression and repression in religious language has gone, then, hand in hand with the oppression of nonwhite people and women and the exploitation of workers across the world. These phenomena have arguably been each other's counterpart in matters of the soul as well, i.e., psychodynamically. They had to do with the channeling and mastery of our own and other people's energies. Thus, just as we, or our kind, publicly subjected white working and colored people to a certain discipline, so we put down certain feelings and responses of our own. Boys didn't cry, whatever the cause; by the same token, my lady was presumably to weep no more at seeing or hearing a slave lashed—if possible, she was not to notice it. This way, human energies could be directed to getting the job done: better, my energies could do the directing and yours, the job. In the literature and art of the time, the triumph of "self-control" parades at the celebration of bourgeois self-aggrandizement and empire. On the other hand, Freud could write of *Civilization and Its Discontents* at a time when European imperialism was at its height. It was a time when white people were persuaded, appalled, and titillated that what was suppressed in themselves cropped up again in the "unbridled lusts" of the "natives" and the inhabitants of the shantytowns.

Not the lone but the chief purveyor of this ideology was, of course, Christianity. The man who had mastered himself was lord of all. This is the dominant white male, the finest piece of work of Western Christian ideology, Nietzsche to the contrary notwithstanding. But Nietzsche was onto something: contemptuous of Christianity as the "religion of women and slaves," Nietzsche was surely seeing not the effective actuality of Christian faith in his day but the truth of its origins and intent. These lay in the struggle against domination and injustice, going back at least to the bondage of the children of Israel under the Egyptian empire and to the comparative emancipation of women in circles around Jesus of Nazareth and the early church. In these themes, the sort of struggle finally emerges that the ideology of faith has for so long covered up. And Christians who do not happen to be white men have been liberating theology by stripping it of its ideology. I want to propose a certain white corollary to that task.

3

Liberation theologies are the God-talk of Christians who are not white North Atlantic men. It is a product of the lives and thought of Christians in Latin America, Africa, and Asia, as well as the children of these continents inside North America, and of women from all over. It is a product above all of their struggle and of their striving to tell the truth about it—the truth in love, as Christians like to say. As a result, Liberation Theology amounts to the purging of ideology from the faith. What Christians believe can no longer be spoken from the top down or from Europe and North America to the rest of the world. It must rise from the people from whom Jesus came, and with whom he lived in solidarity from cradle to cross: the poor and the oppressed.

Women have been naming the places and the feelings and possibilities left silent in men's theology, often as not reconstructing a faith-source all their own in those deep and turbulent quietnesses. Black theologians and Latin Americans have spoken out from spaces that, in white theology, were margins on the border of a white or Northern agreed-upon complex called "the world" (in my elementary school, mapped in a few bright colors for the British, French, Dutch, Portuguese, etc., empires). African and Asian writers are doing comparable work. These theologies, it is clear, can go directly to Scripture to bring back the realms of the oppressed—

like refugee slaves around Moses, the poor around Jesus—and set them out where they belong, at the center of God's kingdom and Jesus' good news. They can require us, who would be Christian, to be first that black or that poor in spirit, as Jesus was. I understand that to mean to be so in solidarity with the Gospel's poor that powers like Rome will want to take us, too, to the gallows hill. Meanwhile, among their own, the theologians of liberation have raised the struggle up directly on the portions of Scripture most overlooked—that is, most suppressed—by white theology: the crowds, the poor. For it is to these that Jesus preached, and these that most white Christians cannot talk to, not wanting to know they are there. But they are here, visible, audible, and eloquent in the language of liberation. That language does not need our help.

This leaves male white Christians with the need to face up to, and articulate for ourselves, the struggle implicit in libraries full of pre-liberation theology. It also hands us the task of clearing up and declaring just where and how the struggle lies for us. In my opinion, we neither could nor should attempt to junk the European theological heritage in its entirety. As its heirs in the churches of the United States, we are probably bound to carry it on. But I do believe that we can henceforth labor to expose its ideologization, root and branch, and in this way be liberated in our faith as well as in our life with women and other men.

What would that process look like, applied, for example, to some of the concepts of the tradition? Not treating here some of the central themes like justice (righteousness) and grace—so thoroughly and well expounded by Liberation Theologians—let me hold up, as a couple of instances, a term and a concept: "lord" and the "law." The aim is to get on with the discovery of the origins of these terms in struggle.

It will help to look at these terms first as received concepts, second as historical ones, with origins in a certain political economy, and third as signs with certain psychological effects.

"LORD." Thomas, called "Doubting," on putting his fingers into the wounds of the risen Jesus, hailed him as "my Lord and my God!" (John 20:28). Not just a spontaneous excess of adulation, this etiquette had been claimed exclusively by the emperor of Rome for himself. For Thomas to use it of a rabbi so poor he had no place to lay his head, one who, by being crucified, had died the death of a rebel or runaway slave, was subversive irony. From high-church "Our Lord" to low-church "Yes, Lord!" it has become a key word in Christian piety today. But it is not *biblical* unless it has the ring of Thomas's subversion; its user must sound suspect.

The Old Testament word translated as "lord" was *'adon*, "master" (more often *'adonai*, "masters," an honorific for the holy and unutterable name "Yahweh"). The New Testament Greek was *kyríos*, which meant owner of possessions, a master, sir. The Latin *dominus* we rightly associate with dominate, dominion, dominance, proceeding from the name *domus*, house. This lord was the owner of a house and of the family in it. "Lord" thus bespoke at bottom a property relationship, as of a man to things or to persons, viewed as things, that are his.

The title, lord, then, stems from political and economic relations of power, themselves based on ownership. The rights of ownership were at first gained, and continued to be maintained, through violence and the threat of violence. In Old Testament as well as in New Testament times, princes became lords by conquering or inheriting territories and towns, that is, by virtue of their own or their forebears' violence. This was true of Pharaoh, of Israel's other foes, of Israel and Judah themselves. In Jesus' day it was certainly true of Rome, the master of the Mediterranean world, including Palestine.

This relationship is not unknown to North American whites. In the twentieth century, those in power in the United States bear a similar relationship to much of the world. They are dominant there; they are in a position to "lord it over" others. And how did they come to possess this power? In the first place, their forebears took it: goods from Asia, land and life from the natives of North and South America, men and women from Africa—the three pillars of pillage on which, after Columbus, European and American empires were raised, industries founded, and fortunes made. These origins comprise the open secret of U.S. dominion today. The unheard-of size of the U.S. war establishment and its budget in the 1980s—a "potential" aggressively active at many points of the globe—testifies to the perceived need to maintain this dominance by violence or the threat of it.

Ideology hides these origins of U.S. dominance from its citizens, and not least from its Christians. Ideology also contrives to make mysterious, while reinforcing, a certain psychological process of identification: namely, the identification of the relatively powerless with the powerful, upon whose beneficence the powerless depend. Religious ideology thus associates the glory of rulers with that of God ("God's country," "In God we trust"), missing faith's subversive irony altogether.

Jesus, however, was unequivocal. "No servant can serve two *kyríois*"—masters, lords. "You cannot serve God and mammon," i.e., riches (Luke 16:13). At stake here is life shared, that is, life as a good abundantly shared all around, as Jesus shared it; versus that death which is the taking-away of both goods and life, heralded by the threat to penalize or to kill ("Give it here, or else"). Thomas, calling the tormented and slain teacher "my Lord and my God," chose this Jesus over Caesar: the one who gave life by sharing over him who ruled it by taking. Again, Jesus' lordship is for Thomas cosmic and final ("my God") as well as inwardly commanding: the disciple wants no two masters in his world or heart, but one only. Although as the Doubter, Thomas feels the struggle within, he has touched and been touched by Jesus' suffering and he has chosen sides.

Against such a background—which I have really no more than indicated—it seems to me that white men would do well not to try to suppress the title "lord" from our vocabulary. Instead, we should be willing to do at least three things: look at the structures of dominance that this ancient word can evoke now, as then; face the struggle over domination that came to a head in Thomas's acclamation of Jesus; and having, like him, felt the suffering, take our stand.

LAW. Law as a concept has a more complicated and ideologized history than "lord," although it possesses many elements in common with it. "Law" connotes the imposing of order on chaos, as with the divine order on the face of the deep at creation (Genesis 1), so that Genesis is the "the first book of the Law." Similarly, law refers to the imposing of a civil order on men and women for whom simple tribal custom no longer suffices, their numbers and their social divisions having become too great. Because such positive law reflects a distribution of power—chiefly the lords' ownership—law tends to act as a conservative force, as in "law and order." In its essence, though, biblical law reflects a radical struggle for justice. Jesus' "Think not that I have come to abolish the law and the prophets; I have come not to abolish them but to fulfil them" (Matthew 5:17) is a challenge to the social order to make way for the advent of the kingdom of God, i.e., for justice.

If this radical quality of biblical law is a thrust we scarcely know, that is because its political and psychological origins have become so ideologized. In Old Testament times, when a king through war became lord of a city, the order he then worked out with his counselors and those of the defeated was often a "covenant" (in Hebrew, *berith*).[1] It was a treaty, a bargain struck with the inhabitants and their leaders concerning their mutual obligations. It told what they owed each other, spelled out in the terms, "If you . . .

then I." The covenant reflected the fact—the gains and losses—of struggle and amounted at bottom to a sort of armistice.

Israel's covenant-law was founded in struggle,[2] and detailed the mutual obligations of the participants. One such struggle comprised the revolt and flight of slaves from Egypt around 1250 B.C.E. and, at about the same time, the insurrection of peasants, seasonal herders, and an ancient urban proletariat (used as mercenaries) against some of Egypt's vassals, the princes of the city-states of Canaan. All those forces appear to have allied themselves against, first, Egypt (whose empire included Canaan), and second, "those who sit" in judgment in Canaan's cities. The revolutionary covenant of these allies was in effect the constitution of a new people, "Israel" (itself a name connecting *isra,* "he struggles," with *El,* "God"). It was also the basis of the new nation's law.

The covenant of the law thus defined undertakings between the people and their victorious god Yahweh (originally the god of Moses and the slaves), among the confederates, and between the people and their rulers. Unfulfilled or broken, these obligations became debts: what one owed to him who owns. Hence, on the one hand, property relations issuing from strife and conquest gave this law its shape; and, on the other, it was such "debts" that had to be forgiven right down to New Testament times and the Lord's Prayer (Matthew 6:12).[3] For at stake in the law was the question of who should own that Promised Land, that covenanted, war-won commonwealth, along with its bodies and lives. Would it be a people committed to God, or rulers, foreign or domestic?

The common territories won collectively in the period of the Judges turned in time into the private property of generals and ranchers, so that homeless and landless men and women sold themselves into bondage or once again filled the towns with troublesome riffraff.[4] By the advent of the monarchy (1050 B.C.E.), the law had to settle accounts between these classes as well.[5] Grounded in such conflicts and having to change and grow in relation to one social crisis after another across the centuries, this law too consisted basically of the terms of truce in the course of a struggle about justice.

Given their pact with Yahweh, Israel's law was always understood religiously. The people owed their early freedom and national existence, and therefore themselves as a people, to Yahweh—the Lord. By the New Testament era, this lord was also "our Father . . . in heaven" and "your Father who sees in secret" (Matthew 6:9, 6). Thus the Lord participated in and governed through symbolic reminders, not only of great confrontations between the powerful but also of the earliest conflicts in human experience, namely, the intrafamilial and even oedipal ones. Along such avenues the law, like the social order generally, would have penetrated into the interiority of individuals growing up in the ancient family complex. Moreover, it would have entered people full of the good and the bad, the ambivalences and tensions, of familial bonds; and, at the same time, it would have been loaded with the larger societal tensions that parents and elders brought home and communicated to family members within their four walls. Religious grownups would have communicated the contradictions of their day, as they do now, through the material-social medium of their equivocal speech in connection with a thoroughly ambivalent practice.

This kind of law lives in modern Christians as the code of a struggle for justice, but one equally full of contradictions that can be religiously ideologized away.[6] Our hope in positive law gets expressed in drives for remedial legislation (e.g., amendments to the U.S. Constitution).[7] So understood, the law is not an order imposed from the top by alien owners or lords. Nor is it utopia. It is the best deal that a more or less pitched battle can win from the rulers—until there is no ruler but God.

But faith to carry on such a struggle is the opposite of the easy conformity or even the painful resignation sometimes suggested by religious ideology. For to call on God as "Father" or "Lord" is not the same as to suppose that an earthly "father"—or, for that matter, President—knows best or that the optimal way to live together has already been defined by "law-abiding citizens," so that all the rest of us need is a good dose of "law and order." Values emerged from the people of Israel's quarrels with Pharaoh and Rome, with David's court and Herod's temple, and with others of the enemies of justice, foreign and domestic: results that comprise the Scriptural law of God. By contrast, much about the economic and political order North American Christians live with today is equivalent not to a divine order of things but to moral chaos. Now, as in Jesus' day, acting so that the law and the prophets can be fulfilled and kingdom expectations accomplished may well be how Christians can best take part in bringing a new creation out of that deep morass.

Once again, the struggle for justice, like the other dynamics of the law, has made its way into our hearts through media of communication, both public and intimate. These mediations are full of conflict, as is and because of that struggle; so are our hearts. Religious language dramatizes the struggle inside us and out, but it also distorts and obscures it. Specifically, when the language of faith itself encourages believers to identify psychologically with the powerful of this world—with the given system's lords and with their readings (if not imposings) of the law; when their struggles are made ours, instead of being questioned and perhaps opposed in the name of justice; when in this fashion the real conflict is warped or quashed in our own thinking—then religion has served mammon perfectly as ideology, but it has also betrayed itself and its true Lord.

In today's encounters with power, faith is being offered and tested. It is a gift to believers, on the order of grace, offered through those people in the world who are becoming free from old oppressions. But the opportunity is also ripe with judgment, especially for North American Christians, and all the more so the while males among us, who today are the heirs of the wealth of centuries, won from those oppressions. These are real, historical circumstances; and I know of no others so apt to wean us at last from ideological subjection and delusion. But in getting ready for such liberation I think we have to go to our own texts and seek out and apply the evidence of struggle right there. For these texts have made their home in our souls as well. They also invest the temples and the hearts of pious, conservative, middle America, where their use is purely ideological. Faith and hope and love may impel us to take the struggle there, so that if the language of a tradition—which has become one of dominance—is still to be used, we can rightly divide the Word of God in behalf of God's just reign.

Thomas could salute in Jesus his one Lord and God when Jesus made it possible for Thomas to touch his suffering. The third world, living inside and outside the United States, and not least third world Christians, are enabling white U.S. Christians to feel their pain and grievances: witness South and East Africa, Central America, undocumented aliens in U.S. cities, even U.S. cities as such. North American white believers respond in solidarity through such moves as sanctuary for people in flight, or as a peace watch on Nicaragua's frontiers. But to do so, these Christians must first be freed by grace from their law-abiding, good-citizen inhibitions; as we can be, in my opinion, with the help of the serious analysis of our most traditional terms. We are freed then to take our stand on the law of God in the struggle for justice.

4

At the outset, I mentioned the repositioning of corporate capital across its world front. This has been accompanied, of course, by phenomena at home. Among these were the national elections in

1968, when there was a deliberate effort to "repeal the 1960s" in the United States. After World War II, anticolonial wars of independence in the third world had rolled onto U.S. shores in the form of the civil rights movement, causing, among other things, cultural and political tremors among the North American white population. As it seems to me, capital needed to get a grip on these movements at home as well as abroad. To secure the submission, if not the help, of white middle and working classes in this domestic project, capital had to update its established use of their paranoias vis-à-vis nonwhites. "Here they come . . ." was the motto, "after our jobs." The line from the people of color in the United States to those outside it was already drawn. The vote for Richard Nixon was a vote of fear of the third world at home and abroad. Subsequent political campaigns have stirred and augmented the same fear, adding to them a humiliated, job-losing, working-class patriarchy's anxieties over women's persons and roles. These moves come at the same time as, and look like they fit, the expansion of capital overseas, requiring the taming of white payees at home, coupled with an aggressive stance toward people of color everywhere.

There are religious ramifications. Taking a position with regard to once oppressed, colonized, and exploited people inside and outside of the United States is a basic element in reactionary, evangelical Christianity today, in my view. Born again is the hegemony (lost only temporarily, it is hoped) of the white old-timers (and of others persuaded of the blessings of their regime). An abiding feature is the repudiation not only of change in the future but still more so of every close analysis of the present—on cultural, sociological, and psychological levels ("secular humanism"). Any religion that mystifies in this way is ideological through and through, as we have used the term in these pages. What is the struggle going on under, over, and in the lives of conservative Christians, so threatening that it provokes this adamant obscuring of itself all the way down deep, even to the life of prayer? But begin more gently. What were the struggles at the foundation of their own gospel? The believer's struggle was and is not against the world's poor.

It may be at that level that while male theologians with a will to demystify by facing and welcoming the struggle are called on to help out.

The ideology of faith is one of those uses of language that, imbibed from society, steers us back to it and through it. If nothing else, the campaign to purge our faith of its pro-dominance, anti-struggle ideology may express the desire and enhance the freedom of white men, too, to live together, live fully, and live at peace with every child of God. It will not take the place of the acts of struggle for justice. It will help us help our peers to reflect in faith.

Notes

1. See in particular the study by Delbert R. Hillers, *The Covenant: The History of a Biblical Idea* (Baltimore: Johns Hopkins University Press, 1969).
2. For the history of these origins of the nation of Israel in struggle, see Norman K. Gottwald, *The Tribes of Yahweh: A Sociology of the Religion of Liberated Israel, 1250–1050 B.C.E.* (Maryknoll, NY: Orbis Books, 1979).
3. For the importance of the debt-code throughout Scriptural law, and of redemption from it, see Fernando Belo, *A Materialist Reading of the Gospel of Mark* (Maryknoll, NY: Orbis Books, 1981).
4. "Mercenaries," "riffraff," "urban proletariat": all these are descriptions of the *'apiru* who drifted through the Fertile Crescent in patriarchal times. Gottwald, cited above, favors the evidence equating *'apiru* with *ivri (ivrit, ivrim),* a rootless motley group speaking the *lingua franca,* Hebrew, which became the dominant language in the thirteenth-century confederacy. See his pp. 401–409.
5. David's outlaws (including "every one who was in distress, and every one who was in debt, and every one who was discontented" [I Samuel 22:2], as well as runaway slaves [I Samuel 25:10]) settled affairs by taking the kingdom over. M. Lurje suggests that the four-year civil war in Israel, between the followers of Omri and Tibni (876–872 B.C.E.), could in no way have lasted that long without the participation of this class. Civil war breaks out again under Zechariah, from 746, and rages for two generations until Sargon destroys Samaria in 721. Four of the last six Israelite kings die by regicide, two (Zechariah, Shallum) within seven months, which says something about the social conditions of those years. M. Lurje, *Studien zur Geschichte der wirtschaftlichen und sozialen Verhältnisse im israelitisch-judäischen Reiche von der Einwanderung in Kanaan bis zum babylonischen Exil* (Giessen: Verlag von Alfred Töpelman, 1927).
6. Romans 13:1, "Let every person be subject to the governing authorities," is usually made the basis for religious submission to the rulers' administration of the law. But Scripture contradicts this stand in Jesus' higher (more philanthropic) fulfillment of the law and in Peter's "We must obey God rather than men" (Acts 5:29). The contradiction gets absorbed into Christian life, where it cannot be expunged but needs to be recognized and lived out in terms of faithful options.
7. From the "⅗ of a person" compromise (Art. 1, Sec. 2) and toleration of slavery (1,9) in the U.S. Constitution to the Jim Crow laws after 1880

(Plessy-Ferguson, 1896), racial discrimination has been legislated in the United States. Against appeals for civil rights laws in the 1950s and 1960s, however, reaction was couched in the religious sentiment, "You can't legislate love!" It is an egregious example of how religious talk can blunt the struggle undertaken within the concept "law." Pro and con, the law remains an arena of struggle.

The Catholic Church's Contradictory Stances

Gregory Baum

It is not easy to interpret the recent changes in the Catholic church's social teaching. On the one hand, there is the claim of Liberation Theology that the divine promises recorded in the Bible include the liberation of people from economic and political oppression. Christians are called to a radical commitment in the struggle for social justice. This claim has been confirmed by the Latin American Bishops' Conference meeting at Medellín, Colombia, in 1968 and at Puebla, Mexico, in 1979.[1] The technical term for the new commitment is "preferential option for the poor." In speeches given in Latin America, including the opening address at the Puebla conference, Pope John Paul II fully endorsed the preferential option for the poor and the commitment to liberation, as long as liberation was not understood in purely economic and political terms. This new orientation, amplified in John Paul II's encyclical *Laborem Exercens*, influenced the Canadian and the American bishops in writing their pastoral letters on economic justice. In their own way they too adopted the preferential option for the poor.

There are signs, on the other hand, that this new orientation should not be taken too seriously. There is, first of all, the massive indifference of the majority of Catholics and their priests to the new teaching. Most Catholics in North American parishes have only the vaguest idea of the new movement. The preferential option is supported only by a minority of dedicated Catholics. The Canadian bishops call them a "significant minority," significant because they summon the church to greater fidelity. There are also those of John Paul II's public statements that appear to be at odds with the orientation he recommends in *Laborem Exercens*. He has been critical of Liberation Theology and he has insisted that priests not assume leadership positions in political organizations. Sometimes this demand has given the impression that priests should not be involved in politics or be politically committed. Then there are the actions of the Roman Congregation of the Doctrine of the Faith, the former Holy Office, against Gustavo Gutiérrez and Leonardo Boff, two influential Liberation Theologians who have the support of their own bishops' conference. Finally, there is the 1984 Instruction of the Holy Office, signed by its president, Joseph Cardinal Ratzinger,[2] which warns Catholics, especially in Latin America, of the dangerous trends in Liberation Theology, trends that surrender theological reflection to Marxism and thus undermine the church's unity and the integrity of the Christian faith.

But the Instruction does not invalidate the new orientation in the church. In fact, it specifically confirms that the divine promises revealed in Scripture include the liberation of people from economic and political oppression, and fully endorses the preferential option for the poor, thereby approving the substance of Liberation Theology.

Divergent Interpretations

Political analysts and social philosophers who attach importance to the Catholic church's historical orientation have come to divergent conclusions as to what the new movement means. Carl Marzani's "The Vatican as a Left Ally?" published in *Monthly Review*, offered an optimistic interpretation.[3] His analysis of the new movement in the Catholic church—beginning with Vatican Council II (1962–65), strengthened and sharpened by the Latin American bishops, and climaxing in John Paul's *Laborem Exercens*—leads him to conclude that the "Catholic church is consciously, though slowly and deliberately, disassociating itself from capitalism and its institutions as presently structured."[4] And what is John Paul's new teaching? The Pope holds that workers are entitled, thanks to the dignity of their labor, to participate in the decisions affecting the goods they produce and the organization of the productive process itself. According to John Paul, all ownership of capital, whether private or collective, is conditional, depending on the use of the capital, on whether or not it is used in the service of labor, i.e., whether it serves the people working in the industry, the improvement of the machinery of production, and eventually the entire laboring society. John Paul offers a pejorative definition of capitalism: capitalism is any economic system, by whatever name it may present itself, in which the priority of labor over capital is reversed.

At the same time, Marzani argues that John Paul is not a socialist. Why not? Because he has no clear concept of class and class struggle. Marzani notes that John Paul recommends a social analysis of economic exploitation and quotes the words uttered by the Pope during his 1979 American visit, calling upon Americans to move beyond conventional charity "to seek the structural reasons that foster or cause the different forms of poverty in the world and in their own country." He argues that the Pope nevertheless opposes class struggle and hence simply offers an idealistic view of what the world should be like, but then argues that in the present historical situation—defined by American empire, the Cold War, the nuclear arms race, and the threat of world destruction—socialists should engage in dialogue with Catholics and look to the Pope as an ally.

A few months later, Joel Kovel's "The Vatican Strikes Back," also in *Monthly Review,* offers a different interpretation.[5] For Kovel, whatever success the new movement in the church may have had, Cardinal Ratzinger's Instruction of 1984, published with the approval of John Paul II, offers clear evidence that the Vatican is determined to define Marxism as enemy number one, opposes cooperation between Catholics and Marxists, and is intent on destroying Liberation Theology, supposedly tainted with Marxist ideas.

At the same time Kovel offers a sympathetic interpretation of Liberation Theology, a sounder interpretation, in my judgment, than Cardinal Ratzinger's. Kovel recognizes the essentially religious and theological inspiration of Liberation Theology; he acknowledges that theologians such as Gutiérrez and Boff stand in the Catholic tradition and that their use of Marxism is tangential. Liberation Theology takes the class struggle seriously, at least to the extent that it recognizes that churches are historically located and hence in one way or another take sides in the Latin American liberation struggle. Kovel even acknowledges that Liberation Theology has a message for Marxists. Liberation Theology, in line with the Christian tradition, takes personal consciousness and interpersonal relations seriously. Marxists, Kovel argues, tend to overlook subjectivity: "For Marxism the challenge is to widen the spiritual opening through a deeper appropriation of subjectivity: what is nonrational, aesthetic, tragic, moral, and sacred."[6]

At the same time, Kovel offers a devastating analysis of the 1984 Instruction. He interprets it as the last word from the Vatican, the unambiguous expression of the Vatican's intention to crush Liberation Theology and in doing so to undo the new movement in the church that links Christian faith and commitment to justice. Marxism is to remain the principal enemy. While recognizing various forms of Marxism, the Instruction concludes that all of them, in one way or another, share the essential structure of Marxist thought: a determinist understanding of history, a materialist ontology, and the idea of class struggle as cause of history's forward movement toward ultimate freedom.

Kovel thinks that the Vatican's analysis of Marxism is false. "Unless one adheres to the by-now discredited scientism of Althusser, it is impossible to read Marx and Engels as giving credence to the Vatican's image of Marxism."[7] Kovel seems a little too sanguine here. A deterministic version of Marxism, what Germans call "vulgar Marxism" remains strong in the Soviet bloc countries. Even in the West a purely scientific Marxism, a minimally qualified economic determinism, a positivism of the left, is still widely accepted among Marxist social scientists. Moreover, the influence of Althusser has by no means been overcome, especially in Latin America. Still, Kovel is basically correct: Ratzinger's Instruction offers a caricature of Marxism. More than that, it presents the wholly unbelievable thesis that those who accept certain aspects of Marxism inevitably assimilate, whether they intend to or not, the entire Marxist problematic.

What Kovel does not notice is that the Instruction avoids setting itself directly against the new movement in the church. The Instruction endorses the teaching that salvation includes emancipation, and therefore praises the preferential option for the poor. And abandoning perfect consistency, it refers to the dangerous trend in Liberation Theology as the "insufficiently critical use" of Marxism, hence acknowledging by implication that a sufficiently critical use of Marxist concepts might be perfectly all right. After all, John Paul's own social thought is strongly influenced by his dialogue with Marxism. The purposeful ambiguity makes the Instruction a mean-spirited and devious ecclesiastical document. Kovel has every right to be angry with it. Where he is wrong, I think, is to interpret this document as the definitive judgment of the Vatican and the Pope on the liberation movement in the church.

How can one make sense of the contradictions in the Catholic church in this area, as well as in others? To shed some light on this confusing situation allow me to introduce a useful distinction, drawn from the sociology of organizations. What follows is a tentative proposal.

Organizational Logics

Two logics are operative in every organization, the logic of mission and the logic of maintenance. The logic of mission deals with the purpose, aim, and function of an organization, for the sake of which it has been established; the logic of maintenance deals with the well-being of the organization itself, its upkeep, security, and perpetuation in the years to come. Both of these logics are essential. Contrary to some people's idealistic impulses, an institution cannot survive if it overlooks the logic of maintenance. At the same time, there is inevitably some tension between the two. In discussions on how to pursue the institution's aim and purpose, how to allocate resources and plan for the future, the logic of mission finds itself easily restricted by proposals representing the logic of maintenance. Sociologists have argued that there is a trend in every organization, a trend that must be resisted, to put an ever greater emphasis on the logic of maintenance.

Sociologists argue that when the concern for the institution's well-being begins to overshadow the commitment to the institution's functioning, a dialectic begins to operate according to which the excessive concern for maintenance becomes dysfunctional and undermines the institution's well-being. Robert Merton has called this phenomenon "goal displacement."[8] The orientation of the organization is now its own perpetuation and support, rather than the purpose for which it was established.

But when this happens the organization loses credibility, weakens its hold on reality, and, paradoxically, fosters its own decline. Merton offers a social-psychological theory to explain this phenomenon. He speaks of "professional deformation." He argues that the fidelity of bureaucrats and administrators to the tasks that have been defined for them, their desire to do everything correctly in accordance with carefully designed plans, and the effort to detach themselves from personal feelings to make the organization operate more efficiently, all create a mindset among the staff so that it becomes increasingly insensitive to its clients, i.e., the group of people it is intended to serve. Excessive preoccupation with maintenance makes the staff increasingly unaware of the world in which the organization exists and they undermine the viability of the organization they so desperately serve.

New Catholic Social Teaching

What happens when we apply Merton's distinction between the logic of mission and the logic of maintenance to the understanding of the Catholic church? I will argue that the church's official teaching, including its social teaching, tends to be formulated in accordance with the logic of mission. Official teaching derives from church councils, papal encyclicals, and national bishops' conferences. Here the church tries to express the meaning of Jesus Christ and his message of salvation in the social conditions of the times. Here the church wants to be faithful to its mission in the world. While this official teaching may not be free of all ideological elements, it is produced and communicated at moments of solemnity when church leaders, in dialogue with their people, try to distance themselves from institutional self-interest and seek renewed fidelity to the gospel, which they regard as a transcendent gift to the church. At these moments popes and bishops have a sense that they do not own the truth but serve it.

Special moments of distancing and fidelity take place even in secular societies and political parties that define themselves according to principles they regard as universal and depend for their success on the vision and dedication of their members. Even secular institutions are able, at certain special moments, to formulate the ideals they stand for—even if these ideals are inconvenient to the organizers. But moments of this kind are more frequent in religious institutions since they have available a language of conversion, forgiveness, and new life that summons the leaders to the required commitment. The church believes that at such special moments the guidance of the divine Spirit is present.

In recent years the Catholic church's official social teaching has changed significantly. I have repeatedly interpreted this change as a passage from an "organic" to a "conflictual" view of society.[9] The organic view, expressed from the time of Leo XIII to the time of Vatican II, presumed that society was a mutually interdependent, hierarchical community, united by common values, in constant need of reform and the enhancement of the common good. This reform was to be promoted by governments, situated above the conflict of classes, and translated into reality by the moral conversion of all citizens, including owners and workers, to the same values of justice and equity. This was the Catholic version of the widely held Tory social philosophy. From this perspective, Catholic social teaching was able to criticize modern liberal society: its concept of minimal government, its excessive reliance on the market, its individualism and utilitarianism, and its indifference to the plight of wage earners and the poor.

When the Latin American bishops met at Medellín to apply the directives of Vatican II to their own continent, they realized that it would be absurd to look upon their own societies in organic terms. They recognized that their continent was caught in patterns of dependence that pushed the great majority of the people into ever greater poverty. Medellín analyzed the "external" and "internal" colonialism" responsible for the economic and social orientation of the Latin American continent.[10] The bishops opted for a conflictual view of society. Society was seen as divided: there were the masses of the people, the great majority, living at the margin, lacking power and hope; and opposed to them was the network of the mighty, linked to the world capitalist system which controlled the economic life of nations. All the relatively small middle class could do was to choose between the two. In this context the bishops no longer used the language of reform and development, proper to a more organic social philosophy: they preferred to speak of "liberation." Social ethics, inspired by the gospel and seconded by practical reason, demanded a struggle against the forces of oppression. In a society in which oppression is institutionalized, love transforms itself into a yearning for justice: love longs for the removal of the burdens inflicted on the oppressed. Love issues forth as solidarity in a common struggle.

I have argued elsewhere that this conflictual perception of society was adopted by two Vatican documents in 1971, the declaration *Justitia in Mundo* of the Synod of Bishops, and the letter *Octogesima Adveniens* of Paul VI.[11] In his encyclical *Laborem Exercens* (1981), John Paul II fully endorsed this approach. For him, the dynamic element of modern society, in the West and the East, is the labor movement faithful to its historical vocation. He advocates the "solidarity *of* labor" supported by the "solidarity *with* labor" as the social movement capable of bringing about the priority of labor over capital in existing capitalist and communist societies.[12] The Canadian bishops, over a period of a decade, have developed a conflictual theory of social change for their own society.[13] The U.S. bishops, not going quite that far, have nonetheless endorsed the preferential option of the poor in their pastoral letter on economic justice, even if this option expresses a commitment to the welfare of the poor rather than solidarity with their struggle for justice.[14] According to the church's official teaching, most strongly expressed in John Paul's *Laborem Exercens*, the people themselves are to be the subject of their history.

This claim does not transform the Christian message into a Promethean myth, man as the author of his own salvation. Christians hold that people are the subject of their history because God has created them for this and because God is graciously active in their lives, possibly in a hidden and unrecognized way, as the mysterious presence that calls them to enlightenment and empowers them to act responsibly and with courage.

The shift in Catholic social teaching has been considerable. To understand this evolution it would be necessary to analyze the historical period in which it took place, and there is no space for that here. It is of interest, however, that John Paul II wrote his encyclical *Laborem Exercens* at a time when it appeared that the Polish trade union movement, Solidarity, was about to transform the Polish system into a more participatory socialism. Nevertheless, the majority of Catholics have not assimilated this doctrinal development. There is hesitation among many Catholics, including bishops, who are still committed to the older, organicist understanding of society and the mildly reformist proposals associated with it. And there is vehement opposition to the new orientation by Catholics committed to the triumph of Western capitalism, whatever the social cost. In the United States, vast sums of corporate money are available to finance opposition to the teaching of the U.S. bishops.

In search for conceptual tools to deal with the preferential option for the poor in a theoretical and practical manner, dialogue with Marxism is a natural step. This has been recognized in ecclesiastical documents. Paul VI argued that Marxism as a total world philosophy and as a political system cannot be reconciled with Christianity but that Marxism as a method of social analysis is a useful partner in dialogue, as long as the Christian partner recognizes the danger of reductionism—that is, the reduction of human consciousness to its economic base.[15] Several national hierarchies, including the Canadian bishops, have followed Paul VI in this recommendation.

The Logic of Maintenance

To understand ecclesiastical statements, and above all ecclesiastical practice, it is important to examine the institutional logic of maintenance. The church is obliged to be concerned with the requirements of its own institutional life. If the church leadership neglected this, the church's mission—the proclamation and service of the gospel—would rapidly decline. At the same time, there is a trend in the church, as in all organizations, to assign priority to the logic of maintenance. *I argue that the contradictions in the Catholic church are due to the as yet unresolved conflicts between the logic of mission and the logic of maintenance.* Defensive, narrow and sometimes paranoid institutional concerns make church leaders speak out and act against principles that are in fact part of the church's official teaching. This is particularly obvious in four areas. (1) The logic of maintenance demands that the church protect its international unity, and this often prompts the Vatican to disregard the principle of subsidiarity, a constitutive element of Catholic social teaching. (2) The logic of maintenance demands that the church protect its internal cohesion, and this often prompts the Vatican and regional bishops to condemn class struggle in terms that are at odds with the new teaching on solidarity of and with the poor. (3) The logic of maintenance demands that the church protect the authority of the ecclesiastical government, and this often prompts the Vatican and regional bishops to speak out and act in a manner that contradicts the new teaching on human beings as subjects. (4) Finally, the logic of maintenance demands that the church protect its economic base, and this often prompts popes and bishops to manifest their solidarity with the powerful and affluent sectors of society, again putting them at odds with the preferential option for the poor.

Whenever the logic of maintenance gives rise to obsessive preoccupations, it not only weakens the logic of mission but it undermines the maintenance of the institution. Church membership decreases, the priesthood and the religious life attract fewer candidates, and the church's public credibility declines. Secular observers may believe that these contradictions are intrinsic to the Roman Catholic church, symptoms of a chronic illness. As a Catholic, a Christian believer in the Catholic tradition, I hold that these contradictions can be resolved, not once and for all, but as part of an ongoing process of religious conversion, dialogue, and institutional change.

Allow me to pursue these four lines of thought. First, the church has the right and duty to protect its organizational unity. The Orthodox and the Protestant churches have chosen to organize on a national basis. Their international fellowship is created by councils and federations. By contrast, the Catholic church has committed itself, in accordance with its reading of the New Testament, to be a world church with a central authority, the papacy. To exist as a vast international organization demands a high price. It necessitates a central government that has the authority to steer ecclesiastical developments in the different parts of the world. The logic of maintenance demands that the differences between regional churches, between their respective visions, their ethos, and their practice, do not become too great. If this happens, or if it is believed to be happening, Rome intervenes to slow down the particular development, however valid it may be in and of itself. Usually this intervention restricts the freedom of those regional churches that are moving ahead and undergoing transformation, rather than those churches that cling to the practices and attitudes of the past. (Although the change of the liturgy from Latin to the vernacular demanded that Rome intervene among Catholic groups caught up in the past.) But because the shift in Catholic social teaching is so substantial, little effort is being made by the Vatican or by the regional bishops to make Catholic parishes, Catholic schools and colleges, and diocesan Catholic organizations follow the new path, in particular the preferential option for the poor. The transition must be made voluntarily, through personal conversion. When prominent Catholics—lay people, priests, or bishops—publicly criticize the church's social teaching, no ecclesiastical pressure is put on them to conform. On the other hand, when bishops or bishops conferences are felt by the Vatican to be too radical in their dedication to justice or to peace, the Vatican either intervenes directly, as in the case of Raymond Hunthausen, the pacifist archbishop of Seattle, or attacks the prominent theologians who help the bishops articulate their social teaching, as in the cases of Leonardo Boff in Brazil and Gustavo Gutiérrez in Peru.

Concern for church unity has often been exaggerated, however. Confronted by what they interpreted as the nationalist culture of modern Europe, the popes and bishops defended the Latin liturgy as the powerful symbol of the church's visible unity. Only at Vatican Council II did the church opt for a more pluralistic image, and present itself as the community of communities—although, the Vatican now seems a little unhappy about the church's pluralistic self-understanding. Vatican Council II also welcomed the worldwide ecumenical movement: Christians are meant to be united in their worship of God and their mission in the world. Yet to this day the Vatican has discouraged liturgical symbols that celebrate and foster this unity among Christians, Catholic and Protestant. An exaggerated logic of maintenance stands here against the free exercise of the church's mission as defined by Vatican Council II.

Secondly, the concern for the church's internal cohesion demands the rejection of a rigid, deterministic concept of class struggle. For if consciousness were wholly determined by class location, then the poor Catholics, especially those of the third world, could tell the popes and bishops that they have no teaching authority over them: for then the consciousness of these church leaders would be wholly shaped by their identification with the powerful and their class interests. The logic of maintenance demands that the popes and bishops resist the idea that the class struggle passes right through the church, except in an attenuated form, a form that does not destroy the unity of faith. This point is made very clearly in Cardinal Ratzinger's Instruction.

Does this contradict the church's social teaching regarding the conflictual nature of society and the need for preferential solidarity? To live up to the exigencies of the two logics, of mission and of maintenance, Catholics want to express themselves on this point in a very nuanced fashion. They want to avoid the Marxist thesis that the class struggle is the key to people's self-understanding and the motor force of the forward movement of history. In *Laborem Exercens,* John Paul II offers a conflictual view of society that is voluntaristic enough to escape the label of Marxism, and yet sufficiently rooted in the material conditions of society to escape the label of idealism. The Pope calls for the solidarity of workers and with workers, and in the third world for the solidarity of the poor and with the poor. The solidarity struggle is here not simply generated by the contradictions between the forces and relations of production: it is a struggle of those who are exploited by the ruling system in various ways, joined by all who love justice whatever class they belong to. This sort of solidarity struggle does not just happen: it must be created by an effort that is a political—and in fact an ethical—achievement. This is the voluntaristic element. This solidarity is not produced by simply following the thrust of people's class interest. People's collective self-interest must be accompanied by a new ethical vision of society. In fact, a solidarity movement of this kind becomes powerful only if each group is to some extent willing to limit its own collective self-interest in order to protect and promote the solidarity among all the groups involved.

The solidarity struggle conducted in this sense resembles the class struggle, but it also differs from it significantly. It includes an ethical dimension and hence opens itself to a wider base. It even acknowledges the possibility that the church itself may join in the solidarity struggle. "The Church is fully committed to this cause [the solidarity struggle]," wrote John Paul II, "for it considers it to be its mission, its service, the proof of its fidelity to Christ, so that it can truly be 'the Church of the poor.' "[16] The Pope here follows the logic of mission.

But in its concern for internal cohesion and unity, often exaggerated and sometimes pathological, some ecclesiastical documents, among them Cardinal Ratzinger's Instruction, repudiate class struggle in an unnuanced manner that leaves hardly any room for the church's official teaching of preferential solidarity.

Thirdly, the logic of maintenance has prevented the Vatican from applying to the church itself the official Catholic social teaching that human beings are meant to be the subjects of the societies and institutions to which they belong. John Paul II insisted on this teaching. He argued that workers are to be the subjects of the industries in which they labor: they are to be co-owners and co-responsible for decision making. He also demanded that the socialization of ownership, which he clearly differentiated from state ownership, must always protect what he called the "subject character" of society: people must remain free and responsible agents, sharing in decisions that affect their lives.[17] This teaching undoubtedly applies to the church itself.

The logic of maintenance demands that the church protect the authority of its ecclesiastical government. Without an appropriate authority demanding obedience, an organization falls apart. But it is an exaggerated, if not pathological, expression of the logic of maintenance to refuse the integration of dialogue, consultation, conciliarity and synodal responsibility into the exercise of ecclesiastical government, in greater fidelity to the church's own social teaching. When the logic of maintenance separates itself from the logic of mission, it undermines the maintenance of the organization. The Catholic church is paying an enormous price for the protection of its authoritarian style of government. Catholic teaching counsels greater collegiality and participation. So would a sound sociology of organization.

And finally, the logic of maintenance that is concerned with the economic base of the organization has led the church to ally itself with the rich and powerful. Some sociologists have argued that churches by their very nature are identified with the dominant classes. This was Ernst Troeltsch's view, and he was no Marxist. Yet to remain consistent, Troeltsch had to call the *ecclesia* prior to Constantine a sect. While churches in the Constantinian age have undoubtedly been identified with the establishment and the interests of the powerful, there are signs that this age has come to an end and that the churches have won a new freedom to seek their location in society in accordance with their theological vision.

Carl Marzani correctly points to the emergence of new Catholic orientation that tends to separate the church from its alliance with the capitalist establishment. He notes the practice of Catholic groups and movements, often supported by priests and bishops, that reveal this tendency. Just recently, the Catholic bishops of Cuba have, for the first time, asked for dialogue with the Cuban Marxism and for the right of Catholics to participate in the building of a socialist Cuba.[18] Here it may be the logic of maintenance that counsels the bishops, but in most instances the logic of maintenance and its economic concern impede the courageous application of the church's new social teaching. We must admire the determination of the Canadian and American bishops to publish pastoral letters that question the existing economic order and arouse the anger and hostility of the political and economic establishment.

Conclusion

What do we conclude from these brief reflections? What direction will the Catholic church follow in the future? Will the trend observed by Marzani continue? Or is Joel Kovel correct in his view that the Vatican has decided to crush the new liberationist trend in the church? In my opinion, the church's commitment to the preferential option for the poor (the logic of mission) is definitive and irreversible. I regard this as an extraordinary happening, possibly of world historical importance. At the same time, we must expect a good deal of opposition to this trend in the church, inspired by institutional concerns and inherited ideological commitment. Yet this opposition, in my opinion, will not try to undo the theological basis of liberation theology: it will not try to sever the redemption brought by Christ from economic and political liberation or repudiate the preferential solidarity with workers and with the poor. Instead, the opposition will try to give these commitments a more moderate or more spiritual interpretation. The liberation movements will not be crushed. They will continue their struggle in church and society, protected by the teachings of Medellín and Puebla and encouraged by papal teaching and many episcopal conferences. Despite occasional setbacks, the movement will gain power. For the religious authority of the preferential option for the poor, ultimately derived from Scripture, is simply overwhelming: it commands the Christian conscience.

In North America, moreover, the presence of the Hispanic Christians, the black church, and the native peoples, as well as the women's movement and the peace movement in the Christian churches, constantly call church leaders to critical reflection and institutional change. These are historical factors that prevent

Catholic bishops from settling into a routine understanding of their ecclesiastical office. These critical forces do not reach the Vatican in the same way, however, and at this time there seems to be emerging at the Vatican a new interest in promoting Christian Democratic parties and cultural groups, and presenting Christianity as the protector of a unified and strong Europe.[19] Nevertheless, the Vatican has become the centre of a world church. The Latin American church and other third world churches will continue to demand that the Vatican live up to the new Catholic social teaching—its own teaching—and that it allow the church, at different speeds in different countries and continents, to become identified with the poor and oppressed sectors of society, or, to use John Paul II's phrase, to "become the church of the poor."

Notes

1. See Donal Dorr, *Option for the Poor: A Hundred Years of Vatican Social Teaching* (Maryknoll, NY: Orbis Books, 1983), pp. 157–62, 205–12.
2. For text of the Instruction, see R. Haight, *An Alternative Vision* (New York: Paulist Press, 1985), pp. 269–91.
3. *Monthly Review* 34 (July-August 1982): 1–41.
4. Ibid., p. 27.
5. *Monthly Review* 36 (April 1985): 14–27; included as chapter 13 in this volume.
6. Ibid., p. 27.
7. Ibid., p. 19.
8. Robert Merton, "Bureaucratic Structure and Personality," in *Reader in Bureaucracy,* ed. Robert Merton et al. (New York: The Free Press, 1952), pp. 361–71.
9. See Gregory Baum, "Class Struggle and the Magisterium," *Theological Studies* 45 (1984): 690–701.
10. Dorr, *Option for the Poor,* p. 159.
11. Gregory Baum, "Faith and Liberation," in *Vatican II: Open Questions and New Horizons,* ed. S. Duffy (Wilmington, DE: M. Glazier, 1984), pp. 75–104, esp. pp. 88–93.
12. Gregory Baum, *The Priority of Labor: A Commentary on "Laborem Exercens"* (New York: Paulist Press, 1982), pp. 41–56.
13. Gregory Baum, "Beginnings of a Canadian Catholic Social Theory," in *Political Thought in Canada,* ed. S. Brooks (Toronto: Irwin, 1984), pp. 49–80.
14. Gregory Baum, "A Canadian Perspective on the U.S. Pastoral," *Christianity and Crisis,* 21 January 1985, pp. 516–18.

15. *Octogesima adveniens,* nn. 32–34, in J. Gremillion, *The Gospel of Justice and Peace* (Maryknoll, NY: Orbis Books, 1976), pp. 500–1.
16. *Laborem Exercens,* n. 8, in Baum, *Priority of Labor,* pp. 110–11.
17. Ibid., n. 14, p. 124.
18. Cf. *Latin American Press,* 14 February 1985.
19. Ed Grace, "The Churches Behind a United Europe," in *Neo-Conservatism,* ed. Gregory Baum and John Coleman (New York: Seabury Press, 1981), pp. 19–24.

From Biblical Economies to Modern Economies: A Bridge over Troubled Waters

Norman K. Gottwald

Religion in this country has been overwhelmingly Christian and Jewish.[1] The memories of how religion and society related in ancient Israel entered the United States partly by way of Jews who stood in continuous succession to biblical Israel, and on a larger scale by way of the Christian majority who brought the traditions of ancient Israel as a part of their heritage from Europe. Jews and Christians in America continued to think of themselves, and often of the nation they lived in, as the heirs or continuators of biblical Israel, much as they had in Europe. Here, however, there was a particular impetus to invoke the biblical concepts of chosen people, covenant, kingdom, and mission to the heathen in terms of new exoduses, new wanderings, new conquests, new prophetic proclamations, and a purer embodiment of the kingdom of God on earth. The native Americans, unbiblical nuisances or threats, were wiped out or expelled westward. In time secular counterparts of the biblical phrases emerged in such catchy terms as "manifest destiny," "melting pot," "American dream," "last best hope on earth," and "guardian of the free world."

Though often dormant, this kind of biblical messianism applied to the United States has had a way of bursting forth in times of crisis and social struggle, especially when people are searching for scapegoats—as witnessed by the recent Moral Majority phenomenon. Abundant illustration comes from the founding period of our nation and makes engrossing reading. When Nicholas Street preached his 1777 New Haven sermon on "The American States Acting over the Part of the Children of Israel in the Wilderness and

Thereby Impeding Their Entrance into Canaan's Rest," he was striving to encourage and enlarge the ranks of the patriots by isolating the Tories and winning over vacillating colonists to the revolutionary cause. When Samuel Langdon delivered his sermon to the General Court of New Hampshire at the Annual Election of 1788, entitled "The Republic of the Israelites, an Example to the American States," he was pitching for the adoption of the proposed new federal Constitution of the United States by the state of New Hampshire, which—being the ninth state to approve—would put the plan into effect.[2]

If space permitted, it would be easy to illustrate how religious, and biblical, grounds have been cited on all sides of every major socioeconomic and political issue and crisis since the founding of our nation. This running religious commentary on American life is as current as the most recently heard sermons and political speeches or the most recently read denominational resolutions, religious journals, newspaper editorials, and letters to the editor, and we will come back to it at the end of this article. But first let us turn to an examination of the origins of ancient Israel in order to establish a view of the relation between political economy and religion in biblical times.[3] This understanding can serve as a touchstone for evaluating the capitalist version of biblical faith in our own time.

The long-standing view of early Israel, studied by most of us in seminary, took the Israelites to be an ethnically distinct group of pastoral nomads that invaded Canaan. Research has shown this conception to be utterly untenable. Moreover, there is a far more soundly based alternative explanation of how early Israel developed. Simply put, the early Israelites developed as an agrarian social movement whose driving spirit and rationale was a religious faith in Yahweh. The chief features of this revolutionary movement within Canaan, which in time became a separate society and nation, were as follows:

(1) In origin, the first Israelites were largely members of the lower or marginal classes within the powerful Canaanite city-states. Their agricultural and pastoral products went to the bureaucrats, merchants, and large landowners, all of whom lived as parasites on the people at large. Thus the Israelites were not pastoral nomadic outsiders or invaders who took over what belonged to others, but depressed "insiders," claiming the wealth that they produced by their own labor.

(2) These Israelites were a people of mixed ethnic and cultural identity. Socioeconomically, they were mostly peasants who became

freehold farmers, but they also included herders, artisans, mercenary soldiers, and priests. Their ethnic identity as Israelites, as the people of Yahweh, was forged in the process of their coming together and creating a new society.

(3) Israel thus emerged into history as a revolutionary social movement, taking the means of production in land into its own hands, breaking the iron grip of the state and its client classes over the life and goods of the populace. The nearest analogies to Israel's manner of waging this struggle appear to be such successful peasant wars of the twentieth century as those in Mexico, Russia, China, Vietnam, Algeria, and Cuba.

(4) Israel arose as a coalition of peoples whose movement for liberation was made possible by large-scale social cooperation among a diverse set of previously unempowered groups. These cooperative ties were not easily developed and could only have been achieved by constant recognition of the need for unity and by a larger, and alternative, vision of communal life than the vision of the city-states or that of peasants looking only to their local concerns.

(5) Israel constituted a village-based tribal people, who organized self-rule, self-defense, mutual-aid networks, and cultural self-expression in cooperative terms that delegated necessary leadership, all the while struggling to restrict this leadership so that it did not usurp the means of production and undermine the equality of the people.

(6) The people of Israel were of approximate equality, living in large extended families and protective associations (often called clans), a people with basically the same rights to resources, which for them meant land and its produce and raw materials. They paid no taxes in kind, nor did they render military service or draft labor to kings or ruling classes. In Marxist terms, they benefitted directly from the use-value of their free labor.

(7) In order to break free from the city-states and overlords and form a viable community of their own, these first Israelites had to conduct a people's war for freedom and to forge a people's culture expressive of their self-confidence, self-determination, and shared values of at-homeness in their world.

(8) The sharpest form of cultural self-expression among the Israelites was a people's religion. This religion, often called Yahwism after the name of the deity Yahweh, affirmed the unity of the people and their commitment to prevail in history as a society of mutually supportive equals. The faith in Yahweh, the delivering and blessing God, affirmed their belief that they were supported by

the highest existing power—a power immediately experienced in the common life of the people.

This formative social revolutionary era of biblical society and religion set a standard and tone for the later phases of Israel's life. The immediate accomplishments of this new society were set back and even reversed when Israel became a state, but the survival of elements of that society of equals under one God continued in prophetic voices and in the organizational communal strategies by which Jews survived down the centuries in colonial situations under great world powers. Jesus and his followers likewise tapped those stirrings for justice and equality under God among Jewish commoners.

When advocates of capitalist inequality look to the Bible for support, they turn to the Isrealite monarchy and to those periods when a Jewish state had great power. They claim the laws of Israel and the apocalyptic visions of Israel, which originally either served to protect the poor or to picture a new world where the poor would be delivered. The biblical apologists of capitalism have the audacity to apply these prescriptions and promises to the rich leaders of America, thereby turning the biblical social visions and values upside down. Or, if you will, they take only those parts of the Bible as normative which imagine power and justice to be fully at work in an existing regime, while ignoring how most of the biblical witnesses tell of the disjoining of power and justice and insist that they will only be conjoined when the people, the whole people, are given their rightful place in the world.

So I conclude that there are two different biblical heritages that refer to God and economics:

The first is the original Israelite notion of God as the direct enabler and protagonist of the poor. This notion "goes underground" as Israel becomes a kingdom and is subjected to foreign kingdoms, but it never disappears for it erupts in the prophets and the Jesus movement, and even the elite Jewish rulers had to pay lip service to justice and equality. Let us call it the notion of *God as the empowerer of the poor.*

The other notion is secondary in Israel, although primary in the ancient Near East and in later Jewish and Christian mainstream theologies whenever they felt comfortable with the prevailing economic and political authorities. In this view, God is the lover of the poor at a safe distance who helps them indirectly by encouraging the rich to care for them charitably. Let us call it the notion of *God as the pacifier of the poor.*

In the former notion, God challenges and disrupts the existing power relationships; in the latter notion, God works to ameliorate their worst effects. The ethical and policy implications are these: believers in the former God are *constrained* to challenge and change social structures on behalf of the poor; believers in the latter God are *restrained* from changing social structures while they do what they can to soften their harsh effects.

Thus if capitalist ideology wishes to claim that capitalism in America has brought biblical power and justice together, it must not only answer to the "pacifying" God but also to the "empowering" God who was not impressed by the claims of Assyria, Babylonia, Greece, or Rome, nor swayed by favoritism toward Jewish kings and rulers, landowners and priests, who thought they had God's blessing because they meant well and used the proper religious language.

To attempt a reading of religion and society in this country comparable to my reading of ancient Israel is not so easy. To be sure, we have a shorter time span to consider, and we possess much fuller information on U.S. society and religion than we do on biblical Israel. The problem is that any penetrating analysis of U.S. society runs against the dominant accounts of American exceptionalism and triumphalism which would have us view U.S. history as the march of unbroken material and spiritual progress based on widely shared democratic principles. The official version of U.S. history which I first received in the public schools of Chicago and which is never far from everyone's hearing, is not unlike the praises of Israel's royal establishment encountered in parts of the books of Samuel, in some of the Psalms, and in the books of Chronicles. A critical version of U.S. society like that of the early biblical tribal texts, or the law codes, or the prophets, or the Deuteronomic history, though often expressed throughout our history, only again become prominent in the late 1960s and 1970s. When we do manage a clear-eyed structural analysis of U.S. history and society, it is often amazingly at odds with the lavish religious explanations of this country widely circulated by so-called civil religion and echoed in mainstream churches and synagogues.

So where does all this analysis leave us? Attempts to equate biblical Israel and the United States are certainly mistaken, but the feasibility of instructive comparisons and analogies within the framework of a rigorous analysis are not only possible but necessary in the sense that past history informs the imagination and is indispensable to any analysis and strategy for social and political commitment.

As a basis for such comparisons, I believe it essential to recognize that U.S. social and political practice began and has continued on a more divided and circumscribed basis of peoplehood and of equality and justice than in the case of biblical Israel. This is because Israel actually began as a victorious social movement that achieved large-scale economic and sociopolitical equality. This social fact put a decisive imprint on Israel's continuing thought and practice, even when it later succumbed to domestic and foreign oppression. In the United States, on the other hand, economic and sociopolitical equality has never held sway over the shaping of public institutions, policies, and the major streams of thought. This is true in spite of the equally true fact that large numbers of people in this country have repeatedly struggled to achieve such justice and equality in the public domain. The federal constitution and the dominant political theories, whether conservative or liberal, value property—or more exactly the property-holding aspect of persons—more than they value persons in their full range of needs and powers. Put another way, persons who are validated by property, especially productive capital, have the primary say about the values, goals, priorities, and resource uses of this society.

In the face of a sober analysis of U.S. society, we must recognize that there is a deep disjunction between this capitalist society and biblical Israel. Equally important for Americans who are Christians and Jews is a frank recognition of the expressed will of the biblical God with regard to the economic and social preconditions for the enhancement of human life. The clear will of God, as expressed again and again throughout the greater part of the biblical record, is in sharp opposition to private monopolies on wealth—inasmuch as the earth's goods belong essentially to the community at large and not to self-appointed expropriators. The much heralded "acts of God" in the Bible aim at establishing communities where everyone can and does experience full physical and spiritual development. It can be said straight out, I believe, that the biblical God wants to see persons adequately funded with food, clothing, shelter, health, education, and all the entitlements and empowerments that make for a full life. God seeks fully human partners in covenant. I do not think that we are talking about God in a centrally Jewish and Christian sense if we ignore the control of world resources and the domination of masses of people by small privileged elites, even if those elites decide to justify what they are doing by using religious explanations derived from the Bible.

The political dimension in biblical interpretation is vividly illustrated by the experience of a North American Christian teaching the Bible in Latin America who decided to make a study of the category of oppression in the Hebrew Bible.[4] He discovered to his surprise that oppression is one of the basic categories of biblical thought, as demonstrated by the great number of Hebrew words (10 basic terms; 16 words in all) and the frequency of their occurrence (more than 300 times). Moreover, he found that while biblical thought is not strongly analytical or causally reflective, a reading of the texts concerning oppression provides us with adequate means to conclude that in the Bible oppression is viewed as the basic cause of poverty. The vocabulary fields for poverty and oppression are extensively related, with oppression viewed as the cause of poverty in some 122 of the more than 300 texts examined. Of the many other causes for poverty suggested here and there in the Bible (e.g., laziness, vice, natural catastrophes such as famine, etc.), none occurs more than a few times.

By contrast, when this biblical scholar turned to classical theology, both Catholic and Protestant, he discovered a virtual absence of the theme of oppression. These theologies appeared to him highly deficient, if not heretical, in this matter. Nor did he find oppression studied in biblical commentaries, dictionaries, and theologies. He also observed that the biblical identification of oppression as the basic cause of poverty directly contradicts the standard view in our churches, where laziness, vice, and racial inferiority are commonly held to be the natural causes of poverty. Finally, the usual English translations of Hebrew and Greek words for oppression frequently obscure the blunt force of the original by the choice of soft, ambiguous terms such as "affliction," "suffering," and "tribulation." Contrary to his starting viewpoint, this biblical scholar came to the regretful conclusion that cultural and class prejudices among Christians in developed capitalist countries have drastically censored the biblical view of poverty and oppression.

This rather striking instance of socioeconomic and political distortion of biblical interpretation is of course far from the last word on the subject. It is possible that, on analysis, one might concur with the biblical view of poverty and oppression in the world of its time but go on to conclude that conditions have greatly improved in our world and that at least the United States is no oppressor of the rest of the world, while this country's ruling elite is no oppressor of the rest of us Americans. What I mean to say is that any connection between poverty and oppression in the biblical world and in our world will only be as convincing as a full analysis of the two situations is able to demonstrate. The Bible does not connect meaningfully with our world just because we claim that it ought to. Only a systematic examination of religion and society in the biblical setting and in our setting can accurately and fully reveal to us in what respects biblical Israel's ways of mixing religion and politics are exemplary or cautionary for us.

However, even if this sort of restoration of biblical views on social and political life is not the last word, it is an absolutely vital *first* word—especially vital for those who take their religious bearings from the Bible. I underline this point because if the Bible's grasp of social and political life is fundamentally misperceived or distorted by the prejudices of our social position, then it follows that all our reasoning derived from the misunderstanding is in serious jeopardy.

As I see it, the Bible and our Jewish and Christian heritages free us to examine, without inhibition, the full range of economic realities and possibilities. As Christians, our faith gives us the basis—and the courage—to speak truth to power and cut through the taboos and sacred cows of capitalist ideology, latter day idols that they are! Our faith enables us to look at socialism as one serious economic option, one that is pushing itself insistently onto the modern scene. We must refuse to settle the matter by comparing the worst features of socialist societies with the best features of our own, on the assumption that all we have to choose from is what now exists in the United States or the Soviet Union or some underdeveloped third world country.

In thinking about economics we need a lot more clarity in our concepts and care in our reasoning. If capitalism is an economic system in which individuals privately own the means of production and appropriate the surplus of everyone's labor privately, then what is socialism? Can we imagine and find ways to work toward an economic order in which people together own and operate the means of production for ends they choose? Along precisely this line, H. D. Dickinson has framed the following straightforward definition of socialism:

> Socialism is an economic organization of society in which the material means of production are owned by the whole community and operated by organs representative of and responsible to the community according to a general economic plan, all members of the community being entitled to benefit from the results of such socialized production on the basis of equal rights.[5]

This vision of socialism gives occasion for further thought. Can we all own the means of production without the organs that operate them taking control by forming a new bureaucratic class? What are the practical means by which we can democratically take part in the economy, a real part, beyond voting for one or another person to represent us? How can we hold these representatives answerable to the community? What if capitalists will not give up their private ownership? What social, cultural, and religious incentives might spur people to work for economic sharing rather than to continue to play the odds that they will be eventual big winners in an unequal economy?

If these seem like undiscussed, even undiscussable, questions in contemporary America, it is in large measure because capitalist ideology has worked well enough to ban them from consciousness and from the public forum. Unfettered capitalism wants to be seen as consonant with—even as the fulfillment of—Jewish and Christian assumptions about human nature and the moral foundations of society. The economic free play of capitalism is supposed to reflect and embody regard for individual personhood and for the free exchange of goods, services, and ideas among equals in society.

The terms on which this much-sought capitalist/Jewish-Christian alliance is being forged involve a dangerous combination of individualistic piety and nationalist self-righteousness. The resulting profile is an America led by "saved" or "pure" persons who together form a self-justifying nation within the larger nation and whose wealth and power, generated by rampant capitalism, are entitled to the fullest possible expression throughout the society and, indeed, across the world. Moreover, capitalist funds are being spent in large amounts to flood the media with this reactionary religious ideology, an ideology that penetrates the circles of government, to the point that sectors of the Reagan administration seriously think about our foreign policy toward the Soviet Union in terms of dispensationalist eschatology, seeing Russia as an "evil empire" while totally oblivious to any biblical judgment on American wealth and power.

This capitalist war of ideas, aimed at claiming religious ground and the support of church and synagogue, is well thought through and vigorously prosecuted. It is apparent that the Jewish-Christian justification of our capitalist economy is carried out not only by overtly reactionary rightists but also by more sophisticated neoconservatives and neoliberals. Since the sacralizing of the economy plays upon and distorts religious truth, it is vital to answer it with a counteroffensive just as well thought through and to which religious communities can and will devote more of their resources than they are now doing.

As Christians and Jews we are both at liberty, and obligated, to break with this pattern. Even to be good reformers, assuming that we remain content to work for changes within capitalism, it will be necessary to think big enough to address all the presuppositions and possibilities of economics. For it is clear to me that capitalist ideology works just as hard to prevent major reforms in capitalism as it does to prevent socialism.

Whether we seek meaningful socialism or a significant change in capitalism for the human good, we will have to learn that economics is more than economics. It is politics, thus political economy. But it is also psychology and culture, and we must overcome the notion that a humane economics will fall on us out of heaven or that it will be presented to us as a gift. Dickinson's definition of socialism speaks of "all members of the community being entitled to benefit from the results of such socialized production." To me this implies another and equally important factor in any genuine socialism or any genuine capitalist reform: in order to benefit dependably and in the long run, all members of the community must take responsibility. The attainment of an economy that truly serves people is a process of culture building and socialization to self-empowerment which at the same time calls for mutual trust among people. It is this self-empowerment and mutual trust of all the people that capitalism, by its very working, systematically destroys, as do presumably socialist economies that keep control in the hands of a small elite.

Here is where the Jewish and Christian heritages come in. Rooted in the Bible, they can nourish and empower us for the long struggle to achieve a humane society, culture, and economy. The Jewish and Christian faiths have never said, if I read them rightly, that we must content ourselves with what is immediately and easily at hand, with only what greed and selfishness will allow. The originative God-who-empowers-the-poor was at least "one down" most of the way through biblical times, and has been so the greater part of post-biblical history.

Suppose we were to admit this God of justice from the theological clouds to our savage earth? What if we permitted God into the length and breadth of this murderous egocentric capitalist society? We are fond of "calling down" our God on the closed socialist societies. Do we realize what we are doing when we try to pull splinters out of the eyes of socialist societies, which we have already done everything possible to destroy, while we see not the logs in our capitalist eyes?

It really does take faith, faith with the sweep of biblical vision, to grasp that humans at large can manage themselves better than you or I, or any small group, in power can manage them!

Notes

1. This paper draws upon a theological reflection on economics in response to an address by Bennett Harrison, "The Conservative Strategy to Rebuild the American Economy—Why It Won't Work," at the Ohio Pastors Convocation, Columbus, Ohio, 28 January 1985, and on an earlier lecture entitled "Church and State in Ancient Israel: Example or Caution in Our Age?" presented at the University of Florida, Gainesville, under the auspices of the Department of Religion, 12 January 1981.
2. The texts of the sermons by Nicholas Street and Samuel Langdon are printed in full in Conrad Cherry, ed., *God's New Israel: Religious Interpretations of American Destiny* (Englewood Cliffs, NJ: Prentice Hall, 1971), pp. 67–81, 93–105.
3. Norman K. Gottwald, *The Tribes of Yahweh: A Sociology of the Religion of Liberated Israel, 1250–1050 B.C.E.* (Maryknoll, NY: Orbis Books, 1979) and in briefer compass in idem., *The Hebrew Bible—A Socio-Literary Introduction* (Philadelphia: Fortress, 1985), chap. 6. For the theological and ethical imiplications of this historical-sociological analysis of the origins of Israel, see N. K. Gottwald, ed., *The Bible and Liberation: Political and Social Hermeneutics* (rev. ed. Maryknoll, NY: Orbis Books, 1983), pp. 166–200.
4. Thomas D. Hanks, *God So Loved the Third World: The Bible, the Reformation, and Liberation Theologies* (Maryknoll, NY: Orbis Books, 1983).
5. From H. D. Dickinson, *The Economics of Socialism* (London: Oxford University Press, 1939); cited in H. Smith, *The Economics of Socialism Reconsidered* (London/New York: Oxford University Press, 1962), p. 113, and in George Lichtheim, *A Short History of Socialism* (New York/Washington: Praeger, 1970), p. 318.

Part III

Marxism and Religion

There are two issues that claim our attention in this section. The first is the way in which theological inquiries that appear critical of mainstream religion have been linked with Marxism as a way of discrediting them. The most notable current effort to do this has been the attempt by conservative forces in the Vatican to discipline Latin American Liberation Theologians who have used, or been accused of using, Marxist analysis as part of their analytical tool kit.

The second is the question of the true relationship between Marxist thought and liberation theologies, and involves an examination of the usefulness of Marxism to those committed Christians who have sought the assistance of Marxist analysis to understand their reality as an adjunct to—but certainly not as a replacement for—their theology.

In the first essay Phillip Berryman, a Maryknoll missionary, describes the ways in which Marxism and religion came together for him. Berryman went to Central America, became radicalized by what he saw, and increasingly came to believe that the analytic tools he had were ill-suited to helping him understand what was happening there. What he describes for himself has been true for many in Latin America: while Marxism is for them a tool for analysis, and socialism is often the goal, it is a socialism that is modeled on biblical ethics and has little in common with what the Soviet Union calls socialism (or communism). Dom Helder Camara, a Brazilian priest who is scorned by the ruling class of his country, states a view that is accepted by most Liberation Theologians: "I don't see any solution in capitalism. But neither do I see it in the socialist examples that are offered us today, because they are based on dictatorships and you don't arrive at socialism with dictatorship. My socialism is a special socialism, a socialism that respects the human person and goes back to the Gospel. My socialism is justice."[1] As members of the religious community read Marx and meet more Marxists who are not followers of the Communist Party (which has long represented itself as the only faithful interpreter of Marxism in Latin America), they find that many (and in the United States, most) Marxists agree with Dom Helder's characterization of the Soviet Union.

Liberation Theologians thus seek to avoid a reductionism that would oversimplify class analysis and so become mechanistic, or that would remove both human agency and divine will from history. If this analysis leads them to focus on such concepts as alienation, exploitation, imperialism, and class struggle, this is because both they and secular Marxists begin with the same end in mind: how to understand the plight of the oppressed. As Gustavo Gutierrez has said: "What the groups in power call 'advocating' class struggle is really an expression of a will to abolish its causes, to abolish them, not cover them over, to eliminate the appropriation by a few of the wealth created by the work of the many and not to make lyrical calls to social harmony. It is a will to build a socialist society."[2]

Approaching these issues as a theologian, T. Richard Snyder draws on the notion of class struggle to shed light on what is meant by the concept of atonement in the Christian faith, offering us an example of how Marxism can enrich the work of theologians.

Those who defend the status quo suggest that the interface between Marxism and theology is evidence of a growing Communist influence that must be repulsed. But those who start with a faith commitment have a different priority—for if the new theologies of liberation are faithful to the biblical message, any tools that assist them in doing what they understand to be God's will must be used—critically and carefully as all tools should be used, but not rejected because of criticism for the company we keep. For what is at issue is the substance of the critique liberation theologies make of the society; and while those who do not appreciate the challenge to the status quo may cry "Communist," they rarely wish to discuss the validity of the analysis.

The Vatican in particular has entered the fray because Liberation Theology has developed in a part of the world that will contain most of the world's Catholics by the twenty-first century. It has acted through the Congregation for the Doctrine of the Faith, the body that is charged with protecting church dogma against heretical revisionism. Joseph Cardinal Ratzinger, prefect of the congregation, acting with the authority of the Pope, has in recent years instituted a series of attempts to discipline leading members of the Liberation Theology movement and to determine what aspects of their thought and practice are acceptable to the church. Joel Kovel, in his essay in this section, sees the Vatican's current attempt to deal with this problem as part of an ongoing effort to domesticate Liberation Theology and to separate the faithful from those aspects of Marxism that are deemed heretical.

In the next essay, Dorothee Sölle, a German theologian who teaches frequently in the United States, describes the Christian-Marxist dialogue that developed in the post-World War II period and flourished in the 1960s, and how that cross-fertilization helped to improve the climate for new dialogues in the 1980s. Harry Magdoff and Paul Sweezy then examine Karl Marx's famous comment about religion being the opium of the people. They make clear that although for Marx religion was, like alcohol or opium, used as a narcotic to ease suffering, this does not mean that Marx (and subsequent Marxists) did not understand the positive potential of religion (although there are important exceptions, including those influenced by Soviet Marxism). In the final essay, Cornel West, a Marxist theologian, discusses the way some of the most influential thinkers in the Marxist tradition have contributed to our understanding of the cultural centrality of religion. All of these writers understand Marxism as a way of analyzing the present as history from the viewpoint of the oppressed.

It will be seen from a reading of these contributions that those critics who see Marxist ideas as the significant subtext in liberation theologies are both right and wrong. There is an important overlap, but not because liberation theologians are more Marxist than Christian. Rather, the Marxist method, and Marx's own goals, deal with the same issues and share the same orientation as the new liberation theologies. But this does not mean—contra the Vatican in its more extreme pronouncements—that Liberation Theologians are either Marxists or Communists. Some of them have read a great deal of Marx, but others are even hostile to what they understand Marxism to be about—an understanding that would, in any case, be considered erroneous by many Marxists. What is clear, however, is that the structural analysis with which these Christians are comfortable is for the most part consistent with, and to a great extent—consciously or not—indebted to, Marxism. And if we are open to a free discussion of ideas, what is important is not the label but the validity of such ideas.

To do justice in many parts of the world today can lead to trouble with the authorities and (in the non-Communist world) to accusations of being a Communist (although in the East one is apt to be charged with being an agent of capitalism!). As Dom Helder says, "I brought food to the hungry, and people called me a saint. I asked why people were hungry, and people called me a Communist." It is enough to lead people to examine what it is they are accused of being, especially when such ideas seem so important. To quote Dom Helder again: "When a man attracts millions of human beings, especially young people, when a man becomes the inspiration for the life and death of a great part of humanity, and makes the powerful of the earth tremble with fear and hate, this man deserves to be studied."

Because third world churches increasingly take this perspective, the more conservative hierarchy finds that it must respond. Yet it must do this with the utmost care because to be an apologist for capitalism is a costly course, one that lost a major part of the European working class to the church in the last century. The church is well aware that an inability to deal with Liberation Theology's radicalizing message could have a similar impact today.

Notes

1. From an interview in *The Sign* (July–August 1976): 12, cited in John C. Cort, "Can Socialism Be Distinguished from Marxism?" *Cross Currents* (Winter 1979–1980): 431.
2. Quoted in Walter Goodman, "Church's Activist Clerics: Rome Draws the Line," *New York Times*, 6 September 1984, p. A14.

How Christians Become Socialists

Phillip Berryman

The "how" is meant in two senses: the process by which Christians come to see themselves as socialists, and what sort of socialists
they tend to become. They are socialists not in the sense of having a
blueprint for society—especially that of the United States—but in
having a profound sense that our ills are systemic and that the
system is called capitalism. (That does not mean, however, that
capitalism necessarily subsumes patriarchy or racism.)

Of course there were Christian socialists around the turn of the
century, and Karl Barth, Paul Tillich, and Reinhold Niebuhr all
regarded themselves as socialists, at least during significant periods
in their lives. Here, however, I want to focus on a growing sympathy with socialism among significant groups of Christians since the
1960s, outlining first the process that leads in that direction and
then the reinterpretation of Christianity it involves. An underlying
question here is whether there is an underlying affinity between
Christianity and socialism.[1]

Radicalization

To come to a profound critique of capitalism while living in the
midst of capitalist society one somehow needs to step out of it, to
have some experience of being alienated and estranged from it. For
some Christians, living in other countries has provided such an
experience. I have in mind particularly church people who have
gone to Latin America since the 1960s.

Some went to do pastoral or missionary work, while others went to aid in development projects (seen as an expression of the church's mission). Many sought to come closer to the poor by moving away from the traditional parish house, convent, or mission compound and into modest homes or even shacks in villages or barrios. Although they could not share the ultimate insecurity of poverty, they could share some of its conditions.

This sharing the condition of the poor was itself aimed at entering into real dialogue with them. The starting point was often a Bible discussion or a concrete problem in the village or barrio, or simply an effort to bring people together to consider their situation. Two things could happen: people could develop a greater critical awareness of their situation and the reasons for their problems, and they could develop ties among themselves and so become something of a community. If their motive for meeting was explicitly religious, they could become a *communidad eclesial de base*, or "Christian base community," with their own lay leadership. At the local level they could start a cooperative, or lobby the government to build a school, set up a health post, or get them drinking water.

Yet such activity soon ran up against limits. People began to see that the real problems were not due to their own "backwardness," but to inequality in wealth and power, especially as manifested in land tenure systems. They often became more militant. Before too long they ran up against the power structure, whether in the form of the local landholding class or the army and police, which threatened them or actually used violence against them.

In this process, church workers themselves experienced firsthand the anguish of the poor. For example, a priest might be called on to baptize infants who were dying, either because of a lack of elementary health services or of illnesses caused by undernourishment. Those church workers got a widening sense of the problem and saw, for example, that local landholders, the army, and the police were simply part of a larger class structure—and that the nation's whole agroexport system was itself part of a world economic system.

In the late 1960s and early 1970s such church personnel might have been "slow learners." The process sketched out often took years and considerable experience. In other words, people were radicalized by living with poor people and seeing what happened when those people tried to organize and pressure for change; they were not radicalized by reading Marx or Marxists. If they did any such reading, however, it tended to reinforce what they had experienced and intuited, and bring it into sharper focus.

Overseas experience led many people to question their previous assumption that the United States was the world's benefactor. They became aware of U.S. intervention, whether subtle or overt, to maintain its hegemony, and of the U.S. role in maintaining the world capitalist system. Such an experience led to a feeling of estrangement vis-à-vis the United States and to conflict. I recall how, during a visit home in California in 1969, I was invited to address some "mission circles" in an Orange County parish. After I showed some slides and gave a talk, someone began the question period by asking, "What can we do for those people down there— perhaps send clothes?" I tried to explain the Latin American perspective on "underdevelopment," and suggested that rather than sending clothing they might examine U.S. foreign policy. As the evening wore on, I encountered an increasing hostility breaking through the surface cordiality. Obviously I had touched on something very deep—their own identity as Americans. It struck me that these people were much more offended by my criticism of the United States than they would have been if I had suggested that the doctrine of the Trinity be revised to include a Fourth Person. In other words, there was something "religious," something of ultimate value, in their attachment to their country. By the same token, the experience brought home to me how estranged I was becoming from mainstream America.

Some church personnel have been close to highly politicized and conflictive events, such as Chile during the Unidad Popular years, or under repressive military governments, or in the struggles of Central America. Under such conditions the radicalization process can be much quicker.

In the United States, many church people undergo a comparable, though perhaps less dramatic, experience without going overseas. Entry points have included direct grassroots contact with the poor, involvement in the civil rights, feminist, anti-Vietnam war, and anti-nuke struggles. The crucial step is recognition of the systemic nature of these things. (Again, I am leaving open the question of how patriarchy, racism, and capitalism intersect.) The process also involves the recognition of the contradictions within the churches themselves and how they function to provide religious legitimation to existing society.

The political practice inherent in this radicalization process can vary enormously. Church workers in Latin America have generally not become directly involved in leftist politics, but they have defended people's right to organize and supported them when they did so. In some cases they have come into direct contact with revolutionary organizations, sometimes collaborating with those organizations, occasionally even becoming militant members.

An option for socialism often makes sense for people who have been exposed to Latin America, who have seen genuinely revolutionary organizations and have a rough idea of what a socialist revolution could look like. In the United States, on the other hand, things are much less clear. No society in the world offers anything like a model for a transition to socialism—not even of what to avoid; nor is there much sense of what kind of process could lead the United States beyond capitalism.

Christians in the United States may sense that profound changes are needed and may have an intuition that what is required is a new kind of order, which may be called "socialism." But since socialism is far from the agenda of mainstream politics, their everyday political practice will continue to be working on a set of issues and struggles. Here they will find themselves side by side with those whose route into those struggles was not religious. In other words, in their political practice, the criteria they use, the organizations they join, and the struggles they engage in, they will be "secular."

A New Understanding of Christianity

Those whose radicalization process has been nonreligious can nevertheless find familiar landmarks in what I have just described: experience with the poor, the violence used by power structures, the growing awareness of systemic connections. Those Christians I have in mind, however, also see this process as a "conversion." The word may conjure up a dramatic emotional event—St. Paul struck on the way to Damascus, or revival participants "repenting and declaring for Jesus"—but the biblical word refers to a basic shift in mindset, attitude, and life-orientation. That is what the experience I have been outlining is all about. As such it calls for a new and deeper understanding of Christianity.

The claim of Christianity is that God has acted in human life in the whole series of events contained in the scriptures, and particularly in Jesus Christ. As embodied in the churches, that conviction has taken cultural forms throughout history and has gone through periods of reformation or renewal. Every such reform movement has been in some sense a retrieval of something in the scriptures, e.g., Francis of Assisi seeking to return to the poverty of Jesus and his first followers.

A key biblical symbol being retrieved today is the Exodus. Whatever the original event was—apparently the escape of a group of slaves from Egypt under circumstances that would, at least later, be recalled as miraculous (plagues, passage through the Red Sea)—the Exodus became a paradigm for faith, that the true God hears the cry of his oppressed people, sends them a liberator named Moses, and goes before them, leading them to freedom. All the events, their wandering in the desert, fidelity/infidelity/repentance, the covenant, etc., became paradigmatic for what Israel should be as a people.

In Latin America, at least, people can make a direct translation of the Exodus, seeing themselves under oppression—whether the Pharoah has a name like Somoza or is an entire oppressive system—and they yearn for liberation. Similarly, the voice of the Hebrew prophets sounds very contemporary, even down to the denunciation of how the wealthy take land from the poor or cheat them with crooked scales.

At first glance the Christian scriptures (the New Testament) might seem less "political" than the Hebrew scriptures. It is true that Jesus did not advocate revolution (in the modern sense) against the Romans—it would be anachronistic to expect him to have done so. Yet the experience of repression today, especially in Latin America, has alerted people to the conflictive aspect of Jesus' life. From the very start, the gospels present Jesus as standing in conflict with the authorities. His message is one of hope for the poor and the outcast, and that message eventually brings his own death—by an execution in which both "church" and state have a hand. The resurrection can then be seen as God's vindication of the truth of Jesus' life and message.

Inspired by their faith, many Latin American Christians have indeed given up their lives out of commitment to an ideal of a more just society, a commitment that frequently began with the kind of village-level pastoral work mentioned above. In the serious life-and-death context of Latin America today, many find a deep meaning in the Christian conviction of resurrection—that God is on the side of life and evil cannot ultimately stamp it out. Archbishop Oscar Romero of San Salvador said, "If I die, I will rise in the Salvadorean people." His belief was orthodox—that is, he regarded the resurrection as something real and not simply a metaphor for the memory of posterity—but he also linked his faith in resurrection to the people's struggle.

I could go on at some length giving examples of the kinds of reinterpretation of the scriptures arising out of experience today. However, rather than assembling further examples, it seems more important to point out what this new kind of interpretation means.

In the first place, it is a reading from the situation of the poor. In fact, it is often the poor themselves who are looking at the scripture and giving their own reading. Liberation Theology seeks to grasp the message of scripture from the side of the poor. Part of the conversion process of church pastoral workers is that they find themselves being "evangelized by the poor," that is, the poor teach them the meaning of the Christian gospel.

It is a reading that takes the material world and human society seriously. Until roughly a generation ago religion and religious symbols essentially affirmed the existing order, including the class system. Although many versions of Christianity continue to do that, this new reading subjects existing societal arrangements to a critique whose standard is how it affects the welfare of the poor. Not only does this reading not see the existing order as fixed by God, but it sees human beings as responsible for the earth, including the societal arrangements they live under.

In this sense we can speak of a "transformative" (in William Tabb's term) way of reading the scriptures, and indeed of understanding Christian faith. In Latin America one frequently hears the notion that human beings are called to be "subjects of their own destiny," "co-creators in history." Although such language may sound Promethean or naively overconfident in the United States, it expresses something central in the new religious vision developing in Latin America.

An option for socialism may make certain symbols or images in the scriptures take on new meaning. I am thinking particularly of all the scriptural images about unity. To begin with, the Bible itself has a very "corporate" understanding of humanity: it seems far more interested in the fate of the "people" (both Israel and the church) than the fulfillment of individuals in our modern Western sense. Various analogies are applied to the church: Paul speaks of the church and Christ being joined into one body, so that if one member suffers, all do. John has Jesus say, "I am the vine, you are the branches" in the same discourse in which he repeatedly urges his followers to love one another.

Throughout the history of Christianity these startlingly collective symbols of unity have either been ignored, or have been applied to the church as institution, or have been given a mystical interpretation, namely that we are united in Christ, despite our apparent differences. A "transformative" reading of the scripture holds not only that there is a mystical unity in Christ, but that we human beings must work to make it something real in human history.

The intuition, then, is that the ideals sketched in the New Testament, including the "primitive communism" described in the Acts of the Apostles (early Christian communities that held their possessions in common), not only express a mystical truth—that despite appearances we are one in Christ—but are an affirmation that human beings can live as sisters and brothers, and that Christians must work to make that possible.

This intuition was not the original understanding of the New Testament authors. They were thinking primarily of the Christian community, the church, although there are some hints of a wider— even cosmic—interpretation. However, their horizon was limited by their conviction that the Lord was due to return soon. They could not have envisioned the transformation of society as a task flowing from the gospel.

Thus a radical or socialist reading of the Bible no doubt goes further than what the original authors consciously intended. Yet it need not be regarded as simply a product of fancy or imagination. The New Testament sees the Spirit as present in the church, providing the basis for new interpretations for new situations.

It is clear that such a reading was impossible at the time of the New Testament, as well as during most of the history of Christianity. It became possible only when material conditions began to make it conceivable. To a great extent it was Marx who signaled a shift in human consciousness. In that sense, what we are talking about amounts to a theological paraphrase of Marx's Eleventh Thesis on Feuerbach: "The theologians have only interpreted the world in various ways; the point is to change it."

Anarchism or Socialism?

Perhaps we can see that there is some affinity between some strands in Christianity and socialism. Not all radicalized Christians become socialists, however. Some believe that what the gospel demands is radical witness to the Kingdom now, with no direct concern for societal transformation. Moreover, they may believe that it is normal for Christians to be in tension with all forms of power— perhaps interpreting this in terms of what the epistle to the Ephesians calls "principalities and powers." Being a Christian then becomes a matter of standing in a small community of faithful witnesses over against the world.

In political terms, such an option can be called anarchism. People who make such an option emphasize the purity of witness and not political effectiveness as such. They would regard an option for socialism as an illusion. For them political power and how it is exercised is the problem, not the solution. They may believe that the example of "really existing socialism" bears out their position.

Church Institutions

So far we have been describing a radicalization that has affected a small but significant minority in the churches. These are lay people, priests, sisters, and pastors, whose experience and reflection lead them to the conviction that today Christianity itself calls for structural change in society. At one point, in the immediate aftermath of Vatican II, people who were thus radicalized tended to transfer that radicalism to the institutional church itself, and to assume that their option inevitably meant a head-on confrontation with church authorities. And indeed, many actions within the church institution, such as the Vatican's assault on Liberation Theology, seem to bear that out.

Nevertheless, things are not quite so simple. Many of the church people who have been radicalized themselves occupy positions in the church structures. For example, those who deal with missions or with issues of international justice have had frequent occasion to meet with people from the third world or representatives from sister churches, and have been able to get something of a third world view of issues. Consequently, ordinary churchgoers in the pews are often more conservative than church bureaucrats. That is not because those officials take on an a priori left mentality, but because they have had to confront the issues directly and repeatedly.

In Latin America and elsewhere, at the institutional level, churches have often taken positions against the worst abuses, especially against governments that violate human rights (e.g., in Brazil, Pinochet's Chile, Central America, South Africa, the Philippines, South Korea). This has not always been the case—the Argentine Catholic hierarchy preferred to ignore the "dirty war" of the later 1970s and is now largely discredited. In some instances Catholic hierarchies have not simply condemned abuses, such as murder, abduction, and torture, but have gone on to point out the structural cause of violence in the unjust distribution of wealth and power.

The stumbling block seems to come over the question of formulating alternatives, that is, the possibility of other economic and political systems, as well as political struggle involved in bringing about change. A most eloquent example was furnished by Pope John Paul II in 1983: in Haiti, where there were no prospects for change on the horizon, he said boldly, "This has to change!" while in Nicaragua he could not accept change when it was staring him in the face. Fear of Marxism (due partly to the experience of the church under Marxist regimes) impels church hierarchies into advocating some sort of vague hypothetical model for society that will avoid the negative features of both capitalism and communism. Hence the great attraction of Christian Democracy, which seems to promise the best of all worlds but which in practice is simply capitalism paved with good intentions.

The pastoral letter of the U.S. Catholic bishops on nuclear weapons (1983) and the final draft of the letter on the economy (forthcoming) are another illustration. The peace pastoral expressed clear opposition to Reagan administration policies and devoted considerable attention to pacifism as a legitimate option for Christians. Nevertheless, its general policy framework remained well within establishment liberal parameters. Similarly, the letter on the economy, which some thought might raise fundamental questions about the capitalist system, again remains liberal, although somewhat to the left of the Democratic Party mainstream. What is most intriguing about its first draft is the insistence that the criterion for judging an economic system should be its impact on the poor.

Radicalized Christians are aware of the many ways the churches are a part of the existing order—from investment portfolios, to the partriarchy and racism in their own practice, to the legitimating power of Christian symbols. Yet they believe that the churches offer important political space, as well as symbols that form the basis for a critique of that order. Most important—from the viewpoint of faith—they believe the church itself can, and must, be converted if it is to be faithful to its own message.

Faith and Political Commitment

During the 1960s there were a number of Christian-Marxist dialogues, often between well-known theologians and prominent Marxist thinkers. The aim was to find points of convergence and outline areas of difference. Such a type of dialogue seemed to imply that persons holding two more or less integral world views were meeting across the table.

What has happened recently in Latin America and elsewhere is rather different. As a result of the process sketched above, Christians have moved toward a systemic understanding of injustice and also a kind of political practice that fits their new understanding. In Latin America, at least, that practice is Marxist to some degree. However, Marxism is viewed not as a world view but as an "instrument of analysis," a kind of engaged social science, and as a method for political struggle.

Consequently, faith and politics operate at different levels. Politics, even when it is about a dreamed-of future society that is in no way on the horizon, is somehow concerned with means, while faith deals with the ultimate grounding and final end. If this is true, there should be no real basic conflict between Christianity and politics—even Marxist politics. Political strategies and tactics should be judged primarily on the basis of whether they offer the means whereby people can achieve justice and peace and expand freedom.

Faith has little to say directly about criteria for political struggle, e.g., about whether it makes sense to work toward socialism within the Democratic Party. Any criterion is primarily secular. In that respect, radicalized Christians are as secular in their political options as their nonreligious colleagues. Like those colleagues, they may be perplexed about how a genuine broad mass movement for change can be built, and despite their own intuitional sense that systemic change is needed, they put their energies into those particular issues they feel called to work on: against intervention in Central America, for a nuclear freeze, against apartheid, etc.

What their religious conviction supplies is a sense of ultimacy, something that goes deeper than any particular issue, and indeed than political struggle as a whole. As an ultimate frame of reference, it can provide a basis for a critical attitude toward Marxism— which is not regarded as an ultimate frame of reference but rather as a heuristic framework, a method that is fruitful but always open to testing and revision. Some Christians may make options that do not seem to make sense in terms of sheer political calculus but do make sense in terms of faith, e.g., opting to work with people simply because they are poor, even disregarding to what extent they may or may not be a "proletariat" and therefore potential agents for change.

Hence a final question: If Christians who become radicalized are essentially "secular" in their political positions and options, is it possible that those who see themselves as nonreligious, or secular, nevertheless have as their ultimate grounding not simply a world view or a method for critique and political action, such as Marxism, but something akin to a faith? I will not presume to put a name on it, but I would like to know whether they would.

Note

1. I have preferred to remain within my own Christian, and specifically
   Roman Catholic, tradition. The question of whether there is an underlying affinity between socialism and other religions, especially Judaism,
   is obviously of great interest but will not be addressed here.

Class Conflict and Atonement

T. Richard Snyder

Class conflict is not a household word within the Christian community. For that matter, any kind of conflict is eschewed by the majority. Yet within recent years the subject appears with increasing frequency in the writings of the Theology of Liberation, most especially among the Latin Americans. Some speak of the necessity and even the inevitability of class struggle for the sake of the Kingdom of God.[1] Others couch the notion more generally in terms of joining God in taking sides with the poor or engaging the forces of oppression in conflict.[2]

Enthusiasm for dealing with class struggle is not generally shared by most other Christians. Pope John Paul II sounded reactionary to some of us when he denounced class struggle, but his condemnation surely represents the majority opinion, both now and in the past. This rejection is quite in keeping with the fundamentalist tradition in which I was raised and the mainstream Protestant theology in which I was trained at Princeton Seminary.

Why is there such an overwhelming rejection of class struggle within the Christian church? In this essay I would like to do three things: first, to address that question, with special focus on the doctrine of the atonement, one of the central teachings of the church regarding the process of reconciliation; second, to indicate how the Marxist emphasis on class struggle has significantly altered my own thinking about the atonement; and finally, to suggest a challenge to Marxist theories of class struggle from the perspective of the atonement.

Anyone other than a devoted theologian must wonder about my

decision to focus on the doctrine of the atonement to answer the question why Christians so uniformly refuse to accept the notion of, or self-consciously join in, class struggle. Obviously the bottom line is that they refuse to do so because they are so aligned with the forces of privilege and oppression that they do not perceive the true nature of things; nor do they understand the ways in which they themselves have been alienated. The rejection, at its base, is due to a class option. And so it is for many. But how do we explain those Christians who are among the marginalized, the oppressed, being also so inclined? I believe it is because the ideological function of much Christian tradition has been to contribute to false consciousness, and that central to the rejection of class struggle has been the doctrine of the atonement. This doctrine, at least as it has generally been interpreted, has led to the obscuring of class conflict and to passivity in the face of it. The doctrine stands in need of serious reconstruction if it is to address the reality of our world.

I was raised in the fundamentalist tradition. My church and my family emphasized the need to avoid conflict, the importance of accepting one's lot in life as God's will, and the affirmation that the endurance of suffering will eventually be rewarded by God in this life or in the life to come. This resignation was reinforced by, if not rooted in, a particular theology of atonement.

Atonement is a coined Middle English word (at-one-ment) signifying the reconciliation God has accomplished through the death and resurrection of Jesus. According to the doctrine, we human beings are in a condition of fundamental alienation from God and from each other. We are lost, in a sinful state that is so total that only God can bridge the gap, can make at one that which has been torn asunder. In the sacrificial offering of Jesus on the cross (derived from the Hebrew ritual), God substituted a perfect offering for our sins, paying the price (either to appease his own wrath or to purchase a ransom from the devil). Jesus, the perfect sacrifice, died for us, the totally unworthy sinners, and in that act brought about atonement. What is left for us is to accept this loving and gracious action on our behalf, give thanks to God, and share the good news with others. There is no call in this tradition for us to engage in conflict to bring about reconciliation or atonement, for that has already been done by Jesus—that was the meaning of one of his final words from the cross, "It is finished."

To the extent that there was any conflict for us to engage in, it was a purely internal one: to become more pure, more spiritual, more like Jesus. Whatever guilt we felt (and we felt plenty) was not due to the basic situation of alienation in our world, but rather to our own failure to be spiritual enough. We did not rend our clothes and wring our hands about the racism of our society, or about world hunger, but rather about our lust, our pride, and our envy. Our conflict was privatized and not seen as essential to the direction of world history, which God had taken care of.

The journey from fundamentalism to a more classical theology, which occurred during my training at Princeton and my entry into the Presbyterian church, did not essentially challenge these basic ideas. The emphasis changed somewhat, however, to one that saw the world in terms of a war being fought by God against the forces of evil—against sin, the devil, and death.[3] In the crucifixion and resurrection of Jesus the final victory had been won, despite the few skirmishes still being fought by those who had not yet discovered the truth.[4]

Though many who shared this doctrinal view engaged in significant actions for social justice, by and large when the issue of conflict in general (and class conflict in particular) was raised, there was a quick rallying around the themes of reconciliation and love. This was most noticeable in discussions of racial conflict, which is a distinctive form that class struggle takes in the United States. When James Cone related the theology of the black church to the concept of black power and called for an option for blackness, the lines were clearly drawn; most Christians, white and black, saw such a claim as eccentric and even heretical.

But to admit such an essential conflict would be to admit that Jesus' atoning work was unfinished. *In a word, the traditional understanding of the atonement had removed Christians from any responsibility for world history.* That responsibility is God's. Of course, most Christians recognize that there are some serious problems in our world, and few would deny that there is conflict. What they would tend to deny, or to ignore, is the class nature of this conflict. Even more importantly, they would deny class struggle a role in the process of transformation or in the process of reconciliation. This denial is not born out of an understanding of the complexity of the debate about class struggle going on within Marxism or out of an appreciation of the complexity of the American "exceptionalist" situation, but rather comes from an outright rejection of fundamental conflict of any kind as a strategy for change because the fundamental conflict has already occurred, "once-for-all."

Yet as I continued to participate in the various struggles for justice, both here and abroad, to read in Marxism and in liberation theology, and to attempt to make sense of the ongoing nature of oppression in our world, I became convinced that Christians must think and act in terms of class and class struggle. In so deciding, I had to rethink what the atonement means. While no Marxist would claim me as a thorough-going adherent, and while I still have much to learn about Marxist theory, nonetheless my views of the atonement have been substantially altered by the experience and theory of class struggle.

As noted above, the theory of class struggle, like the doctrine of the atonement, has had a variety of interpretations. Today the debate about the significance of class, the nature of class reality, and the possibilities of class solidarity and action is intense. In the United States, the phenomena of the middle class, widespread affluence, the rise of various coping mechanisms, the coopting of the trade unions, and so on, have prompted revisionist interpretations, such as that of Herbert Marcuse, while the experience of dissidents in Eastern Europe has raised questions about traditional formulations there. But despite this questioning and debate, there are some central aspects of the notion of class struggle that have provided direction for me in thinking about the way in which alienation and oppression can be overcome. Central to these is the understanding that there are divisions within our world caused by the exploitation and control of the many by the few, and the belief that human beings have the responsibility to participate in the transformation of the world through a change in their relation to the means of production (though this term is frequently expanded to include political and cultural processes, not merely economic ones), thereby ending exploitation. Such a transformation demands taking sides and developing solidarity among the exploited against the exploiters. While it is true that many are confused and coopted, it is impossible to remain neutral. One's thought and actions inevitably have an impact on the struggle. The challenge is to become self-consciously engaged on the side of the workers (a term that is also constantly being revised) and against those who control the means of production. In so doing we shall alter the course of history. The picture may be fuzzy because of the changing nature of capitalism, but the essential lines have been drawn and the direction of world history sketched out. In other words, while there is no blueprint encompassed by the notion of class struggle that can be applied universally and uniformly, the direction is clear.

Even this sketchy a presentation of the concept of class struggle makes it clear that those who accept its broad outlines may have difficulty making sense of the idea that in Jesus the Christ, God has once-for-all changed the course of history and achieved reconciliation or atonement. On the other hand, while the concept of atonement may not be understandable to those outside the Christian faith, for those of us who have encountered Jesus and the power of his life and death and resurrection as mediated by the church, it is impossible to dismiss the centrality and importance of his work. Thus I am forced to make sense of him and what was accomplished through his death, while at the same time affirming class struggle as an essential and ongoing reality.

My conclusion, in a word, is that in Jesus the Christ we have a revelation of the essential truth about life, about world history, about the process of reconciliation. This revelation does not alter world history once-for-all, as many claim. Rather, it presents (or declares) the fundamental way in which reconciliation is occurring within history. It points to the ongoing struggle that must continuously be waged by those who, like Jesus, choose to be in solidarity with God and the oppressed.

Without attempting an exhaustive defense of this position, let me set forth an interpretation of a key text in the New Testament that has helped lead me to such a conclusion, the letter to the Colossians. This letter, to one of the early churches in Asia Minor, begins with a doxology (a hymn of praise to God) which portrays Jesus as the center of all creation, eternal, and the instrument of God's atonement through his crucifixion. No higher Christology or claim about the person and work of Jesus is made anywhere in the New Testament. The hymn ends with the words, "For in him all the fullness of God was pleased to dwell, and through him to reconcile to himself all things, whether on earth or in heaven, making peace by the blood of his cross."[5]

This text, and others like it, serves as the foundation for traditional Christian claims that the war against evil and death has been won and only a few minor skirmishes remain. In Jesus, they claim, all that is essential for atonement has been completed.

It is precisely this emphasis upon—or this interpretation of—*completeness* that has become suspect to me. My experience of both fundamentalism and orthodoxy has been that the general consequence of such interpretations is a certain political quietism and even fatalism. As mentioned before, the essential task is seen to be a striving for purity rather than a striving for justice and a new world as the means for becoming more Christ-like. In so saying, I do not wish to impugn the numerous Christians who, holding to this traditional view, have nonetheless sacrificed and struggled heroically. The critical test is not the orthodoxy of our theology, but the class option we make, our *orthopraxis*. Jesus made clear that the final judgment is not based upon our theological claims but upon our faithful service to the needy.[6] Further, we are all painfully aware of how often our theory and our practice diverge. Despite these disclaimers, it seems safe to say that for the majority the traditional understanding of the atonement has led them to opt out of the struggle, and therefore to side with those in power.

But if we keep reading in that same letter to the Colossians, there is a statement that opens up another possible interpretation. The author writes, "Now I rejoice in my sufferings for your sake, and in my flesh I complete that which is lacking in Christ's afflictions for the sake of his body, that is, the church."[7] While I might want to take issue with the limiting focus upon the church, the important point is the claim that there is something lacking in Christ's afflictions. The crucifixion of Jesus was not an act that removed us from the struggle; rather, it thrust us into a life of suffering.

The suffering spoken of here, however, is not just any suffering. It is not the long endured suffering of those who shoulder poverty as their cross to bear. It is suffering for the sake of others. There is some suffering that is neither chosen nor redemptive: the anguish of Africans wrenched from their homeland to serve as chattel slaves in North America, the decimation of the Jewish community in the Nazi gas chambers, the torture and death of Central American peasants by U.S. -backed forces. This suffering is imposed and has no merit, no right to exist, no redemptive possibilities. But because imposed suffering exists, we are called upon to *choose* to suffer on behalf of those upon whom suffering has been imposed, in order to end that imposition. That is what class struggle is about: to end the divisions and restore us to wholeness as a world people. *Class struggle is the contemporary form of completing that which is lacking in Christ's afflictions.*

There is not, there cannot be, a once-for-all solution to the problem of oppression, not even by God. Jesus did not bring about a change in world history, but rather revealed its essential truth: that atonement is possible and that is an ongoing process which involves constant struggle and suffering, even crucifixion. He revealed this truth by engaging in the struggle of his day, which was against a priestly caste that dominated Jewish life and had formed an uneasy alliance with the Romans.[8] And the consequence of his struggle was crucifixion.

Some Christians will see this interpretation as a reduction in the centrality and importance of Jesus. They will assume it is harking back to the theology of Abelard and some of the Enlightenment theologians, who held up Jesus as the example par excellence of the way life is to be lived—the way that, if all would follow it, would lead to atonement. That is not my intent.

To say that Jesus *reveals* is far different from saying that he *serves as an example*. To reveal something is to do more than simply to set forth a fact or idea. Revelation is an act that occurs only in relationship and, in the process, changes the very nature of the relationship. It is a way of knowing that moves beyond the factual to a level of intimate engagement and vulnerability that leaves nothing the same. The Hebrew scriptures speak of the act of sexual intercourse in terms of "knowing" another person. This implies a mutuality that changes both parties. Such knowledge is closer to what Marx had in mind, I think, when he said, "Philosophers have only interpreted the world, in various ways; the point is to change it."[9] A genuinely revelatory experience is one in which understanding and change are inextricably linked. Hence to know Jesus is not primarily to know *about* his atoning work, but to become so caught up in that work that we complete what is lacking in his afflictions through our struggle and suffering.

The completeness of Jesus' action is in its fullness, not in its finality. It is full in what it reveals about the atoning process in world history and it is full in the deep grounding it offers those who open themselves to that revelation. This is not a claim, then, that excludes other revelations, but rather one that describes the reality of life for those who have experienced Jesus.

In summary, I now understand atonement to be a world-historical process of the most concrete and material sort, one for which the ongoing crucifixions of those engaged in the class struggle are a necessary condition. The life, death, and resurrection of Jesus reveal this truth in the fullest possible historical (incarnational) manner.

Finally, let me set forth an element of the Christian doctrine of the atonement which I believe makes a contribution to the debate going on within Marxism. Leslek Kolakowski has raised the question as to whether changes in economic and political structures are adequate to deal with all the aspects of life that plague us. Even under a classless society, there will be sickness, tragedy, and death. Has Marxism dealt seriously enough with the fullness of life and history in its theory? I think not.[10]

Marxism is a scientific attempt to understand and to change history. The early Christian doctrine of the atonement was also often set in scientific language, the language of cosmology. Cosmology was their form of science. In the letter to the Colossians, we have a case in point: with the science then at their disposal, the early church tried to show that all creation—the entire cosmos—was alienated and in need of atonement. Herein lies a challenge for Marxism. The rigidity and reductionism of some contemporary forms of Marxism and state socialism often belie such an encompassing understanding. This is evident, for instance, in the unbending political bureaucracies, the use of the arts for purely propaganda purposes, the denial of the importance and legitimacy of any form of religion, and the emphasis on production at the expense of ecology.

The fullness of the work of Jesus as described in the cosmic portrayal of the atonement lends support to those voices within Marxism which seek to expand the vision of what is necessary and of what is possible in the struggle to restore our alienated condition. And it certainly gives those of us who are Christians special pause lest we unwittingly capitulate to a rigid and narrow understanding of, and commitment to, the Kingdom of God.

Notes

1. Gustavo Gutiérrez, *A Theology of Liberation* (Maryknoll, NY: Orbis Books, 1973), and Jose Migues Bonino, *Doing Theology in a Revolutionary Situation* (Philadelphia: Fortress Press, 1975).
2. Robert McAfee Brown, *Theology in a New Key* (Philadelphia: Westminster Press, 1978).
3. For a fuller treatment of the various views of the atonement, see Gustav Aulen, *Christus Victor* (New York: Macmillan Press, 1969).
4. This position is most developed in the theology of Karl Barth. See, for instance, *Dogmatics in Outline* (New York: Philosophical Library, 1947), p. 123.
5. Colossians 1:19, 20.
6. Matthew: 25.
7. Colossians 1:24.
8. See George Pixley, *God's Kingdom: A Guide for Biblical Study* (Maryknoll, NY: Orbis Books, 1981).
9. Karl Marx, "Theses on Feuerbach," XI, in Karl Marx, *Early Writings* (New York: Vintage, 1975), p. 423.
10. See Rudoph J. Siebert, "Jacob and Jesus: Recent Marxist Readings of the Bible," in Norman K. Gottwald, ed., *The Bible and Liberation* (Maryknoll, NY: Orbis Books, 1983).

The Vatican Strikes Back

Joel Kovel

The Vatican's *Instruction on Certain Aspects of the "Theology of Liberation"* (Dublin: Veritas Publications, 1984; henceforth referred to as *Instruction*) is doleful but essential reading for those of us who have begun to rethink the traditional hostility between religion and the left. The work of one of Catholicism's leading ideologians, Joseph Cardinal Ratzinger, *Instruction* is a key link in Pope John Paul II's counteroffensive against the challenge to orthodoxy represented by Liberation Theology, and is to be seen in context alongside other recent events, such as the trial of Fr. Leonardo Boff of Brazil and the attempt to set the Peruvian church against Fr. Gustavo Gutiérrez.

Instruction is of special interest because it attempts to thwart an association between Liberation Theology and Marxism. This is all the more remarkable since, as anyone familiar with Liberation Theology can attest, its actual proponents are anything but systematic Marxists. For example, Gutiérrez, the most influential of the group, keeps his remarks concening Marxism strictly tangential to theological discourse.[1] As Arthur McGovern has put it, "direct references to Marxist analysis occur much less frequently than one would be led by critics to expect, and references to Marx tend to be qualified when they are made."[2] The same observation has been made by Phillip Berryman: "None of [Liberation Theology's] major exponents have devoted systematic attention to Marxism as such, with the exception of José Porfirio Miranda" (of whom more below).[3] Certainly the great majority of Christian base communities, those spontaneously arising collectives of believers who comprise the social base of Liberation Theology throughout Central and South America, cannot be said to have *any* kind of consciously Marxist perspective.

And yet *Instruction* is suffused, one might even say obsessed, with the notion that Marxism is either incipiently or actually taking over the Liberation Theology movement and turning it to its sinister purposes. Does the Pope know something that no one else does? What is the point of this curious diatribe, its logic honed over centuries of fending off heresy, and turned here toward what at first glance appears to be a largely imaginary threat?

Instruction is not a particularly long document, and its principal argument can be readily summarized: the phenomenal injustice in the world that has given rise to Liberation Theology (and, of course, to Marxism as well) is recognized, and the causes of this injustice are described, as are the alleged inadequacies of Liberation Theology–Marxism for dealing with them. Finally, the Catholic church is affirmed as the true champion of liberation. Embedded in the text, then, are distinct critiques of Liberation Theology and Marxism, a defense of the traditional church, and a theological conception of history that ties the whole argument together. It is perhaps best to begin with the latter, as it provides the underpinning for the rest of Ratzinger's discourse.

The Vatican's position may be represented as follows: the world groans under a burden of horrible crime and inequities against which humanity is justifiably outraged. The church joins fully in the outcry; it insists, however, that a priority of causes be established, and the ultimate cause of injustice be given its proper place. This cause is sin: "Liberation is first and foremost liberation from the radical slavery of sin. Its end and goal is the freedom of the children of God, which is the gift of grace" (p. 3). Or again, "The root of evil . . . lies in free and responsible persons who have to be converted by the grace of Jesus Christ" (p. 12). Everything else in *Instruction* flows from this presupposition, for only the true church is qualified to judge those lapses from God that constitute sin, and only through the church can grace be achieved. Even the massive maldistribution of wealth which underlies revolutionary ferment ultimately derives from sinfulness. Thus the fulcrum of all change is the individual: "The source of injustice is in the hearts of men. Therefore it is only by making an appeal to the *moral potential* of the person and to the constant need for interest conversion, that social change will be brought about which will truly be in the service of man" (p. 31; italics in original). Marxism, which not only does not recognize this truth but insists upon the contradictory dogma of historical materialism as well, is therefore not only inadequate as an answer to injustice and a science of history—it becomes another kind of sinfulness as well. And Liberation Theology, seduced by the basic materialism of Marxism, even if not espousing the whole party line, is guilty of the same. Q.E.D.

Why, then, the appeal of Marxism? In their eagerness to act, people demand a scientific analysis of society as a guide. And indeed there are places on earth, notably "certain parts of Latin America" (p. 20), which seem to conform, however superficially, to a Marxist analysis. Marxism, however, is nothing but despotism masquerading as pseudoscience. Nor should we be misled, the cardinal continues, by the fact that there seem to have been many different strands of Marxism. For however variegated the surface, there is an essence to Marxism which damns all varieties: "To the extent that they remain fully marxist, these currents continue to be based on certain fundamental tenets which are not compatible with the Christian conception" (p. 18). The flaw of historical materialism is epistemological: "All data received from observation and analysis are brought together in a philosophical and ideological structure, which predetermines the significance and importance to be attached to them" (p. 17). And what is this structure? Nothing but the central presupposition of Marxism concerning the unity of theory and praxis, the overriding recognition of history as the main determinant of human life and class struggle as the main determinant of history.

It is this essence which lends Marxism its atheistic character, denies the value of the individual, and leads inexorably to the totalitarianism which characterizes all Marxist societies. For whereas the true Christian regards the ultimate criterion of truth as theological, i.e., rooted in faith, the Marxist sees truth emerging from partisan engagement in the class struggle: "There is no truth in the struggle of the revolutionary class" (p. 21). This is necessarily a violent doctrine. Since the existing class society is the product of violent expropriation, a truth exclusively on the side of the proletariat necessarily justifies amorality and revolutionary violence. It thus denies "the transcendent character of the distinction between good and evil" (p. 22).

The fundamental sin of Marxism and Liberation Theology, according to Cardinal Ratzinger, is therefore historicism. The conviction that human reality is fully disclosed in history empties the theological reality of Christianity: faith, hope, and charity become subordinated to what one does here in this world. They become the province of a "temporal messianism" (p. 27) instead of the divine;

and the very symbolic structure of Christianity is inverted: "The Eucharist is no longer to be understood as the real sacramental presence of the reconciling sacrifice, and as the gift of the body and blood of Christ. It becomes a celebration of the people in their struggle" (p. 29). And so the unity of the Catholic church is denied.

So much for Marxism, revealed once again, as the rightwing press loves to blather, as "godless, atheistic communism." There is a singular difference, however, between the Vatican's dismember-ment of Marxism and the customary assault by the right. For we are now asked to believe that the criticism comes from a leftward direction. Along with its frequent reminder of the countless mil-lions who have been impoverished and sold into slavery by the Marxists, comes a stentorian claim that the church "hears the cry for justice and intends to respond to it with all her might" (p. 29). There are some interesting subtleties in the grammatical tense of this sentence, which suggest that the church may not have been doing all it could to right earthly injustice in the past, but that it (or she) is now about to throw everything into the fray. If so, it would be a major development indeed, and one for which we may thank the very Liberation Theology being excoriated. Can it be that the Catholic church has genuinely shifted to the left, swallowing and destroying the substance but ultimately absorbing the impulse of Marxism in the process?

What Does the Vatican See in Marxism?

I think that a close reading of *Instruction*—not to mention a look at what the Vatican is actually about—will settle this question firmly in the negative. But before we turn to this, we should consider the adequacy of *Instruction*'s critique of Marxism. Is there any merit in what the Pope and the Cardinal say?

Essentially, the Vatican is claiming that Marxism has failed, and that it has failed because of its materialism. Both parts of the proposition are open to some doubt. However, assume for the moment that all socialist societies have been in fact as much of a disaster as the Pope thinks. One would then have to demonstrate that it was "Marxist materialism" that was responsible for the fail-ure: a challenging intellectual task, worthy of a Vatican ideologue. However, *Instruction* never begins to look at the real connection between ideology and history. It simply assumes that there is a hidden materialist essence to Marxism that somehow infects so-cialist societies and drives them in a totalitarian direction. All of the passionate discussion within Marxism as to the nature of historical materialism, all of the concrete and tangled history of socialist societies—all this gets buried by simple fiat of theological damnation.

In fact, since *Instruction* never actually begins to look at the real world it is judging, there is no point in considering existing socialist societies in order to assess its critique. If there is something worth disputing in *Instruction*, it is its opinion of historical materialism, since it is here that Cardinal Ratzinger concentrates his attack.

Many serious questions can be raised about historical materialism. Unfortunately, the questions raised by *Instruction* are not among them, for the simple reason that it does not address historical materialism as such, but some concoction of it suitable for the Vatican's war against communism. Recalling that *Instruction*'s main contention about Marxism is that it subordinates the individual and all higher values to history and the class struggle, let us consider some of the views held by those reasonably well-known and authoritative nineteenth-century German expatriate Marxists, Karl Marx and Friedrich Engels, to see whether this is in fact what historical materialism holds.

Unless one adheres to the by now discredited scientism of an Althusser, it is impossible to read Marx or Engels as giving credence to the Vatican's image of Marxism.[4] There is no point in dredging through the texts for the endless examples that could be brought forth in support of this position. Two may suffice as a basis for further discussion, each chosen from the author's mature "scientific" phase.

In *Theories of Surplus Value*, Marx wrote:

> Man himself is the basis of his material production, as of any other production he carries on. All circumstances, therefore, which affect man, the subject of production, more or less modify all his functions and activities, and therefore too his functions and activities as the creator of material wealth, of commodities. In this respect it can be shown that all human relations and functions, however and in whatever form they may appear, influence material production and have a more or less decisive influence on it.[5]

There can be no more positive statement of the humanist core of Marxism, and hence no more vigorous denial of the Vatican's claim that Marxism subordinates "man" to history and denies the transcendent value of the human being. The point for Marx is that the material mode of production is decisive, but that it itself is a human process, subject to the full range of human relations.

Consider next this passage from Engels:

We therefore reject every attempt to impose on us any moral dogma whatsoever as an external, ultimate and forever immutable moral law on the pretext that the moral world too has its permanent principles which transcend history and the differences between nations. We maintain on the contrary that all former moral theories are the product, in the last analysis, of the economic stage which society had reached at that particular epoch. And as society has hitherto moved in class antagonisms, morality was always a class morality; it has either justified the domination and the interests of the ruling class, or, as soon as the oppressed class has become powerful enough, it has represented the revolt against this domination and the future interests of the oppressed. That in this process, there has been on the whole, progress in morality, as in all other branches of human knowledge, cannot be doubted. But we have not yet passed beyond class morality. A really human morality which transcends class antagonisms and their legacy in thought becomes possible only at a stage of society which has not only overcome class contradictions but has even forgotten them in practical life.[6]

Here is the Vatican's "subordination of morality to the class struggle." But is Engels denying a transcendent dimension to morality, as *Instruction* claims? Obviously not. He is rather asserting that a transcendent morality—that is, "really human morality which transcends class antagonism"—can exist. Engels' point is that if one is seriously interested in bringing this about, then one should not be mystified by actually existing class moralities but press for overcoming them: an objectively revolutionary prospect, and, I might add, a profoundly moral one as well. It follows also that the basis for "really human morality" has to be the universality denied by class morality—including, one might add, the class morality of the proletariat itself. Thus even if the morality of the proletariat may be more universal than, and so superior to, that of the bourgeoisie, this fact does not—nor should it—justify any and every crime in the name of the revolution. Undoubtedly, people in real history who may have called themselves Marxists have concluded otherwise, but they have no authority from either Marx or Engels (not to mention a host of others within the Marxist tradition) for doing so.

Interestingly, this point has been pursued with great energy from within the Liberation Theology movement itself, in a remarkable work written by the aforementioned José Porfirio Miranda, a Mexican and one theologist who can be unequivocally classified as a Marxist. Miranda has an indisputable advantage in any discussion of what Marx and Engels really meant, since he appears, like so few others, to have bothered to read every word they ever wrote. His work *Marx Against the Marxists* (Maryknoll, NY: Orbis Books, 1980) establishes, without vitiating any of the scientific content, the deeply humanistic, moral, and indeed spiritual core of Marxism as conceived by its founders. From the *Theses on Feuerbach* to the *Critique of the Gotha Program,* Miranda demonstrates that the materialism of Marx is—as the passage quoted above from *Theories of Surplus Value* indicates—a materialism of the active, hence moral and spiritual, human subject. Such happens to be the way things are for human beings; and Marx's greatness consisted in bringing a scientific vision to bear on human reality, thereby opening up the prospect for consciously changing history. As Miranda says, "For Marx, sound science presupposes the existence of a subject. It is an inescapable datum, because such a subject [i.e., a being with "interiority"] does exist in reality, and because the mind of the scientist cannot prescind from it" (p. 35). And, "If there is no subject to engage in revolutionary activity, then materialism consists in contemplation and we are stuck with a philosophy that proposes to interpret the world rather than to change it" (p. 29).

If this is the essence of Marxism—and I cannot see how any other reading can be supported—then the Vatican's critique becomes vacuous. Marx does not put history over the human spirit, as an absolute, final category. He says rather that the human spirit is locked inside historical domination, i.e., alienated from its true potential. It is true that Marx does not seem to regard our potential as spiritual in the religious sense of that term. In other words, he sees no need to relate the human spirit, essence, or subject to any kind of Godhead. For Marx, the notion of a deity belongs to the prehistory of humankind. God is a projection of alienated human power into the heavens. Once this power is reclaimed, the idea of God, now so omnipresent, will wither away, like the state under communism. This may indeed be a problem for Marx and Marxism: it is a question that deserves the most careful scrutiny. What it does not deserve is an argument at the level of distortion and sophistry found in *Instruction.*

What is *Instruction* really about? Not a principled and reasoned critique of Marxism, unless Marxism is considered identical with the works of Joseph Stalin; nor of "really existing socialist" societies, all of which get tarred with the same brush and reduced to the level of Pol Pot's Kampuchea. Nor is it more than a coarse caricature of Liberation Theology. No, the true purpose of this document, I am afraid, is much more mundane than this—and vastly more mundane than the Pope and cardinal would ever admit.

It is nothing less than a defense of the Vatican's authority in a situation that Pope John Paul II evidently perceives to be slipping out of his grasp. Of course, he would not say that it is the grasp of the Vatican and what it stands for that is involved. No, it is the grasp of the True Faith which is at stake so far as the pontiff is concerned, and he, merely Faith's custodian on earth. For what is Liberation Theology, tinged with Marxist materialism? It is a "challenge to the *sacramental and hierarchical structure* of the Church, which was willed by the Lord Himself" (p. 25, italics in orginial). And the class struggle, adherence to which damns Marxism once and for all? "The class struggle thus understood [i.e., by Marxism] divides the Church herself, and that in light of this struggle even ecclesial realities must be judged" (p. 22). And again, "Building on such a conception of the Church of the People [a major tenet of Liberation Theology], a critique of the very structures of the Church is developed" (p. 25).

Now as we have seen, the class struggle for Marx is not a metaphysical category standing above history, but only the determining principle for history itself. In other words, there is, despite *Instruction*, room within Marxism for a spiritual dimension, whether or not Marxists have chosen it. I would not recommend, however, trying to inform the Pope of his misconception. The above passages make very clear why this would be a waste of time. The Vatican is interested solely in putting itself *above* the judgment of history. Absolute faith, of which the Pope is of course the sole arbiter, is to be the ultimate criterion: "The ultimate and decisive criterion for truth can only be a criterion which is itself theological. It is only in the light of faith . . . that one can judge the validity . . . of what other disciplines propose . . . as being the truth about man, his history and his destiny" (p. 19).

It begins to appear as if *Instruction* is an attempt to claim an exemption from the judgment of history by discrediting anything which would call into question the worldly role of the church. By sealing itself up in its tautological cocoon, the Vatican is behaving somewhat as the U.S. government did when it refused to allow the World Court's jurisdiction in the suit over the mining of Nicaraguan harbors. That was a "political" not a legal matter; here we have a veto of "faith" overriding rational scrutiny. In a classic instance of the pot calling the kettle black, the Vatican accuses Marxism of subordinating all to the iron law of class struggle when this is precisely the kind of maneuver it engages in by setting itself over all other means of getting at the truth through its monopoly of the "light of faith." John Paul II is a kind of technocrat of faith: one gets away with anything one pleases, since one acts according to a "value-free" principle.

Faith in itself should give us no cause for outrage, neither as a guide to action nor a source of intuitive insight. Quite the contrary. Given the reality of subjectivity, a degree of faith is probably essential, and certainly desirable, in human affairs. But for someone to proclaim oneself *infallible* on the basis of faith is another matter entirely. For here is a human, and an institution, being held over the rest of humanity. This is not an affirmation of faith but an excuse for domination.

Essentially, the Pope is denying that the Catholic church is implicated in class struggle. That the Vatican should act this way is of course no surprise. It has been doing so for more centuries than one cares to count. Still, it is a wonder—or rather, an indication of the power of mystification—that people take the claim seriously. We do not have to be dogmatic about Marxism to recognize the power of class struggle in history. This is simply a fact, as is the need of ruling-class ideology to say it isn't so. Liberation Theology—whether it adopts a fully Marxist attitude or not—does take the fact of class struggle seriously. In this sense, the Pope is correct to call attention to what is at least a potential union with Marxism. He is entitled to dislike the idea, but not to deny the fact of the Vatican's role in the class struggle—nor, of course, that such a role would motivate it significantly.

To claim that the Vatican is above class struggle is like claiming it does not use a cathedral known as St. Peter's in Rome. It means, for example, denying that the Vatican engages heavily in banking, or that it meddles politically wherever and whenever it can. The problem for John Paul II, of course, is that recognition of class struggle, and the Vatican's role therein, would be highly embarrassing. For say what you will about Marxist discourse, it does have the annoying tendency to throw things into sharper perspective. Once one starts talking of class struggle instead of the "social stratification with all its inequity and injustice" (p. 22), which is the term *Instruction* would have us use, one is committed to an engaged view of history: society is not just a collection of data, but a struggle with sides to it and no bystanders. *Instruction* deplores above all else the way Liberation Theology cum Marxism "divides the Church herself." But neither Liberation Theology nor Marxism divides the church. The church divides itself, through its participation in class struggle—and Liberation Theology and Marxism do no more than unmask the reality. Of course, this is quite an accomplishment, whence John Paul II's undying enmity.

A word about the recent worldly activities of the Vatican may be in order here, to cast more light on why *Instruction* came to be written. There should be no doubt that the present Pope is a highly reactionary and authoritarian man who represents the right wing of the Catholic hierarchy in its effort to roll back the liberalizing forces set into motion by Pope John XXIII and Vatican II. Unfortunately, there is not only doubt but confusion about the subject, owing to John Paul II's high visibility and skill at coopting progressive rhetoric. Needless to add, the customary boost to confusion is provided by the bourgeois media, pleased pink by a glamorous figure who sweetens traditional authority with the jargon of emancipation. He has been hailed as a great reformer and "a kind of social democrat," as he barnstorms about Latin America, flailing away at the Marxist Antichrist and talking up land reform and parliamentary democracy, then leaving with promises of heavenly reward, and the existing system of oppression intact.[7]

Instruction is a set of rules to play the game John Paul II's way. If one accepts its terms, one does not have to worry about any contradictions in the Vatican's position—for example, the fact of the ascendancy during his reign of the ultraconservative group, Opus Dei, a secret society with its roots in Franco's Spain and its branches throughout the Catholic world.[8] Then there is the slight matter of the Vatican bank, with its dummy companies in Panama funneling money to neofascist groups throughout Latin America, presumably according to God's will.[9] This is not the place to go into the interesting shenanigans of this organization and its many connections in the first and third worlds. One quotation, however, may drive home some of the unseemly reality behind the Pope's attack on Liberation Theology and Marxism. As Penny Lernoux writes in her study of banking, citing no less an authority than Michele Sindona, the imprisoned international financier and erstwhile adviser to the Vatican Bank:

> Sindona also insisted that Marcinkus [the Archbishop in charge of the Vatican Bank] knew and generally approved of Calvi's [the shady banker found hanging in 1982 under London's Blackfriars Bridge] Latin American ventures, although he was unaware of the details. "I had told Calvi to tell Marcinkus that if they [the Vatican] can help, it is in their interest. South America is Catholic. They don't want to lose this big a part of their account."[10]

To regard a continent as "part of an account" may be too vulgarly materialist an interpretation to be placed upon the complex affairs of a great church. Yet it has the refreshing feel of truth when placed against the cant of *Instruction*. Indeed, the Pope has real cause for alarm in Latin America. For centuries the Catholic church has been a rock of oppression, providing ideological support for an endless succession of vicious rulers by artfully weaving together the spiritual yearnings of the masses with a morality of submission to authority. Now all that is coming undone, the rock is crumbling, and John Paul II is racing frantically about trying to glue it together. He perceives accurately enough that what has dissolved the old compact is the radical spirit of emancipation brought forward by Liberation Theology—and knows, too, that no matter how much the liberation theologians try to deny it, there is a convergence between their doctrine and Marxism. The Pope is right, then, and does sense something truly: a showdown will come, if not now, then later. Liberation Theology necessarily must challenge the church's role in oppression if it is to be serious about emancipation—and it cannot challenge this role unless the concept of class struggle is taken seriously. It is not the present appropriation of Marxism but the inevitable future one that *Instruction* seeks, probably vainly, to forestall. For it seems that the Pope is caught in a trap. John Paul II cannot risk an actual split in the Latin American church, yet overt policies of repression seem to lead only in this direction. The failure to discipline the Frs. Boff and Gutiérrez, and the Pope's continuing inability to bring the priests serving Sandinist Nicaragua into line, testify to the relative strength of the religious left in Latin America. Hence the two-pronged strategy of *Instruction:* attempting on the one hand to discredit the Marxist appropriation, and on the other to steal its thunder by proclaiming the Pope the true liberator. However, it is doubtful that the first strategy will appeal to more than the already convinced; while the second runs the substantial risk of raising expectations and legitimating Liberation Theology once the fraudulence of the Pope's offer sinks home. It promises to be a hard decade for the Pontiff.

A New Reformation?

The shabbiness of *Instruction* is no ground for complacency among Marxists. If, as seems incontrovertible, a historically momentous transformation is now being contested within the Catholic church (and, to a different degree, which we cannot take up here, other churches as well), then Marxism is in a position to play an active role in the development of this struggle. But this requires the most rigorous self-critique. It is not enough to become convinced once again that the Vatican is an enemy. The challenge is rather to recognize the significance of a "friend": Liberation Theology.

What is startling here is the degree to which an organic unity has been created out of spiritual and revolutionary appeals. For centuries the church had preempted the dimension of spirit in the cause of reaction. Now, suddenly, these limits have been shattered. No wonder the Vatican is alarmed.

And no wonder Marxism is taken aback as well, but with less grounds for fear. For, as Miranda and many others have shown, there is no inherent contradiction between spirituality and a historical materialism both scientific and revolutionizing. There is, however, historical inertia to be overcome.

For Marxism the challenge is to widen the spiritual opening through a deeper appropriation of subjectivity: what is nonrational, aesthetic, tragic, moral, and sacred. One does not have to accept Cardinal Ratzinger's repressively idealistic view of sin, for example, to recognize that he is calling attention to a dimension of existence slighted in fact, if not in principle, by historical materialism. The frankly reactionary treatment of this theme by the Vatican requires no further comment here. It should not blind us, however, to the truth that Marxism has fallen short by being unable to relate itself practically to the spiritual dimension of life.

Here is where Liberation Theology enters to address spirituality in a revolutionizing mode—one audible to Marxism if only it will listen. The Protestant Reformation gave capitalism its "spirit." Will what is taking place in the Latin American church be recognized one day as having begun the same process for socialism?

Notes

This article originally appeared in *Monthly Review* 36, no. 11 (April 1985), and is reprinted with permission. Copyright © 1985 by Monthly Review.

1. Gustavo Gutiérrez, *A Theology of Liberation* (Maryknoll, NY: Orbis Books, 1973), and *The Power of the Poor in History* (Maryknoll, NY: Orbis Books, 1983.

2. Arthur McGovern, *Marxism: An American Christian Perspective* (Maryknoll, NY: Orbis Books, 1980), p. 184.

3. Phillip Berryman, *The Religious Roots of Rebellion* (Maryknoll, NY: Orbis Books, 1984), p. 29.

4. See, for example, Louis Althusser, *For Marx* (New York: Vintage, 1970).

5. *Theories of Surplus Value* (Moscow: Progress Publishers, 1963–71), vol. 1, p. 288.

6. *Anti-Dühring* (New York: International Publishers, 1972), p. 104.

7. See, for example, E. J. Dionne, Jr., "Pope and the Poor: Doctrine Defined," *New York Times,* 1 February 1985.

8. Fred Landis, "Opus Dei: Secret Order Vies for Power," *Covert Action Information Bulletin* 18 (Winter 1983): 11–15. See also T. M. Pasca, "The Vatican Flops in Latin America," *The Nation*, 26 January 1985, pp. 76–79.

9. Penny Lernoux, *In Banks We Trust* (Garden City, NY: Doubleday, 1984), pp. 169–74.

10. Ibid., p. 209.

The Christian-Marxist Dialogue of the 1960s

Dorothee Sölle

It may be useful to survey briefly the development of the Christian/Marxist dialogue which took place in the 1960s between East and West Europeans.

Christianity and Marxism were long hostile to each other and there seemed to be little that could bridge the gap between them. Deep-rooted mistrust and fears on both sides had to be overcome before the step from "anathema to dialogue," as Roger Garaudy put it, could finally be taken. In the 1970s we entered a new phase of this development, which I would call "from dialogue to alliance."

A retrospective look at the dialogue that was developed by Christian and Marxist intellectuals at the end of the Cold War has to start with de-Stalinization and Vatican II as the historical turning points. The ice of Cold War mentality began to melt. Two important forerunners and exponents of this dialogue, both Italians, should be mentioned: Palmiro Togliatti, head of the Italian Communist Party, and Angelo Giuseppe Roncalli, later Pope John XXIII. Both broke the taboo of not acknowledging or addressing the other, except in terms of virulent clichés. Although the first steps of approach were taken from a tactical-political perspective, there was a deeper insight on both sides—the insight that neither religion nor socialism could be suppressed by mere violence. Religion continued to exist, even deepened its meaning, in the Eastern European countries; socialism did not die through fascist concentration camps and CIA machinations. The dialogue, however, meant and still means not only to live side by side, but to grow together, to learn from each other.

It is not possible here to go into the details of this phase of dialogue, which took place in hundreds of articles and pamphlets, conferences and personal encounters. What is important to recognize in this backward glance is the ideological shift that took place on both sides through the dialogue. What was the mutual give and take? What did Marxists learn from Christians and vice versa?

As long as religion continues to be seen by Marxists as a hindrance for the building up of a human society, as a category of alienation, as the opiate of the people, as illusion and mere fraud, the Christian-Marxist dialogue is meaningless. The new insight into the Christian faith which came about on the Marxist side of the dialogue was to recognize it, in the words of Cesare Luporini, as "a doctrine of the liberation of man." This necessarily implied a shift of the Marxist epistemology from a vulgarized determinism, which renders all forms of superstructure totally dependent on the basic economic conditions, back to the original Marxist dialectic of being and consciousness. If there is a dialectical interplay between base and superstructure, then religion, too, like other forms of the cultural superstructure, is empowered not only to mirror the given facts, but to change them. Religion, too, has to be understood dialectically in its double function: as apology and legitimation of the status quo and its culture of injustice on the one hand, and as a means of protest, change, and liberation on the other hand. What was seen anew by Marxists in the dialogue was this double function of religion, its veiling power which serves the interests of bourgeois injustice, but its liberating force as well. In regard to the problem of religion, de-Stalinization meant abandonment of the undialectical forms of criticism of religion. Vulgar materialism, as opposed to a historical materialistic outlook, sees religon simplistically as an enormous swindle invented by priests in order to take profit from superstitious people. Feuerbach developed his criticism of religion out of a deeper philosophical materialism that is capable of understanding dialectical contradictions; religion in his view is a projection from earth into heaven, a projected illusion. The young Marx agreed with Feuerbach's statement, but he wanted to know why and under which social conditions people begin to project the best of their inner life into heaven. Thus Marx added the historical dimension to materialism. Unfortunately, many of his followers fell back either into the Feuerbach position or even into the naïveties of the eighteenth-century materialistic tradition. For Marx it was superficial to maintain that religion is nothing but an illusion, a mere projection from earth into heaven, because Feuerbach's critique did not even raise the question why people need to project and to dream and to create myths. Marx himself went back to the needs and interests of people, which is a much deeper category of human existence than Feuerbach's reason and the rational capacities of humanity.

The Marxists who were involved in the Christian-Marxist dialogue were seen by their bureaucratic party leaders as "revisionists," although they were actually the ones who followed the best Marxian tradition, namely to take seriously the needs and questions of human beings, which cannot be suppressed by a monocausal worldview that reduces any phenomenon to economic reasons.

True Marxism understands itself as the heir of humankind's history, and therefore it also inherited such eternal questions of humanity as the search for the meaning of suffering, guilt, and death, and the need for fulfillment of each individual existence. Therefore the dialogue taught Marxist philosophers to look anew for "a theory of subjectivity which is not subjectivist and a concept of transcendence which is not alienated." Transcendence here means not a state but an act, the capacity of creatively overcoming the given set of conditions in a historical situation. The transcendence which Marxists learned from Christians or, to put it more correctly, which was given back to Marxists by their Christian brothers and sisters after it had been stolen by the rigid and reductionist guardians of orthodoxy—this transcendence is not conceivable in a dualistic worldview. It happens here and now, rather than hereafter and later. This transcendence is the deepest because it is the most creative fulfillment of human beings on their way toward humanization.

The Christians gave their philosophical dialogue partners a new understanding of *transcendence.* What did the Christians learn from the Marxists? In terms of traditional language, I would answer that Christians relearned the meaning of *incarnation.* The encounter with Marxism deepened their understanding of the historical and social dimensions of human existence. As we all know, the Christian God very often remains a non-incarnated heavenly being who stays out of the victories and defeats of history and is perceived only by individuals for purposes of individual fulfillment. This God is perceived in an idealistic way, for he lacks both the bodily and the social dimension. God is not concerned with what happens to the body and to the structures of society. By being confronted with philosophical materialism, Christians learned to take material existence more seriously in this twofold sense of body and society. Hence hunger and joblessness, the industrial-military complex and its consequences for everyday life, advance into theological themes. No longer can incarnation be understood as an event that happened once and was completed, but rather as a process of God's ongoing self-realization in history. The Marxist critique of Christianity as idealistic and superficial in its understanding of human victory was now answered by a new grasping of the word that became flesh, which means body and society. Marxists helped Christians to understand better the deep this-worldliness of Christian faith that Bonhoeffer spoke of.

What does this concept mean to Christians who are living in socialist countries? These Christians in East Germany, Poland, Czechoslovakia, and other countries have a new chance to live out their faith without being rewarded and privileged by society, as is the case in capitalism. They have experienced the end of the Constantinian era with their own bodies: their privileges were taken from them, their schools were closed, their buildings were no longer maintained by the state, they lost tax reductions and tax-free and labor-free income. What was perhaps most hurtful of all, their society had little respect for church people. The dirty fists of a construction worker were more highly esteemed than the lily-white hands of a bishop giving blessing. Christians became only one group among others in society. The dialogue encouraged Christians in East Europe to understand the historical shift of life after 1945 in a theological perspective, rather than in a noncritical worldly one, which sees only the loss of power. Christians began to understand what had happened to them as they returned from the Palace of Herod, where they had had a nice time for nearly two thousand years, and came back to the stable and manger. Instead of complaining about this new historical situation and denouncing it as "persecution," as Radio Free Europe and other CIA-based institutions did, they learned, in a painful process that is not yet completed, to understand and to accept what was going on. Theologically they learned to discriminate between Christian faith and church-connected privileges, between the stable and the palace, between a rich and mighty church, which is paid off by society for legitimizing social oppression, militarism, discriminatory laws, and a small, poor, and sometimes underprivileged church that only now has the chance of becoming more Christlike.

From this perspective Christians also received a new understanding of church history from the dialogue. Marxists such as Friedrich Engels and Rosa Luxemburg had devleoped, more clearly than most church historians, criteria of distinction between the Constantinian and the apocalyptic Christian tradition. There is an inner dialectic in church history: on the one hand, there is the Constantinian tradition, which emphasizes sin in order to legitimize the state and its rulers as willed by God, because the people are not capable of freedom and self-determination. On the other hand, there is an apocalyptical tradition, which is revived wherever the masses become conscious of their power; here the emphasis is on the fact that the son of man has defeated sin. The Constantinian tradition has sanctioned all forms of class domination, from slavery to serfdom to wage labor, and it has placed the church in solidarity with the different ruling classes. The apocalyptic tradition, however, has inspired uprisings from Jan Hus to the contemporary Christian socialist movement in Latin America.

This dialogue between Christians and Marxists was brutally ended in 1968, when the Russians invaded Prague and suppressed the "socialism with a human face" (Dubček), which was dreamed of by many participants in the dialogue. The historical attempt to reconcile socialism and democracy was crushed down by one of the imperialist superpowers, as was later to happen in Chile through the other. At the same time, the most open-minded and progressive positions of Vatican II were watered down or withdrawn from. The Catholic reform movement in the Netherlands was suppressed, rebellious priests were transferred, radical books and articles could not be printed by Catholic publishing houses. Paul VI followed John XXIII. The time of hope seemed to have passed and solidification took place. But meanwhile other forms of cooperation between Marxists and Christians began. They were carried out less by intellectuals, university teachers, pastors, and journalists than by people who organized themselves into resistance groups around the central political and social issues in Western and first world-dominated countries, such as the increasing deterioration of the conditions of life in capitalist societies, the Vietnam war and its open and hidden military and financial support, and perhaps most importantly the increasing resistance to the economic exploitation of the third world countries. In the 1970s Marxists and Christians found each other more and more frequently allies in different forms of the struggle. The struggle may be described as a spiral of violence. The first and predominant form of violence consists in the denial of a humane life for the majority, cutting them off from jobs, housing, food, health, and education. The second form of violence is the counterviolence of the oppressed. This leads to a third form of violence on the part of the state and the police, and the consequent repression and destruction of the democratic rights for which the people had struggled so long. This third form of repressive violence today characterizes an increasing number of Latin American countries; it is a process of creeping fascism, which starts with the cutback of democratic rights, such as freedom of opinion, speech, press, assembly, and organization, and ends in overt terror and torture.

The phase at which most Christians enter the struggle is not during the counterviolence of the oppressed, although there are some Christians working on strike committees side by side with their Marxist comrades and in alternative forms of cooperative production, but rather when they become aware of the overt growing fascism in their countries in the third phase of violence. To mention one example, I recall the Peace Committee in Chile between 1972 and 1975, until it was forbidden and dissolved, a group of mostly Christians led by Cardinal Silva and Bishop Frenz, who became active on behalf of the political prisoners and so-called missing persons. It is a bitter fact that fascism brings about the alliance between Christians and Marxists which the softer forms of capitalism, though they are as murderous in their aims, fail to do. In any case, the new alliances were prepared and made easier by the former dialogue and its insights into the common struggle. What is overcome today is the uncommitted, merely academic dialogue, and it is the street, the urban slum, and sometimes the prison cell rather than the conference room where Christians and Marxists meet and continue growing together.

The march route is drawn up: from anathema to dialogue was a first step, from dialogue to alliance is a second; yet there is a third step, which many of us have taken, others are still reluctant to take, a step into a new Christian-socialist identity.

Note

This article originally appeared in the special issue of *Monthly Review* 36, no. 3 (July-August 1984), entitled "Religion and the Left." Copyright © 1984 by Monthly Review.

Marxism and Religion

Harry Magdoff and Paul M. Sweezy

Radical movements and religion have not always been strangers, let alone antagonists. In fact, as Friederick Engels pointed out, Christianity itself began as a protest against oppression:

> The history of early Christianity has notable points of resemblance with the modern working-class movement. Like the latter, Christianity was originally a movement of oppressed people: it first appeared as the religion of slaves and emancipated slaves, of poor people deprived of all rights, of peoples subjugated or dispersed by Rome. Both Christianity and the workers' socialism preach forthcoming salvation from bondage and misery; Christianity places the salvation in a life beyond after death, in heaven; socialism places it in this world, in a transformation of society. . . .

> The parallel between the two historic phenomena forces itself upon our attention as early as the Middle Ages in the first risings of the oppressed peasants and particularly of the town plebeians. These risings, like all mass movements of the Middle Ages, were bound to wear the mask of religion and appeared as the restoration of early Christianity from spreading degeneration; but behind the religious exaltation there was every time a very tangible worldly interest. This appeared most splendidly in the organization of the Bohemian Taborites under Jan Zizka, of glorious memory; but this trait pervades the whole of the Middle Ages until it gradually fades away after the German Peasant War to revive again with the workingmen Communists after 1830. The French revolutionary Communists, as also in particular Weitling and his supporters, referred to early Christianity long before Renan's words: "If I wanted to give you an idea of the early Christian communities I would tell you to look at a local section

of the International Working Men's Association [The First International]."[1]

The association in earlier history of the struggle over religious issues with economic and social protest was inevitable in view of the hold that theology and the church had on everyday life. This was especially so in the Middle Ages when politics, jurisprudence, and education were in the hands of the clergy, who provided the institutions and the ideology on which feudal domination relied. Revolt against feudal oppression could not be separated from revolt against the sanctity of the established church. Heresies and social rebellion were part of the same struggle.

With the weakening of feudal power and the rise of capitalism, however, new ideological trends emerged that were independent of religious controversy or directly challenged religion by advancing atheistic or agnostic positions. In an important sense, Marxism is the main inheritor and continuer of the secular, an anticlerical tradition that goes back to the Renaissance and the Enlightenment. For this reason alone organized religion and organized radicalism, overwhelmingly influenced by Marxism, became increasingly separated.

Early in the development of his philosophical views, Marx explained his approach to theology in the following way: "We do not turn secular questions into theological questions. We turn theological questions into secular ones."[2] A corollary belief is that it is not God who created human beings, but that God (or Gods) was created by human beings in different parts of the world and under different historical circumstances.

Marx's thought is of course thoroughly materialist. Materialism, as opposed to idealism, asserts that matter is not a product of mind or of a supernatural being; instead, mind is seen as the highest product of matter. These philosophical concepts have often been confused in the popular mind with another set of meanings for the same terms. In everyday language, the terms materialism and idealism are used to characterize personal behavior. According to this view, a materialist is one who tends to be more concerned with material than with spiritual goals and values, and an idealist is one who behaves according to his or her ideals. In this sense, philosophical idealists may conduct their personal lives and politics as materialists, while there is nothing in the philosophical materialism of Marx and Marxists that conflicts with the idealistic behavior of its advocates. That is especially true of Marxists who are committed in thought and action to creating a more humane society.

Marxist materialism in no way denies the role of ideas and ideals in moving people to action and influencing the course of the action. Misconceptions about this have arisen in part because of occasional generalizations in the writings of the founders comparing the processes of historical change with laws of nature. Analogies of this kind have been taken by some Marxists, as well as by critics of Marxism, to mean that changes in material conditions (notably, technology) automatically or inevitably bring about clear-cut, uniform social transformations. This interpretation ignores a vital core of the Marxist historical vision, that social change occurs through the medium of class struggle. Class struggles, however, take place in given circumstances and can only accomplish tasks that are circumscribed by the realities of time, country, and the inherited past.* Yet despite these ever present limits, the course of history is not foreordained. What matters is the way class struggle develops concretely, which in turn is strongly influenced by the ideas that guide the participants. And it is because of this perception that Marx and Engels devoted their lives to theoretical clarification and advocacy. "Material force must be overthrown by material force," Marx wrote, and then added, "but theory too becomes a material force once it seizes the masses."[3]

The role of ideas assumes unusual significance in socialist revolutions because the creation of a socialist society, ideally, requires a self-conscious working class that participates in the design of a new social system. And although the revolution—and the building of a new system—is rooted in the self-interest of the working class and its allies, its full realization requires the pursuit of ideals that go far beyond immediate self-interest. Thus the *Communist Manifesto* proclaims the aim of the proletarian revolution in these words: "In place of the old bourgeois society, with its classes and class antagonisms, we shall have an association, in which the free development

*Much of Marx and Engels's writing was devoted to combatting contrary philosophical and socialist trends as well as to popularizing their own views. These efforts led them to stress what was new and different in their world outlook and historical perspective, resulting at times in broad, oversimplified generalizations. Engels admitted as much in a letter to Joseph Bloch (dated September 21–22, 1890): "Marx and I are ourselves partly to blame for the fact that the younger people sometimes lay more stress on the economic side than is due to it. We had to emphasize the main principle vis-à-vis our adversaries, who denied it, and we had not always the time, the place, or the opportunity to give their due to other elements involved in their interaction. But when it came to presenting a section of history, that is, to making a practical application, it was a different matter and there no error was permissible." An excellent example of how they analyzed a concrete historical process in all its complexity, including the interplay of ideas, classes, and material circumstances, can be found in Marx, *The Eighteenth Brumaire of Louis Bonaparte.*

of each is the condition for the free development of all." Furthermore, the ultimate fulfillment of this goal assumes the adoption of extraordinarily high moral principles in relations among people. As Marx put it in the *Critique of the Gotha Program:*

> In a more advanced phase of communist society, when the enslaving subjugation of individuals to the division of labor, and thereby the antithesis between intellectual and physical have disappeared; when labor is no longer just a means of keeping alive but has itself become a vital need; when the all-round development of individuals has also increased their productive powers and all the springs of cooperative wealth flow more abundantly—only then can society wholly cross the narrow horizon of bourgeois right and inscribe on its banner: From each according to his abilities, to each according to his needs!

The point to be emphasized here is that Marx's materialism was in no sense a denial of the spiritual side of human existence. Furthermore, although Marx himself did not deal with the problems of private life, there is nothing in Marxism that denies the psychological needs of people. The popular image of Marx (and by extension Marxists), assiduously propagated by the mass media, is that of a mortal enemy of religion in general. It is of course totally false. Marx's attitude toward religion in general—though not toward all religious institutions—was one of understanding and sympathy. His famous statement that religion is the opium of the people, read in context, is the best illustration. Here is what he said:

> *Religious* distress is at the same time the expression of real distress and also the *protest* against real distress. Religion is the sigh of the oppressed creature, the heart of a heartless world, just as it is the spirit of the spiritless conditions. It is the *opium* of the people.
>
> To abolish religion as the *illusory* happiness of the people is to demand their *real* happiness. The demand to give up illusions about the existing state of affairs is the *demand to give up a state of affairs which needs illusions*. The criticism of religion is therefore in embryo the criticism of the vale of tears, the halo of which is religion.[4]*

Clearly Marx thought of religion not as an evil but as a necessary human reaction to oppression and misery. For him religion was a symptom of an unacceptable state of affairs, of a world that had to be changed. Whether or to what extent religion fulfills other deep-seated human needs are questions Marx never addressed. Nor need we do so here, since they have no bearing on the subject that is

---

*The German word *Eland,* translated as "distress" in the first sentence, would be more appropriately rendered as "misery." Distress often connotes a specific and transitory mishap (e.g., a ship in distress), while misery usually refers to a lasting condition.

the focus of our present concern. It is sufficient to recognize that Marx was in no sense an enemy of religion as such, and the same goes for those who can reasonably claim to be Marxists.

Nevertheless, antagonism and conflict between Marxism and religion did ensue. These have in large measure been due to the debasement of religious values as reflected in the practices of religious institutions, and to the degeneration of Marxist principles in states that fly the Marxist banner. Where churches are or have been large landowners, they exploit the peasants who work their land and join with other large landowners in upholding the laws and institutions that sustain the oppression of tenant farmers, sharecroppers, plantation workers, and virtual serfs. Beyond that, most religious organizations have served as major defenders and rationalizers of the existing order. And the ruling classes in turn support and rely on the dominant religions in their countries to blind the exploited masses to the causes of their misery and to keep resistance in check. Where this is flagrantly the case, rebellions, whether led by Marxists or other radicals, have often been vigorously anticlerical and have attacked the church as an integral part of the ruling class that had to be overturned.

This was especially so in Russia before the revolution. There the official church was a crucial part of the ruling establishment, strongly identified with the evils against which the people of the tsarist empire rebelled. The church and the monarchy were twin institutions that relied on each other to maintain their legitimacy. Exploitation of the peasants on the vast landed estates owned by the church was as harsh as on those of the nobility and other large landowners. The conservative clergy exercised a decisive influence in keeping the people subservient to their secular masters. Finally, in the years of revolution and civil war, the church as a whole aligned itself with the counter-revolution. The Soviet regime, not surprisingly, treated the church hierarchy as an enemy whose power and sway over the minds of the masses had to be destroyed. Thus along with the revolution came confiscation of church property, closing of churches, elimination of church schools, etc. In addition, militant campaigns were conducted to wean the population from religious views and to convert them to atheism. As a side benefit, it was hoped that the spread of atheism would help replace widespread superstition and mysticism with respect for science.

Over the years, however, the antireligious trend, interrupted during World War II, became rigidly embedded in the ruling ideology of the Soviet Union and in most other countries that consider themselves socialist. The sentence about religion being the opium of the people, isolated from its context, is declared to be the cornerstone of the Marxist outlook on religion; and this in turn is associated with a one-sided view of religion as an instrument of oppression, ignoring the appeal of religion to deep-seated spiritual needs.

The animosity aroused among religious people by these developments naturally widened the gulf between them and Marxists. But that was not all. Practically every other seemingly unfavorable feature of Soviet-type societies was seen in religious circles to be an inevitable outgrowth of Marxism. Thus, the concentration on a rapid rise of the productive forces, along with an underemphasis of spiritual factors, are taken to be inherent in materialist philosophy, a view that fails to take into account the enormous tasks facing postrevolutionary societies, emerging as they have in underdeveloped countries where the large majority of the population live in wretched poverty. But the fact of the matter is that meeting the basic needs of the people—for food, clothing, housing, medical care, education—can only be achieved by a mobilization of human and natural resources and an intensive, almost military, campaign to expand productive capacity.

On this score, the achievements of the Soviet Union deserve special attention. The proper way to appreciate these achievements is to measure the condition of the Soviet people against that of the masses in the underdeveloped areas of the third world. For example, even though Mexico's revolution preceded the Russian Revolution, there is no comparison between the mass misery prevalent in Mexico today with the way the Soviet people live. Equally pertinent, if not more so, is the comparision of the living standards—including educational and cultural facilities—on both sides of the borders in the Soviet Asian republics. Before the revolution there was little difference; now they are worlds apart.

The issue, as we see it, is not the all-out effort of postrevolutionary societies to raise as quickly as feasible the material and cultural standards of their peoples. It is rather their departure from socialist and Marxist principles that is at fault. In their desperate struggle to overcome backwardness, they have developed institutions and an ideology that stand in the way of moving toward the goals outlined by Marx in the *Critique of the Gotha Program.* What is needed now is not the identification of the course of postrevolutionary societies with Marxism, but rather a critical—yes Marxist—analysis of the nature and potentialities of these societies.

History has thrown up this challenge to radicals if they expect to do better in the future. At the same time, developments in religious circles, responding to the crisis of our times, have opened up new perspectives for radical movements. In some respects a class struggle has emerged on the theological front, between those who continue to see the church as a mainstay of capitalism and those who call on it to participate actively in the battles of the poor and downtrodden for social justice, to bring the kingdom of heaven down to earth.

With changes thus occurring on both sides, there is a growing basis and need for cooperation between Marxism and religion. Each can learn much from the other that can be useful in the struggle. For those who see their church as a mission to the poor and oppressed, Marxism has a good deal to offer in helping to understand historical processes and the nature of capitalism. And Marxists need to learn to distinguish between the religious hierarchies that prop up capitalism and aid counter-revolution, on the one hand, and those in the church who side with revolution and progress on the other. Still more important, Marxists have to strive for a greater understanding of the role religion plays in the private lives of people and how to incorporate spiritual needs and imperatives with advances in material well-being.

It would be a mistake, however, to underestimate the many obstacles that impede cooperative efforts. Suspicions on both sides, arising from past experience and from differences in style, are bound to persist. But the real test of the possibility of cooperation is practice. There is of course no guarantee of success, but it is already clear that the potentialities are enormous. What the world needs above all else in these closing years of the twentieth century is a reborn revolutionary movement that understands the nature of the global crisis and reaches into history for the elements in both religion and Marxism that can provide the spiritual energy for a new beginning.

Notes

1. Friedrich Engels, "On the History of Early Christianity," first published in *Die Neue Zeit,* vol. 1 (1894–95), and reprinted in Karl Marx and Friedrich Engels, *On Religion* (Moscow: Foreign Languages Publishing House, 1957), pp. 313–15.
2. "On the Jewish Question," in Karl Marx and Friedrich Engels, *Collected Works,* vol. 3 (New York: International Publishers, 1975), p. 151.
3. "A Contribution to the Critique of Hegel's Philosophy of Law. Introduction," in Marx and Engels, *Collected Works,* vol. 3, p. 182.
4. Ibid., p. 175.

Religion and the Left

Cornel West

Notwithstanding the secular sensibilities of most left intellectuals and activists, religion permeates the lives of the majority of people in the capitalist world. And all signs indicate that the prevailing crisis in the capitalist world is not *solely* an economic or political one. Recent inquiries into racism, patriarchy, homophobia, state repression, bureaucratic domination, ecological subjugation and nuclear exterminism suggest that we understand this crisis as a crisis of *capitalist civilization*. To extend left discourse about political economy and the state to a discourse about capitalist civilization is to accent a sphere rarely scrutinized by Marxist thinkers: *the sphere of culture and everyday life*. And any serious scrutiny of this sphere sooner or later must come to terms with religious ways of life and religious ways of struggle.

In this brief essay I shall pose three crucial questions to contemporary Marxism regarding religion. First, how are we to understand the character and content of religious beliefs and practices? Second, how are we to account for the recent religious upsurges in Latin America, the Middle East, Asia, Africa, Eastern Europe, and the United States? And third, in which ways can these upsurges enrich and enhance—or delimit and deter—the international struggle for human freedom and democracy? In the present historical moment these queries strike me as inescapable and important.

Religion and Marxist Theory

The classical Marxist understanding of religion is more subtle than is generally acknowledged. Crude Marxist formulations of religion as the opium of the people, in which the religious masses are viewed as passive and ignorant objects upon which manipulative religious institutions impose fantasies of otherworldly fulfillment, reveal more about the Enlightenment prejudices and arrogant self-images of secular intellectuals than about the nature of religion. Contrary to such widespread crypto-Marxist myths about religion, Marx and Engels understood religion as a profound human response to, and protest against, intolerable conditions. For Marx and Engels, religion constituted alienated forms of human cultural practice under circumstances not of peoples' own choosing. In this view, religion as an opium of the people is not a mere political pacification imposed from above, but rather a historically circumscribed existential and experiential assertion of being (or somebodiness) by dehumanized historical agents under unexamined socioeconomic conditions. Marx and Engels characterized religion as alienation not primarily because it is "unscientific" or "pre-modern," but rather because it often overlooks the socioeconomic conditions that shape and mold its expression and thereby delimits human powers and efforts to transform these conditions. In short, the classical Marxist critique of religion is not an a priori philosophical rejection of religion; rather, it is a social analysis of, and historical judgment upon, religious practices.

For Marx and Engels religion often overlooks the socioeconomic circumstances that condition its expression principally because the religious preoccupation with synoptic vision, abstract pronouncements on human nature, and personal morality hold at arm's length social and historical analysis. Hence religion at its worst serves as an ideological means of preserving and perpetuating prevailing social and historical realities and at its best yields moralistic condemnations of, and utopian visions beyond, present social and historical realities—with little insight into what these realities are and how to change them. The Marxist point here is not simply that religion alone is an impotent and inadequate form of protest, but also that without a probing and illuminating social and historical analysis of the present even the most well-intentioned religionists and moralists will impede fundamental social and historical transformation. In stark contrast to crude Marxists, Marx and Engels do not claim that only a substitution of a rigid Marxist science of society and history for false religion and glib moralism can liberate humankind, but rather that a Marxist social and historical analysis can more effectively guide transformative human praxis, motivated in part by moral and/or religious norms of human freedom and democracy.

This more nuanced understanding of religion has rarely surfaced in the Marxist tradition, primarily because of the early Eurocentric development of Marxism. In Europe—where the Enlightenment ethos remained (and still remains) hegemonic among intellectuals and the literate middle classes—secular sensibilities were nearly prerequisite for progressive outlooks, and religious beliefs were usually a sign of political reaction. The peculiar expression of critical consciousness in Europe focused on a corrupt and oppressive feudal order which the institutional church firmly supported and buttressed. And though the advent of Marxism itself bears traces of this Enlightenment legacy, the deep sense of historical consciousness nurtured and promoted by Marx and Engels led them to understand religious beliefs as first and foremost cultural practices generated from conflictual and contradictory socioeconomic conditions, rather than as ahistorical sets of philosophical arguments. Of course, Kant, Fichte, and especially Hegel and Feuerbach, contributed to such an understanding.

The Marxism of the Second International—with its diverse forms of economic determinism, Kantian moralism, and even left Social Darwinism—viewed cultural and religious issues in a crude and reductionist manner. Karl Kautsky's monumental work, *The Foundations of Christianity* (1908), is an exemplary text in this regard. The major antireductionist voices in this deterministic wilderness were those of the Italian Marxist Antonio Labriola and the Irish Marxist James Connolly. Lenin and Trotsky undermined the crudity and reductionism of the Second International, but they confined their efforts to the realms of politics and the arts. Neither provided serious and sustained antireductionist formulations in regard to ethics and religion. In fact, the Third International also remained quite reductionist on such matters.

The centrality of morality and religion loom large in the works of Antonio Gramsci. For the first time a major European Marxist took with utter seriousness the cultural life-worlds of the oppressed. Though still tied to a rationalist psychology that reglected unconscious impulses, and to a revolutionary teleology that uncritically promoted industrial working-class agency, Gramsci highlighted the complex elements that comprise the cultural ways of life of oppressed people and the fragile, ever changing character of these elements in response to contradictory socioeconomic circumstances.

Gramsci understood culture as a crucial component of class capacity. Like James Connolly before him and Raymond Williams in our own time, Gramsci examined the ways in which cultural resources both enabled and disenabled political struggle among the exploited and excluded in capitalist societies. While Georg Lukács disclosed the reified character of contemporary capitalist culture— the way in which processes of commodification and thingification are shot through bourgeois thought, art, and perception—Gramsci focused on the cultural means by which workers and peasants resisted such reification. And while Karl Korsch enunciated his principle of historical specificity—the need to acknowledge the materiality of ideology and the diversity of conflicting social forces in a particular historical moment—Gramsci applied this principle and specified the nature of those conflicting social forces with his seminal notions of hegemony and historical blocs.

Ironically, the major figures of so-called Western Marxism were preoccupied with culture, but none were materialist enough to take religion seriously. Whether it was Teodor Adorno and Herbert Marcuse on the subversive character of highbrow music and po- etry, Jean-Paul Sartre and Louis Althusser on the progressive pos- sibilities of avant-garde prose and theater, or Walter Benjamin and Mikhail Bakhtin on the revolutionary potential of film and the novel—all rightly viewed the cultural sphere as a domain of ide- ological contestation. Yet none highlighted religion as a crucial component of this cultural sphere.

It is important to note that it has been primarily third world Marxists—for whom issues of praxis and strategy loom large—who have confronted the religious component of culture in a serious way. Peru's José Carlos Mariátegui, China's Mao Zedong, and Guinea-Bissau's Amilcar Cabral were trailblazers on such matters. All three shunned the reductionism of the Second International, eschewed the excessive hostility toward religion of the Third Inter- national, and transcended the Enlightenment prejudices of West- ern Marxists. Mariátegui, Mao, and Cabral—whose cultural concerns inspire black Marxists, feminist Marxists, gay and lesbian Marxists in the first world—recovered and refined the classical Marxist insights regarding the materiality and ambiguity, the rela- tive autonomy and empowering possibilities, of cultural and reli- gious practices by grasping the existential and experiential content of such practices under capitalist conditions. In our own time, Marxist historians such as Christopher Hill and E. P. Thompson in England, W. E. B. Du Bois and Engene Genovese in the United States, Marc Bloch and Henri Lefèbvre in France, Manning Clarke in Australia, and Enrique Dussel in Mexico have begun to come to terms with the complex relation of religious practices to political struggle. In other words, the age of crude Marxist reductionist treatments of religion—along with the European secular condescending attitudes that undergird such treatments—is over. Concrete social and detailed historical analyses of the relation of religion to revolutionary praxis is now a major issue on the agenda for contemporary Marxism.

Religion and Marxist Politics

The fundamental challenge of religion for Marxist politics is how do we understand religious practices as specific forms of popular opposition and/or subordination in capitalist societies. Recent religious upsurges around the world—in postindustrial, industrial, and preindustrial capitalist countries—call into question bourgeois theories of secularization and crude Marxist theories of modernization. The world-historical social processes of rationalization, commodification, and bureaucratization have generated neither a widespread "disenchantment of the world," a "polar night of icy hardness and darkness," nor a revolutionary class consciousness among industrial workers. Instead, we have witnessed intense revivals of nationalism, ethnicity, and religion. Modern capitalist processes have transformed traditional religious worldviews, intimate *Gemeinschaft*-like arrangements, and customary social bonds, but have not eliminated the need and yearning for any of these. Recent nationalist, ethnic, and religious revivals constitute new forms of these worldviews, arrangements, and bonds, with existential intensity and ideological fervor.

This is so primarily for three basic reasons. First, the culture of capitalist society has, for the most part, failed to give existential moorings and emotional assurance to its inhabitants. The capitalist culture of consumption—with its atomistic individualism, spectatorial passivity, and outlooks of therapeutic release—does not provide meaningful sustenance for large numbers of people. So in first world countries religious responses—often in nostalgic forms but also in utopian ones—are widespread. Given the relative lack of longstanding ties or traditional links to a religious past, these responses are intertwined with the prevailing myths of European modernity: nationalism, racism, anti-Semitism, sexism, anti-Orientalism, and homophobia. This is why religious revivals (as well as nationalist and ethnic ones) are usually dangerous, though they can also be occasions for progressive opportunity. *Such opportunity is significant in that religious impulses are one of the few resources for a moral and political commitment beyond the self in the capitalist culture of consumption.* These impulses often require commitments to neighbor, community, and unknown others, though such commitments are ideologically circumscribed.

The second reason religious revivals emerge is that they constitute popular responses to intense capitalist domination of more traditional societies. This is especially so in third world countries in which the cultural forms are either indigenous or colonial and the capital is primarily external or international. The boomtown character of industrialization, urbanization, and proletarianization demands the cultural ways of life—usually religious—provide strategies for new personal meaning, social adjustment, and political struggle.

The emergence of the most important third world development in religious practice—the Liberation Theology movement—consists of such strategies of new personal meaning, social adjustment, and political struggle. This movement began in Latin America primarily in response to rapid capitalist penetration, quick yet painful industrial class formation, rampant state repression, and immense urbanization. This response was not only rooted in Christian thought and practice; it also flowed from the major "free" space in these repressive regimes, the church. And given the overwhelming Roman Catholic character of this movement—with the monumental reforming impetus of Vatican II (1962–1965) and the groundbreaking counterhegemonic posture of the Medellín Latin American Bishops' meeting (1968)—these new strategies became more open to personal meanings, social adjustments, and political struggles informed by prophetic elements in the Scripture and ecclesiastical tradition, as well as progressive social and historical analyses.

Liberation Theology in Latin America—put forward by Gustavo Gutiérrez, Reubem Alves, Hugo Assmann, José Miguez-Bonino, Victorio Araya, Ernesto Cardenal, Paulo Freire, Elsa Tamez, José Miranda, Pablo Richard, Juan Luis Segundo, Enrique Dussel, Beatrice Couch, and others—is generated and sustained by popular religious opposition to the consolidation of capitalist social processes. It is in part an anti-imperialist Christian mode of thought and action. Similar Liberation Theology outlooks—with their own contextual colorings—are found in Africa (especially South Africa), Asia (especially the Philippines and South Korea), the Caribbean (especially Jamaica) and the United States (especially among black and feminist theologians). Yet in terms of widespread concrete praxis, none yet rivals that of Latin America.

The last reason such religious revivals emerge is that they constitute anti-Western forms of popular resistance to capitalist domination. This is especially so in those third world countries (or pockets in the first world,as with indigenous peoples) in which a distinct cultural and religious way of life still has potency and vitality over against Western modes of religion. For example, in the Middle East and parts of Asia and Africa, Islam, Buddhism, Hinduism, or traditional religions still have substance and life. Hence these religions serve as cultural sources against not simply Western imperialism, but also against much of Western civilization—especially Western self-images, values, and sensibilities. Such resistance, like all forms of resistance, can be restorative and reactionary (as in Iran) or progressive and prophetic (as among many Palestinians).

In short, the religious revivals, along with nationalistic and ethnic ones, fundamentally result from the inability of capitalist civilization to provide contexts and communities wherein meaning and value can be found to sustain people through the traumas of life. And since without such contexts and communities there can be no potent morality, these religious revivals represent an ethical challenge to Marxism. Instead of the promised autonomy and progress of the European Enlightenment, the modern West has bequeathed to the world—besides ingenious technological innovation, personal liberties for some, and comfortable living for the few—mere fragments and ruins of a decaying and declining civilization. This decay and decline owes much to the captivity of its ways of life to class exploitation, partriarchy, racism, homophobia, technocratic rationality, and the quest for military might. Of course, many of these remarks—and even more in the realm of personal liberties—can be made of "actually existing" communist civilization. But our focus in this essay is the capitalist world. And as this capitalist world continues its deterioration, religious revivals will more than likely persist. But will such revivals enable or disenable the left in its struggle for human freedom and democracy?

Religion and Marxist Strategy

Religious upsurges in the third world (and second world, as in Poland) may quite clearly contribute to the building of a left movement. As we have seen in Latin America—where over 200,000 Christian base communities exist as concrete praxis-centers for social change, communal support, and personal sustenance—and parts of Africa and Asia, religion plays an important role in liberation struggles. The prophetic church in Nicaragua, with its healthy and unhealthy tensions with the state, is the best recent example of this crucial role.

The major contribution religious revivals can make to left strategy is to demand that Marxist thinkers and activists take seriously the culture of the oppressed. This fundamental shift in the sensibilities and attitudes of most Marxists requires a kind of indigenizing of Marxist praxis, a laying bare and casting off of the deepseated Enlightenment prejudices that shape and mold the perspectives and perceptions of most Marxists. This shift does not demand a softening of critical consciousness, but rather a deepening of it. It does not result in an antiscience stance, but rather in antiscientism (the idolizing of science). It does not yield an antitechnology viewpoint, but rather an antitechnologism. Nor does it produce a rejection of reason, but rather a specifying of liberating forms of rationality.

Such a shift is necessary because after over a century of heralding the cause of the liberation of oppressed peoples, Marxists have little understanding and appreciation of the culture of these people. This means that though Marxists have sometimes viewed oppressed people as political or economic agents, they have rarely viewed them as *cultural* agents. Yet without such a view there can be no adequate conception of the capacity of oppressed people, the capacity to change the world and sustain the change in an emancipatory manner. And without a conception of such capacity, it is impossible to envision and create a socialist society of freedom and democracy. It is in part the European Enlightenment legacy—the inability to believe in the capacities of oppressed people to create cultural products and oppositional groups of value—that stands between contemporary Marxism and oppressed people. And it is the arrogance of this legacy, the snobbery of the tradition, that precludes Marxists from taking seriously religion, a crucial element of the culture of the oppressed.

Needless to say, shedding the worst of the Enlightenment legacy does not entail neglecting the best of this European tradition. Relentless criticism and historical consciousness remain the benchmarks for any acceptable emancipatory vision, just as protracted class struggle and an allegiance to socialist democracy remain indispensable features of any recognizable Marxism. So the call for overcoming European bourgeois attitudes of paternalism toward religion does not mean adopting religious viewpoints. Religious affiliation is not the mark of ignorance or intelligence. Yet it is the mark of wisdom to understand the conditions under which people do or do not have religious affiliation. In this sense science neither solves nor dissolves the issue of religious beliefs. Instead, history provides us with traditions against which we must struggle yet within which we must critically abide. The grand quest for truth—which will ultimately separate religionists from secularists—

is a thoroughly historical one that takes the form of practical judgments inseparable from value judgments upon, and social analytical understandings of, prevailing socioeconomic realities. There are indeed standards of adjudication, but such historically constituted standards yield multiple viewpoints worthy of adoption. Hence the quest of truth continues, with only human practice providing provisional closure.

If Marxists are to go beyond European bourgeois attitudes toward the culture of the oppressed, without idealizing or romanticizing these cultures, it is necessary to go beyond a "hermeneutics of suspicion" and engage in hermeneutical combat. In other words, Marxists must not simply enact *negative* forms of subversive demystification (and, God forbid, mere bourgeois forms of deconstruction!), but also *positive* forms of popular revolutionary construction of new personal meanings, social adjustments, and political struggles for human freedom and democracy. These new forms can emerge only after traversing, transforming, and building upon the crucial spheres in society—religion, family, labor-process, state apparatuses—in order to consolidate and unite multiple organizational groupings for fundamental social change.

So to take seriously the culture of the oppressed is not to privilege religion, but to enhance and enrich the faltering and neglected utopian dimension of left theory and praxis. It is to believe not simply in the potential of oppressed people, but to believe also that oppressed people have already expressed some of this potential in their actual products, their actual practices. To be a leftist is not only to envision and fight for a radically free and democratic society; it also is to see this society in the making as manifest in the abilities and capacities of flesh-and-blood people in their struggles under conflictual and contradictory socioeconomic conditions not of their own choosing. This is the fundamental message regarding the relation of religious practices to a revolutionary praxis beyond capitalist civilization.

Note

Part IV

Theology Rooted in the Community

The essays in Section I dealt with the theologies of liberation that have developed in Latin America and among black theologians and feminists in the United States, and which are beginning to be developed among Jews out of their particular historical experience. What is striking about these efforts is that they all had deep roots in the experiences of a particular people *in community*. The essays in this section further develop this theme, focusing on the development of liberation theologies through work in and with different communities in the United States.

There is among many at this point in time a pessimism about our situation: responsibility to others, and for others in the community, seems on the way out, while a "mean and lean" selfishness is gaining public acceptance as a way of life. Americans seem to have moved from a belief in the ability of the individual to develop in a caring context to a condemnatory attitude toward those who are not winners. And because Americans, including most churchgoers, are not used to analyzing their society, they tend to blame some devil for this malaise—either the "evil empire" (the Soviet Union) or "big government"—rather than examining how injustices are perpetuated or how alternatives can be developed. Even liberal churches, whose members are more likely to think in terms of institutional reforms, assume that the private economy will produce wealth which the government can redistribute to those in need. And when this fails to happen, they still hesitate to examine and question the core structures of the economy.

Those who live in less liberal contexts, on the other hand, and those who face the harsh competitive world without middle-class resources—and indeed see the wealthier Protestants as the owners, the underminers of the security of their own world—are often attracted to an other-world escapist religion or a political conservatism that tries to replace the sense of loss with the kind of faith that is proferred by some of the pentacostal, evangelical, charismatic, and fundamentalist churches. There is an ironic class dimension to the long-standing animosities between the mainstream liberal churches and the evangelical and fundamentalist Protestant denominations: these latter are viewed by the mainstream churches as hopelessly conservative, while the liberal churches that would be in solidarity with the poor and oppressed are identified by the lower classes with the bosses and governing elites. But this need not happen, and the way a shared sense of community and the feeling of being embattled by hostile external forces have led to different results in different racial and ethnic communities is what is discussed in the articles in this section.

It may surprise both mainstream churchgoers and members of fundamentalist denominations to learn that the latter have a radical history. This is what Donald Dayton, who comes from the Holiness Church tradition, argues in the first essay. He believes that "redneck religion," the white working-class, member-controlled churches, may have a liberating potential that has not yet been realized. Gil Dawes, in the next essay, shows how the potential for a progressive politics with a liberation theological base is indeed present in working-class churches. While not minimizing the difficulties, the example of his work suggests what socially committed Christians can achieve in a seemingly hostile environment.

The importance of race in the United States is underscored when we examine examples of how oppression that has been translated into a sense of group identity can result in a new response to marginalization. Gayraud Wilmore, in the next essay, discusses the black church in its relation to both a socially enforced and group-created sense of identity and religious experience.

In the following essay Norman Fong describes how a uniquely Asian-American theology has emerged out of the experiences of the Chinese community in San Francisco, which has brought its own culture with it to this country. The community's response to discrimination has been somewhat different from that of blacks, Hispanics, and others. Indeed, these articles can only introduce some of the complexities of religious experience, differing as they do according to group and personal experience. Even within one group, there are divisions: so that among Hispanics in the United

States, Cubans, Chicanos, Puerto Ricans, and Filipinos are distinct from each other and divided among themselves by class, gender, region, denominational dogma, and so on. Nevertheless, an effort is being made to elucidate an encompassing Hispanic theology, building it out of community. Virgilio Elizando tells us:

> We find our unity in new expressions of the church growing out of the roots of people, which we call *las comunidades ecclesiales de base* or *comunidades populares*. . . .These grassroots communities are "church" because they are communities of service. They do not build community for the sake of their own self-development. They are held together by the word of God as they exercise their common mission to the world. It is of the essence of the *comunidades* to have a collective commitment to their neighborhood of their cities. They ask themselves, "What can we do as a group to better conditions in this area?" It is of the essence of the community to pray together because they realize in their own weakness that without prayer the community can never accomplish what they hope to accomplish. They are a community of study, a community of commitment to service, a community of prayer, a community of celebration. A community that does not celebrate will die. In coming together, faith must be celebrated.
>
> This unity, which is already being lived in the church, is expressed, proclaimed, and transmitted, not so much in theological vocabularies but in a new way, in the language of the people. The common faith is expressed, proclaimed, and transmitted primarily through poetry, dance, music, songs, art, imagery, murals, festivity. This is the language of the renewed church, perfectly comprehensible to those who belong, but for those who are not a part of it, no explanation will be adequate. It comes out of the experience of common struggles, common suffering, common hope. Believe me, if you want to know the new thought coming out of Latin America and from the Hispanics in the United States, don't limit yourself to the theologians who write so that theologians of the West and East can understand them. They are doing this well. But if you want to go to the real theology of Latin America, go to the poets. Go to the songwriters. The songs bring forth theology: the songs of joy, the songs of hope, the songs of faith. These are common songs for all of us, Catholic and Protestant. They are common songs we can sing together.[1]

The very complex question is What *is* community? How identities are molded and changed through complex interactions of personal growth in social and economically changing situations, and in the presence of ongoing and strongly held group identities, is an issue that goes beyond the scope of this volume. Yet the question of personal identity as a part of community of faith is important, because it is often the group that—to some extent at least—shelters its members from the impersonal market forces that grind them down and attempt to strip them of any identity except that of worker and consumer.

But where does this insight leave us when we also know that each larger group can be divided and redivided in terms of identity? We can ask, for example, what is the relationship of Black Theology to Rastafarian beliefs or to traditional African religions? Are we, any of us, sure we know what "blackness" is? And if we are one world, all sisters and brothers, then to do justice is a universally encompassing commandment, which means that there can be no strangers, no ethnic or racial groups that are outside the human family. But can our communities be open to the others in our midst? And does such an acceptance include Buddhists and Moslems? Are they children of the same God? Do they worship the same creator? If so, how are Christians—a minority of the human family, after all—to communicate with them? If we communicate, what do we talk about? And if we succeed, what will the church become? Who will this threaten, who will it encourage?

The theologies of liberation that are developing out of specific communities, tied to particularistic identities and histories, are increasingly recognizing the larger shared experience of being members of a single family. But beginning with the particular and recognizing the universal is far different from presuming a universal theology modeled on an exclusively Euro-American white male reality.

Note

1. Virgilio Elizondo, "Ecumenism: An Hispanic Perspective," *The Ecumenist* (July–August 1984): 73.

The Radical Message of Evangelical Christianity

Donald W. Dayton

Sometimes I think I was born to be skeptical of reigning shib-boleths, and as I grow older the problem seems to get worse. I am becoming increasingly convinced of the inadequacy, and even the perniciousness, of the usual paradigm by which the contemporary religious (especially American Protestant) world is interpreted with regard to questions of social change and social transformation. This paradigm understands American Protestantism in terms of a "two party" system, a party on the right and a party on the left. The current popular term for the party on the right is "evangelical," and according to the paradigm this party consists of apolitical or conservative types who, because of the peculiar shape of their piety, are either uninterested in social transformation or resist it from a reactionary position. On the left is the other wing of Protestan-tism—variously called liberal, ecumenical, or just "mainstream"—that contains the progressive social vision of the churches.

There is, of course, some usefulness to this paradigm, but the more I try to use it to understand myself, the current situation, and the historical dynamics that have gotten us where we are, the more the paradigm disintegrates in my hands (or in my mind—or wher-ever such paradigms might be said to disintegrate). Since my grow-ing dissent on these questions is rooted very much in my own experience, let me describe that briefly so that the reader will be better able to filter out the distortions of my pilgrimage.

I was born and reared in the Wesleyan Church, a small and to all appearances archetypal example of the right side of the paradigm. The denomination was the original founder of Wheaton College in

Wheaton, Illinois, in many ways the symbol of the modern "evangelical" culture, but lost control of the college in a moment of financial weakness and later replaced it with my *alma mater,* Houghten College, widely known as the "Wheaton of the East." In this denomination and in this college I was reared on the reigning paradigm.

My dissent began early. This religious tradition was unable, at the time, to mediate its values to me; I was unable to "connect" and secretly cultivated a secular world view. By a strange set of circumstances, however, I was pulled out of this context by the Woodrow Wilson Foundation, which decided I was the perfect candidate (bright but with limited educational advantages and obviously "culturally deprived") to provide the token integration for a program at Columbia University that had been designed to facilitate the transition of black students into graduate schools. This program, which required an extra year in order for these black students to qualify for the fellowships, was perceived as racist by many blacks, and the foundation was forced to focus instead on the "culturally deprived"—and prove its new orientation with my presence. It was at Columbia University that Christianity first really began to make sense to me and that I first learned about racism from the way in which the program was administered.

These were the early and mid-1960s, and I was profoundly shaped by the rise of the civil rights movement. I could not escape the questions it was raising, especially after I spent the summer following the Columbia program living with two black roommates on the edge of Morningside Heights, just a few blocks from the urban riots of that summer, entertaining, as I remember, my visiting parents with the sound of sirens and gunshots in the background. This led, during my seminary years, to direct involvement in the civil rights movement, and to such powerful memories as hiding from the police in the bushes in Biloxi, Mississippi, and trying to sleep on the floor of the Jackson civil rights office as the white citizens' council cruised the streets outside.

These experiences led to a long struggle to integrate such social concerns into the heart of my theology. In this I found common cause with people on similar pilgrimages, and we channeled our thinking into such journals as *The Other Side* and *The Post-American* (now *Sojourners*), attempting to articulate a form of "biblical radicalism." I pursued these issues in a doctoral program in theology and ethics at the University of Chicago, but was sidetracked by what was intended to be a quick exploration into the origins of the denomination in which I had been reared. I was surprised to discover that my church—archetype of the evangelical cuture that it was—had been founded by a group of social radicals who had withdrawn from the mainstream Methodist church because of its willingness to compromise on the question of slavery. My own denomination had been one of the clearest precursors in all of Christian tradition to many of the themes of Liberation Theology in our time. This discovery led me deeply into these questions, and with each step I have had to radically revise my view of the inherited paradigm. Let me illustrate briefly.

The paradigm under which most of us operate suggests, for example, that the "mainstream" Protestant churches, members of the National Council of Churches of Christ (NCCC), under the influence of contemporary feminism, have been in the avant garde in incorporating women into the ministry. The counterpart of this, again unusually assumed without investigation, is that the other Protestant churches—the "evangelical" groups that are members of the National Association of Evangelicals (NAE)—are "conservatives" on this issue because of their opposition to feminism. Indeed, I have heard this aspect of the paradigm expressed by representatives of both wings of the church. The truth of the matter, however, is that most of the member churches of the NAE ordain women, that they did so for a century before the NCCC, and that they have had women ministers in numbers as yet uncontemplated in most NCCC churches—in some cases a third to a half of clergy have been women. Further, this has often been done on explicitly feminist grounds, though it is not the only path to egalitarian visions.

In pursuing some of the ironies of this fact, I have learned a great deal about how ideology determines the way we see and understand the world, how scholarship serves ideology, and how evenly bigotry is distributed throughout the culture. But this fact is not allowed to surface because it cannot be—it upsets our fundamental assumptions about how the world is put together. Scholarship on the history of women in the church is elaborated largely on the basis of the assumptions of the accepted paradigm and any other perspective is precluded.

As another example, take the way in which we use the word "pietistic." "Pietism," a religious movement that originated in Germany in the seventeenth century in reaction to the intellectualism of the existing church, is not understood to be "socially transformative," even though historically the opposite was the case. As Paul Tillich commented in his lectures on the history of Christian thought, Pietism's two greatest gifts to modern Protestantism were the missionary movement and a concern for the poor and oppressed. Classical Pietism can be described in many ways, but was at heart an intensification of Christian piety—an effort to make Christians more Christian. The emphasis on "sanctification" led to efforts to love more, to sacrifice for the poor, to identify with those in need, and so on. In fact, the history of social concern in modern Protestantism is largely the history of the rise and impact of Pietism, from classical Pietism in the seventeenth century, to the rise of Methodism in the eighteenth century, to the conjunction of revivalism and social reform in the nineteenth century—and even including the extension of these into the "social gospel" of the American Baptist Walter Rauschenbusch in the first part of this century, which was deeply influenced by contemporary social movements in German Pietistic circles. This conjunction is also clear in England, where there seems to have been a clear connection between the rise of "evangelical religion" (in the sense of being in the line of Pietism) and various efforts at social reform.

There are many reasons for this conjunction of Pietism and visions of social transformation, not all of which fit our stereotypes of how the world is put together or of the roots of religiously based social transformation. The emphasis on religious and spiritual conversion that was at the core of Pietism might have led away from social change; in fact, it did just the opposite, and it was Pietism that taught modern Protestantism to think of God's grace and activity as bringing *change,* as ushering in the new, rather than sustaining the old, maintaining stability, and keeping order in the world. Conversion involves a "before" and an "after," and this necessarily involves change and movement. These ideas overflow the dimensions of personal experience and affect our understanding of the world. Thus Pietism has generated millennial and utopian visions that have had a powerful influence on shaping and reshaping the world.

I was just beginning to contemplate these ideas during a sabbatical in 1980 when I sat in on lectures given by Jürgen Moltmann, the Tübingen theologian who articulated a "theology of hope" as the basis of modern political theology. I was stunned when he attributed his ideas, especially the concept of "hope," to Pietism. Since then I have come to understand that he was not just playing to the gallery in Tübingen—historically a center of Pietism—but that Pietism has been one of the most powerful motive forces behind social change in the modern world.

But the ironies go even deeper. Pietism is often dismissed because of its "ethical precisionism" and over-scrupulosity, which led to attacks on drinking, dancing, card-playing, etc., and thus to a supposedly socially irrelevant ethic. Theologically the struggle was over the extent of the *adiaphora,* or morally neutral aspects of life. The "mainstream" of the time tended to maximize the *adiaphora* while the Pietists (and later the evangelicals and revivalists) tended to minimize the category, putting a moral value on everything. This issue became crucial as sentiment against slavery grew. Theologians at Princeton Seminary, the major Presbyterian center of theological education, included slavery and political despotism among the *adiaphora,* and it was the revivalists, often despising such centers of power and education, who concluded that slavery was a sin and had to be done away with—and salted the mid-West with such convictions, turning the tide of popular sentiment against slavery. Thus it was precisely this moral over-scrupulosity, with all its quaintness, that broke the back of slavery.

We need to re-read the "evangelical heroes" of the past with a new set of questions. Recent study of Frances Willard, the major figure behind the Women's Christian Temperance Union, has shown, for example, the extent to which her fight against the liquor trade was part of a larger constellation of socialist, pacifist, and labor-oriented convictions that would be considered radical in our own time. It may even be that we owe women's suffrage to her astute campaign to link the issue of temperance with "home protection": women needed to get the vote because only they were concerned enough about the home to vote prohibition in. And whatever we think about prohibition itself, we need to understand it as a massive social campaign to stamp out a "social evil," a campaign that has parallels in the abolitionist and civil rights movements. Similarly, we have been misled by the seemingly innocuous charity of the Salvation Army and have failed to grasp founder William Booth's devastating critique of bourgeois church life. The Salvation Army is probably the most egalitarian of the various manifestations of Christianity, having broken both class and sexual barriers. The Army's work with prostitutes is often dismissed as a concern for personal "virtue" and therefore not socially relevant, an attitude that ignores Booth's social critique of a society that paid clerical wages too low for survival and forced its women into prostitution.

I have also been surprised to discover the extent to which some currents of religious socialism have been rooted in Pietism. There are a number of illustrations of this, but I have been especially impressed with the Blumhardts of Germany, father and son, who lived in the mid- to late nineteenth century. Clearly latter-day

Pietists of a most intense sort, their writings are used today in German "evangelical" circles as devotional books for morning prayer. Almost unknown in this country except through their profound influence on Pentecostal and charismatic doctrines of divine healing and demon possession, the Blumhardts made a lasting impact on European theology (Karl Barth, Paul Tillich, Oscar Cullmann, and Jürgen Moltmann) and its recovery of eschatological themes, and were also a major source of religious socialism in Europe, especially Switzerland. This is understandable, because the heart of both religious socialism and Pentecostal doctrines of divine healing is the same conviction: that the kingdom of God breaks into human life in such a way as to transform it in accordance with the divine intention of wholeness and redemption.

Such illustrations could be extended, but I have said enough to illustrate my growing conviction that not only is the Pietist and evangelical tradition within Christianity just as ambiguous as other strands with regard to questions of social transformation, but that a strong case can be made that this tradition has been among the most productive of visions and motivations for social transformation.

On the other hand, it is also possible to critique the "liberal" traditions in Christianity and their role in social change. This became clear to me when I studied the anti-slavery controversies of the nineteenth century. There is no doubt that liberal Christianity has made important contributions to questions of social transformation, but it also has a soft underbelly with regard to these questions, for liberal religion is often that part of the religious tradition most assimilated into the reigning values of the culture—that most accommodated to modernity. Through this assimilation liberal religion gains credibility, but it can also lose much of its creativity and the leverage through which it is able to offer a fundamental critique of the culture in which it resides. It can extend the application of the values of the controlling elite, but it does less well in articulating new visions that are not on the current intellectual map.

Thus we are left, for example, with the impression from the hegemonic historiography that the Unitarians played a determinant role in the abolition of slavery—they were, of course, the great "liberals" of their time. But although very important contributions to the anti-slavery struggle were made by Unitarian leaders, if we move beyond such figures we discover that Unitarianism was much more assimilated to the culture than is generally assumed. On the other hand, when we move down to the grass roots of revivalism, we find an intensification of anti-slavery sentiment that is rooted, as I have indicated, in the idea that slavery was a "sin" in a very old-fashioned sense and therefore deserved "immediate abolition." There is certainly some "cliometric" evidence that there was a close correlation between revivalism and the emergence of anti-slavery voting patterns in the antebellum era.

Having tried to overturn some of the categories by which we approach all these questions, I must now admit that the present scene provides much evidence to support the reigning paradigm. The political and social consciousness of many modern Pietistic and evangelical groups is not particularly creative or productive of new visions. But there are reasons for this that are peculiar to our own time, and we must not let ourselves become prisoners of the paradigm—in part because our analyses can gain a life of their own and then create the very realities that they are attempting to describe. Let me therefore indicate some of the factors that I believe are at work; without understanding these, we cannot unravel the extent to which evangelical and fundamentalist Christianity is, or can be, creative and progressive.

We often read the recent past as a struggle between conservative and liberal, progressive and reactionary. But a better understanding of the religious issues of social transformation in the last few centuries can be found in the variations in millennial visions that have been such an important part of the U.S. Protestant experience. Pietism and Puritanism were related movements, and both taught a doctrine (based, as already noted, on the belief that God was bringing something new and better into existence—a necessary assumption for any religiously based vision of reform) of a future reign of God that came to be identified with the biblical image of the millennium, a thousand-year period of peace that would come at the end of history, in anticipation of its consummation. This vision was a powerful force in American religious life and formed a large part of the motivation for social transformation up until the Civil War—and the more intense the commitment to the doctrine of the millennium, the more radical the vision of social reform. What is particularly significant, however, is that the present-day "evangelical" and "fundamentalist" movements are the great-grandchildren of these radical movements of the nineteenth century: the modern Protestant "mainstream" consists in large part of the descendents of the "moderates" of the nineteenth century. Similarly, much of the secular and liberal social vision of the last century is, at least in part, a secularized version of this "moderate" millennialism.

But the vision of the radicals fell on hard times. Instead of the millennium, the late nineteenth century brought civil war, pluralism, secularism, urbanization, and other acids of modernity that eroded the great hope. Ironically, it was the most ardent advocates of the millennium who despaired most at its failure to arrive. They had hoped beyond the possibility of history to deliver (though they made significant, and ambiguous, contributions along the way). After the Civil War these radical groups fell increasingly under the influence of a new eschatological vision, that of premillennialism, which believed that the world would get worse and worse until the return of Christ would provide the transition to the millennium, which would have no continuity with history. In this scheme efforts at social amelioration were counterproductive because such attempts to overcome human sin by human effort would only postpone the real solution, the "blessed hope" of Christ's return.

Many fundamentalist and evangelical groups are the direct heirs of this tradition, and the emergence of social and political involvement on their part (which is of all political stripes, in spite of the impressions left by the media) can therefore be seen as a hopeful sign: these Christians are rejecting the most extreme forms of the premillennial vision and are beginning to take responsibility for the shape of social life in a way that overcomes the apolitical and otherworldly character of the eschatological vision. This way of looking at it seems to me to explain more of what is happening today than the more common interpretations.

But it is also true that evangelical and Pietistic groups have in recent years adopted forms of theology that have undercut their social creativity. In the nineteenth century socially radical evangelical visions were part of millennialist and perfectionist theologies—and were ardently opposed by theologians such as those at Princeton. Ironically, but reminiscent of the unfortunate way in which oppressed peoples take on the characteristics of their oppressors, these groups have lusted after the respectability of the supposedly superior intellectuality of these theological traditions and have allowed themselves to be assimilated into them. The result is that evangelicalism has come to be dominated by a theology and historiography that is not only foreign to its own historical experience but that also blocks social creativity. We desperately need a "hermeneutic of suspicion" to unmask the ideology, social reality, and apologetic manipulation of much recent interpretation of evangelicalism. Categories that are false to history and cannot fully explain present reality are defining the terms of the debate.

It is also important to grasp the social dynamic that underlies much of the contemporary scene. One aspect of Pietism and its related currents has been a profound commitment to a "preferential option for the poor," and this flowered in the nineteenth century after John Wesley turned to the neglected working classes of England. Methodism was the dominant religious force in nineteenth-century America not only because it became the largest Protestant denomination at a time when Protestantism dominated the culture, but also because it convinced much of the rest of Protestantism to act like Methodists. And many of the evangelical churches that arose in the nineteenth century did so in reaction to the *embourgeoisement* of Methodism and its imitators among the revivalists, so that the modern evangelical and fundamental experience is rooted in the indigenization in the lower social classes of a form of the Pietist tradition—a consciously articulated "preferential option for the poor"—that was in opposition to the churchly neglect of those classes. What we are seeing now, however, is the *embourgeoisement* of these same groups that were born in opposition to this same dynamic.

Sometimes I think one has to have grown up in these groups to understand the experience of alienation and the desire to belong that erodes any ability to withstand the dominant ethos. One of the reasons that these traditions are so "conservative" in one sense is that their members are now entering the middle class and professions and are for the first time reaching for the levers of power that are at the center of the society. There is also a parallel with the black community's reaction in the 1960s to its radicals: "Don't tear down the system until we get our piece of the pie." Another way of saying this is that we are seeing the emergence of another "ethnic" and "alienated" tradition into the mainstream of American life, claiming a piece of the action and insisting that at least some of the game be played by its rules. What we are experiencing in much of the religious conflict of our time is class-based and needs to be understood as such.

The issue is complicated, but I have found it helpful to use an image used by George Marsden, a prominent historian of the evangelical experience, who argues that these groups should be understood as being "immigrants in their own land." Living with subliminal memories of a time when the "evangelical" vision was *a,* if not *the,* determinative shaper of American experience, these groups have lived for a century in exile within their own country. I have in recent years become increasingly sympathetic to their complaints about being invisible in their own culture—or, when they are noticed, of being caricatured and maligned by those with no

sympathy or understanding for popular religion and this particular Christian tradition. I am also beginning to take more of
their complaints about the media seriously. It is only recently, for
example, that the *New York Times* woke up to the fact that its weekly
list of bestsellers represents only a part of the culture and does not
include titles that have sold literally millions of copies in subcultures
that it apparently either does not know exist or does not take
seriously. And I could not help being amused during Jimmy Carter's presidency at the number of phone calls I got from such
papers as the *Village Voice* desperately seeking help in understanding one of the largest subcultures in American life. I was told that
they could not find anyone in New York to help them unravel what
was going on. Such claims were obviously overstated, but they make
the point nonetheless. Much smaller subcultures dominate the media. If such caricatures and ignorance continue to be perpetuated,
we will have much more anger and conflict than we do now. It is not
too much to say that we are experiencing a "liberation movement"
among groups that will no longer tolerate the psychic oppression of
their culture and the constant violation of their own ethos. I think
that much of the polarization of the present scene is rooted in the
overreactions created by this dynamic.

While these observations may help us understand the contemporary scene, they do not speak directly to the original question of
whether these groups and traditions can have a creative influence
in the future. I am still uncertain about this. My own studies have
convinced me that the religious dynamic that has produced many
of these movements has been socially creative, and may therefore
become so again. On the other hand, I am doubtful that anything
significant will come out of the current realities: these groups'
embourgeoisement and assimilation into the dominant liberal culture
makes this unlikely. I am also skeptical about reversing some of the
powerful social forces and psychic experiences that lie behind
many current developments. Yet I also wonder what hidden potential lies buried in this community that might cause it to rise up and
alter the shape of the future by deciding that some other aspect of
the culture (say, the arms race) is "sin" and launching an abolitionist
campaign comparable to that launched against abortion. I am not
ready to predict what lies ahead.

Much depends, of course, on how we analyze the future of the
dominant liberal ethos and the extent to which we are committed to
its present shape. Here again I am uncertain, but I am impressed
with the discussion of the emergence of a new "post-modern" era,
with the proposition that we are at some fundamental turning

point that involves the disintegration of the values and ethos of the modern period and a movement toward a new synthesis. Some theologians, such as Harvey Cox and Jeremy Rifkin, are suggesting that the evangelical and popular religious traditions may play a key role in this. Only time will tell, of course, what the future will be, but in anticipation of that future I believe that we need to begin to destroy the confining paradigms with which we think about questions of religion and social transformation.

Bibliographic Note

I have written this piece in the manner of an essay, without documentation. But since the subject matter is not well known outside certain circles, I am adding a few bibliographic items for those who wish to pursue the questions discussed here further, or perhaps check up on my reading of the material. I myself have written a popular book, *Discovering an Evangelical Heritage* (New York: Harper and Row, 1976), an effort to expose the radical past of various strands of evangelicalism. I have also edited a volume of source material from my own denomination, *Five Sermons and a Tract by Luther Lee* (Chicago: Holrad House, 1975; available from the editor), which illustrates the increasing radicalization of the Wesleyan Methodists during the slavery controversies. Much of the analysis of millennialism is taken from my *Theological Roots of Pentecostalism* (Metuchen, NJ: Scarecrow Press, forthcoming).

Dale Brown's *Understanding Pietism* (Grand Rapids, MI: Eerdmans, 1978) is a good introduction to that subject. I have also edited a small volume of papers from a section of the American Academy of Religion, called *Contemporary Perspectives on Pietism* (Chicago: Covenant Press, 1976). The literature on Methodism and social issues is vast. The classic study of the U.S. scene is Timothy Smith, *Revivalism and Social Reform* (New York: Abingdon, 1957), but this should be supplemented with a book by his student Norris Magnuson, *Salvation in the Slums* (Metuchen, NJ: Scarecrow Press, 1977). The cliometrics to support the thesis about revivalism and slavery are to be found in John L. Hammond, *The Politics of Benevolence: Revival Religion and American Voting Behavior* (Newark, NJ: Ablex Publishing, 1979). Along similar lines, see Lawrence T. Lesick, *The Lane Rebels: Evangelicalism and Antislavery in Antebellum America* (Metuchen, NJ: Scarecrow Press, 1980).

The Blumhardts are given their place in the history of religious socialism by James Bentley, *Between Marx and Christ* (London: Verso,

1982). A recent anthology of the Blumhardts' work has been edited by Vernard Eller, *Thy Kingdom Come* (Grand Rapids, MI: Eerdmans, 1980); this relies to some extent on a German anthology by Leonhard Ragaz, who is in turn anthologized in Paul Bock, *Signs of the Kingdom* (Grand Rapids, MI: Eerdmans, 1984).

George Marsden's interpretation of fundamentalism is in various earlier writings, which are climaxed by *Fundamentalism and American Culture* (New York: Oxford University Press, 1980). Jeremy Rifkin's projections are found in *The Emerging Order* (New York: Putnam, 1979) and Harvey Cox's in *Religion in the Secular City* (New York: Simon and Schuster, 1984).

Working People and the Church: Profile of a Liberated Church in Reactionary Territory

Gil Dawes

For thirteen years, a local United Methodist congregation in Camanche, Iowa, has maintained solidarity with local, national, and international struggles for liberation.

- Time and again the congregation spoke out and demonstrated against the war the Vietnam.
- Members of the congregation picketed locally in support of Native Americans at Wounded Knee.
- The pastor, with congregational support, went to Wisconsin in solidarity with members of the Menominee Tribe who had seized a Roman Catholic novitiate.
- Members picketed local department stores for the boycott of Farah slacks.
- The congregation as a whole channeled strong financial support to the Patriotic Front in Zimbabwe.
- The 1979 Communist Party state convention was held in the church fellowship hall.
- The congregation supported a local wildcat strike, and later a year-long strike through weekly picketing, donations, and public advocacy.
- In conjunction with the strike, it hosted Angela Davis at the church when she came in support of the union.
- The pastor was beaten by the police, arrested on charges of riot and interfering with the police, put on trial, and later acquitted of all charges by the jury, all the while whole-heartedly supported by the local congregation.

The above is by no means an exhaustive list, but is indicative of the range and depth of concerns commonly responded to by this congregation. As a result of such stands, the group was sometimes jokingly referred to by its friends as "St. Mark's with a 'k'." Its enemies usually called it "that Commie church."

To most people, the description above is almost unheard of for a church in this country. It is perhaps conceivable in some well-endowed, large West Coast church, or in a campus ministry at a university in a metropolitan area. But the church in question acted out of very different circumstances. It was a group of 170 members, located in a small town of five thousand in the heart of the Bible Belt. It is part of a larger industrialized area along the Mississippi River, known for its reactionary traditionalism.

The existence of such a progressive Christian community in that setting was not an aberration or a fluke. It came about as a result of deliberate planning, hard work over many years, and sustained effort in the face of relentless opposition.

The history of the area in which the church is located has not always been conservative or reactionary. Iowa was part of the abolitionist movement during the period preceding the Civil War. One of the trunk lines of the underground railroad was the Mississippi River, with the Clinton area being one of its stations. The Methodist church itself had split over the question of slavery fifteen years before the Civil War, and did not reunite as a denomination until 1939, nearly one hundred years later. The local congregation in Camanche began meeting in 1839, with visits from a roving circuit rider. However, there is no indication what position, if any, the congregation may have taken regarding the issue of slavery.

By the turn of the century the area was divided over a number of issues, including that of slavery. The Reconstruction era following the Civil War gave rise to the Ku Klux Klan not only in the South but also among this northern river population. Its target for intimidation was not just the few black residents, but an immigrant population of Catholic background and the growing movement for unions. On one side of this struggle was a socialism that spawned two local newspapers (the *Clinton County Socialist* and the *Merry War*) and elected members to the city council. On the other side of the struggle, along with the KKK, was the American Protective Association, born in Clinton, Iowa, spreading from there across the nation. Coming out of a reactionary business sector, the organization compiled the blacklists used by Attorney General Palmer to round up, detain, and in many cases deport an estimated ten thousand activists.

Though union organizing began around the turn of the century and maintained a lasting presence in the area, the strength of the local establishment, along with Iowa's "right to work" laws, has preserved a business stronghold. Any hint of the early socialist movement has long been forgotten. Following the McCarthy era the place would have been described by most people as a typical "redneck" river town. The churches do not seem to have distinguished themselves in any way from the usual evangelistic and moralistic participation in the status quo. The church in Camanche was a garden-variety small-town congregation, made up primarily of working-class people, plus a few professionals and a handful of management and farmers. It swung between outright fundamentalism and confused liberalism, depending on the theological leanings of the pastor at the time. It was hardly considered a plum of an appointment, and had during its entire existence until 1971 been part of at least a two-point circuit. Since the town seemed to be growing in population as a kind of bedroom community for the Clinton area, the denomination decided to make the local congregation a single appointment, with missionary support to get it off the ground. It was at that point that I was designated as pastor to the congregation in Camanche. The fact was not considered a stroke of luck for the congregation or a feather in my cap. Camanche was viewed as a kind of cultural desert, in spite of local pretensions to the contrary, and I as a returned missionary from Latin America had been making speeches since my return derogatory of U.S. foreign policy. The hierarchy of the denomination seemed to be of the opinion that the congregation and I deserved one another!

Parenthetical Reflection on the Author's Rationale

For my part, the pastorate in Camanche was an experiment to see if Christians in a typical small-town setting in the United States would respond to the gospel message from a Liberation Theology perspective. My feeling was that "if it played in Camanche," it would play almost anywhere. This was not an academic experiment for me, but something to which I had been deeply committed for a number of years. I knew that Christians in Latin America responded to that message, but I did not know if, given the same opportunity, North Americans would do the same. Was the local church a lost cause, as most progressive Christians and non-Christians seemed to feel, or was it an untested mission field in both a theological and ideological sense? I had to know the answer for myself. I could not justify from either a Christian or a Marxist point of view wasting my life on something that would be unproductive from either perspective.

"Productive" for me did not mean having the freedom to act in a "Lone Ranger" individualistic sense. It meant creating a community of faith in action. Knowing the religious roots of this country, and having grown up in Iowa, I was convinced that such an effort was crucial. It was clear to me that unless such a religio-political connection could be made, fundamentalist Christianity had the very dangerous potential of becoming the mythological base for an American fascism. After all, Hitler did not gain control of Germany just by exercising a charismatic personality in a time of runaway inflation and national loss of identity. Nor did he simply deceive the workers while secretly making a deal with the major industrialists. While all of this is part of the story, what is often neglected, particularly on the left, is the appeal of Hitler to the masses through his manipulation of Germanic tribal and religious mythology. He was able to take hold of them at the roots of their social and cultural formation, individually and as a people.[1]

What I strongly suspected then, and believe has been confirmed since, is that the roots of an emerging fascism in the United States are to be found in Christian fundamentalism. Recently, liberal and left political and religious groups have tended to underestimate the danger of the linkage between fascism and fundamentalism. They suggest, for instance, that the Moral Majority is really the creation of a few right-wing ideologues, with computerized mailing lists and some well-funded charismatic TV evangelists as fronts. There is no doubt that such a conspiracy of the few exists and has been very effective. However, that does not explain the reverberations their strategy has sounded in broad segments of the public. It should be noted that it has touched a tap root of cultural formation deeply enough to create a working coalition out of such traditional enemies as conservative Catholics, fundamentalist Protestants, and Zionist Jews. One can cynically conclude that this is an opportunist coalition that accurately demonstrates the superficiality of the religious commitments involved, as compared to the profundity of their commitment to capitalism. However true that may be regarding the public leadership of the Moral Majority, it does not sufficiently explain the response of masses of people.

A second tendency to underestimate the danger posed by the linkage of fundamentalism and U.S. fascism is to see the link as the isolated product of certain "miniscule" right-wing paramilitary groupings. The bizarre religious expressions of the KKK's "Kingdom Identity" or The Order's "Church of the Aryan Nation" should not blind us to the religious roots they share with the broad base of American fundamentalism. Nor should we underestimate the influence of fundamentalism on the mainline denominations, which makes them very weak opponents of the pressures of militant fundamentalism.

Clearly, what was and is needed is a much more profound study of the social and political role of religion and cultural mythology.[2] We urgently needed to question the role religion plays in the life of its adherents, in order to more accurately assess the potential of differing religious motivations regarding change. Does a particular religious point of view speak to the hopes, aspirations, dreams, and visions of a better, more just, and more peaceful world? Or does it speak to the fears, insecurities, resentments, and self-justification of its believers? Does it press toward an as-yet-unfulfilled potential in the future, or the protection or recapturing of real or imagined good in the past? Is it directed toward otherworldly compensations for this-worldly deprivations, or is it a religious justification for overcompensated, earthly power, wealth, and privilege? Such questions suggested to me the kind of inquiry needed to differentiate the stance of differing religious motivations.

Prior to going as pastor to Camanche, I had found that the answers to such questions do not necessarily follow lines of denominational preference. In fact, I had seen the same denominational preference associated with profoundly different motivations. For instance, for large masses of people belonging to fundamentalist churches, any hopes they have for a better world are projected onto an otherworldly future after death. Their aspirations have been translated into an otherworldly compensation for this-worldly deprivation. Over and over again fundamentalist music makes this clear.[3] Along with the displaced hopes of heaven is a heavy guilt trip over natural human desires for sexual and material satisfactions.

At the same time that the masses of the people religiously influenced by fundamentalism are motivated by alienated hopes and frustrated desires, much of the leadership (and some of the membership) has quite a different motivation. They quite literally have "had it all" on the face of this earth, and their religious motivation is to religiously defend and justify having "had it all." They may or may not be hypocrites, but in either case, their motivation is decidedly different from the mass of those professing the same faith.

With the rise of an American fascist religious component on the one hand, and the growth of Liberation Theology on the other, it was then and is now vitally important to learn to distinguish between the religious sheep and goats. The importance of this is not just to tell our friends from our enemies, but also to see and experience the world as it is understood by the masses of religiously motivated people. Without such an understanding, fascism always seems to inexplicably appear out of nowhere. Instead, the assumption of myself and many others is that it is a product of certain specific historical conditions that we have not sufficiently investigated.

In addition to the forgoing political rationale, I came to the church in Camanche with a theological perspective that was almost unknown in the Midwest. There had been some antecedents for my point of view in the Social Gospel movement and the Epworth League Methodist youth fellowship, which were remembered by one or two persons in Camanche. However, the church, like most of those I had served, had a mixture of fundamentalist and orthodox theologies, with an occasional liberal or progressive minority. In general it was conservative and indistinguishable from most lower and middle-class congregations. What this meant was that the thinking of the congregation as a whole tended to be a moral and religious justification of the American way of life.

The roots of that way of thinking were not as the congregation supposed them to be—in the life and teachings of Jesus. Instead, they came from the strange syncretism of Jewish mysticism, Greek philosophical idealism, and Greco-Roman mystery religions that came together probably in the first and second centuries A.D. When the mother church of what later came to be called Christianity was destroyed in 70 A.D. along with the city of Jerusalem, whatever survived was widely scattered throughout the Mediterranean world of that day. Prior to that crushing blow, Christians were known as Ebionites, meaning "The Poor," because they shared all things in a kind of primitive communism under the leadership of Jesus' brother, James.[4] This way of life is pictured not only in the account of the lifestyle of Jesus and his disciples in the gospels, where they are depicted as sharing a common treasury, and in scattered fragments mentioned in the book of Acts, but also in the attitude evidenced in the book of James. The title of this latter book does not necessarily mean that it was written by James, but that it purports to reflect his point of view.

The view of Christianity held by James and the mother church in Jerusalem was decidedly different from that of the chief proponent of Christianity in the Gentile world. The gospel preached by Paul, a Jew of Pharisaic persuasion whose family had Roman citizenship, was not based on the life and teachings of Jesus. In fact, it is difficult to find anything at all about the teachings or ministry of Jesus in the writings of Paul. Instead, he spoke of "the death of Jesus on the cross for the forgiveness of our sins, and Jesus' resurrection from the dead as the basis for life after death for those who have faith in him." In essence it was similar to the message of the mystery religions which promised "salvation" to those who participated in the cults. However, the language and thought forms that Paul used to communicate his message were those of Greek philosophical idealism.[5] It was a dualistic view of human life and the world in which soul, mind, and spirit were seen as part of the real and eternal world of ideas above, while body, flesh, and the material world were a passing illusion. The goal of life was therefore to cultivate the world of ideas, while disciplining and resisting the desires of the material world. Plato symbolized this worldview of idealism by saying that the mind and soul and spirit are like a bird in a cage. The cage was the body, flesh, and matter of this world. If one's efforts were dedicated to the real world above, then at death the bird would fly out of the cage to be a part of that real world above.

This dualistic view was the philosophical justification for a slave-based economy. The "democracy" of the Athenian city-states did not rest on the will of the people, but on the will of an elite from which women, propertyless males, and slaves were excluded. Both the philosophy and economic base of that culture have come down to present-day America, transmitted principally through the teachings of Paul. And the hierarchical ordering of patriarchy and the repression of human sexuality has also come as an integral part of that teaching. Paul speaks of the spirit and soul as opposed to the flesh and body, and out of this dualism he portrays sexuality as at best a necessary evil for those who lack "the gift to resist the fires of desire." Sexual "immorality" clearly takes on the image of deadly sin in his writing. The "real" world for which one saves oneself increasingly takes on otherworldly and after-death dimensions, so that resurrection is the centerpiece of his theology. In the meantime, before that cataclysmic end, one is to obey the hierarchy of established order. "All authority comes from God," and therefore those who exercise earthly authority do so by the will and for the restraining purposes of God. The hierarchy of authority in descending order is: God—rulers—men—women—children—and slaves. Slaves are explicitly told to be obedient to their masters, and to serve them as though serving God. Women are instructed to be submissive to their husbands, while husbands are urged to love their wives. Children are to be disciplined, though treated kindly in exchange for obedience. All of the forgoing hierarchical order is a perfect reflection of the cultural milieu of the Greco-Roman world in which Paul was preaching.

The fundamentalist churches of today make no apology for such teaching by Paul, and instead seek to perpetuate this same hierarchical order as "ordained by God." The Vatican asserts much the same position, though with more careful rationalizing to make it palatable in the present-day context. Mainline and liberal churches say very little if anything about Paul's dualistic, patriarchal, sexually repressive, and slave-based morality. Instead, they focus almost entirely on the one place where Paul speaks of the new man in Christ for whom there is neither male nor female, Jew nor Greek, slave nor free. They fail to acknowledge that this consciousness of the "new man" was not to change the hierarchical order in the church, let alone the society. When this inconsistency is pointed out, the response is that Paul believed that the end, when God would make all things right, was near, and that in the meantime one must avoid all social conflict and any antagonizing of the authorities. Whatever Paul's intent may have been, this interim ethic in view of an apocalyptic end has been extended by the church to all time, without end. As a consequence, for the fundamentalists the "Kingdom of God" has been projected into heaven. For the mainline churches, the "Kingdom of God" has become a state of mind rather than a just state of affairs on earth.

Over against this synthesis of Greco-Roman culture, Greek philosophical idealism, and religious salvation cults resulting from Paul's missionary work was the starkly contrasting religion of the Ebionites ("The Poor"), with James, "The Just" (Jesus' brother), as their leader. Its philosophical base was a form of Hebrew materialistic theology, rooted in the tradition of Moses and the prophets. It had surprisingly little to say about life after death. Instead, it spoke of a "promised land," flowing with milk and honey, here on this earth. It spoke not of "peace in your heart," but of shalom— that earthly peace which comes from lacking no good thing and being in harmony with nature and human nature. It taught that this world and the human body were good—the gift of God. Therefore, human sexuality was not an unfortunate evil, necessary for the begetting of children, but was a form of re-creation. They could unabashedly celebrate erotic love, as in the Song of Solomon, which rabbis urged their people to go home and read on the Sabbath night. This materialistic theology is so far removed from what passes for Christianity today that fundamentalists try to explain away things like the Song of Solomon by claiming that it is an allegory, teaching the love of Christ for his bride, the church.

Since the gap between the Pauline tradition in which the church of today has been formed and the materialistic theology of ancient Judaism and the early church was so wide, my role as pastor was to find a way to bridge these conflicting worldviews. I did not see that task as consisting only of theoretical study and consequent testing of those ideas in action on the raw data of everyday experience. I also expected that the human condition of those participating would assert itself. It was at this point that I assumed that the religious motivation of those who participated would be crucial. If the motivation for their religion was the hope or longing for a better and more fulfilling life, then they might be expected to move from otherwordly compensation to the realization of the Kingdom of God and its justice on earth. On the other hand, if the motivation of the participant's religion was to justify the unjust distribution of wealth and power, to confirm the status quo, then conversion was unlikely.

The second human condition that could be expected to assist the process was the natural desire of human sexuality. In our social and religious formation, attempts to restrain, repress, or harness sexuality have led to the manipulation of sex for profit in the advertising of consumer society, control of mores and behavior by false guilt, and the sadism so characteristic of fascism. However, if in the process of religious clarification the impulse of sexual desire were recognized as natural and good, then a kind of personal liberation might accompany the struggle for social liberation. If people were able to celebrate the fact that they are by the hand of God part of the animal kingdom as well as citizens in the Kingdom of God, then they might in the long run be less subject to manipulation by advertising, false guilt, or repressed sexuality leading to sadism.[6]

A third natural impulse undergirding the struggle for religious liberation is the will to survive and the instinct of self-preservation. When religion teaches resignation in the face of oppression and violence, it does so by cutting off this natural response of all living things, including human beings. However, once religion demystifies the nature of oppression so that it is clear that it represents the will of an oppressor and is contrary to the will of God, then the reservoir of the will to survive quickly refills. The human animal, like other animals, is very resourceful in self-preservation if religion has not alienated him or her from their true human nature. U.S. imperialism has had to relearn this lesson the hard way in Vietnam, where supposedly backward people have fought the most technologically advanced nation on earth to a halt.

Each of the abovementioned human conditions could be expected to act as a catalyst in the struggle for religious clarification if the awareness of the congregation were sharply enough focused on the two mutually contradictory worldviews.

Methodology

The first thing I did in Camanche was to request that we put Bibles in the pews, so that people would see as well as hear. I said, "You're not going to believe what you hear unless you see it with your own eyes!" Whenever I read the scripture lesson for a particular Sunday, it was as part of its larger context. There was to be none of that fundamentalist habit of stringing quotes together out of context! By "larger context" I mean not only the setting within the Bible itself, but also the historical moment out of which the book and specific concern had originally come. From this approach to the Bible and the socioeconomic and the political history out of which it arose, it became clear that we were taking the Bible more seriously. This was not the old fundamentalist "hunt and peck" literalism or the liberal "topical" approach. Only when this was clear did we move on to ask about the meaning of a passage for our present historical situation.

Obviously, such a different approach is not something that can occur as a result of twenty minutes sermon time per week. Even when the sermon was followed, as it always was, with a time of questions and clarification relating to the biblical text and my interpretation of it, it simply was not sufficient. Out of this need for further reflection came the weekly Wednesday night study group. In that session the first hour was used to study the biblical passage that would be used as the basis for the sermon the following Sunday. It would be read aloud, historical background and clarifications would be given, and then we would discuss its meaning and significance in the original context and now. Background included such things as the fact that Moses' time was one of slave revolt in Imperial Egypt, that Jesus lived during a time of protracted insurrection against the Roman Empire, and that the Protestant Reformation cannot be understood apart from a class war that included the Peasants' Rebellion. The value of all of this was not just a more lengthy explanation of my viewpoint, but a shared understanding of our biblical and theological roots. I learned from them and they learned from one another, and on many occasions their insights and questions caused me to change the direction of my remarks for the sermon the following Sunday.

The second hour of the study group each week was spent in a sharing and analysis of current events and trends. The presupposed question underlying this part of the session was: "What important things have happened locally, nationally, and on the world scene this week?" The key word of course was "important." It meant that we had to learn to distinguish the important from the unimportant. Week after week and month after month, as people shared with one another their idea of what they thought was important, some viewpoints proved to be accurate in the long run as explanations of what was happening and others did not. This meant that on a weekly basis we were undergoing an ideological transformation together. When trends began to appear, raising questions for which we did not have adequate answers, we would do a study of that specific concern. One of the concerns that came up repeatedly was the lack of accurate information about other social, economic, and political systems. As a result, we studied *Introduction to Socialism* by Leo Huberman and Paul Sweezy; *World Hunger: Ten Myths* by Frances Moore Lappé and Joseph Collins; *Peoples and Systems,* a study of the United States, the People's Republic of China, Tanzania, and Cuba; and *The Enemy* by Felix Greene.

These two aspects of the study group, the theological and the ideological, were not kept strictly separate but were often woven back and forth together in the discussion. What evolved from this form of study and its content was an awareness that the Greek division of life between mind and matter, body and soul, flesh and spirit, individual and community, was a false division. It further became clear that the early church, as it moved out into the commercial cities of Asia Minor in the Roman Empire, had become synthesized with Gnosticism and the mystery religions, with their underlying philosophy of Greek dualism. We saw that historically Hebrew theology had struggled against that dualistic worldview arising out of Greek philosophical idealism. The Judaic understanding has as a result been called the most materialistic of all religions. This was also the base of early Christianity, but our discovery of that fact was due to a study of Marxist critiques of later Christianity. We came to see that the Kingdom of God movement with Jesus and the early church had formed a primitive communist subculture that persisted to varying degrees for several centuries. It came naturally out of the wilderness sects, such as the Essenes and

John the Baptist's movement, but it also took a significant step beyond them. For the first time, primitive communism was not based on the extended family, tribalism, or a federation of tribes. In effect, these discoveries meant that Marxism was not just a channel for the expression of our Christian motivation, but also a means to understanding our Judeo-Christian roots.

Clearly, the discussion of such themes made the study group very lively. It was serious, but it was also enjoyable, because we could argue and laugh as well. That kind of development allowed us to become a community of faith in action. The sizable percentage of the congregation that participated regularly in the study group became the core group that knew what it was doing and why. The members could "give a reason for their faith" on theological and ideological grounds.

Since not everyone was willing or able to participate in the study group, it was necessary to create a means for those who were sympathetic to be a part of things beyond mere attendance at the Sunday service of worship. What evolved was a coffee hour in which forty to fifty people would stay to discuss in an informal setting following the Sunday worship service. While the children were in Sunday school, the adults, including high school youth, would start with the subject of the scripture lesson and sermon, but go on from there in a wide-ranging discussion. It was exciting enough that it was difficult to get adults to teach Sunday school since it meant that they would have to miss the coffee hour. As a result, we had to rotate Sunday school teachers frequently.

The adult education resulting from the study group, Sunday worship hour, and the coffee hour following were sufficiently effective that visitors assumed that they had stumbled into a discussion among college-educated people. The fact was that very few had a college background, some had not finished high school, and a few were totally illiterate. These differences in formal education did not create a barrier to discussion in the group because the subject was life as people had experienced and understood it.

From an organizational point of view, the coffee hour formed another concentric circle of commitment around the core group at the center. Sympathizers who participated helped to inform those whose only contact was the worship service and those who lived in the community but who had no direct relationship with the church.

Baptism of Fire: Immersion in Struggle

If the study and discussion had not been followd by appropriate action, the course of events at St. Mark's would have inevitably gone in circles. Without testing of conclusions and persons, we would have simply developed in ivory-tower or stained-glass separation from reality. As it was, the actions described at the beginning of this article carried us to deeper understanding and questioning with each step. With most of the actions described, individuals would leave the group, but those who stayed and participated were strengthened. People also were added to the church with each of the public actions. Evangelism by deed is more powerful than that of the word. Our understanding was clearer and our commitment to a Christian and a Marxist perspective was successively deeper each time it was put to the test. That is not to say the process we experienced was easy or painless. Each time someone left, it was very painful because we had become very close. In fact, the division between family and friends is probably the hardest thing such a group has to face. The words of Jesus about the inevitability of division in the family as a result of such commitment had particular significance for us after going through that kind of experience each time we practiced what we preached.

The reflection and study which the congregation engaged in was crucial to tie the various causes on which we decided to act into their common root. Without such study, people would soon burn out in the effort to pursue the myriad of seemingly unrelated concerns. Both Liberation Theology and Marxism, each from its own point of departure, is radical in the sense of going to the root of the problem. Each attempts to pursue things to the point where they come together, so that as we traced particular issues they broadened and deepened our understanding and strength, rather than weakening us. A liberal approach to the same causes usually leads to burnout, because there is no alternative vision that ties the pieces together. As a result, liberalism either has to limit the depth or the number of concerns on which it will act.

Defining who we were as a group resulted not only from studying and acting together. It also came about over against opposition. From the very first Sunday I preached in Camanche, that opposition made itself known. The wife of a local lawyer and slumlord, who had been one of the self-appointed pillars of the church, began a whispered campaign to the effect that I was a "communist." Since I had not used any scare words in the sermon, and clearly was basing what I said on the Bible passage, this left other people with questions about her rather than about me. Their reaction was to say, "I don't know who he is or where he is coming from, but if she is against him, then we're for him."

The next stage of opposition was a financial boycott by conservatives unhappy with the direction of my preaching. These were people who condemned the idea of boycotts by working people against companies, but the idea did not bother them when they used it to make me shut up or get out. Though their financial withholding was felt in a small congregation, it was not decisive. In fact, it proved to the rest of the group that it was not the wealthy, but the workers and poor who carried the financial responsibility for the church. When the working people found out what was happening, they increased their giving to offset the loss from the boycott by the wealthy.

When the financial boycott did not work, the next step was withdrawal from leadership by those who were thought to be indispensable to the running of the church. Though this was somewhat frightening to those who remained, it soon became apparent that others could do the jobs, and that for the first time in years there was a spirit of cooperation. Things never ran better!

Beyond the opposition within the congregation, the business and social "elite" tried to pressure the bishop to move me elsewhere during the time of the wildcat strike. On one occasion this came to a crisis, and I was requested to appear before the bishop and the thirteen district superintendents of the state. This was an unprecedented kind of demand on the part of the hierarchy of the church, so I responded that I would like to bring a fellow pastor to the hearing with me. My district superintendent replied that that would be impossible because it would "violate the confidentiality of the appointment process." I answered that perhaps he could sit in on the discussion until the question of appointments came up, but was told, "Absolutely not!" At that point I said that I would like to record the meeting, since it sounded like a labor/management meeting in which I was outnumbered fourteen to one. In shocked tones I was told that this seemed to indicate a lack of trust in the brotherhood, and that I most certainly would not be allowed to record the discussion. Finally I said, "I guess you leave me no option but to speak to the news media." They ignored this comment as inconsequential.

That afternoon I participated in a rally of some fifteen hundred strikers in which the business agent for the union announced my summons by the church hierarchy. The strikers immediately responded saying, "Let's take a bus caravan to Des Moines and picket the state headquarters of the church, talking to the news media outside while Gil talks to the hierarchy inside." An informer apparently called the bishop immediately, because when I got home the phone range and the district superintendent said, "That meeting has been indefinitely postponed—we weren't planning a media event."

The significance of describing the kind of opposition we faced is to point out that its result among us was to clarify our minds and strengthen our solidarity. It made clear to all that a class struggle was taking place in the church as well as in the community, and this in turn made such struggle around the world much more understandable.

Two years later, having stayed on as pastor to help people put the pieces of their lives together after the strike and decertification of the union, I voluntarily requested transfer to another church. I had been in Camanche for ten years, and felt that it was time for a change, both for myself and the congregation. In my place, the bishop appointed a young pastor, with the instruction to bring back and "reconcile" those who had left St. Mark's with those who had remained and gone through the struggle. This class collaborationist approach of "unity above all" was pushed by the opportunistic young pastor over against the solidarity of the existing congregation. Within a few months those who had experienced a new understanding of Christianity during the years of study and action together decided to leave St. Mark's, and organized themselves as a subgroup of the Methodist Federation for Social Action. For the past three years, that group of seventy to eighty persons has continued to meet and carry on as before. They have no pastor, but they take turns leading the study group on Wednesday night and preaching on Sunday morning. They have experienced many kinds of harassment and opposition, but they are now free to use their time and money toward the concerns and actions they believe in rather than in keeping up a building or in paying per capita to the denominational structures. They have clearly learned that the "church" is not to be equated with the pastor, a building, or a denomination, and in so doing they are stronger than ever before.

We have all learned that the gospel which is good news to the poor is usually experienced as bad news by the rich; that our lives are not "justified by faith" but by faith in action; that Jesus and the prophets lived and died for the sake of God's rule of justice on earth, in which there is to be "abundant life" for all, and in which "the last shall be first, and the first last." Finally, we learned that Christianity and Marxism are not antithetical, or simply two sides of the same progressive movement in history, but complementary aspects of who we are in the struggle.

For myself, the questions I had about the church thirteen years ago have found some answers. Yes, it was possible in Camanche, beyond all my expectations or those of others. Yes, it is possible to split the monopoly of religious myths and symbols intended by fundamentalism and the "Moral Majority." Yes, Liberation Theology can take root here. Furthermore, it gives promise around the world as far-reaching in its impact toward the rise of socialism as the theology of the Protestant Reformation was for the rise of capitalism. And yes, fundamentalism does seem to be the mythological component of an emerging American fascism that must be vigorously and intelligently opposed before it is too late.

Notes

This is an expanded version of an article that originally appeared the special issue of *Monthly Review* 36, no. 3 (July–August 1984), entitled "Religion and the Left."

1. See Jean Michel Angeberg, *The Occult and the Third Reich: The Mystical Origins of Nazism and the Search for the Holy Grail* (New York: McGraw-Hill, 1974).
2. Very useful, in spite of what seem to be strange categories, is Wilhelm Reich, *The Mass Psychology of Fascism* (New York: Farrar, Straus, and Giroux, 1970).
3. Two examples are the following:

No Disappointment in Heaven

There's no disappointment in heaven,
No weariness, sorrow, or pain;
No hearts that are bleeding and broken,
No song with a minor refrain.
The clouds of our earthly horizon
Will never appear in the sky,
For all will be sunshine and gladness,
With never a sob nor a sigh.

We'll never pay rent for our mansion,
The taxes will never come due;
Our garments will never grow threadbare,
But always be fadeless and new.
We'll never be hungry nor thirsty,
Nor languish in poverty there,
For all the rich bounties of heaven
His sanctified children will share.

I'm Going Home

My heavenly home is bright and fair;
Nor pain nor death can enter there;
Its glittering towers the sun outshine;
That heavenly mansion shall be mine.

My father's house is built on high,
Far, far above the starry sky;

When from this earthy prison free,
That heavenly mansion shall be.

Let others seek a home below,
Which flames devour, or floods o'erflow,
Be mine the happier lot, to own
A heavenly mansion near the throne.

4. Acts 2:44–45 and 4:32–5:11.
5. Mainstream biblical scholars have tended to justify Paul's use of this language by saying that he gave it a more holistic content by the way in which he used it. However true their contention may be, Paul was obviously much too subtle, if that is the case, because the church through the centuries has followed the obvious meaning rather than the subtle toning that Paul is said to have intended.
6. The fact that we are able to conceive of such a possibility only in terms of libertinism is in itself an indication of how much we have been victimized by a dualistic formation that separates flesh and spirit—or, on the other hand, that we try to deal with sexual liberation apart from the social transformation of life as a whole.

Spirituality and Social Transformation as the Vocation of the Black Church

Gayraud S. Wilmore

Two familiar criticisms of the black church are that it exaggerates parochial spirituality and otherworldliness at the expense of social action in the wider society, and that it behaves too much like a secular community organization, with the consequence that the basic religious purposes of a church are obscured by partisan politics and a dubious quest for black power. The first criticism has often been voiced by liberals, the second by conservatives. The fact is that the black church has exhibited both of these characteristics over time.[1] But what is even more important is that within the Afro-American churches, perhaps more than within any other large group of churches in the United States, these two tendencies exist side by side in a precarious balance. The genius of Martin Luther King, Jr., was that he understood as well as anyone this paradox of the religion of an oppressed people and was able to meld the two tendencies into one of the most successful mass movements of the twentieth century.

My thesis is that what we call the black religious tradition nurtures and promotes both spirituality and militancy for social change in varying and complex ways; that both in the official actions of the denominations and in the black church as a mass-based, folk institution, religion and politics are inseparable; and, further, that spirituality and social transformation are not only two sides of the same coin, but are so interpenetrated that the black religionist cannot rest comfortably without both.

The black religious tradition holds that God brought this particular church into existence for extraordinary purposes and that one of those purposes was to combat racism. Thus throughout most of its history the black church has recognized a cultural vocation expressed in terms of what we may call a "pragmatic spirituality"—the ability to live and struggle in this "world of hard knocks" and secular demands and at the same time transcend that world in the ecstasy of worship and the security of Christian communalism. Unfortunately, however, the black church of today has an insufficiently developed sense of its own tradition. One of the tasks of the Christian leadership concerned about the pluralism and vitality of the ecumenical church in the United States is to help black Christians regain a sense of cultural vocation that relates to their experience of struggle in terms of both spiritual formation and social transformation.

1

The religion of most Afro-Americans was originally laced with an attenuated spirituality from West Africa. It was soon sprinkled with a liberal measure of Southern U.S. white revivalism and pressure cooked for the next two hundred years in the cauldron of slavery, political disfranchisement, and an entrenched color prejudice on the part of white Christians. Such a religion had disabilities as well as strengths, and one of its notable strengths was that it had no squeamishness about politics once it became possible for blacks to act politically. Black Christians have rarely taken the view held by most white Christians that "religion and politics don't mix." Black church members almost never express misgivings about the interrelationship between marching together down the aisle on Sunday and marching together to the polls on Monday. Even when they have appeared to be politically regressive, it was usually because of a lack of opportunity or an illusion caused by using a white ruler to measure black behavior.

The paradox that sometimes serves to obscure the issue is that because we have always had to fight for sheer survival our churches have been, at one and the same time, the most radical and the most conservative institutions in our communities. But one must exercise caution in speaking of the social and political conservatism of the black church at a given point in history. Unlike the white church, black religious conservatism has been oriented to survival and has fought so many rearguard actions that it has given the impression of being apolitical and otherworldly. We must remember that its emphasis upon personal transcendence in the throes of conversion and spirit-filled worship experiences has only partly been in response to social, economic, and political deprivation. Shouting and "getting happy" are also residual expressions of a spontaneous and liberative African spiritual inheritance. Despite the obvious diffusion of evangelical religiosity between Southern blacks and whites over many years of intimate contact, even a casual observer will note the differences between the way black and white congregations of the same denomination or ecclesial family tree worship and respond to political guidance from the pulpit. In many black churches of the past, particularly in mainline urban congregations, the emphasis upon personal religion and sanctification was usually accompanied by an equally powerful, if covert, desire among the people for basic social change that broke with the guilt-laden, moralistic orthodoxy of white fundamentalism to express more inclusivistic and world-affirming values. The desire for social change and the realism about white people that accompanied it created a tough-minded this-worldliness underneath the raw emotionalism that characterized Southern black revivalism.

James S. Tinney of Howard University has identified this as a "hidden theology" in black Pentecostalism.

> This strain of hidden theology in black Pentecostalism represents a certain psychological "hardness" resulting from realistic pessimism occasioned by experiences of racism. It represents a certain psychological "mellowing" resulting from much suffering at the hands of western culture, capitalist institutions, and white persons. . . . Hidden theology is a closer identity with black people everywhere than with universal Christianity, and a built-in tolerance for all deviations from what that universal Christianity pretends to represent.[2]

I am convinced that this "hidden theology" is not exclusively Pentecostal, but is found in the religion of the black masses generally. Moreover, it has subtle—perhaps even radical—political implications. We usually think of radicalism among blacks in terms of the Douglass-Trotter-DuBois tradition and identify conservatism with Booker T. Washington. In those terms the black church at the turn of the century was more supportive of Washington and was therefore conservative in the sense that it separated fervent religion from overt political action. But since 1900 the ethos of black religious institutions, as reflected in sermons, biographies, local histories, and the secular and religious press, includes evidence of a persistent ideological attack against what blacks have always regarded as the root problem of the United States, namely, the problem of racial justice—the great sin of white oppression. Such an attitude has enormous and radical political significance. It may be expressed not only by organized political activity, but by the subversion of politics by nonparticipation, the continuation of politics by other means. Scholars, in my judgment, have overplayed the so-called passivity of black Christians in the political arena during the first half of the twentieth century.

In a recent book Peter J. Paris argues that because black religious leaders were deluded into thinking that the self-development of their people would eventually convince whites that they deserved full citizenship rights, "in that sense, the black churches have not been radical."[3] His conclusion may, however, be the result of a too simplistic understanding of the nature of radicalism. What Paris fails to take seriously in his own explication of the social teachings of these same churches is the revolutionary significance of their critique of white Christianity. He contends that what he calls the "black Christian tradition"—by which he means the principle of nonracism—contains the doctrine of the parenthood of God and the kinship of all people. In short, the black Christian tradition posited a fundamental moral and religious dilemma in the heart of white Christianity and, in fact, was born in opposition to the problem."[4]

In my view this characteristic of black religion represents a radical confrontation with the essence, the very being, of America and not only in official pronouncements and episcopal addresses but in black talk, folk sayings, day-to-day communications of the wisdom and understandings of local preachers and their congregations—what the late Howard Thurman meant when he wrote of the "throbbing reality of the Negro idiom" that gave him inspiration and vitality, i.e., the *culture* of the black church.[5] This black Christian tradition, which Paris believes is nonradical, was in fact the crucible out of which the weapons of our struggle were forged and honed for three centuries. If being radical has anything to do with getting at the root of an issue, the tradition must be judged to have had radical as well as conservative dimensions.

It is interesting that a few secular scholars, including Charles Hamilton, Manning Marable, and Cedric J. Robinson, are showing curiosity about the political salience of the black religious tradition just at the time when some black religious scholars are becoming more dubious about it. In *Black Marxism: The Making of the Black Radical Tradition,* Robinson defines that tradition as the historic struggle for liberation that began in Africa and was grounded in the charismatic and metaphysical orientations of black folk culture in the United States. He writes, in a tone that is surprisingly reminiscent of the Pentecostal theologian James S. Tinney, of a "collective consciousness informed by the historical struggles for liberation and motivated by the shared sense of obligation to preserve the collective being, the ontological totality."[6]

I take this to be a rather backhanded way of affirming that religion has played and continues to play an indispensable role in the long struggle of African and African-American people for humanity and liberation. In this respect it is more accurate to speak of the black *religious* tradition than the black *Christian* tradition. In doing so recognition is given to the fact that one must, in any discussion of the relation between spirituality and social transformation, include the experience of the Moorish Science Temples, Father Divine's Peace Mission, the Black Jews, Garveyism, the Black Muslims, Rastafarianism, the neo-African religions of the ghetto, such as the Yoruba cults, Kawaida, and other religio-political movements that have, from time to time, mounted radical attacks upon Western civilization and white Christianity.

Spirituality and social transformation go hand in hand in this tradition, one that far exceeds the boundaries of the black Christian churches. It could not have been otherwise. The very humanity of the masses was threatened by U.S. racism and the only meaning that could sustain an authentically human life and motivate political struggle was religious meaning—or what Cedric Robinson has called the "ontological totality"—a thoroughly African way of relating to the cosmos that the black religionist translated for the North American milieu.

If we have sufficiently established the connection between spirituality and social transformation, or religion and politics in the black religious tradition, let us now turn to what may be the most critical question of all: the purpose of the black church and its sense of cultural vocation. What is the nature and purpose of the self-conscious, voluntary accountability of the black church as a cultural institution? To what extent does it acknowledge a God-given vocation to provide both spiritual and political direction to the embattled black community? And if such a vocation is accepted, to what extent does the mission convey a message for the society as a whole—a message about God's action in history and the human response of pragmatic spirituality that points to the fundamental transformation this nation sorely needs and human survival demands?

Certainly the black church of the nineteenth century had a sense of such a vocation because our foreparents had the audacity to see themselves in the pages of the Old Testament. It was a truly amazing achievement for a poverty-stricken and half-literate people. They assumed from an oral tradition that compared them with the people of Israel that God either had a valid reason for their affliction, one that was somehow related to their non-Christian African past, or a mysterious purpose connected with their future in America, and indeed beyond America to the redemption of Africa. This assumption of a vocation to transform America and redeem Africa won out in the protracted debate among black religious thinkers about the proper interpretation of the "Hamitic hypothesis" and why a just God had permitted them to be enslaved by the very people who called themselves their brothers and sisters in Jesus Christ.

Albert J. Raboteau has examined the importance of Psalm 68:31 as one of the keys needed to unlock the secret of the providential relationship that many black religionists of the nineteenth century thought existed between themselves as a race and God—a relationship that gave the black church a signal importance, a special destiny and sense of vocation related to both the United States and Africa. Unfortunately, in my opinion, the Revised Standard version of the Bible obscures the prophecy that is quite clear in the King James version. The latter reads: "Princes shall go forth out of Egypt and Ethiopia will soon stretch forth her hands unto God." Raboteau makes the point that the tantalizing ambiguity of this biblical reference to the future of black Africa gave the children of the Diaspora full range to apply it to the idea of the divine mission of black people to do a great work for God in North America and Africa:

> In the destiny of the black race, predicted in Psalm 68:31, Afro-American Christians thought they could read the meaning of black suffering. But they confronted an immediate problem: unlike the book of Exodus in which the events were clear and easy to interpret, Psalm 68:31 was obscure. . . . Yet, the very obscurity of the prediction extended its explanatory range. Consequently, nineteenth-century interpretations of Psalm 68:31 differed widely. *They all, however, clustered around three major themes: the African Race, the Redemption of Africa, and the Mission of the Darker Races.*[7]

The prophecy that black people have received a special gift from the hand of God to contribute to America and Africa continued into the twentieth century and came to symbolize for many the mysterious, inner meaning of blackness that is essential to the self-understanding of black people. We find it in African Methodism under the influence of such powerful leaders as Bishop Reverdy Ransome (AME) and Bishop William J. Walls (AMEZ); in the National Baptist Convention during the presidency of E. C. Morris; of course in Garveyism and the African Orthodox Church of Bishop George A. McGuire; and in many of the smaller churches of the 1920s and 1930s that had their origin in the Pentecostal revival. We should not, therefore, be surprised to find Martin Luther King, Jr., asserting in *Where Do We Go from Here: Chaos or Community?* that black Americans have a responsibility "to imbue our nation with the ideals of a higher and nobler order." King is speaking out of a long tradition of black vocational consciousness when he writes:

> This is our challenge. If we will dare to meet it honestly, historians in future years will have to say there lived a great people—a black people—who bore their burdens of oppression in the heat of many days and who, through tenacity and creative commitment, injected a new meaning into the veins of American life.[8]

Walter Hollenweger, one of the leading scholars of black and third world Pentecostalism, has reminded us that C. H. Mason's Church of God in Christ (COGIC) welcomed Dr. King to Memphis in 1968 and made Mason's Temple the nerve center for the movement in support of the strike of garbage workers—most of whom were members of the denomination. Hollenweger believes that the attraction that COGIC laymen in Memphis had for King strongly indicates the potential in black Pentecostalism for revolutionary activism, based not on some secular rationale for political power but on a concept of empowerment by the Holy Spirit that is considerably more militant and socially relevant than what can be found, for example, in the white Assemblies of God.[9]

This is an important insight into the nature of black "fundamentalism" and fits well with my own observation that in both the United States and England black Pentecostals—coming out of historic roots in Wesleyan Holiness and W. J. Seymour's emphasis upon charismatic spirituality—are beginning to play a determinative role in movements for social justice and liberation in their respective contexts. This is a role that in some communities has already challenged, and threatens to eclipse, the "mainline" black denominations in terms of aggressive leadership and mass participation. One thinks immediately of ministers like Arthur Brazier, Tom Skinner, Franklin Florence, Columbus Salley, and particularly in these days, of Herbert Daughtry, John Perkins, James Forbes, and Leonard Lovett. In Great Britain the New Testament Church of God, a black Pentecostal transplant from the West Indies, is not only the fastest growing Christian body in the country but, under the leadership of younger theologians like Ridley Usherwood of their new Overstone College in Northampton, has been introduced to Black Theology and a social praxis calculated to combat the increasingly overt racism of British society.

Black Pentecostal scholar-activists in the United States are giving a new vitality to the Black Theology movement. At a January 1985 consultation at Virginia Union University in Richmond a group of black theologians and church leaders produced a theological statement concerning the search for a common expression of apostolic faith that was transmitted for discussion to the meeting of the World Council of Churches Commission on Faith and Order in August 1985. The section of the statement dealing with the holiness of the "One, Holy, Catholic, and Apostolic Church" was primarily influenced by Pentecostal theologians, and the fact that it was enthusiastically adopted by the overwhelmingly non-Pentecostal consultation shows the growing influence of Pentecostal theological emphases upon other sectors of Afro-American Christianity. A few random quotations from the document may suggest how the black church as a whole is being called back, not to some new evangelical pietism but to a cultural vocation in the world in which holiness and secularity cohere in a new consciousness of the meaning of blackness in the context of Trinitarian theology:

> The Holy Spirit is not an abstraction of Trinitarian theology but participates dynamically in what it means to be a human being and to suffer and struggle with the assurance of victory in this world as in the one to come.
>
> Holiness is a criterion of the church's theological authenticity. It creates a theology that is "hummed, sung and shouted" in black churches, and contrary to white fundamentalism, has more to do with how Christians treat one another than how strictly they hold to biblical literalism or ascetic lifestyles.
>
> We know that to struggle in the midst of the world is to experience the glory of God that is thwarted by racism and oppression, but we also know that we need to praise God in the sanctuary in order to struggle. One of our spirituals has the refrain: "Have you got good religion?" The response is, "Certainly, certainly, certainly Lord!" *Good* religion is, therefore, understood to make worldly things that were formerly dubious better, and *bad* religion ruins the best of all possible worlds where there is no acknowledgment of God's presence. Without holiness no one shall see the Lord.[10]

It should be clear that this approach to the idea of holiness infers a mission in the world that goes far beyond the "snatching of brands from the burning" that was once thought to be the hallmark of black Holiness and Pentecostalism. The Richmond statement, representing a rare ecumenical consensus among black theologians and church leaders, sets a new horizon for understanding the inseparability of spirituality from social transformation in the evangelical witness of the black church. It indicates also that such an evangelical witness is understood to be the special vocational responsibility of black Christianity.

It is important to note that while the critique and reformation of the political order (social transformation) is basic to what black theologians have set forth in the Richmond statement and in other statements in recent years, the basic strategy is *cultural.* This is to say that the controlling concept has to do with the whole gamut of human activity and involves a structural and dynamic renewal that goes beyond the pragmatic ends and shallow motivations of electoral politics. This does not, of course, mean a rejection of electoral politics. Far from it. But what is invoked here is a more profound vision and responsibility of the Church as "custodian and interpreter" of the Afro-American religious and cultural heritage, not only in behalf of the black secular community but on behalf of the nation as a whole.[11]

To speak of the mission and strategy of the black church as cultural rather than political is not to deny the political, but to subsume it in a larger context; and it is precisely in such a context that we can see how the spiritual dimension of life impinges upon the problems and possibilities of social transformation. This means that we intend to encompass the entire scale of perceptions, meanings, values, behavioral patterns, etc., all integrated in that system of symbols we call culture, by which people formulate "conceptions of a general order of existence" and take passionate actions on the basis of such conceptions.[12] This broad understanding of culture as the context of self-consciousness and vocation is necessary for the church to recover that "gift of blackness" of which W. E. B. DuBois wrote so powerfully—that sensitivity to the "ontological totality," the fusion of the spiritual and political that goes deep into our cultural roots as an African people and was enlivened again and again in our long fight for survival and liberation in North America and the Caribbean.[13]

The problem of being dependent upon electoral politics is that people trapped in the resistance-absorbing and ameliorative qualities of the status quo are insensitive to the fact that the realities of the U.S. political economy will not respond to superficial remedies, court decisions, and legislation, but call for deep-lying cultural transformations on a world scale. What is required, therefore, is not more segmental political action according to the rules laid down by the brokers of white power in one region or community in competition with another, but access to the deepest sources of the disaffection and revolutionary consciousness of all national groups of marginalized people. Black Christians, as the most unified and largest of these groups, need a self-definition that breaks with traditional American individualism and an awareness of Afro-American peoplehood that negates the false assumption that blacks must be integrated into middle-class America and adopt the culture of white evangelical Protestantism before they can be considered "normal," assimilable Americans.

Before the recent development of a black theology the church had never seriously considered a worldview and value system that sought to transform the collective consciousness of black Americans rather than permit them to be satisfied with manipulating political structures which change every four years only to remain the same. Thus the sickness of a large sector of the black middle class, most of whom are in the churches, is its commonplace moralism, its value orthodoxy, its obsequious imitation of the conservative Protestant culture that the mainstream white denominations seem to be attempting to resuscitate—its lack, in other words, of what Jesus called the righteousness that "exceeds that of the scribes and Pharisees." Such a demon cannot be cast out by court decisions and electoral politics, but only by prayer and fasting—so to say, by a revitalized religion and culture informed by a more radical theology of world-affirming spirituality and eschatologically oriented social transformation than has yet been formulated by white Christianity.

But what Black Theology offers is more than a new Afro-American cultural nationalism afflicted with the same moralism, sexism, classism, and imperialism that afflict white civil religion. One of the dangers in the present situation is cooptation. A temptation that bedeviled the Jackson campaign and in the end may have possessed it was coloring the liberal wing of the Democratic Party black, turning on a little soul music at rallies and persuading the folk that because of this, "our day has come." Black Theology has serious misgivings about conventional politics. It builds upon a tradition that presents a counterculture to the American mainstream. An enumeration of some of the abiding characteristics of that black counterculture would have to include radical protest and agitation, Jesus as liberator of the oppressed, pragmatic spirituality, the dialectic of redemptive suffering and concrete victory in struggle, relativity and an openness on the question of violence, identification with the poor and victimized of all groups and cultures, a hermeneutical suspicion of racism as a constant in Western theology and church history, an openness to heterodoxy in dialogue with African traditional religions and independent churches, and an appreciation of and willingness to learn from other non-Western forms of spirituality. All of these concepts or motifs cluster around the present Black Theology movement, as represented, for example, by the Black Theology Project, Inc., of Theology in the Americas. They comprise the essential content of what many of us who have continued to struggle with white racism and black apathy believe necessary for the preservation and enhancement of black culture and its role in bringing about a new consciousness and quality of life for all struggling people in the United States and abroad.

2

That the tradition we have discussed is woefully absent from the majority of Afro-American churches today is a reality of our situation that must be acknowledged before it can be corrected. Only here and there do we find congregations that are reminded week after week of the rock of black Christian consciousness from which they were hewn, that have an educational program for children and adults emphasizing black culture and the themes of Black Theology, and that is engaged in a praxis demonstrating the coherence between spirituality and politics. In most cities where there is a critical mass of blacks in the population one can, perhaps, name one or two laypersons and clergy who are struggling against the internal and external pressures in their situations that make for this grievous evaporation of the historic nature and purpose of the black church. They are, in any case, an embattled minority. One of the reasons for the founding of the Black Theology Project, Inc., was to identify these persons, build them into a national network of men and women of similar concern and commitment, and provide them with a variety of resources for reflection and action that are usually unavailable within their respective denominations. The work is agonizingly slow and painful on at least three scores.

First, interdenominational movements of this kind have always needed more money than was available from traditional sources in order to provide staff, travel, regional structures, and other institutional expedients that are necessary for the promotion and development of such services to individuals and congregations.

Secondly, neither the predominantly black nor the predominantly white theological seminaries are producing a sufficient number of men and women who have any knowledge of or commitment to the kind of church and ministry that the Black Theology Project envisions. Most seminarians are being equipped to fit into the grooves of "professional" ministry as understood by denominational headquarters. That usually means preaching, counseling, and keeping the wheels of congregational life oiled and functioning smoothly and obediently to the norms and values of conventional Christianity. In this regard there is little difference between the black and white ministers graduating into the church each year. They are equally uninformed, success-oriented, and ill-prepared to assume leadership in a church that seeks to be the vanguard of revolutionary change.

Thirdly, the few people who somewhere along the line have been inspired by the way the black church of the past troubled the waters of its era and who are committed to the radicalization of black religion today are usually neutralized by being pushed to the fringes of their denominations. They soon become nuisances to their superiors—marked men and women because they threaten the ecclesiastical hierarchies and bureaucracies that expect everyone to march in lock-step toward the same institutional goals.

If this picture seems so pessimistic as to leave in doubt any possibility of the renewal and radicalization of the historic black church, we can only conclude by saying that "Christian hope springs eternal." Moreover, one continues to be surprised by the God who is never left without a witness and continues to call prophets and martyrs for the reformation of the church and the healing of nations. There are such men and women today in the pews and pulpits of local congregations, denominational and ecumenical agencies, and in our divinity schools. They may be few and sorely pressed, but they are there, by the grace of God toward them and us, and they are the hope of the future.

The black church has helped to keep a part of a universal church faithful and a part of America human. It continues to have an awesome vocation today with respect to a witness that binds together spirituality and social transformation, which is a requirement of our authentic humanity. It must keep constantly before its members that God did not call it into being for exclusive, narrow purposes, but for the whole world. But it cannot realize those purposes, either for itself or others, unless more black religionists reappropriate the usable past that motivated and inspired not only Denmark Vesey and Nat Turner, but some of its more recent warriors—the immortal Benjamin E. Mays, Adam Clayton Powell, Jr., Fannie Lou Hamer, Malcolm X, and Martin Luther King, Jr.

Nor will the black church be able to build upon that past until it catches a vision of the future that includes all men and women, of every race, culture, and nationality.

We do have a great inheritance, but it can only be preserved and enhanced if the black church accepts its vocation to be the custodian and interpreter of what God has taught us "from the days when hope unborn had died." Because that lesson has to do with both spirituality and social transformation, it is a wider task than the institutional church can perform. Actually, what we have to preserve belongs not to the church but to black people as a whole— to the poets and the politicians, and street people and the new middle class that still desires a black identity, to the NAACP and the Republic of New Africa, to the "blues people" and the gospel choirs, to the thousands of young black men and women in the nation's prisons, and to the thousands who are still in church on Sunday mornings. The cultural vocation of the black church and of Black Theology is to prevent what God has given to Afro-American people from evaporating and being lost forever to the world—to keep the music going and the soul free, to keep the poets preaching and the preachers writing revolutionary poetry, to conserve, correct, and embellish the gift of blackness so that its riches will be available to all people who want to be human and free.

Notes

1. Hart M. Nelsen and Anna K. Nelsen, *Black Church in the Sixties* (Lexington, KY: The University Press of Kentucky, 1975), pp. 134–35; Seth M. Scheiner, "The Negro Church and the Northern City, 1890–1930," in *Seven on Black: Reflections on the Negro Experience in America,* ed. William G. Shade and Roy C. Herrenkohl (Philadelphia: J. B. Lippincott, 1969), pp. 109–16; C. Eric Lincoln, *The Black Church since Frazier* (New York: Schocken Books, 1974), pp. 105–10.
2. James S. Tinney, "Competing Strains of Hidden and Manifest Theologies in Black Pentecostalism," paper presented to the Society for Pentecostal Studies, Oral Roberts University, 14 November 1980, p. 11.
3. Peter J. Paris, *The Social Teaching of the Black Church* (Philadelphia: Fortress Press, 1985), p. 35.
4. Ibid., pp. 11–12.
5. Howard Thurman, *The Luminous Darkness* (New York: Harper & Row, 1965), p. x.
6. Cedric J. Robinson, *Black Marxism: The Making of the Black Radical Tradition* (London: Zed Press, 1983), pp. 245–46.

7. Albert J. Raboteau, "'Ethiopia Shall Soon Stretch Forth Her Hands': Black Destiny in Nineteenth Century America," a University Lecture in Religion published by the Department of Religious Studies, Arizona State University, Tempe, 1983, p. 5; italics added.

8. Martin Luther King, Jr., *Where Do We Go from Here: Chaos or Community?* (New York: Harper & Row, 1967), p. 134.

9. Walter Hollenweger, *Pentecost Between Black and White: Five Case Studies on Pentecost and Politics* (Belfast: Christian Journals Limited, 1974), p. 17.

10. "Toward a Common Expression of Faith: A Black North American Perspective," statement of the Richmond Consultation of black theologians and church leaders sponsored by the Commission on Faith and Order of the National Council of Churches, 14–15 December 1984, p. 5.

11. "Urban Mission in a Time of Crisis," a statement of the National Committee of Black Churchmen, in Gayraud S. Wilmore and James H. Cone, eds., *Black Theology: A Documentary History, 1966–1979* (Maryknoll, N.Y.: Orbis Books, 1979), p. 64.

12. My understanding of culture is influenced largely by the writings of Clifford Geertz. See particularly *The Interpretation of Cultures* (New York: Basic Books, 1973), pp. 87–125.

13. W. E. B. DuBois, *The Gift of Black Folk: Negroes in the Making of America* (New York: Washington Square Press, 1940).

Chinatown: Theology Emerging out of Community

Norman Fong

I hope to share with you, in this essay, some of my attempts to deal with the following questions: How does one theologize within a community that is largely made up of recent immigrants and second and third generation immigrants? How does one live with the tensions of "moving slowly" with a community without losing sight of the overall goal of transforming society? What does our struggle have to say to broader movements for social change? Related to all three of these questions, I hope to share with you my own story of becoming more radical, both politically and theologically.

Theology Is for Community

As long as theo-logy (talk about God) is based on abstract bodies of knowledge or systems of thought, it remains a tool for oppression, or at best an ideology fused with biblical rhetoric. Theology is first and foremost a theology for and with a community. It must be rooted in a people's story, giving direction for and with that community. A theology that does not take into account a people's story (i.e., the social-political-economic and cultural context) is a theology that is imperialistic because it imposes the theologian's ideology as "truth." Missionaries to China, for example, in seeking to transplant Christianity into China also transplanted a cultural and imperialistic ideology.

As nice and expedient as it would be to have *the perfect theology* based on *the correct political–economic analysis*, the resultant theology

254

would still be prescriptive and imperialistic if it did not take into account a people's story. *Theology for community,* then, is evocative! The biblical story and the people's story must "bounce off each other" so that a theology for and with the community emerges.

"Wandering theologians" and some Christian activists often assume that the theology they carry applies to every situation they encounter. I, too, have been guilty of such elitist sentiments. "If only *they* had the correct analysis or 'my' theology," I would think to myself. Radicals in the 1960s, for example (mostly middle-class white students), made this mistake when they wandered into Chinatown (and other communities) expecting everyone to understand the *"Problem."*

Theologians and Christian activists must first be rooted in a community before they can begin to evoke a theology meaningful and challenging for and with a community. As painfully slow as the process may seem at times, anything less than this would still be elitist or paternalistic. Even in the broader movement for social change in the United States, I would hope that our story—the story of Pacific Asian-Americans—would be included. At times I have felt that Asian-Americans were being excluded from various activities (i.e., Theology in the Americas, Detroit Conference I) because we were considered "too slow," or "too race-oriented without a class analysis," etc. to be included in the "movement." Of course, not to be judgmental, maybe people "in the movement" did not know our story of struggle.

A Community's Story as the Basis for Theology

> A Chinaman is cold, cunning, and distrustful; always ready to take advantage of those he has to deal with; extremely covetous and deceitful; quarrelsome, vindictive, but timid and dastardly. A Chinaman in office is a strange compound of insolence and meanness. All ranks and conditions have a total disregard for truth.
> —*Encyclopedia Britannica* 1842

The above definition of a "Chinaman" in 1842 reflects American attitudes toward the Chinese at the time of the first Opium War, when China's "closed door" policy with the West was smashed open. Racist attitudes toward the Chinese were operative in the United States even before the Chinese started coming in the late 1840s. Racism and imperialism are both integrally related in the story of Chinese-Americans. Racism helps to explain why the Chinese faced such intense persecution in the United States (1850s–1940s) and imperialism helps to explain why the Chinese were impoverished enough to leave the "homeland." Western penetration into China resulted in poverty that forced many Chinese to emigrate at a rate not known before in China's long history. Before the Opium Wars few Chinese left their homeland.

Of course, as always economic needs were the prime reason for the coming of the Chinese, not only to the United States but to countries all over the world:

> Emancipation has spoiled the Negro, and carried him away from the field of agriculture. Our prosperity depends entirely upon the recovery of lost ground, and we therefore say let the coolies come, and we will take the chance of Christianizing them.
> —Editor, *Vicksburg Times* (1869)

With the end of the slave trade, and later of slavery, the so-called world coolie trade emerged, using the Chinese as a source of cheap labor to develop and till the new lands. California did not enter the union as a slave state. Through the organization of immigrant labor, the lands were developed, railroads built, fruits and vegetables picked. The Chinese, like later Asian groups and Mexican-Americans, came as contract laborers. The Chinese, contrary to popular myths, did not come to "exploit the land and gold mines." That was the exclusive right of white Anglo-Saxons and "assimilable aliens." The Chinese came as contract laborers who were excluded, kicked out, beaten, and killed when the work they were contracted for was done. White working-class racism also emerged as a way to unify the working class at the expense of the Chinese. There's a street in Chinatown named after Dennis Kearny, who led the Workingman's Party with the slogan, "The Chinese must go."

The Chinese, from their beginnings in this country until World War II, were used as economic scapegoats in times of depression. In the 1870s, for example, the Chinese comprised about one-twelfth of California's inhabitants. Since Chinese women were not admitted ("God forbid the idea of Chinese families becoming a part of America"), the Chinese actually comprised about one-fourth of the labor force! When the 1873 depression hit, just as the railroads were reaching completion and Chinese labor became expendable (due to the influx of nearly 1 million migrants from eastern parts of the United States), the anti-Chinese movement rose to unbelievable heights. During the 1870s and 1880s the Chinese were not safe anywhere. Anti-Chinese riots became the "in thing" and were legally sanctioned. The Chinese were increasingly blamed for the economic slumps of the 1870s. And in the 1870s and 1880s all kinds of ridiculous laws were passed aimed at the Chinese—for example, a law making it illegal to use a pole to carry things (Chinese style). In 1879 the second constitution of California gave the legislature "unlimited power" to remove all Chinese from towns and cities and to proscribe areas outside city limits where they were unwanted. Legally sanctioned anti-Chinese riots increased as numerous Chinatowns were burned to the ground and many Chinese were lynched, beaten, and chased out of town.

As many prominent persons have stated (i.e., Kennedy and Carter), the United States was and is a nation of immigrants (i.e., pro-North and Western European and anti-Communist). In the Chinese Exclusion Act of 1882, the Chinese were officially excluded from immigrating to the United States and white working-class racism played a major part in bringing about their exclusion. The Chinese were also excluded occupationally (even worse), as is reflected in the second constitution of California—which prohibited the employment of Chinese by any corporation and "any state, county, municipal or other public work." In 1880 there were 105,465 Chinese in the United States. By 1900 there were only 39,963 left (while European immigration had skyrocketed). It was not until 1943, when China became a U.S. ally in World War II, that the Chinese Exclusion Act was repealed. It was replaced with a meager Chinese quota of 105 per year which lasted until 1965, when the racist National Origins Quota System was abolished.

In light of the very brief historical background given above, questions like "Why are the Chinese so apolitical?" or "Why do the Chinese like to do laundry and restaurant work?" (because we were excluded from all other occupations) or "Why don't Chinese get organized and join unions?" reflect an ignorance or insensitivity on the part of the questioner. *They don't know our story.* However, it was not until the late 1960s that many of us, even in Chinatown, began to relearn this story. Our history has been so distorted by myths and stereotypes created by the white "establishment" that a major struggle for our community in the past decade and a half has been simply to destroy myths! (By the way, did you know that "Charlie Chan" is coming back on the screen?)

Story Versus Myth

There is a myth in this country that every person who works hard can "make it." This myth is the basis for the "American dream." After the black riots in the 1960s, this myth was applied to Asian-Americans. The *New York Times, U.S. News & World Report, Time, Newsweek*, etc., began to print stories about how "successful"

Chinese- and Japanese-Americans have been. Titles like "Out-Whiting the Whites" and "Success Story: Japanese Style" began to appear in the headlines. Quoting from a 1966 *U.S. News & World Report:*

> At a time when Americans were awash in worry over the plight of racial minorities—one such minority, the nation of 300,000 Chinese-Americans, is winning wealth and respect by dint of its hard work. . . . Still being taught in Chinatown is the old idea that people should depend on their efforts—not a welfare check—in order to reach America's "promised land." In any Chinatown, from San Francisco to New York, you'll discover youths at grips with their studies.

Implied in this "Asian success story myth"—and it is a myth—is the dangerous idea that any person, no matter what color he or she is, can achieve material wealth and success if he or she works hard enough. There are no racial barriers. This myth justifies the ghetto conditions of minorities by shifting the burden and blame upon them and denying the white institutional racism and economic system that created the ghettos. The myth frees whites from assuming responsibilities for white establishment oppressiveness by saying, in effect, "See, the Asians have made it so the blacks must be lazy or something."

The myth also exerts a kind of social pressure within Asian-American communities because if you are a poor Asian-American, there must be something wrong with you. Growing up in Chinatown, I felt the heavy burden of this myth because my family was poor. We did not have that car, home, or any of those things associated with the so-called middle class. Worse than that, I grew up ashamed of my parents because obviously they were failures, and what's more, my dad couldn't speak English very well. *I didn't know our story!*

With the rise and fight for ethnic studies in the late 1960s, for the first time in schools, we got the chance to relearn our story. The ethnic movements in the 1960s were a liberating experience for many minorities. For the first time in my life, I began to ask my mom and dad about their experiences in the United States. My dad arrived in 1919 and was placed in the Angel Island Detention Center (prison) because the Chinese were unwanted in this country. He came alone, a teenager, and ended up picking tomatoes in southern California. His story, like that of many other early immigrants to this country, used to be a story so painful and shameful that nobody ever talked about it. Yet that same story of shame has become a story of pride and struggle for many Asian-Americans today! The ethnic movement helped me and many others to re-learn our story, and it was that liberating experience that radicalized me politically and theologically.

Knowing our story invalidates old theologies that were based on myths or on a distorted establishment ideology. (I believe that not only minorities, but whites as well, must relearn the story.) Theologies based on the old story tend to celebrate the wealth and prosperity of America as a "God-given gift," ignoring the social injustices that go along with it. For Asian-Americans, theologies based on the old story (the American dream) tend to push "assimilation" and "acculturation" ideologies and theologies. Since the rise of the Asian-American movement, and of the Asian-American Caucus movement in the major denominations, new theologies have emerged for our communities. One Asian-American Christian Education Curriculum project recently published for our churches stresses the sojourner theme: "You shall not wrong a stranger or oppress him, for you were strangers in the land of Egypt" (Exodus 22:21). We must remember our oppression as aliens so that we can seek to implement a society that does not use "aliens" as an expendable labor force to serve "Pharoah." More than remembering our oppression-history as aliens, we as biblical people must remember that we are forever "sojourners" before the Lord and the land belongs to God "and shall not be sold in perpetuity" (Lev. 25:23). Our biblical and historical identity as "aliens" or "sojourners" shapes our attitude toward other newcomers and about land-use. Based on this new theology and story of struggle, Asian-Americans should be concentrating on justice concerns and land-use issues rather than striving for "assimilation" and "thanksgiving" for our nation's wealth.

Another Asian-American Christian Education Curriculum project is an alternative interpretation of the Book of Judges. Rather than accepting the standard theology which interprets Israel as, through the grace of God, conquering the people of Palestine to reach the "promised land," another interpretation is proposed.

Rather than pushing the "assimilation" type ideologies and theologies (i.e., Israel assimilating into Canaan), a more appropriate theology presented by Norman Gottwald and Marvin Chaney, that the Israelite minority joined forces with other marginal people in the "hill country," and with the oppressed peasantry, to implement a revolt and overthrow the unjust and oppressive Canaanite establishment. For Asian-Americans this approach to the Book of Judges implies that we should seek to join forces with other marginal and oppressed peoples in the United States to seek justice, rather than to "assimilate" into a fake "melting pot" accepting the status quo. Both of these Asian-American theological perspectives are based on "our story" in this country. Both remind us of our story of struggle and make justice concerns a top priority for our church and community.

For Asian-Americans our story bounces off the biblical story in new and revolutionary ways once theology is rooted in a people's story. Of course the movement is slow—the myths are still around. Our story needs to be understood and shared among different communities, in order to create and move in a direction for and with the broader movement for social change in this country. Hopefully, unlike our past experiences in times of economic slump, we will not be excluded or discarded from the larger movements (i.e., anti-alien or anti-Asian exclusion). Our story and struggles are hopefully a part of the larger struggle for economic and political justice in this world.

Chinatown: Moving from the 1970s to the 1980s

> If there is one thing that the people of Chinatown fear, it is the bulldozer to tear down and replace that which they know, own, and occupy.
> —Chinese Community Fact-Finding Report (1979)

A decade ago the 1970 census revealed statistics concerning Chinatown, San Francisco, that blew the minds of many people outside our community (especially those who believed the Asian success myth). For example, Chinatown was revealed as having the second highest population density in the United States. The Chinatown core area had 912 persons per residential acre over against San Francisco's citywide figure of 79 per residential acre. Another revealing finding was that Chinese women workers were recorded as having the lowest income compared to other women workers categorized by color/national origin. This reflects the exploitation of women in our communities by the garment and electronics industries. Language barriers, sexism, and racism make the vulnerability of Chinese women workers quite high (not to mention their alien status, which guarantees a passive worker for fear of deportation). The census also revealed the fact that a very high percentage of the Chinese elderly in both New York and San Francisco's Chinatowns live below the poverty line. Fifty-eight percent of all Chinese elderly living in the United States live alone (reflecting the racist exclusion laws that did not permit wives of

Chinese-Americans or single Chinese women to come to the United States.

In terms of health, housing, education, suicide rates, etc., Chinatown is very much a ghetto. But what is unique is that it is one of the few ghettos that has become a "tourist attraction." Why white Americans want a "fake China" is beyond my understanding. Yet we are stuck with the situation and now many Chinese business-persons are capitalizing on it. What is worse is the fact that the "fake China," with parking lots and tourist shops, is encroaching upon our residential needs—housing! To make matters worse, the finan-cial district next door is also encroaching upon our community.

A decade ago, my family was evicted from our $90.00 a month rented flat. It was a scary situation not knowing where to go. My parents work and shop for food daily in Chinatown and it was difficult finding another place to rent nearby. The old landlord died and some other guy bought the building. He evicted us and doubled the rent for the flat below us, which chased out my aunt and uncle's family as well. "Eviction" is a terrifying word in Chinatown.

A few years ago, a hotel and community center for elderly Chinese- and Filipino-Americans (International Hotel) was torn down to make way for an overseas corporation that hoped to make a profit in Chinatown by investing in a parking lot. For nine years, the tenants and people in our community fought successfully against the attempted eviction. In 1978 an army of three hundred police, sheriffs, and deputies, some on horses, broke through a human barricade in the middle of the night to evict the elderly tenants. How the needs of an overseas corporation with extra capital to spend can become more important than the needs of our community's elderly clearly demonstrates just whose interests the laws are protecting and, further, the screwed-up priorities of our economic and political system. Profits first, people second.

Our community has learned a lot in the past decade. There have been a number of tenant-organized rent strikes and protests for better housing maintenance. When a women was raped and killed in the *Ping Yuen* (Chinatown's public housing project), the tenants organized and pulled a rent strike for months demanding new lighting facilities for the dark balconies and walkways. They also demanded that a security guard be assigned to the Ping Yuen. Their demands were finally met, after four long months. Also, the site of the International Hotel (where the elderly Chinese and Filipinos were evicted) has been targeted for a new low-cost housing project with space for some community organizations and some commercial interests. The long International Hotel struggle is still alive! In terms of labor organizing, there is now a Chinese Committee of the Hotel, Restaurant, and Bar Tender's Union.

Our church in Chinatown has also been involved in the struggle for more low-cost housing and after eight years of tedious weekly meetings, picketing HUD and City Hall, it looks like our church-sponsored housing project is going to be built. Responding to the needs of our community, we recently started a bilingual afterschool program to help immigrant youth and we sponsor a senior citizens' program with good and inexpensive Chinese food for the elderly. We've also begun a daycare program. Yet the struggle to keep up with the needs of the community is overwhelming, and it looks like it will become harder in the light of attempts to cut public assistance and badly needed social services for the sake of an increased military budget and tax breaks for corporate interests.

How does one begin to move toward that "radical vision" of a society based on people's needs rather than commercial interests and profits? How does one keep those "radical goals" of a "new heaven on earth" in sight when you're fighting hard to survive? The day-to-day struggles and tasks seem so "reformist" in that it means dealing with victims most of the time, leaving little time to challenge the overall structure that creates victims. For me, as "slow and tedious" as it may seem at times, I believe that it is at those very moments of working in a community and struggling with people to get their basic needs met that talk of radical social change can have any meaning. In other words, I believe that the struggle for change in the 1980s means getting involved in community struggles where the contradictions of our society are most concretely felt. I guess some people call it a "bottom up," rather than a "top down," model. Sure I'd like to form a radical subculture at times to mouth off "revolution," but from experience and seeing how that style has alienated people in our community, I'd rather not. I believe that in the long term, this process of rooting oneself in community struggles has a better likelihood of social change.

Getting involved in community-story and bouncing that story off the biblical story can have tremendous "consciousness-raising" power. It may seem slow, but when the right moment comes to shove those bulldozers through that capitalist wall, we'll have the community and other communities ready to break through. The movement is slow, but the story will never die, and it is the story that motivates people to struggle.

As long as people are taught to forget the story, we'll keep making the same mistakes. As long as people are fed myths which distort the story, we'll never end our nation's oppressiveness. I can't believe all the war-hawk talk being soaked up nowadays . . . and the draft is back! Have so many "Americans" today forgotten the story? Have they forgotten Hiroshima, Korea, Vietnam, Kampuchea, etc.?

We bombed the hell out of Kampuchea a decade ago and now our hearts are pouring out for those "poor refugees." Contradictions, contradictions, contradictions—that is our starting point. The story must be retold, retold, and retold until the message finally gets through. Asian suffering as well as Asian-American suffering is part of the same story that must be retold and heard in the 1980s.

Note

This article originally appeared in a special issue of *Radical Religion* 5, no. 2 (1980), entitled "Theology and Politics in the 1980s," and is reprinted with permission. Copyright © 1980 by the Community for Religious Research and Education, Inc.

Part V

Political Activism and the Mission of the Church

Theologies of liberation are characterized by their concern for the poor, the afflicted, and the oppressed, and by their emphasis on the need to strengthen the communities of God's children through conscious praxis, by acting in this world. They are premised on the understanding that each of us—women, men, and even nations—are to be judged by our commitment to justice and our concrete activities. This stance increasingly involves the church as an institution in social issues, and it is this participation that the essays in this section discuss.

Richard Gillett, a long-time church activist and worker for economic justice, provides an overview of the church's involvement in the effort to bring a moral perspective to corporate decision-making, in this case to the decision as to when (and if) a plant should close and/or move away. He argues that decisions such as these, which affect the lives of millions of working people, their families, and the communities in which they live, should not be "private matters" decided by boards of directors, but should be subject to social priorities established democratically.

The commitment to justice has affected all branches of religion, including some that have heretofore been considered very conservative. The U.S. Conference of Catholic Bishops powerfully enunciated this position in its 1985 pastoral letter, "Catholic Social Teaching and the Economy," discussed by myself in the next essay in this section. The major intervention by the bishops was a shot in the arm for the movements devoted to economic justice, but at the same time it avoided going the necessary step further and making an analysis that would seek to explain *why* our system works the way it does—a fact that can perhaps be understood in terms of Gregory Baum's distinction between the prophetic and institution-maintaining roles of the Catholic hierarchy. But the relation of the official church to the U.S. political system suggests that it is not ready to go further than offering moral advice which, however inspiring, will not challenge the institutional sins it describes.

On a less global but no less dramatic level individuals within the church are also taking on a role in the community that challenges the established order, both religious and secular. The piece by Paul Burks shows the extent to which individuals, congregations, and even whole communities have committed themselves to reach out beyond their narrow confines to challenge what they believe to be unjust laws and policies by sheltering strangers fleeing death squads and armies sponsored by the U.S. government. The activists see their actions as emerging out of their faith: political activism is the consequence, but does not provide the impulse. Personal witness to a shared faith commitment is shaping a social movement.

What these activists see as offering assistance to the strangers in our midst, to the poor, the homeless, to widows and orphans, the U.S. government has called a conspiracy to smuggle aliens into the United States, and it has indicted twelve people in Tucson, Arizona. In building its case, the government has used paid informers (who, according to pre-trial testimony, had previously been arrested for illegal smuggling and managing a prostitution ring) to spy on the sanctuary activists, using hidden recording devices in church services and during Bible study meetings.

Why has the government pursued this case, especially since there is a widespread sense that those offering sanctuary have moral right on their side? Sister Darlene Nicgorski, one of the twelve indicted, says:

> The indictments are an attempt to silence the truth by silencing refugee witnesses to atrocities, by silencing church workers assisting refugees and by silencing truth's entrance into the courtroom. As long as the war in Central America can remain technological, clean, and distant, the reality of the people's suffering there does not become real to our people.[1]

The Reverend Jesse Jackson's decision to run for president and to become the catalyst in the creation of a "rainbow coalition" was the first modern-day move by a religious figure into mainstream electoral politics in the United States. The issues that were stressed by the media during the Jackson campaign obscured many of the important aspects of Jackson's candidacy. Sheila Collins, in the next essay, looks at the significance of the campaign as a potential unifying force, a new movement with grass-roots strength among the poor, people of color, and progressive whites. Her essay is complemented by that of Gayraud Wilmore, which shows how the black experience, and particularly the black churches, spawned the concept of politics rooted in community values which is embodied in the Rainbow Coalition. We do not have to agree with the positions Jackson took on every issue to recognize that the idea of a rainbow coalition was a progressive development, a positive counter-response by members of the religious community and their secular allies to the use of religion to promote a rightward drift in U.S. politics. Many themes competed in Jackson's campaign rhetoric, but the aspirations of the poor, the marginalized, to a place in our society commensurate with that required of the majority by the Judeo-Christian commandment that justice be done is an important development in our nation's politics.

Note

1. Renny Golden, "Sanctuary Movement Exposes Secret War," *In These Times*, 4–10 September 1985, p. 17.

The Church Acts for Economic Justice

Richard W. Gillett

History seldom if ever permits advocates of social change the luxury of planning, gathering the resources, and then strategically deploying the agents to implement such change. On the contrary: groups and individuals who conceive a new vision and proceed to implement it must invariably contend immediately with the full weight of events and forces seemingly concocted precisely to snuff out any such vision or resultant strategy. Thus the massive wave of plant closures which began in the United States in the late 1970s gathered momentum and destructiveness even as the first stirrings of a revived church consciousness about the plight of working people and communities flickered into visibility in Youngstown, Ohio. The ecclesiastical pronouncements resulting from Youngstown, and from subsequent areas of the churches' engagement with labor in the 1980s, were cast directly into the teeth of a veritable gale of proclamations and policies paying tribute to the glories of the unfettered marketplace as supreme arbiter of justice, jobs, and prosperity. In our communities, churches, and work-places, we do not have the luxury of working methodically and purposefully to assess situations, plan responses and apply for grants for programs—all the while writing solid theological treatises to explain our actions.

Therefore it is all the more astonishing, given the adverse circumstances, that a surprising array of church-related action programs addressing the economic crisis has been lauched in almost every part of the country. In addition, a number of strong and sometimes highly insightful theological statements have been issued, coming even from high church levels.

Here I will look at a sampling of these programmatic responses, acknowledging it to be by no means complete. A reflection on their effectiveness and some further directions for action will be suggested for deepening involvement and theological reflection.

Programmatic Responses

It was the catastrophic closure of the steelmills in Youngstown, Ohio originating in 1977 with the Campbell Works shutdown, that began to bring the churches back to the concerns of labor and working people they had espoused in the 1930s. The suddenness of the closures, their widespread impact upon the community, and the brazenness with which the steel companies pursued their economic objectives shocked the community and brought the churches together across denominational lines. With ecumenical leadership fully involved and with the community behind them, the churches collaborated with community and local labor leadership to seek federal government assistance to keep the mills open. A major feasibility study proposed local joint community-worker ownership but proclaimed the need for huge capital investments in steelmill modernization. Yet not only did the national union, the United Steelworkers of America, refuse to back the takeover proposal (thus going counter to the desires of its local union), but the federal government ultimately turned thumbs down on any bailout assistance. Still, the churches learned a great deal from their involvement, and began to see that an entire region was suffering from the precipitous decline in the steel industry. The Tri-State Conference on Steel, focusing on steel's collapse in Ohio, West Virginia, and Pennsylvania, subsequently emerged as a regional attempt by the churches to address the issue.

As the 1980s dawned, and before the economic policies of the Reagan administration had had a chance to take hold, religious groups in other areas—such as New England, Chicago, Philadelphia, and California—began to become aware that the economic dislocation was nationwide. In California, a major Western International Conference on Economic Dislocation was initiated by religious, labor, community, and academic groups in 1981. It demonstrated that the presumably prosperous West, from below the Mexican border up to Canada, was also suffering severely from closures and capital flight in the automobile, rubber, forest products, food processing, and other industries. The conference spawned a statewide California Coalition Against Plant Shutdowns. It had seven projects, the most active being in Oakland, Los Angeles, and Eureka. These church-labor projects had notable successes in generating wide support for state plant-closure legislation, in obtaining the passage of a landmark city ordinance in Vacaville denying public financing for plant relocations except under stringent conditions, and specific plant closure battles across the state.

In the South, church involvement in the work arena revived. Several small cooperative projects in North Carolina, for example, focused on worker participation, worker ownership, and job creation for low-income workers, particularly blacks. And as other projects came into being around the country, the groundwork was laid for the creation of a national Interreligious Economic Crisis Organizing Network, which was officially inaugurated in early 1982 with the active support of several Protestant, Roman Catholic, and Jewish religious bodies. It followed the National Conference on Religion and Labor, an annual convocation of organized labor (principally AFL-CIO leadership) and religious leadership from Roman Catholic and Protestant churches. The conference, convening annually since 1980, has facilitated useful networking.

A particularly significant struggle in the steelmaking Monongahela Valley near Pittsburgh has highlighted several crucial aspects of the involvement of the churches in the economic crisis. Within that compact region, massive layoffs and plant closings have cast about twenty thousand steelworkers out of their jobs in the last five years, and further shutdowns were scheduled in late 1984. Working first to provide relief to unemployed workers, the churches became involved in the Mon Valley Unemployed Committee, among others. As increasing numbers of jobless workers had to foreclose on their homes for failure to meet the payments, the committee began to up the ante by picketing the public auctions where the workers' homes were put up for sale. Ultimately they were successful in stopping such sales, and the Pennsylvania legislature set up a program to fund mortgage relief loans. Pursuing the root causes of the failure to invest in modernizing the closed mills, another group, the Denominational Mission Strategy (DMS), focused on the Mellon Bank. They charged that while the bank was refusing to invest in the Mon Valley, it had been lending hundreds of millions of dollars to foreign steelmakers. The DMS has used confrontational tactics which have resulted in turning off virtually all church funding, but several clergy have remained deeply involved. And at least one prominent Pittsburgh Roman Catholic clergyman, Monsignor Charles O. Rice, believes the group is on the right track. "I would not be surprised if the DMS suffers more defeats than victories in the near term," he is quoted as saying, "but if what I foresee comes to pass, in ten or twenty years we will be glad for religious revolutionary leadership." (Nevertheless, the highly confrontive tactics used in 1984 by a Lutheran minister may have gone beyond reasonable protest and humiliated both potential supporters and opponents. The utter humiliation and degradation of opponents moves beyond a redemptive outcome and engenders a gridlock polarity.)

Another project gaining support from religious leadership is the Ecumenical Great Lakes/Appalachian Project. Building on previous religious collaborative efforts in the region, it has support from Episcopal, Presbyterian, Roman Catholic, and United Church of Christ sources. Its focus is on education and on broadening the participation in shaping the region's economy, including the goal of empowering the unemployed themselves.

A potentially significant effort which would join the labor, peace, and religious constituencies in addressing the militarization of the economy as a major aspect of the economic crisis may be developing. An international economic conversion conference held in Boston in June 1984 saw the joining of these three groups in a new attempt to understand the relationship of peace to economic policy. The need for planning for productive civilian employment in conjunction with religious groups' efforts to halt the arms race has the potential of opening up the peace movement to the hard realities of the seeming "economic determinism" of military production. Thus the need for people working in military-related production to find useful civilian employment may become clearer to the churches as such connections are pressed.

Meanwhile, various religious groups have begun to issue statements on the economic crisis. Nationally, the Episcopal Urban Bishops issued a Labor Day Pastoral Message in 1982. The statement questioned whether work defined primarily as "competition" can build local security and stability. It called for the beginning of a process of democratic control of work in local communities and warned of dangers to the community posed by corporate structures which remove control of resources and decision-making from the people most affected. In January 1983 the Canadian Conference of Catholic Bishops, through its Commission for Social Affairs, made a strong pronouncement titled *Ethical Reflections on the Economic Crisis,* which had wide impact. It drew scornful comments from Canadian Prime Minister Pierre Trudeau, who said the bishops were meddling in areas where they were not competent. In addition, solid local and regional theological pronouncements on the economic crisis came from Appalachia, Philadelphia, New England, and California.

In perhaps what was the signal religious event of 1984 in the United States, the Roman Catholic bishops issued in November the first draft of a pasₜoral letter titled "Catholic Social Teaching and the Economy." Its release has prompted intense comment and discussion both within the ecumenical religious community and beyond. The third and final draft is scheduled for completion in the fall of 1985, with continuing debate and dissemination.

It is beyond my purview to include an analysis of the 112-page document. Suffice it to say that its primary significance lies in the fact that it was issued at all. More important, it dethrones the "economy" from that lofty autonomous perch where governments and politicians have typically placed it in U.S. history:

> The dignity of the human person is the criterion against which all aspects of economic life must be measured. This dignity can only be realized in relationship and solidarity with others.

If the pastoral letter is taken seriously in our churches, it could well mark the beginning of a historic new role for them: that of questioning some of the long-held beliefs about the nature and assumptions of our economic system. Such questioning must reach beyond economic theory and practice to the moral and religious assumptions underlying human behavior and human aspirations. Perhaps only the churches, using such deeply religious categories as "creation, convenant, and community" (categories used in the pastoral) can call the society to this higher ground of openness to the future.

Where to from Here?

From looking at the ways in which church groups have been drawn into the struggles of working people as they have developed over the past few years, it becomes clear that a crucial maturation has taken place. Many church activists have come to see that the issues of work and economic justice as they present themselves to our era in history must be addressed in ways that go beyond the application of mere correctives to the existing economic system. They are raising questions having to do with the deepest questions of the social well-being of the human community, and the need of human beings to feel fulfilled, productive, and related in a positive way to that larger well-being. They are recollecting that Christian history and scriptural tradition reject the primacy of economic systems and uphold the sanctity of the human person and the community as theological givens. Likewise, some of the theological statements we have referred to have recalled the churches to the foundations of a concern for work as a fundamentally religious issue.

However, these responses have tended to occur at the extreme ends of the social spectrum without touching the middle. At one end are activist clergy working with grassroots labor activists, usually workers who themselves are victims of plant closure. At the other end are some bishops and denominational leaders who likewise have taken the courageous step of identifying with these activists through statements and sometimes through financial support. The vast middle of the American religious constituency, along with its clergy, as yet remains untouched by such activity. An educational task of enormous proportions thus awaits the churches. But if the perception is correct that the restructuring of work is tending to push the American workforce toward the extremes of menial, low-paying, and nonunion work at the one end, and technical, managerial, and high-paying work at the other end, the basic contentedness of the middle class may begin to erode. It is likely that more mainline churches will begin to see their congregations affected.

In addition, the shift toward a service and information society over the past decade means that such churches have an opportunity to become aware of the work lives and experiences of the now numerous members of their congregations who are secretaries, bookkeepers, health-care personnel, computer programmers, and the like. Their experiences of job boredom, sex and race discrimination, the threat to their jobs from automation or other rationalizations in the workplace, and a lack of participation and control make them primary objects of concern for the mainline churches. More important, they may have keen and deeply felt insights into the purpose and future reshaping of work that would be exceptionally useful to the churches as they formulate theological and programmatic responses.

A second weakness in the response of the mainline churches to the recent economic dislocation derives form its origin with mainly white workers and mainly white church leadership. This leadership has tended to see the crisis in the workplace through the eyes of, say, a white autoworker who lost his or her job, to the neglect of the large segment of people who, though of working age, have never worked in the first place. With considerable justification, those in and beyond the churches concerned with the latter group can claim that the poorest in society have been neglected by this new manifestation of concern, and that racism is also involved.

In partial defense of those responding to economic dislocation, it must be pointed out that a very large number of the millions of displaced blue-collar workers in this country are blacks and Hispanics, and that, as indicated in a previous chapter, racism has operated in plant closures too. Nonetheless, the work of plant closure and other church-related groups has suffered from this myopia. Those in both mainline and minority-based churches who have championed the plight of the jobless poor through welfare and legislative advocacy must join with plant closure and economic dislocation projects and coalitions to address one common agenda: *the present and future of work, workers, and community.* In practice, this means that the agendas of restoring the "social safety net" and advocating major policy changes must become one.

In thinking about the specific role of the churches as strategy is planned, it may be instructive to reflect briefly on the churches' experience in the Monongahela Valley and Youngstown. The churches in both places (as in many other situations) began their involvement as providers or enablers of relief for unemployed workers and their families. As their awareness deepened, the church people directly engaged with the affected people examined the deeper causes, and in doing so began to be radicalized. They crossed the important line from church as provider-of-services to church as prophetic advocate. Crossing it, they began—especially in the Monongahela Valley—to experience what prophets have always experienced: rejection and ostracism as their church funding was cut off and the jobs of clergy threatened or terminated.

There is thus no doubting that in the present social context, churches and church people who cross over into advocacy from service can expect opposition. To those in the churches accustomed to peaceful dialogue over differences, the confrontational tactics used in the Monongahela Valley and other places come as a shock. Of course, there can be legitimate differences over specific tactics or objectives used in a given situation; perhaps these were and are present in the Monongahela Valley struggle. But the Achilles' heel of many mainline churches, especially affluent mainline churches, is that their clergy and laity invariably know and are comfortable with the life-style, ethics, and language of privileged people, while being far removed from the grit, oppression, and deprivation frequently experienced by workers. Thus the anger, grief, and hurt experienced by discharged workers and appropriated by sympathetic clergy come across as unmannerly arrogance and exaggeration when expressed in the comfort of a corporate boardroom or rector's study. The call for "dialogue" issued by the well-meaning but well-paid clergy of a posh parish is viewed as fence straddling, or worse, by angry and aggrieved clergy and workers.

This dynamic is in fact far from new. We need look no further back than the civil rights movement to see essentially the same argument. Blacks and Hispanics demanding equality were told they were too aggressive and were asking for too much, and that dialogue was needed instead. It was the genius and vision of Martin Luther King, Jr., to see that while dialogue was always welcome, only nonviolent resistance done with the deeper purpose of uniting the human family in brotherhood and sisterhood would move the hearts of people to accept the claims to equality of their brothers and sisters.

It is thus probably true that similar nonviolent resistance by workers and the unemployed and church people advocating the rights of such workers may now be called for. It may take various forms: occupation of a workplace, strikes, marches, boycotts, or other peaceful means to bring to public attention the plight of working people. In retrospect, we look at Gandhi and King as saints who nobly lifted the hearts and minds of people to new and lofty visions. That is in fact what they did. But we forget that the British regarded Gandhi as a dangerous rabble-rouser threatening basic societal stability and that many white Americans, including prominent churchmen, thought of King as a provocateur, communist, and breeder of violence. Might not the militant worker, priest, or minister who similarly calls for a new day that upsets the prevailing view of things be regarded as a champion of justice?

At the very least, our Christian history and our engagements with social change since the 1960s ought to suggest to us that, in the crisis facing workers and communities, we be open to new insights and new directions. Can the churches, thus reminded of their own history, bring themselves at least to support such advocacy efforts financially and in public statements? It is not necessary to agree totally with a given objective of a specific group (in fact criticism ought to be welcomed), but the principle ought to be honored that a prophetic voice ought to be heard, a new direction explored.

As the crisis in work and the workplace deepens, a gigantic

educational task must be undertaken. Several strategies must be launched:

First, as indicated above, church funding for new and ongoing action projects must substantially increase.

Second, internships, conferences, and seminars must be established and funded to enable church persons, particularly of college and post-college age, to test long-term vocations and involvement in the issues of work.

Third, our theological seminars and colleges, where the churches have a historic presence or influence (in both Roman Catholic and Protestant traditions), must begin to develop solid curricula relating work and economics to Christian tradition. They might explore, among other topics, the following:

- Work and human fulfillment.
- Capital and community in conflict and collaboration.
- Trade unions and their future in society.
- Workplace democracy and government planning.
- Technology and human values.
- The relationship of work to culture and family.

Fourth, the publication of materials relating to work for church-school curricula and adult study groups must begin as a major Christian education enterprise. This must enable the active participation of parishioners *as workers*. The learning value of this kind of give and take would be immense to the churches.

Most important, as heretofore emphasized, is the firsthand involvement of church persons themselves, both as workers and in solidarity with the specific struggles of workers in the workplace.

None of the strategies and opportunities mentioned here, or other strategies which may subsequently evolve, will be long sustained if they rely merely on their own rationale. This is especially true in the midst of such adverse conditions as currently prevail. Rather, the motive power for sustained and effective action over the long term must evolve out of a new vision of hope for the future of work, the worker, and a just community. Such a vision, at least for persons in the Christian tradition, is fueled from the power and promise of the gospel itself. That gospel proclaims work as sacred human activity and the just community as foretaste on earth of the kingdom of God. Through Old and New Testaments it establishes human history as the arena in which those divine plans are worked out. Human systems, philosophies, or specific political or social arrangements which interfere with that working out must be brought into question. Finally, the voices of working people struggling the world over for a new day and a new dignity for themselves and their families must be recognized by us as the voice of God calling us to join God in them.

Note

This is a chapter from *The Human Enterprise: A Christian Perspective on Work,* and is reprinted with permission from Leaven Press, P. O. Box 281, Kansas City, MO 64141-0281. Copyright © 1985 by Richard W. Gillett.

The Shoulds
and the Excluded Whys:
The U.S. Catholic Bishops
Look at the Economy

William K. Tabb

"The dignity of the human person, realized in community with others, is the criterion against which all aspects of economic life must be measured." Is this some socialist group calling for a "new cultural consensus" that all persons have rights in the economic sphere, condemning the concentrated privilege of power and wealth and laying out an alternative vision of "economic democracy"? No, it is the U.S. Catholic Bishops' pastoral letter on *Catholic Social Teaching and the U.S. Economy,* a first draft of which was issued in 1984, a second in 1985, with the final document to be completed in 1986. In most respects this document is more radical than anything that has been, or is likely to be, issued by any mainstream organization in the United States. It represents a major social democratic statement of the sort that we are not accustomed to in this country. This is not to say that it is very radical, however—in major respects it goes no further than Pope Leo XIII's 1891 *Rerum Novarum (On the Condition of Labor).* Sorting out the good news from the not such good news is therefore an important task, because by doing so we can learn much about the limits of renewal from above and about the influence of liberation theologies on the hierarchy of the U.S. Catholic church.

The bishops' statement is a mugwump document. Its project of investigating and judging present economic realities in the light of church social teachings is much needed, as is its implicit willingness to dialogue with the more radical implications of Latin American Liberation Theology, but it fails to have the courage of its convictions and risk the scorn that would result if it were truly to embrace a transformative conception of social justice and join the struggle to put it into practice by challenging economic institutions that are by their nature sinful. It may be that the bishops simply cannot bring themselves to take the next step, but it is likely that their stance is more willful than that, their belief in capitalism and its refor-mability much more secure.

In what follows I will first describe the statement more fully, review the criticism from the right and the left, and say a word about the way in which the statement could allow a more radical interpretation of aspects of theological doctrine. Finally, I will briefly explore the radical implications that can be drawn from the bishops' theological position.

The Bishops' "Shoulds" and the Political Economists' "Whys"

The U.S. Catholic bishops believe in redistributive liberalism. Accepting the logical premise that wealth must be created before it can be distributed, the bishops argue that capitalism is the most efficient system for producing wealth, but that that wealth should be produced by a reformed, more humane capitalism—that gov-ernment is needed to control greed and monopolistic tendencies, and to redistribute some portion of the economic product to those in need.

There is therefore a sharp disjuncture in the document between the theological section on Catholic social teaching and the other sections on economic policy. The former offers a strong and clear moral argument; the latter are limited and inadequate responses. Thus the bishops reject the possessive individualism that proclaims "I worked hard for my money, therefore I can do anything I want with it." No, they say, once our own needs are satisfied, the surplus must go to the poor. The hungry must be fed before the desires of the better-off are indulged. Yet because they stay within the frame-work of the liberal agenda, the bishops do not challenge the struc-tural evils which stand in such sharp contrast to their principles of justice; they never ask *why* things are the way they are (i.e., make a causal analysis of how economic institutions work), and therefore— and this is key—they never address the question of what economic system would allow this principle to operate as the social norm. The approach can therefore be seen as liberal, voluntarist, or utopian socialist, but certainly not Marxist (as some of their critics have charged), since the bishops' critique and goals are admirable, while the methods proposed for achieving them are totally inadequate and there is no *systemic* analysis of the way in which the U.S. economy works.

The bishops begin with a cogent discussion of the social justice teaching of the Catholic church, highlighting key biblical passages in both the Old and New Testaments, placing their pastoral within a wider Judeo-Christian context, and throughout combining a Catholic specificity with a broad ecumenical tone. The inclusiveness of the approach to moral teaching means that the document is congenial with a social democratic vision. It stresses the concept of inclusiveness: the justice of a community is measured by its degree of solidarity with the workers and the powerless, with those who create wealth by their labor and those who are scorned and marginalized. When wealth dominates, the bishops write, it becomes an idol, and the world a place where the possession of things reigns; our freedom to create is then denigrated.

The bishops describe how the United States falls short, by a substantial margin, of being a just society. They argue that current levels of unemployment are morally unjustified. The needs of the hungry and homeless must be met first—not last, or never. They include statistics: the richest 20 percent of Americans have more income than the bottom 70 percent, and that too is immoral. Racial and ethnic discrimination, the feminization of poverty, deindustrialization—all are condemned, and the arguments are persuasive.

The critique of our present welfare system is equally well done. The bishops argue that those mothers who prefer to stay home and care for their children should be able to do so, and should be paid to do it. They also argue that there should be jobs for all who want to work. They endorse the right of workers to form unions, with government encouragement. They understand that we live in a global community and that nation-states must not be allowed to deny or distort this; they therefore encourage international solidarity in terms of concern for sisters and brothers everywhere.

While to much of the American public this document sounds radical in its unfamiliar probing of the consequences of the operation of the economic system, in fact it is not, for the cause of the problem is seen to lie in a lack of concern and an individual selfishness, and the call for conversion is likewise personalistic in emphasis, addressed to the powerful, the decision makers, and the informed middle class. There is no analysis of how relations of production under capitalism are inherently exploitative, and how center and periphery are united by bonds of imperialism.

Yet such a stance is not outside the trajectory of important theological developments within the Catholic church elsewhere in the world. Indeed, the U.S. bishops stop far short of the implicit class analysis found in the Pope's own writing. Gregory Baum writes:

> It is no accident that the U.S. bishops either avoid or offer a minimalist interpretation of the social theories in *Laborem Exercens* that reflect John Paul II's critical and creative dialogue with Marxism. In particular, the U.S. bishops do not follow the teachings of the encyclical (1) that the person should be defined as worker and that human dignity is derived from human labor; (2) that workers are to be subjects, not objects, in the process of production; (3) that labor becomes alienated whenever workers are deprived of participation in the decisions that affect the work process and the use of the capital they produce; and (4) that commodity fetishism or the consumer mentality creates a distorted culture that prevents people from assuming responsibility for their existence and changing the historical conditions of their lives.[1]

Because the Pope himself has already developed these radicalizing conceptions of social relations, a different sort of discussion within the Catholic church could have been developed. But the U.S. bishops confined the debate to one with the conservative business community and those who embrace neoconservative, laissez-faire views. They address the powerful as agents of change, they believe that the world can be made better, and suggest that that alone is their goal. The profit motive, which they acknowledge is the driving force behind much of capitalism's wrongs, is to be moderated but not replaced. There is to be worker participation, but not worker control. Free trade and an open world economy are valued; the analysis of the transnational corporation stresses its potential for good, not its imperialist agenda.

The Conservative Catholic Response

Philip Lawler, a former Heritage Foundation official and president of the conservative U.S. Catholic Conference, a lay group, responded to the first draft of the bishops' statement by in effect telling the bishops to mind their own business and stay out of public discussions of economic policy. He wrote in the *Wall Street Journal*, "It is individuals—not economic systems—that face heaven or hell; so it is the business of the church to save individual souls. Bishops once focused on that."[2]

The editorial accompanying Lawler's blast called for equal time in every parish for a pro-free enterprise lay commissions report. The defense of liberty as an individualistic notion grounded in the alleged superiority of laissez-faire market mechanisms is of course at *odds* with centuries of Catholic social teaching.

Since the demise of feudal assumptions, Catholicism has never successfully provided a convincing alternative to capitalist ideology. As the bishops' statement and numerous papal encyclicals demonstrate, Catholic social teaching remains in profound tension with basic capitalist assumptions. What the conservative Catholics say is simply that the common good is best served by the magic of the market, which will provide growth, because a rising tide lifts all boats, and expanded moral responsibility through charity can meet the needs of those unable to contribute in the dynamic economy.

Both liberal and conservative Catholics—and most of their fellow citizens—accept this Kennedy formulation, but times of slow growth and global restructuring tend to give it a neoconservative translation: We cannot afford so much redistribution now because under current conditions it would come at the expense of growth. There is therefore a necessary trade-off between efficiency and equity. We need supply-side solutions. We need growth to help everybody. Corporations bring jobs, and growth, only if they can invest. We therefore need to help them invest more. The poor must wait. It we help the poor first, they and the rest of us will suffer in the not so long run.

Important elements within the Catholic business community, which organized effectively and had easy access to the media, were exceedingly important in defining how the bishops' statement was understood by the public. The Catholic Lay Commission, chaired by William Simon, former secretary of the treasury, and including as members J. Peter Grace, Alexander Haig, and Claire Booth Luce, issued an alternative report even before the first draft of the statement was made public—an obvious effort to claim an equal role in making pronouncements for (and to) Catholics. Much of the media then treated the two statements together, as part of a debate, thus proving the bishops correct in their analysis of the power and influence money can buy: could thirty welfare mothers or thirty steelworkers have received the media coverage that the Lay Commission document received?

The conservatives' criticism of the bishops' statement—both the first and second drafts—centered around the assertion that the free market is not acceptable as the final arbiter of the allocation of resources in a just society. The conservatives were supported in their defense of the market system by much of the press. A typical reaction was that of *New York Times* economic columnist Leonard Silk:

> The bishops have been modest about their expertise in economics, and their critics will say they have much to be modest about. Certainly there is room to question the bishops emphasis on economic planning, which would be likely to breed inefficiency by substituting political decisions for those of business people, who are better judges of their own problems and opportunities.[3]

In one swift stroke, Silk ignores the economic success of such countries as Sweden and Germany, where political intervention plays a large role in economic policy, and where the "problems and opportunities" are understood to affect *all* citizens, not simply businesspeople. Indeed, the bishops seem to have had such European social democratic practices in mind as they wrote. Only by denying the overall movement toward planning under contemporary capitalism can Silk and other critics be so dismissive of what is in any case only mildly hinted at by the bishops. The bishops, having made it quite clear that they do not have a Soviet-type economic model in mind, are subject to pink-baiting, a milder but none-too-subtle form of red-baiting.

When the first draft of the bishops' statement appeared, many conservative critics objected to what the *Wall Street Journal* called a "view of morality and justice derived from the tables found in the U.S. Statistical Abstract—a sort of means test morality based on an analysis of income percentiles," so that in the end "the bishops' view of American society is reduced almost entirely to numbers." This is an amazing accusation, for although the document does contain facts and figures, they are used to demonstrate the validity of carefully weighed statements about general moral principles and specific church teachings, which is surely the scholarly way of doing things. Is it wrong to call the percentage of the population living in poverty a "social and moral scandal," or to refer to the current level of unemployment as "morally unjustified"? Yes, for mainstream economists and defenders of U.S. capitalism in general it is, because for them inequality acts as an incentive, a spur to the poor to take jobs, a reward to the rich to come up with better mousetraps. And since in the end the statement does call for *measurable* change, perhaps that is what the conservatives really object to.

The Lay Commission report defends the profit motive as the proper central steering mechanism for our economy. "Profit is more than an accounting concept," they write. "It is better understood as a reward for risk-taking and invention, as an incentive for creative growth. Whoever favors development declares for profit. In this sense, the common good requires profit, for without it the needs of the many cannot be met."

According to the commission, the spirit of enterprise is a "needed addition" to Catholic social teaching, and there is not, as Pope John Paul II wrote in his encyclical *On Labor,* a necessary "priority of labor over capital": "The fact of widespread unemployment shows beyond a doubt that, as an efficient cause, labor is not prior to capital but, on the contrary, requires new investment as its own prior cause."

The Response from the Catholic Left

The U.S. bishops' statement said that people are not things, but God's children, and should not be secondary to the preservation and enhancement of things, capital, or wealth, as claimed by the rich. In the face of obvious suffering, morality requires that basic needs be met in a way respecting the dignity of those receiving help.

Could the bishops have gone further? They seem to believe not. They are not economists. They set out moral teachings and expect experts, economists and others, to be convinced by their moral arguments and provide the technical answers consistent with these moral teachings. This stance is encouraged by the intimidating outcry by conservatives when the bishops endorse liberal policy measures to foster the goals of social justice.

Yet the bishops' cautious stance can be contrasted with that contained in a statement on the economy made by a group of Canadian bishops, and with the statements issued by the several conferences of Latin American bishops.

The Canadian bishops are equally clear that the pursuit of profit is *not* the pursuit of the common good, but they spell out in much more detail—with footnote references (omitted in the quote below) to the work of dependency theorists Andre Gunder Frank and Samir Amin, as well as John Paul II and Paul VI—the impact of using the profit motive as a guide to economic choice. The market does not automatically allocate resources in the best possible way. I quote them at some length to make clear a line of development it would be possible for the U.S. bishops to have taken:

> The present recession appears to be symptomatic of a much larger structural crisis in the international system of capitalism. Observers point out that profound changes are taking place in the structure of both capital and technology which are bound to have serious social

impacts on labor. We are now in an age, for example, where transnational corporations and banks can move capital from one country to another in order to take advantage of cheaper labor conditions, lower taxes, and reduced environmental restrictions. We are also in an age of automation and computers where human work is rapidly being replaced by machines on the assembly line and in administrative centers. In effect, capital has become transnational and technology has become increasingly capital-intensive. The consequences are likely to be permanent or structural unemployment and increasing marginalization for a large segment of the population in Canada and other countries. In this context, the increasing concentration of capital and technology in the production of military armaments further intensifies this economic crisis, rather than bringing about recovery.

Indeed, these structural changes largely explain the nature of the current economic recession at home and throughout the world. While there does not appear to be a global shortage *per se*, large scale banks and corporations continue to wait for a more profitable investment climate. Many companies are also experiencing a temporary shortage of investment funds required for the new technology, due largely to an over extension of production and related factors. In order to restore profit margins needed for new investment, companies are cutting back on production, laying-off workers, and selling off their inventories. The result has been economic slow-down and soaring unemployment. To stimulate economic growth, governments are being called upon to provide a more favorable climate for private investments. Since capital tends to flow wherever the returns are greatest, reduced labor costs and lower taxes are required if countries are to remain competitive. As a result, most governments are introducing austerity measures such as wage restraint programs, cut-backs in social services and other reductions in social spending in order to attract more private investment. And, to enforce such economic policies some countries have introduced repressive measures for restraining civil liberties and controlling unrest.[4]

This document reflects, while the U.S. document has only the most distant glimpses of, the influence of Latin American Liberation Theology. The Canadian bishops provided a prophetic reading of the signs of the times, from a periphery-of-the-core perspective, which Gregory Baum has described as follows:

> The Canadian reader notices a difference in the understanding of "the preferential option for the poor." In the U.S. pastoral, the option refers to a principle of social ethics that must be taken into account in the making of public policy. In Latin American and Canadian ecclesiastical documents, the option is given a slightly more radical interpretation: It signifies a double commitment—to look upon society from the perspective of its victims (the epistemological dimension) and to give public witness of solidarity with their struggle for justice

(the activist dimension). According to my reading, the Latin American and the Canadian option for the poor expresses an aspect of discontinuity, a break from the recognized view, a conversion, an emancipatory commitment, which serves as guide even among various social theories and methods of economic research. The option for the poor is here more than a principle that should direct public policies within the inherited institutions; it expresses a more radical imperative, in some instances, to support a political struggle to change the inherited institutions.[5]

Consistent with the Canadian Catholic bishops, and to some extent also inspired by the Latin American bishops—whose bold denunciations of "institutional sin" and radical reading of the gospel from the side of the poor did not find a place in the U.S. statement—North American Catholics have also offered constructive criticisms of the first draft of the statement. (These criticisms were not successful in stimulating changes in the second draft of the pastoral, however.) In the words of the Center for Concern, an important focus of progressive social analysis within the Catholic community, a key problem with the document was that it contained "no overall analysis of why these problems arise and what the *interconnectedness* of the several problems might be. . . . more focused analysis is needed on why things are as they are and what obstacles we face to change the situation." The Center's analysis argued that the "theological reflection offered in the first section does not grow out of a situation experienced and analyzed. The draft begins with only a very minimal reading of the 'signs of the times' and then offers substantial biblical perspectives and ethical norms. The biblical insights, moreover, are not integrated into the central reasoning of the document when applications are discussed."[6]

The language of the Center's critique is awkward and grammatically convoluted, perhaps reflecting self-imposed restraints that the critics feel necessary in an institution which, despite rather dramatic signs of new direction, is still a profoundly conservative and hierarchical body, one that although it invites comment and criticism, can easily marginalize those who are believed to be asking it to move too far, too fast. Leading the Catholic church is like driving a huge, clumsy ship that does not change direction easily: the momentum of the past is not easily overcome. Yet the Catholic church is not the single powerful corporate body it once was; it is riddled with internal dissension. Because it is the Catholic church, formal splits are unlikely to lead to new denominations, as among Protestants, but the strains are nevertheless great. The predominantly white, and exclusively male, hierarchy is being pressed to respond to the needs of diverse currents among the laity, the priests, and the women religious, many of whom work with and are committed to the poor. Bishops also raise money from, and are influenced by, the powerful, who as individuals may be antagonistic to any reform, but may also be socially concerned.

The Catholic church today is thus an important arena of class struggle. As an institution, it does not automatically side with the powerful; nor do its members, who are no longer predominantly conservative Southerners and Eastern Europeans, recent immigrants who need to prove their loyalty to this country. Many have moved up into the mainstream. Some of these, now accepted as Americans, can partake more critically in discussions of what kind of America this will be. Others are unemployed industrial workers. The recent Catholic immigrants are Latin Americans and their churches know of the alternative message of Liberation Theology. Thus in the context of eccesiastical politics, the Center's criticisms are much needed because for a movement to develop in North America that is broadly analogous (bearing in mind the profoundly different historic conjuncture) to Liberation Theology in Latin America, the church hierarchy needs to relate to a model of doing theology which begins from the situation experienced by communities of believers. Such a theological orientation uses versions of the pedagogy of the oppressed, written about by Paolo Friere and others, and actualized in the methods of developing self-awareness through collective Bible study and community-building by believers acting in communities akin to the Latin American base Christian communities. To integrate biblical insights and a reading of the "signs of the times," the realities of life, into an overall analysis of how societies function to deny the claims of the oppressed, and to be empowered by the word of God to take sides, as he does, with the poor, the marginalized, the exploited—that God's will is a just society—this is a revolutionary message for the United States today, as it is for the rest of the world. It is a revolutionary message of hope.

Evaluating the Pastoral

There are, then, at least two ways of interpreting the bishops' pastoral. On the one hand, it can be seen as historically progressive. It has put the concern for social justice back on the agenda for public debate and implicitly criticizes the worst excesses of the Reagan administration and the neo-liberal Democrats. If it were to gain a broad and honest hearing, it could contribute significantly to moving our country off the conservative path. At the same time, the bishops have been realistic: while not compromising their religious teachings on social questions, they have written the document so that it will be as effective as possible in a country where most people form their opinions from the mass media and operate in a framework that is profoundly (if often unthinkingly) patriotic, favors individualistic solutions, and is hostile to the very word socialism.

The second way of looking at the document is less sympathetic. This view suggests that the institutional church is more a part of the problem than of the solution: that urging class collaboration and a moral economy within the capitalist frame of reference misspecifies both the reality of class and the defining characteristics of capitalism as a system. Thus solutions based on appeals to the common interest and the general good—a moral approach—can only yield limited results, because capitalists have only limited reservoirs of good will. Such solutions are therefore impossible under capitalism, defined as it is by the private control of the resources necessary for well-being—ownership by some gives them the "right" to extract profits from the labor of others. This runs totally counter to the biblical demand for justice, which must be a demand for an end to capitalism. Capitalist society cannot be a just society. Similarly, the dependent status of the poor nations of the world will not be relieved by more of the same sort of "help" from the United States. What is needed is more autonomous development within the context of a profound reshaping of interdependence to create just relations among equals. Oppressive military regimes exist for a reason, and serve certain narrow interests. Yet the bishops do not acknowledge this fundamental reality, any more than they acknowledge the other contradictions of the capitalist system.

This may be true, but it portrays a point of view that sees Catholicism from a highly selective perspective, one that minimizes changes in the church over time. Like the state and the trade union movement, the churches are an important arena of class struggle: the ideologies that justify capitalist economic relations are internalized in the structures and belief systems of all these institutions, as well as in the minds of the women and men who interact in and with them.

Although the bishops' statement is less radical and prophetic than many might like, it is nevertheless an exceedingly important step forward for the institutional church, not only in its strong endorsement of principled liberalism at a time when such support is weak, but also because the bishops have chosen a method for developing their statement that goes beyond usual Roman Catholic practice. If process is part of the message, the manner in which the bishops invited input into the formation of the statement from a variety of economists and business leaders, Catholic and not, and then subjected the first draft to the slings and arrows of public criticism, shows an openness to democratic process that could have far-reaching implications for the prospects of greater internal democracy in church matters in general. In fact, the democratic process implied in the method may be as important ecclesiastically as the economics of the letter is politically. In both areas, liberal steps have been taken.

Not surprisingly, even this consultative process has been criticized from within the church. In an article in *Le Libre Belgique,* Michel Schooyans, an advisor to the Pope, claimed that because the process includes a broad dialogue, it weakens the teaching authority of the church hierarchy. Joseph Cardinal Ratzinger, prefect of the Vatican Congregation of the Doctrine of the Faith (the current name for the Inquisition) went even further and denied that a national episcopal conference (in this case, the U.S. Catholic Conference) had any authority to teach on such subjects at all—in the process contradicting some of his own earlier writings and various Vatican and papal policy statements.[7] The chair of the committee that drafted the statement, Archbishop Rembert Weakland, responded by implicitly criticizing such a view:

> Underneath this criticism is a definite concept of ecclesiology. Its proponents see a strongly hierarchical model of church, where the faithful are taught by the bishops, who are in possession of the gifts of the Spirit needed for such authoritative teaching. The model adopted by the U.S. conference believes that the Holy Spirit resides in all members of the church and that the hierarchy must listen to what the Spirit is saying to the whole church. This does not deny the teaching role of the hierarchy, but enhances it. It does not weaken the magisterium, but ultimately strengthens it. Discernment, not just innovation or self-reliance, becomes a part of the teaching process.[8]

How we describe our reality—which aspects we focus on and which we turn a blind eye to—defines what we believe exists. For this reason description and analysis are not separate steps of knowing and deciding. Nor can commitment be separated from knowing and making judgments. As they continue their reflection upon, and consequent involvement in, the quest for economic justice, the U.S. Catholic bishops (like the rest of us) may be pulled—sometimes even against their will—in unexpected directions. Who would have thought that the Latin American bishops would have moved so far so fast? Who in the 1950s would have dreamed that the U.S. bishops would adopt the rudiments of social democracy in 1985? To the religious left the new directions being taken by the church hierarchy are a sign of renewal, of recommitment to the old gospel tenants that promise good news to the poor. Secular critics would do well to be more sensitive to the fact of this wrestling with an issue within the established church and not to preclude the possibility of meaningful movement. Theirs is a theologically mugwump document, its thrust, while hardly a radical embracing of Liberation Theology, is historically progressive and so we have genuine, if qualified, enthusiasm for what they have done.

Notes

1. Gregory Baum, "A Canadian Perspective on the U.S. Pastoral," *Christianity & Crisis,* 21 January 1985, p. 517. See also his essay in this volume.
2. "At Issue Is the Prophet Motive," *Wall Street Journal,* 13 November 1984, p. 32.
3. Leonard Silk, "Bishops' Letter and U.S. Goals," *New York Times,* 14 November 1984, p. D2.
4. Canadian Conference of Catholic Bishops, *Ethical Reflections on the Economic Crisis,* available from CCCB, 90 Parent Avenue, Ontario, Canada KIN 7BI.
5. Baum, "A Canadian Perspective," p. 517.
6. The Team of the Center of Concern, "U.S. Bishops on the Economy: An Exciting and Challenging Call," *Central Focus* (January 1985): 2. The Center for Concern is an independent interdisciplinary team engaged in social analysis, religious reflection, and public education around social justice questions. Its address is 3700 13th Street NE, Washington, DC 20017.
7. Jesuit theologian Avery Dulles documents this in *America* magazine, 11 June 1983. See also Baum in this volume.
8. Cited by James E. Hug, "The Catholic Bishops Pick Up Another Bomb," *Christian & Crisis,* 1 October 1984, pp. 346–47.

This Is Sanctuary:
A Reformation in Our Time

Paul Burks

Sanctuary: n., historically a place of refuge or protection; in Roman and English law fugitives from justice were immune from arrest in churches and other sacred places.

They call them coyotes. They prey on people who are in desperate straits. They are in the business of smuggling. Their cargo is not highly valued illegal cocaine or marijuana for affluent Americans. It is human beings. There is a demand for the coyotes' services because of something called a border—an artificial barrier stretching from the Pacific Ocean to the Gulf of Mexico, a barrier which separates mostly Anglo "haves" from mostly Hispanic "have nots." Like guards in a jail, most coyotes would prefer to make their living some other way than preying on vulnerable "illegals."

They call it the Sonoran desert. Even in winter it swelters during the day and freezes at night. Bone dry to boot, it is barren and hostile to humans who come to it well prepared. It is deadly to those who do not.

You probably read about the tragic incident in 1980 when a coyote took what little money that twenty-six Salvadorans in family groups had, guided them across the border near Nogales, Arizona, by night, took them far enough into the Sonoran desert that they could not find their way back—and deserted them. Within days, half of them—men, women, and children—had died a horrible death; the other half, surviving by drinking their own urine, struggled northward until spotted and helped by a rancher near Tucson.

I met John Fife, forty-five year old pastor of Southside Presbyterian Church, at an Inter-American conference which attracted

1,300 concerned church people, from all over the United States to Tucson, Arizona. The focus of the conference was the plight of Central American refugees.

"It was this tragic incident in the desert in 1980," John Fife told me, "which caused me and other area pastors to get involved. The survivors were bought to Tucson hospitals. We engaged our congregations—Protestant and Catholic—in assisting them. In time we asked them what on earth they were doing two thousand miles from their villages in El Salvador. That's when the incredible stories of terrorism, torture, and death squads in their country began to come out. That's how growing numbers of church people in the Tucson area, through first-hand contact with these refugees, became aware of and sympathetic to these traumatized, exhausted Salvadoran and Guatemalan families. We learned that they were fleeing the violence in their homelands, leaving behind friends, jobs, and whatever possessions they had to seek temporary asylum in the United States. And that's how we became aware that our government, for some reasons, did not want these people here in the United States, even temporarily."

On January 14, 1985, in coordinated raids, federal agents swept down on sixty Salvadoran and Guatemalan refugees in five cities across the United States—Phoenix, Tucson, Seattle, Philadelphia, and Rochester, NY. They were arrested, booked as "illegal aliens," and released on bail or "personal recognizance" pending court action.

Later that day other federal agents—like coyotes, not all are happy with their job—sought out and handed grand jury indictments to sixteen persons who work with a nationwide church-based movement to provide sanctuary in the United States to Salvadoran and Guatemalan refugees who have fled the religious persecution, political repression, and armed strife in their countries. Among these sixteen church people charged with smuggling, transporting, or harboring illegal aliens are two Roman Catholic priests, three nuns, and one Protestant minister—John Fife, pastor of Southside Presbyterian Church in Tucson.

The sixty refugees arrested, all of whom were assisted to find shelter in the United States by one or more of the sixteen, were named by the grand jury as unindicted co-conspirators. Another twenty church-related U.S. citizens were named unindicted co-conspirators in order to gain their testimony against the sixteen in lieu of prosecution.

What lies behind this strong move of the federal government against grass roots church people—lay and clergy?

• In every case the refugees arrested were persons who had fled the violence in their homeland, violence which has taken over forty thousand Salvadoran and twenty thousand Guatemalan lives since January 1980. (These numbers include the life of Catholic Archbishop Oscar Romero in 1980. They do not include four American women—three nuns and one lay worker—who were abducted and killed by Salvadoran soldiers, also in 1980.)

• In every case the refugees had lost children, brothers or sisters, parents, relatives, or friends to soldiers or death squads and had "a well-founded fear of persecution," believing they would be killed if they did not flee. This is the wording of the Refugee Act of 1980, the U.S. law which says refugees who flee to this country under those conditions shall be granted asylum until those life-threatening conditions in their homelands have ceased.

• In every case the refugees are here as sojourners, wishing to return to their homeland, friends, extended family, and jobs just as soon as conditions permit. In total it is estimated that 200,000 Salvadorans and Guatemalans have fled the violence in their countries and sought safety in the United States since 1980.

• In every case the refugees were living in a church facility or with a church family in their home or in an apartment found for them (and the rent paid monthly) by a church committee.

• In every case the refugee family is voluntarily sharing their story, speaking to interested groups in the area of their sponsoring church about the situation which caused them to flee their homeland. (It is their message about a violent, repressive government and military—funded in significant part by the United States—that probably led to Immigration and Naturalization Service (INS) agents singling them out for arrest in the government crackdown on the sanctuary movement.)

• In every case the refugee family had been helped by a network of church people—called the sanctuary movement—which extends from the Mexico border to congregations in the northwest, midwest, and northeast. This network has been likened to the "underground railroad" of the Civil War era which helped slaves escape to the safety and freedom of the northern states. A common first stop on this railroad in Arizona is Southside Presbyterian Church which, according to John Fife, has assisted 1,500 Salvadoran and Guatemalan refugees since it became the first church in the United States to publicly declare itself a sanctuary on March 24, 1982.

• Of the sixty arrested, fifteen had been together the night before as a Bible study group in the basement of a Phoenix church, forming a BCC (Base Christian Community) similar to those in which most of them participated in their home communities.

How was the evidence provided to the grand jury, which met in secret, obtained? Since the actions of sanctuary congregations have been announced in formal press conferences and all meetings have been open to the public, there was no need for the INS or the grand jury to struggle to gain evidence that those indicted had assisted "illegal aliens." However, as the *New York Times* reported in its front page story of January 15: "The indictments were based in part on evidence gathered by four undercover agents who, wearing concealed tape recorders, attended church meetings in Tucson. There they taped discussions helping people flee from El Salvador and Guatemala to the United States." Two of these four "informants" were refugees themselves, hired and paid by the INS to gather data. The information helped INS agents arrest their fellow refugees and to indict those church people assisting them. (The refugee informants probably helped in return for not deporting them back to the violence they had fled. Deporting is done in 97.5 percent of the cases of Salvadorans who request asylum and 99 percent of Guatemalan requests.)

What was the response of those indicted to the actions and charges of the INS and the federal grand jury?

"It is not the sanctuary movement but the U.S. government which is breaking the law. So said John Fife and the other fifteen persons indicted. So says every other person involved in the movement, including some 160 "declared sanctuary" churches across the United States plus over 1000 churches that are supporting the official sanctuary congregations.

They point out that the United Nations Convention and the 1967 protocol agreements on refugees—both signed by the United States—establish the right to refugees *not* to be sent back to their countries of origin. The protocol states: "No contracting party shall expel or forcibly return a refugee in any manner whatsoever to the frontiers of territories where his life or freedom would be threatened on account of his race, religion, nationality, membership of a particular social group or political opinion."

In addition they cited the U.S. Refugee Act of 1980—mentioned above—which requires the granting of temporary asylum to those applicants who have a well-grounded fear of persecution should they be forcibly returned to their homeland.

In response, the Reagan administration contends that the vast majority of asylum applicants from Central America are fleeing poverty, not persecution—simply seeking to better themselves economically. The administration makes no attempt to explain why hundreds of thousands began a chaotic exodus from El Salvador and Guatemala when right-wing repressive governments, supported by the administration, took over in 1980. (The administration also fails to explain what sanctuary workers have long noticed—that the numbers who are fleeing wax and wane with the level of violence in these two countries.)

Of the methods used by the U.S. Justice Department, John Fife observed that the government had placed our INS agents in his church in Tucson, "people who represented themselves as church members working with the ministry." They were equipped with electronic listening devices to gather information on the movement.

"I've always known that in Russia the government put agents in churches to spy on pastors," Fife added. "It's a very sad day. I don't know of any precedent" for such surveillance in the United States.

What has been the reaction to this unprecedented action by the federal government against a grassroots, mainstream church movement with member churches from fourteen denominations—Protestant, Catholic, Unitarian, and Jewish—now found in thirty states all across the United States?

In spite of the fact that support of the movement means knowingly breaking the law (as the Reagan administration is interpreting it), a number of major church groups, including Methodists and Presbyterians, have actually endorsed the sanctuary movement. Most other mainstream denominations have issued statements of strong support for the faith-based action of these Christians on behalf of the poor and oppressed. No denomination, to my knowledge, has taken a strong stand in opposition to the sanctuary movement or the participants' actions.

In politically conservative Phoenix, eight hundred people marched through downtown to the federal building in support of the six indictees who were arraigned there on January 23. Some saw the turnout as evidence that this movement, and the harsh government reaction to it, are uniting church people right across the political spectrum.

On the negative response side, Alan Nelson, director of the INS, has said of the sanctuary movement: "This is not a religious ministry; it is a political movement." INS has also said it has no plans to alter its investigation methods, as approved by the U.S. Justice Department and sanctioned by the courts.

The most difficult response to hear was that of refugees in sanctuaries. A Salvadoran mother who lives at University Baptist Church in Seattle said, "It's impossible to sleep. My nerves are just so tight. They could come here and get us, too."

Frustration, that's what brought sanctuary into being. John Fife in Tucson and Lutheran pastor Gus Schultz in Berkeley, California, almost simultaneously saw the applicability of the ancient church's approach to injustice to the tragic situation of Salvadoran and Guatemalan refugees. By the spring of 1982, pastors and congregation members in Tucson, Los Angeles, and the Bay Area were aware that every week *hundreds* of Central Americans were being apprehended by INS agents and shipped back to El Salvador and Guatemala, to the increased government persecution, probable torture—even death—in retaliation for fleeing. The founder of the modern underground railroad, rancher Jim Corbett—a Tucson-area Quaker, acting in the tradition of Quakers who assisted slaves to flee the South—told me of an entire planeload of refugees who were slaughtered by government troops in 1982 at the San Salvador airport after they left the U.S.-based, INS-funded plane.

For two years Fife, Corbett, and dozens of others, working through the Tucson Ecumenical Council, had driven hundreds of trips to the INS deportation facility in the California desert at El Centro, had bailed out hundreds of Central Americans, and had helped them fill out the complex applications for asylum—only to have 97 to 99 percent of them refused and the individual or family flown back to sure persecution, possible death. The government was not changing its incredibly harsh policy one bit. Over $750,000 had been raised and spent on bail, travel costs, and court fees in this process. How long can you beat your head against a stone wall?

In January 1982 Jim Corbett was invited to submit testimony to a National Council of Churches consultation on immigration meeting in Washington, D.C. He spoke about the 100,000 to 200,000 Salvadorans who, since January 1980, had fled their country, attempted to settle in poverty-stricken Mexico, and, unable to sustain themselves and their families there, had made their way to the United States. Out of his unique role assisting these frightened, exhausted people, he had learned what was going on in El Salvador and Central America. This was his testimony.

"These people are fleeing from military and death squad violence, from guerrilla violence, and from what might be termed bushwhacker violence, but *the situation's generative feature is that their government has instituted a program of systematic terrorism calculated to traumatize the populace into acceptance of established patterns of rule.* In much of Latin America, similar programs of military terrorism exist and are being further developed under a unifying U.S. sponsorship that combines massive arms build-ups, extensive military training, advanced intelligence technology, regional integration of military forces, and destabilization of governments considered politically incompatible. Consequently, the Salvadorans are probably only the first wave of an influx of Latin American refugees fleeing this military terrorism who will reach the United States through Mexico during this decade."

He went on to define what response is needed from the church. "The most urgent need of the vast majority of Salvadoran refugees in the United States is to avoid capture. . . . With people in our midst being hunted down and shipped back, denouncing the terror while ignoring the victims simply teaches the public how to live with atrocity." Jim's ringing call to action was expressed in these words: "Much more than the fate of the undocumented refugees depends on the religious community's participation and leadership in helping them avoid capture. *If the right to aid fugitives from government-sponsored terror is not upheld in action by the churches—regardless of the cost in terms of imprisoned clergy, punitive fines, and exclusion from government-financed programs—the loss of many other basic rights of conscience will certainly follow.*

Two months after Jim Corbett's testimony, Southside Presbyterian Church in Tucson and five churches in Berkeley, California, publicly declared themselves to be sanctuaries for "illegal" Central American refugees: St. John's Presbyterian, University Lutheran Chapel, Trinity United Methodist, St. Marks Episcopal, and Holy Spirit Newman Parish (Catholic). The date was March 24, 1982, the second anniversary of the assassination of El Salvador's outspoken Archbishop, Oscar Romero. Thus was born the public sanctuary movement which has captured the imagination of 50,000 Christians in 160 churches across the nation. In every case the congregation's decision arose from firsthand contact with the refugee victims, from Bible study, and from congregational grappling with a difficult situation in our time.

Less than three years after the movement was publicly initiated, ironically or perhaps by plan on the same day as the first nationwide gathering of sanctuary movement people on January 23, the federal government decided that "they were going to have to deal with us" and acted. On that day, John Fife and Jim Corbett were arraigned in federal court along with fourteen other key sanctuary workers, mostly in Arizona.

Who is this tall, lanky Tucson pastor who with Southside Presbyterian Church made the decision to declare the church a sanctuary?

This pastor, known in church circles across the United States as founder of the sanctuary movement, is a soft-spoken, outgoing, unassuming man, very much at ease as he talks with refugees, with coworkers, with national reporters, and with me. He is a husband, father of two boys ages 16 and 20, and manages to balance his family life and his ministry. He is pastor, for fifteen years now, of Southside Church, which was honored with the 1984 Peace Seeker Award of the Presbyterian Peace Fellowship—"for its ministry in support of refugee victims of the violence in El Salvador and Guatemala."

A big, well-funded congregation? Hardly. "We have 137 members including blacks and Hispanics, Native Americans from three tribes, and a mix of Anglos, some of whom retired to Arizona from icy northern states," Fife said of his multiethnic, bilingual, economically and educationally diverse congregation. "Worship, Bible study and prayer are the center of our life together as we support one another and try to live lives faithful to the Gospel. We currently have seven refugees being housed in our sanctuary, nine in other churches, and four in private homes. When congregation members are asked to help these frightened, fleeing people and have met them face to face, there is little problem in getting them to respond. When Jim Corbett asked us to house some of the many families he was trying to help in late 1981 and early 1982, we had a month's worth of discussion and education, prayer and bible study, then voted by secret ballot—so no one would be intimidated—to declare our church a public sanctuary. Only two members voted against this action."

After this decision, John Fife visited Central America with a group of U.S. church people. He observed not only the conditions under which they live but also the key role in their lives played by their faith, the Bible, and the base Christian communities in which they meet weekly—at the risk of their lives.

"On this trip, already being a Presbyterian minister and pastor of a church, I can honestly say that I was converted to the Christian faith. Since Vatican II in 1963 and the Latin American Bishop's conference at Medellín, Colombia, in 1968, a grassroots Christian reformation has been under way in the church in many of those countries. People's lives are transformed by what they read, for the first time, in the Bible. Following its many examples, they rise up together and question the oppression under which they are forced to live. A new church is emerging in Central America, ecumenical in nature and the sanctuary movement arising in this country is a very clear part of that reformation. The church, to be the church of Jesus Christ, must identify itself with the poor and become poor itself. The church must share with its brothers and sisters and identify with them in their suffering."

The number of frightened "illegal aliens" assisted very personally by Southside stands at 1,500 and rises daily. It has decided where it stands in the growing conflict between the Christian faith and government policy. It has been infiltrated by government agents. The secret grand jury has singled out two members of the Southside Church family, John Fife and Philip Willis-Conger, for prosecution. Their trial lies ahead. In the meantime, their assistance to "illegal aliens" continues unabated.

And who is Jim Corbett? There are many answers. He is the rancher, retired early by gnarled, arthritic hands. He is the Quaker who is called the father of the new underground railroad, the man who asked John Fife and Southside to "get involved." He is the man who, with Fife, when they were overflowing with fleeing refugees, contacted the Chicago Religious Task Force on Central America and asked them to "build an underground railroad." He saw this "railroad" as a series of safe havens stretching from the Southwest to the Midwest and on to the Northeast. And this ecumenical group, which has become so crucial to the sanctuary movement, did just that.

Jim Corbett is a coyote, one of the best, because his faith tells him to do it, with no personal gain involved at all. He, Fife, and Willis-Congers are crucial parts of the Tucson Ecumenical Council, without which the development of the sanctuary movement would have been inconceivable. He is the man who, in January 1982, challenged the National Council of Churches to *act* on behalf of undocumented refugees—and two months later the sanctuary movement got under way in Tucson and Berkeley.

Most of all, Jim Corbett is the man who, with his wife and co-worker Pat, saw the suffering of Salvadorans and Guatemalans, was angered by government refusal to accept them into the United States, and *acted* in 1981 to create an apartment in their home to house frightened refugees seeking safety and help. He and Pat, not the Statue of Liberty, first "lifted their lamp by the golden door" at the Mexican border. In 1984 he and Pat received the Letelier-Moffitt Memorial Human Rights Award for their work on behalf of Central American refugees and their role in creating the sanctuary movement.

The moral authority of Jim Corbett's statements and actions emerge directly from his extensive sojourns with refugees. He insists that his own coyote activity pales before the courage of the actual refugees and Mexican church communities who harbor them. He has heard so many refugee stories of lives sacrificed for others that he feels he has come to experience the meaning of the cross. Like John Fife, Jim Corbett speaks of "the vitalization of religious community—an ecumenically inclusive community—which is now arriving among us in Anglo America. It is not arriving as a new theology or creed or ritual, but in person, as a Central American refugee." It led to his indepth ministry with the sanctuary movement and to John Fife's conversion. It will hopefully produce an entirely new spirit in this troubled land of ours.

Note

This article is taken from *Sequoia: The Church at Work,* newspaper of the Northern California Ecumenical Council. Copyright © 1985 by Sequoia.

Somewhere over the Rainbow: Religion, Class, and Ethnicity in Coalition Politics

Sheila D. Collins

The 1984 presidential campaign of Jesse Jackson and the Rainbow Coalition—the centerpiece of its ideology and the premise of its organizing strategy—offers the secular left and the progressive church a way out of the dilemma posed by the failure of class-based politics to win over the majority of the American people to a transformative agenda. The Jackson campaign planted the seeds for a new kind of moral premise and created a political organizing vehicle appropriate to the history, the cultural context, and the present socioeconomic realities of the United States. For a progressive movement of any significance to emerge in this nation, it will have to understand and appropriate the lessons of that campaign experience.[1]

One of the most important of these lessons is that religion has become, once again, a major means of political mobilization, as it was in the first four decades of the eighteenth century. There is a kind of holy war going on for the soul of the American people. On the one side is the religious right and its political allies, with its racist, sexist, jingoistic, and apocalyptic mythology. On the other side are the excluded, oppressed, and colonized peoples in the United States and much of the third world, who view the world and its future from a very different perspective than do those in the religious right but who nevertheless also view it in religious terms.

The Jackson campaign began to draw these excluded worldviews together into a coherent moral vision and political platform that could contend for state power. In doing so, the campaign challenged not only the religious right's attempts to conform American political institutions to its own image, but also challenged long accepted white liberal and left ideas about the proper role of religion in American life.

The political and religious liberalism which has dominated U.S. society at least since the latter half of the nineteenth century maintains that religion and politics are separate spheres that cannot, and should not, mix. But while the formal, constitutional, separation of church and state has been upheld in law, the separation between religion and politics has been violated in countless informal ways—from prayers that open sessions of Congress, to chaplains provided by the government for its armed forces.

The fact is that the ruling class has always seen religion as its most potent ally. An open alignment of religious and political power served the kings and princes of Europe until the dawn of the industrial age. During the last one hundred and fifty years of American history, the de jure separation of church and state has served much the same purpose for the corporate elite.

What the constitutional separation did was to mask the de facto use of liberal Protestantism by the white elite to legitimize its own rule, as Gayraud Wilmore explains in another contribution to this volume. If religion and politics are seen to be separate, then prophetic religious ethical standards—which in the Bible were as often applied to ruling authorities and nations as to individuals—could not be applied to affairs of state or transactions of the market. Liberal religion had only to do with personal choices, sexual behavior, the state of one's soul. Thus whatever presidents or corporations did internationally, or whatever domestic political decisions were made by senators or congressmen, were according to the dictates of realpolitik or the demands of the market rather than of conscience or religion.

Religion, however, could provide inspiration to individual politicians as they gathered to make laws, or give solace to grieving widows at state-sponsored military ceremonies; and religion could bless everything the state did in the name of the people (hence the words "In God We Trust" on our coins), but it could never criticize those decisions.

Both secular and religious leftists have tended to accept the liberal definition of religion and politics as separate and unmixed spheres. Thus secular leftists have viewed religion as a kind of diversion or drain on political consciousness—an "opiate"—while religious radicals engage in moral suasion and symbolic acts of resistance without expecting to challenge the real levers of power. In their acceptance of these liberal assumptions about the relationship between religion and politics, secular leftists have fallen into the trap of identifying narrow economic or "class" interests as the lever of political change. Ironically, such reductionism is a mirror image of the ruling class's own assumptions about human motivation, which it calls "self-interest." Religious radicals, too, have accepted this assumption. They have acted as if only exemplary individuals (themselves) can be motivated by the higher values of altruism, love of country, the desire for peace, justice, community.

In mixing religion and politics from the perspective of the oppressed and excluded, the Jackson campaign waged the first viable challenge to the politico-religious ideology of the New Right and set the tone and posture for future political organizing. The Jackson campaign was a religious crusade, a mass "people's movement," and a third party campaign waged within the framework of the two-party system. By combining all three forms of activity—which historically had been separated—the campaign stretched traditional definitions of what is politically possible and offered a new paradigm through which to appropriate the American experience.

The Jackson campaign represented a stage in the search for a new consensus of identity—a new guiding myth of what it means to be American. National myths of identity always represent the end product of a political struggle and are usually projected in religious language and symbolism. The Jackson campaign directly challenged the century-long hegemony of the myth that has been central to American politics—that of the great American melting pot, from which there emerged the ideal "American," a self-made (white) male who "pulled himself up by his own bootstraps," and by virtue of hard work achieved material success, thereby demonstrating both his own spiritual salvation and the benefits of American "democracy" and "freedom" to the rest of the world. This self-made man drew on the imagery of the patriarchs of the Old Testament, who were led by God out of "Babylon" (Europe) into "Canaan" (America) to be a "light to the nations" and a "city set upon a hill" for all to marvel at and emulate.[2] President Reagan called upon this imagery in his first inaugural address to the nation in 1980.

Beginning in the late 1950s, a series of events, both in and outside the United States, began to challenge this central mythology. One of the first of these was the rise of national liberation movements in predominantly non-Christian third world countries. Here were people inspired by and asserting in politically effective ways alternative religio-political myths, some drawing on Marxism-Leninism, others upon various forms of socialism indigenous to their own cultures. The rise of these movements had an electrifying impact on the internal colonies of colored peoples in the United States, causing them to begin to value positively their own national histories and cultures, and providing them with a source of authority out of which to critique the dominant American value system.

A second shock to the dominant identity myth were the civil rights and black power movements of the 1960s, both of which undermined the assumption that America had been a melting pot or that it was possible to pull oneself up by one's own bootstraps. These movements asserted the positive value of ethnic particularity, and introduced the notion of collective responsibility for past sins and collective (as opposed to bootstrap) salvation.[3] The black movements of the 1960s led to the development of a series of new lenses through which to view the American experience—lenses that looked at the society "from the bottom up."

In the civil rights movement, for example, redemptive suffering in the service of a whole people—as opposed to rugged individualism in the service of personal gain—became the hallmark of true patriotism. Through the tongues and pens of black Christian theologians, the Exodus story from Genesis became the still unfinished story of a suffering and enslaved people, rather than the self-righteous justification for conquest and empire which it had become as a result of the Puritan experience. In another part of the Afro-American world—in the slums of large northern industrial centers—Islamic nationalism and collective economic self-determination was proving a more effective inducement to self-discipline and material achievement than the Puritan-originated bootstrap theology.

Following the civil rights and black power movements came the women's movement, with its systemic critique of patriarchy; the Native American movement, with its indictment of Western culture's instrumental relationship to the natural environment and its challenge to America's right to the land; the Chicano movement, which positively valued *mestizoism* and bi-culturalism; and the disabled movement, which questioned the Social Darwinism implicit in the reigning American myth of identity. In addition, a new Jewish-American movement sought to recover the prophetic elements in its own faith tradition from a Zionism that was increasingly allied with U.S. imperialism and South African fascism.[4]

Still another challenge to the dominant myth came from the predominantly Catholic countries of Latin and Central America, whose revolutions were inspired by a radicalized reading of the

Bible and imbued with an understanding of class struggle consistent with a local appropriation of Marxist social categories. In Latin American Liberation Theology, the "poor" are seen as the privileged inheritors of God's saving message for the world and as the vanguard of revolutionary struggle. This lens which give status to the poor is in direct contradiction to the ideal American portrayed in the dominant myth. Affluent Americans have come to equate their material well-being with spiritual salvation. The reality emerging out of the Latin American experience, however, and echoed by black liberation theologians in the United States, is that it is precisely those groups that the American norms of success consider marginal, unworthy, and even subhuman that are the bearers of history. They, in fact, hold the key to the development of genuine democracy, to the continuation or destruction of life on the planet.

Starting in the late 1960s, and throughout the 1970s, a series of national and international conferences brought together activists and grass-roots intellectuals from each of the movements from which challenges to the dominant American myth had been emerging.[5] In varying combinations, they began learning from each other, which meant recognizing the cultural, natural, or class biases inherent in their own particular perspectives, recognizing commonalities, and sensing themselves as a collective moral and political force.

From the early 1980s through 1983 the interaction among these groups remained chiefly on the level of dialogue and theory. Though important temporary coalitions emerged which attempted to affect national and international politics (such as the June 12 disarmament rally in 1982, and the 1983 March on Washington), there was as yet no concrete political project that could unite all of the intellectuals, with their constituencies, in a mass expression of the new politico-religious worldview that was emerging from these discussions.

The 1983 Mel King and Harold Washington mayoral campaigns, in Boston and Chicago respectively, were the first tests, on a local level, of the emerging political concept of the Rainbow Coalition. Building on these two campaigns, the Jackson candidacy became the first national political project to test the new national myth of identity.

In the remainder of this essay I want to look at the various elements that constituted the "message" of the Rainbow Coalition and the ways it has challenged both right wing and liberal mainstream assumptions about both religion and politics.

Politics as the Arena of Religious Longing

> Passion: Extreme compelling emotion of burning intensity; great anger, fury, hate, grief, love, fear, joy. To travel with Jesse Jackson is to witness the sudden awakening of the locked out.
>
> —Myra MacPherson,
> *Washington Post,* 21 May 1985

> What does exist [today] is a hunger among a significant number of Democrats for a candidate with a moral dimension—for a spiritual side to politics. . . . This yearning for the spiritual side of politics, this desire to enlist in a crusade, is as old as mankind. Its absence from the Democratic campaign explains why support for the front-runners is soft in the polls.
>
> —Richard Cohen,
> "Jackson's Candidacy Is Feeding the
> Spiritually Malnourished,"
> *Washington Post,* 25 January 1984

Memories from the campaign:

> Ethel, in her late sixties, is a twelve-hour-a-day volunteer at campaign headquarters in Detroit. "Honey, Jesse Jackson has been chosen by God. I knows it. I had a vision last night. I was layin in my bed with my face to the wall. And all of a sudden I had a feelin to turn around. And there he was—God's hand was on Jesse, sayin, "This here's your next president." Yes, honey, this is the year of religion. God callin us back away from all them drugs, that killing. Mondale, Hart—they all got money. Jackson starts down here, but he's comin up. Those other guys, you watch, like Mondale. He goes up, then he comes down. Hart the same.

> A young white minister beams out at his "congregation." He remarks inwardly that the church is fuller than he's ever seen it, even on Easter Sunday. There is no standing room in the back; extra chairs have been brought in to fill the spaces between the front pews and the chancel rail. He has hooked up a loudspeaker to carry the service into the church's gym which is also packed with people. On his way in he passed hundreds of people lined up and down the quiet suburban street in northern Philadelphia. In the chancel he has gathered a rainbow of speakers—Black, Latino, Asian, white. A rainbow of children is there to present flowers to the candidate when he arrives. The young minister begins his sermon: "Can whites build rainbows?"

> They have been waiting for four hours, singing songs and practicing chants. Their church is the last stop on an itinerary that has included six churches, two major television appearances, and a stop-off at an

abandoned housing site. The church is packed from the choir loft to the back of the balcony. Sweat-drenched faces are lifted expectantly. They are young, elderly, and in between. There are mothers with babies in their arms, exultant teenagers. He appears. The crowd roars to its feet: "Win, Jesse, win! Win, Jesse, win!" Two minutes. Five minutes. The thunder is deafening. Hands clap, arms swing and sway in ecstasy. "Praise God!" "Hosannah!" "Let the crowd say, 'Amen.'" A voice from the choir loft begins . . . "Precious Lord, take my hand . . ."

It is the worst blizzard of the season. The streets are filled with about six inches of slush. A freezing rain drives everything indoors. New York's streets are uncharacteristically abandoned. At 8:30 in the morning three hundred and fifty "peace activists" from all over the city have gathered in St. John's Cathedral House to hear Jesse Jackson speak the truth on Central America. They were notified two days before of the event.

The coordinator of volunteers confesses that she has been chronically ill for several years. "But since working on this campaign, I've felt great. Used to be that I couldn't be up for more than half an hour at a time. It's like a miracle."

A young white construction worker nervously confesses that this is the first time he's ever worked for a political candidate. Trembling with emotion and shyness he explains why: "Respect. Dignity. That's why. This god-damn country doesn't give you any respect. All they want to do is use you. I like Jesse Jackson. He talks about respect."

There is no doubt that something extraordinary was going on in the Jackson campaign. The crowds everywhere—even in white New Hampshire—were large, ecstatic, and remarkably patient. People threw themselves into working for the Jackson candidacy with an energy and a passion unequaled except for the civil rights movement. The atmosphere of expectation that the above notes and observations reveal might be compared to Old Testament accounts of the longing for the Messiah, the frenzy with which Jackson was greeted to the palms and hosannas that greeted Jesus of Nazareth as he rode into Jerusalem. The accounts of conversions, of healing, of messages through dreams which abounded throughout the campaign belong more properly to the phenomenology of religion than to American politics.

This longing has no place in traditional American political discourse. There is no language in mainstream or right-wing America—or even in the left—to describe it, because Americans are thought to have achieved all that there is to achieve. We are said to enjoy "democracy," "freedom," and the benefits of the American system. This assumption, and the protection of these fruits, were the basis of Ronald Reagan's campaign.

Yet at least 3.4 million Americans (including 735,000 whites) were not satisfied with the status quo, and in voting for Jackson they were expressing their desire for things that cannot be quantified and measured in traditional terms. Indeed, what they were expressing a longing for could not be delivered even by this political campaign. Knowing that the candidate they had chosen to work and vote for could not deliver jobs, or housing, or a tax reduction, or even peace, they nevertheless affirmed their faith in the things of the spirit that the campaign could, and indeed did, affirm: love, compassion toward human suffering, dignity, respect, solidarity, community, justice, and a desire to end the spiral of violence both at home and abroad.

The sociological characteristics of those who responded to the Jackson campaign's appeal, and who can be expected to be moved by the developing politics of the Rainbow Coalition, do not fit into established categories of analysis—one could not predict, purely on the basis of their relationship to the means of production, which groups would be moved by the Jackson campaign's message.

The bulk of the support, of course, came from the black community's working class—though the reality of that term differs considerably from traditional Marxist definitions of class. The black working class consists of many occupational sectors that have been thought of as "middle class" or "professional" or "managerial" in conventional terms, or, in Marxist terms, as petty bourgeois. These include civil servants, schoolteachers, lower level managers of fast food chains and supermarkets, owners of small stores, nurses, and secretaries. The black working class also includes that great and growing body of nonunionized service workers, sales clerks, and financial sector employees, as well as those employed in the unionized industrial sector. It was this black working class that provided the organized troops for the campaign. Continuing racial discrimination and memory dispose the black working class, and even the more affluent elements in the black community, to a far more progressive consciousness than their white class counterparts. As Manning Marable has pointed out, "Each member of the black majority is a prisoner, and shares the marks of oppression upon his/her shoulders. . . .Acceptance of bourgeois illusions provides no temporal salvation; the crushing blows of the workplace, the police, and the racists form a chorus which proclaims to the black majority: *you are not human beings.*"[6] Even members of the black bourgeoisie belong to churches located in the ghettoes, and black politicians must appeal to a constituency that is increasingly impoverished, if not one job away from poverty. Thus the black community, which voted 85 percent for Jackson, consists of a cross-class spectrum defined by a common experience of racial oppression and responding to a call for dignity and respect.

The Jackson campaign also sought to appeal, with some success, to other groups that define themselves on the basis of their racial or other exclusion from American institutions, though in some instances sections of these groups have attained what we think of as middle-class economic status. These include Latinos, Native Americans, Arab-Americans, Asian-Americans, lesbians and gays, women, and disabled people. Among them were the very marginalized, living on Indian reservations in the Southwest, as well as wealthy Arab and Asian businessmen, some of whom had been registered as Republicans.

Other predominantly white groups responded to the Jackson campaign out of the recognition of their declining class position: white mid-Western farmers who were losing their land, displaced white industrial workers. Still others responded out of the dawning recognition that the American system was not working for them: working- and middle-class families who were being destroyed by toxic wastes, for instance,[7] and other environmentalists.

Finally, white peace activists and religious leaders, as well as an assorted group of other white leftists, responded not primarily out of economic class interest (most are members of the middle class) but out of the recognition that their ideas and values are violated by the American political system. There is a "peace culture" or an "environmentalist culture," located primarily in the white middle class, which responds to political stimuli on the basis of shared ideals and values, much of it drawn from a religious upbringing. This grouping perceives itself to be "locked out" of the centers of power and decision-making, and therefore responds to appeals for greater participation and democracy, as well as for an end to war and degradation of the environment.

Out of all of these groups emerges a demand for conversion of both the American political economy and the American spirit, which have become corrupted by greed, power, and the denial of the darker side of its own history. Jackson responded to this demand with language that was part of his experience as a black preacher. Interestingly, it was part of the experience of the American public as well, because of the historic intertwining of religion and politics in American culture. Although he used modern termi-

nology, Jackson's message was a broad translation of certain endur-
ing biblical themes.

Good News to the Poor

> The Spirit of the Lord is upon me,
> because he has anointed me to preach good news to
>   the poor.
> He has sent me to proclaim release to the captives
> and recovering of sight to the blind,
> to set at liberty those who are oppressed,
> to proclaim the acceptable year of the Lord.
> —Luke 4: 18–19

> My commitment as a presidential candidate is to focus
> on and lift those boats stuck on the bottom full of
> unpolished pearls. For if the boats on the bottom rise,
> all boats above will rise—my views in this regard are
> the exact opposite of the "trickle down" views of Presi-
> dent Reagan. The way I propose to do this is to build
> a new functional "Rainbow Coalition of the Rejected"
> spanning lines of color, sex, age, religion, race, re-
> gion, and national origin.
> —Jesse Jackson, *Philosophy*

> Our mission is to lift up the poor, deliver the needy,
> to see justice done in our land. There is great wealth
> in the hills of West Virginia. The people should share
> in it.
> —Jesse Jackson,
> speech in Charleston, West Virginia

To provide hope for those at the bottom, to energize the locked
out, the disenfranchised, the discriminated against, to build a
movement that utilizes the energy and abilities of those who have
the most to gain from fundamental social change may involve the
use of messages, of symbols, and of metaphors more akin to those
of religion than of traditional party or even left and movement
politics. There is a line that is heard frequently in both: organize
people on the basis of their economic self-interest. The Jackson
campaign and the Rainbow Coalition directly contradict that standard line. Jesus understood that as well. He offered the people not
power and wealth, but dignity, respect, the personal power to
overcome internalized oppression, and, most of all, hope; and
according to the Bible the locked out and disenfranchised followed
him. Christians have tended to overlook the political power that

was inherent in the "Jesus movement." But the ruling authorities understood it, and had its leader falsely accused and then killed. The Democratic Party has attempted to kill the vision and the momentum begun by the Jackson campaign by politically isolating every national leader that was associated with it, reneging on agreements made, framing and indicting local organizers in areas where the potential for building on the campaign is the greatest, and attempting to rewrite history by trivializing the place of the Jackson campaign in American history.[8]

The Politics of Affirmation

> As he drew near to Jericho, a blind man was sitting by the roadside begging; and hearing a multitude going by, he inquired what this meant. They told him, "Jesus of Nazareth is passing by." And he cried, "Jesus, Son of David, have mercy on me!" And those who were in front rebuked him, telling him to be silent; but he cried out all the more. . . .And Jesus stopped, and commanded him to be brought to him; and when he came near, he asked him, "What do you want me to do for you?" He said, "Lord, let me receive my sight." And Jesus said to him, "Receive your sight; your faith has made you well."
>
> —Luke 18:35–42

"Repeat after me: 'I am somebody!' " "I AM SOMEBODY! I AM SOMEBODY!" the crowd shouted. Jackson was speaking to a group of physically and mentally disabled people in a sheltered workshop in Manchester, New Hampshire. Half-blind, in wheelchairs, cerebral palsied, retarded, their incantation of this familiar chant, which I had until then considered gimmicky and manipulative, suddenly took on a new meaning for me. Repeated over and over again, like a mantra, it drove out the reality of their physical and mental limitations, their pariah status in a society that idolizes youth and good looks. "I AM SOMEBODY" connected them with another source of respect and dignity not to be found in the social or political institutions by which they had been defined, labeled, and segregated. It was similar to Jesus saying to the blind, the leper, the demoniac, and the outcast: "Your faith has made you well."

The psychic scars left by centuries of racism and class exploitation are harder for an outsider to see but just as debilitating, and those who carry them are in need of affirmation as well. Everywhere the Jackson campaign went, it brought a message of affirmation to populations and individuals who had been locked out, overlooked, and ill-used by the American political/economic system. Simply by bringing the presidental campaign into the urban slums, the homes of working and unemployed people, onto Indian reservations, into the nation's Chinatowns and Muslim mosques (where no other presidential candidate had ever been), the campaign was affirming in a profoundly important way the basic humanity and dignity of the people who inhabit these places. It was also affirming the particularities of the ways in which they see the world, the histories out of which they came, and the issues and concerns that were uppermost in their communities. This approach contrasts with that of both the right and often of the Marxist-Leninist left, which demand conformity to a particular religious or political line. It also contrasts with traditional party approaches to political mobilizing, which tend to seek the lowest common denominator around which to bring people together.

The Politics of Diversity Within Unity

> There is neither Jew nor Greek, there is neither slave nor free, there is neither male nor female; for you are all one in Christ Jesus.
>
> —Galatians 3:28

> Most people in the world are black, brown, yellow, red, poor, non-Christian, and don't speak English. We must open our eyes and see the real world.
>
> —Jesse Jackson

Chauvinism and ethnocentricity have plagued both religious and political systems for centuries. In the name of universal values and truths, religions and political empires have raped, looted, and destroyed whole peoples. The acknowledgment of racial, sexual, and ethnic diversity and the affirmation of each group in the rainbow was a central message of the Jackson compaign and is at the heart of the concept of building a Rainbow Coalition. To acknowledge diversity is to enable people to see reality more clearly. The U.S. population is now nearly one-quarter nonwhite, yet few of our institutions acknowledge this fact in their daily practices.

But simply acknowledging the fact of ethnic diversity, or mobilizing people on the basis of ethnic identity, will not necessarily move us in a progessive direction. Ethnic consciousness can also be a tool of the right. When the civil rights and black power movements of the 1960s gave legitimacy to the political assertion of national identity, the right moved in to coopt this theme.

In the early 1970s several studies of "white ethnics" were published by people like Daniel Patrick Moynihan, Nathan Glazer, Michael Novak, and Norman Podhoretz, who have since demonstrated their true class allegiances—they are the leading theoreticians of Neoconservatism. These studies purported to discover the lingering effects of ethnic bigotry directed against white ethnic groups by WASP and Jewish intellectuals. Michael Novak's *The Rise of the Unmeltable Ethnics* predicted a new form of "ethnic politics" in which each ethnic group would place its "costs and needs" on a "frank trading basis" and barter with others for pieces of the American pie.[9] While white ethnics were credited with concern for "family," "neighborhood," and "religious values," appeals to universal interests or "higher morality" were held by Novak not to be "ethnic traits," and were anyway useless in the political world.[10]

The attention given by the media and academics to these "forgotten white ethnics" obscured the real class divisions which continued to deepen throughout the 1970s and the disproportionate institutional racism suffered by people of color.[11] It laid the ideological foundation for the development of the concept of "reverse discrimination," which has been used as the rationale for dismantling affirmative action programs and civil rights legislation in the 1980s. Moreover, the presumption that only white ethnics were interested in family neighborhood and religion denied similar aspirations among people of color, and set up poor people ("welfare chiselers"), feminists, and homosexuals as scapegoats in the emerging right-wing politics of family, neighborhood, flag, and religion.

Ethnic diversity is a progressive political theme only when it is accompanied by the acknowledgment that racism, sexism, and class exploitation are evils that continue to plague human societies, preventing such diversity from making a positive contribution to the reshaping of civil and political life. Ethnic diversity is not an end in itself, but the means to a more inclusive conception of the entire "human family"—in religious language, it is the tree with many branches, the body with many functions.

Jackson consistently played on the theme of ethnicity to educate his audiences to the lingering wounds of racism, sexism, class exploitation, and imperialism. He stayed in the homes of the poor—elderly blacks, a white West Virginia coalminer, a Mexican-American single mother, a white mid-Western farm family that was losing its farm, Lumbee Indians, a Puerto Rican family living in an inner-city housing project—to call the public's attention to the multicoloredness of socially induced poverty. He traveled to Cuba, Mexico, Nicaragua, Panama, and Syria to call human those whom our government has labeled "enemies." He used ethnicity to call his listeners to a higher human inclusiveness, looking for the themes in each ethnic group's experience through which it could unite in solidarity with others. The following excerpt from a speech he gave to Arab-Americans in Worcester, Massachusetts, exemplifies this approach:

> As you know, the rainbow is the symbol of our campaign. The rainbow, for us, represents the coming together of many groups, discovering together that what unites us is more important than what divides us. . . . I have come to you this morning after having addressed the B'nai B'rith in Framingham and the Emanuel Baptist Church here in Worcester. With each community there was a sharing. We spoke together of the scourges of racism and anti-Semitism. We spoke of the need to forgive and become reconciled to one another.
>
> As I know of the sufferings of blacks, and Jews, I also know of your pain. Anti-Arab sentiments, so prevalent in Western culture, are but another form of anti-Semitism. The dehumanization of Arab people has, I know, brought great suffering. Because of it, the Crusades and centuries of colonialism and oppression were justified. And even today, killings and occupations are legitimated by anti-Arab racism. . . . There is, in the Middle East today, a cycle of pain and dehumanization and violence. Tragically, Arabs and Jews, both victims of others, have today become victims of one another.
>
> Each of us knows our own pain. Sometimes we draw a circle around our pain and see nothing but it.
>
> I come before you, as I came before blacks and Jews earlier today, to invite you to join me in going another way. We should go out from our own circles and see each other's suffering. We should trialogue together, and become reconciled with one another. . . . I have long felt that it is a tragedy to see the lack of talk in the Middle East—but it is even worse to see it here. . . . For all of the Middle East, dialogue and not violence can open the road to peace. We can help to begin that process right here. The peace we establish among ourselves can be exported to the Middle East. Our peace can be as contagious as their war.[12]

And in a speech before a Hispanic audience, Jackson asked: "What do we have in common?" He answered it in this way:

> First, both of us learned about foreign policy in America and got our foreign policy experience in essentially the same way. Blacks were brought to America as slaves against our will, and Hispanics were annexed to America against their will. Slavery, annexation, and eco-

nomic exploitation form our common foreign policy experience and perspective. We view national life from the perspective of the rejected, the downtrodden, the exploited and the colonized.

Secondly, we were enslaved and are rejected and are exploited because of our skin color. Hispanics were annexed and are rejected and exploited because of caste, culture, and language.

Lastly what has benefited one group has benefited the other and together our progress has benefited the nation. Blacks took the initiative to end segregated education in 1954, but blacks, Hispanics, and whites have benefited from multicultural and bi-lingual education. . . . Ceasar Chavez and the farm workers suffered and struggled for worker's rights, but the entire labor movement and the nation benefited.

When the black and Hispanic foundation comes together, everyone above has to adjust. We are not the bottom of this society where things end up. We are the foundation—where everything begins.[13]

That last phrase, for those who know their Bible, has resonances with the scripture found in both the Old and New Testaments, "The very stone which the builders rejected has become the head of the corner" (Mark 12:10 and Psalm 118:22) By using it, Jackson suggests that those who have been rejected by the American political system are those who have the key to its salvation—not because of any intrinsic superiority, but because they see the world and what needs to be done from an entirely different perspective.

Jackson's use of ethnicity stands in sharp contrast to Walter Mondale's evocation of it in his acceptance speech at the Democratic convention. After invoking the image of a multicolored party— "Just look at us: black and white, Asian and Hispanic, native and immigrant, young and old, urban and rural, male and female— from yuppie to lunchpail"—Mondale went on to enumerate the values his small-town parents had taught him to live by, and referred at the same time to his running-mate, Geraldine Ferraro:

> They taught me to work hard; to stand on my own; to play by the rules; to tell the truth; to obey the law; to care for others; to love our country; to cherish our faith. My story isn't unique. For the last few weeks, I've deepened my admiration for someone who shares those values. Her immigrant father loved our country. Her widowed mother sacrificed for her family. Her own career is an American classic: Doing your work. Earning your way. Paying your dues. Rising on merit.

It was the same old Horatio Alger story warmed over for modern consumption—except this time one of the heroes was a woman.

The Politics of Memory and Truth

It was the Jackson campaign—which emerged from the under-side of American history, appropriating the liberation theology of the black church—which consistently pointed out that the rules were rigged, the law was unjust, presidents lie, no one rises entirely on merit, and sacrifices do not always end in success stories. It was Jackson, the "country preacher," who exposed Reagan's hypo-critical use of religion, and named the real terrorists:

> Grown men and women used the fact that there has been an election in El Salvador to justify funding further terror there. . . . An election in a country where you can be fined $20 for not voting; a country where many people do not see $20 a month. An election, in a country where any evidence that you have not voted is regarded as a direct show of sympathy with the guerrilla forces. An election, in a country where those *suspected* of sympathizing with guerrilla forces are shot at road blocks and "disappear" when they cross the street, much less than when they apply for a job or travel.[14]

It was the Jackson campaign which continually recalled that other American dream, the one that got buried under false history over and over again:

> Many of the leaders of the antiwar movement came from this state [Jackson was talking to the Wisconsin state legislature] in the 1960s. They had a dream—of a nation that would not demonstrate its power in the world by bombing and napalming the people of a small third world nation, fighting for self-determination. They had a dream of a nation that would seek peace and justice among the peoples of the world. Their dream lives on.
>
> Great feminist leaders, fighting for the right to vote, fighting for a decent wage, fighting for the rights of women to raise their children in safety and security, fighting for a dream of equality between men and women. Their dream lives on.
>
> The oldest struggle of all. The fight of the great Indian nations for justice for their people, for ancient treaties to be honored, for the land, its waters, and its people to be treated with respect. The Amer-ican Indians were the first great environmentalists. Their dream—their vision—of men and women living in harmony with nature becomes more critical to our future as a nation every day.[15]

The Politics of Practical Utopia

It was this representative of the locked-out who called upon his audiences to move together to higher moral ground, who proposed policies that would move the world toward justice, peace, and equality:

> My first act as president and commander-in-chief of the armed forces will be to bring all combat troops and advisers home from Lebanon, Honduras, and El Salvador, and cease the illegal and immoral attempt to overthrow the government of Nicaragua. America must return to being a force for peace, for democracy, for human decency. A beacon of hope, not a helicopter gunship of despair.[16]

> Not one more U.S. corporation should be licensed to do business with South Africa, and businesses there must be given a timetable to get out. Choosing dollars over dignity not only in South Africa, but in El Salvador, Chile, the Philippines, and elsewhere is leading us as a nation down the road to moral suicide.[17]

Speaking to unemployed steelworkers in the Mahoning Valley, Jackson proposed national disaster relief for the region, a National Steel Authority that would set up local authorities in depressed areas to maintain facilities that were being abandoned and to facilitate new ownership that would preserve the jobs and the health of the community, and a 20 percent cut in the military budget, to be used for developing jobs in housing, transportation, and human services. To the Navajo and Hopi in Arizona, Jackson pledged to abolish the Bureau of Indian Affairs, to create a new cabinet-level agency to promote and protect the interests of the Indian people, and to develop a system of direct block grant funding to be administered by the tribal governments as each tribe best determined. To hard-pressed mid-Western farmers, Jackson proposed a program of 90 percent of parity, an immediate moratorium on farm and home foreclosures, emergency loans, and long-term renegotiation of the farm debt. Speaking before an Asian audience, he called for reparations for Japanese-Americans and Aleuts who were interned during World War II.

These and other policies proposed by the campaign did not grow out of Jackson's head but were the result of the campaign's commitment to listen to and learn from the movements for peace and justice that exist in the margins and on the periphery of this country and around the world. That commitment to see things from the bottom up did not emerge from a full-fledged Marxist analysis of our condition, but from a spiritual commitment and a life-stance.

It was the theology that has grown, over the years, out of the Afro-American slave community which enabled the Jackson campaign to cut through the varied ways in which race, sex, and ethnicity have been used to divide, distort, and impede very pro-gressive political movement in this country. The black church, which nurtured Jesse Jackson and many of the campaign's key strategists, "has always been that institution that has had its doors open, has practiced a reach-out policy to care for people who suffer, to be a witness in the world," explains the Rev. Ben Chavis, then deputy director of the United Church of Christ's Commission for Racial Justice.[18]

Mondale was defeated in November 1984 because he offered no compelling vision, no new politics that could speak to the despair gripping millions of poor, working-class, lower middle class, and progressive middle-class people. To blame the Mondale defeat on a white male backlash supposedly created by blacks and women—as Democratic Party leaders have been doing ever since—reflects the cynical and bankrupt political and moral vision of the white liberal establishment. It is a vacuity which can only lead to the emergence of a more sinister worldview, a more brutal and fascistic politics—the vision and politics we now see emerging from the political and religious right. This is a politics in which MX missiles are "peace-keepers" and ex-Somocistas are "freedom fighters" (equivalent to our Founding Fathers), in which Nazis and their victims are morally equated, and in which Armageddon is anticipated as the purifying of the world.

The Rainbow Coalition, emerging from the political practice of the most oppressed sectors of American society, informed by the deepest and most universal tenets in all of our religious traditions, using a language that illumines, inspires, and unites, is the only viable antidote to the right—religious or political.

Notes

1. A much more detailed account of the campaign and its implications for the future can be found in Sheila D. Collins, *From Melting Pot to Rainbow Coalition: The Future of Race and Ethnicity in American Politics* (New York: Monthly Review Press, forthcoming in 1986).
2. For descriptions of the development of the dominant American myth see Charles A. and Mary R. Beard, *The American Spirit* (New York: Collier Books, 1962); Conrad Cherry, *God's New Israel: Religious Inter-pretations of American Destiny* (New York: Prentice-Hall, 1971); Richard Slotkin, *The Fatal Environment: The Myth of the Frontier in the Age of Industrialization, 1800–1890* (New York: Atheneum, 1985); William

Appleman Williams, *Empire as a Way of Life* (New York: Oxford University Press, 1980).
3. Though the notion of collective responsibility for the sins of slavery was raised by black abolitionists in the 1840s, the concept did not achieve recognition outside the black community until the civil rights movement of 1960s. The Black Economic Development Conference made the notion explicit in the form of "reparations." Native Americans have called for the restoration of lands taken from them by treaty violations; and Japanese-Americans have called for reparations for their internment during World War II.
4. The civil rights and black power movements of the 1960s stimulated among a number of progressive Jewish students an interest in their own ethnic and religious roots. These young people began forming national organizations to explore their ethnic heritage in the context of a more progessive political and theological agenda than they saw their elders pursuing. The first of these groups was the North American Jewish Students' Network, killed when it was taken over by the old Zionist establishment. In 1973 Breira was established to focus on alternative policies in the Middle East. Intense persecution by pro-Israel Zionists killed this organization after about three years. It was supplanted by New Jewish Agenda, which now has about five thousand members nationwide.
5. Afro-American Christians, Muslims, and Marxists came together through several groupings: the National Black Economic Development Conference; the National Black Independent Political Party; the Black Organizers' Conference; the National Black United Front. Theology in the Americas, begun by an exiled Chilean priest, brought together, over a ten-year period, Christians and traditional Native Americans from the Latin American liberation movements, the Afro-American Christian community, and the Chicano, labor, women's, Puerto Rican independence, and Asian-Pacific people's movements. The Ecumenical Dialogue of Third World Theologians exposed progressive North American Christians to the religiously based revolutionary ferment taking place thoughout the third world. The Religious Left Network of the Democratic Socialists of America brought together progressive Christians and Jews; and Clergy and Laity Concerned, a national peace and justice action network, brought together progressive Christians and Jews, and is now including Black Muslims as well.
6. Manning Marable, *How Capitalism Underdeveloped Black America* (Boston: South End Press, 1983), pp. 27–28.
7. While Jackson never received more than 9 percent of the white vote in any state for which exit polls are available, there is evidence that where the campaign worked vigorously for white votes (meaning going door to door, seeking personal contact with voters) the campaign was successful. Jackson won the city of Homestead, Pennsylvania, where thousands of steelworkers have lost their jobs. He was enthusiastically

received by farmers all over the mid-West who were losing their farms and homes to foreclosure. In New York, Philadelphia, Los Angeles, and Nashville a majority of the leaders of the white peace movement held press conferences to endorse the campaign.

8. In 1985 the Democratic Party regulars refused to accept the Black Caucus's nomination of Richard Hatcher, who had played a key role in the Jackson campaign, as vice-president of the national Democratic Party, choosing instead Roland Burris, who had not been a part of the Jackson campaign. The party also watered down the caucus system and did away with some of the standing caucuses, thus limiting the leverage of the ethnic blocs that voted for Jackson. The Fairness Commission, which the Jackson campaign had fought for through the process of the Democratic Convention, will not contain any of those who supported the Jackson campaign, even though the party had promised that Jackson supporters would participate. In 1985 eight local Jackson campaign organizers in the Alabama Black Belt, who had won that area for Jackson, were put on trial by the federal government, in collusion with state and local Democratic Party leaders, for voting fraud under the Voting Rights Act, and all but one were acquitted (and that one is appealing his conviction). All of the major civil rights groups view these trials as racially and politically motivated.

9. Michael Novak, *The Rise of the Unmeltable Ethnics* (New York: Macmillan, 1971), p. 285.

10. Ibid., p. 215.

11. Colin Greer, "Remembering Class," in *Divided Society: The Ethnic Experience in America,* ed. Colin Greer (New York: Basic Books, 1974), pp. 3–4, exposes the arguments of Novak et al. as a facade to obscure the fragility of America's egalitarian self-image. What Novak attributes to ethnic bigotry, Greer explains as the continuing effects of class discrimination.

12. Jesse Jackson, "A Call to Trialogue," speech delivered at St. George's Orthodox Cathedral, Worcester, Massachusetts, 4 March 1984.

13. Jesse Jackson, "Converging Interests and a New Direction," speech delivered on 16 April 1984.

14. Jesse Jackson, "The Crisis in Central America," speech delivered at Arizona State University, Phoenix, 12 April 1984.

15. Jesse Jackson, speech to the Wisconsin state legislature, 6 April 1984.

16. Jackson, "A Call to Trialogue."

17. Jesse Jackson, speech delivered in New York City, 18 June 1984.

18. Interview with Ben Chavis, 7 March 1985.

Religion and American Politics: Beyond the Veil

Gayraud S. Wilmore

In the writings of W.E.B. DuBois there is a recurring theme: the veil of color that hangs between black existence and American reality. In some places DuBois says that the world we blacks look out on is "beyond the Veil." In other contexts he says that our own world is "within the Veil." I never understood the full meaning of this metaphor until I reflected back on an experience that for many years I tried to blot out of my memory.

It happened when I was in the army during World War II, traveling by train through the South from Shreveport, Louisiana, to Washington, D.C. As we sped through the night, I sauntered back to the dining car to get something to eat. It was full of white people who gawked, forks poised between mouth and plate. I must have looked sharp in my freshly pressed uniform and T/5 stripes. A stonyfaced black waiter ushered me to a table for one. He then reached up and pulled a curtain completely around me and my table so that I suddenly found myself seated in a little world all my own, behind the veil of a Jim Crow curtain.

Beyond that curtain I could hear the chatter of the voices of my fellow passengers and the clatter of their glass and silverware. But I remember something else. Through the slightly opaque scrim that separated us I could make out the natural gestures and postures of the white people without the distraction of accidental and inconsequential detail. In other words, I saw what really mattered—the essential aspect of the reality beyond that curtain. And when I looked the other way, out of the window at my side, with the curtain as a barrier to the glare of the dining car lights, I could see the dark world outside through which our train was moving—instead of my own reflection.

We've heard a lot lately about religion and politics in America. What I am suggesting is that blacks bring to this discussion what is, perhaps, a unique perspective. It may be described as the privileged disprivilege of an outsider, a kind of perception that both deforms and informs our vision as we stand in the shadows, out of the harsh and glaring reality of the American experience—within the veil.

What do we see? Much of the same world that everyone else sees, but from a different perspective. Most of us vote either Democratic or Republican, like most Americans. But I think we see realities about American politics that others may miss. One example must suffice.

For most of our lives we have heard white Christians say that "religion and politics don't mix." And yet from where we sit they seem to mix very well. American religion and American politics seem to make quite comfortable bedfellows even though they like to pretend that they're not really in the same bed. We have found that when that game is being played somebody is going to get screwed and we are usually that somebody! Why? Because both religion and politics in this country are programmed to maintain the ascendancy of white over black, the middle classes over the underclass, males of all colors over females of all colors.

The institutional church has seemed exceedingly unreliable when it comes to trying to understand the relationship between religion and politics in the United States. During the nineteenth century several major denominations protested that because churches had no business mixing religion with affairs of state they could not decently undertake political agitation against slavery. But many churches changed their minds when they saw a profitable economic and political union going down the drain. Similarly, the same churchpeople who did not want to mix religion and politics over the question of slavery joined forces to organize the Anti-Saloon League under strong church sponsorship and succeeded in getting the 18th Amendment ratified in 1920—no mean political trick for apolitical churches. In the South at the turn of the century, many Holiness Christians were politicized within the Ku Klux Klan. Charles Fox Parham praised the Klan for its "fine work in upholding the American way of life." Other conservative Christians who eschewed partisan politics when the labor unions and the civil rights movement tried to get their churches to cooperate had no problem mixing religion and politics in the postwar Christian Anti-

Communist Crusade and, more recently, the mobilization of the Moral Majority behind the election of Ronald Reagan.

I don't want to oversimplify complex issues, but from where we stand it appears that many white churches are inconsistent about when they may or may not soil their hands in the dirty linen of politics. When a fair economic wind is blowing and politicians are preserving white supremacy, controlling the levers of social power and guaranteeing material security for the middle and upper classes, religion and politics are presumed incompatible and the walls go up between church and state. But when Anglo hegemony is threatened by external forces like communism, or by marginated minorities within the society, like blacks, atheists, and women, then it becomes a holy cause to send church lobbies to Washington and march church members to the polls to vote "for the sake of our Lord and Savior, Jesus Christ." One cannot help being suspicious about the theological seriousness of such self-serving inconsistency.

Now to be sure, the black churches have their own problems. It may be that because they lack squeamishness about political activity (with some notable exceptions, like the former Colored Methodist Episcopal church) some of them have been shamefully used by big city machines. But at least they have never pretended that politics could get along without religion. They have rather assumed that it was their moral responsibility to marshal the votes that would force the powers that be to loose the bonds of the victims of poverty, discrimination, and human injustice of every kind.

Nor have black churches expressed the kind of panic recently observed when white liberal Christians, like Walter Mondale, met ebullient conservative Christians, like Jerry Falwell, going to the polls to take an opposing position on presumably religious grounds. Black folks, after years "behind the veil," take such things in stride. When the 1984 presidential election returns were in and we realized that we had again backed the losing side, the general attitude on the street was: "So what else is new? The struggle continues." For many black churches the bottom line has been not so much winning or losing, but being faithful to what they are convinced is the "right thing to do."

As a matter of fact, most black churches probably have more in common with the white Christian right than some of us like to admit. But on fairness and justice issues they are usually on the side of those who expect government to take greater responsibility for those who are hurting the most in our society. If the white evangelicals will open themselves to the spirit of Jesus in using their new political power to minister to the poor and oppressed, blacks will be the first to welcome them. But if not, Brother Falwell and his cohorts had better be prepared for a fight.

Perhaps the major difference between the white Christian right and the mainline black churches with respect to religious attitudes that influence political choices is what may be called the ambivalence of black Christians about what white conservatives like to call the "traditional values of American life," or the "values of our Christian culture," or "bringing America back to God." Such slogans ring false to people for whom religion, for all its exuberance, is something poor, sinful human beings find comfort in at the foggy bottom of life—where judges deal and preachers steal, presidents tell lies and legislators play shady games behind oak-paneled doors. Somehow black folks have always believed that honest religion has to have a strong stomach for the nitty-gritty world we live in and help people survive by keeping their feet on the ground even when their souls may be rising to Pentecostal heights. For such down-to-earth religiosity the new Christian right slogans sound a bit too precious to be real, and just a mite too hypocritical. Beware of people who want to be more religious than God. Frederick Douglass wrote in 1845: "Were I to be again reduced to the chains of slavery, next to that enslavement, I should regard being the slave of a religious master the greatest calamity that could befall me. For of all slaveholders with whom I have ever met, religious slaveholders are the worst."

In an article in *Soundings* (Winter 1970), William H. Becker of Bucknell compares Jews and blacks in terms of their intense ambivalence that "derives from certain basic affinities within the life and thought of each community." We need to recall these affinities during this period of our estrangement. Becker argues that blacks and Jews share an ambivalence about the basic goodness of secular, democratic, and scientific America; about assimilating with this supposedly enlightened nation; about its Christianity and about the vocation of black or Jewish suffering for its ultimate redemption.

I think Becker is dead on target. When black theologians merge the thought of Martin Luther King, Jr., with that of Malcolm X, that is precisely what we get—a hard-nosed realism about America as a den of thieves slightly moderated by a compassionate hope that by the power of God it might someday become better than it is. That is what I like to call "pragmatic spirituality." Malcolm and Martin were developing it together (although quite independently), complementing one another like yin and yang; weaving a tapestry of tough love, a down-home but surprisingly sophisticated religion that is neither fundamentalist, evangelical, nor liberal, Protestant, Catholic, or Jewish. In a way that we have not yet begun to understand, it is Afro-American, deeply spiritual, and unabashedly political.

What kind of politics is the consequence of this kind of religiosity? I want to suggest that it is something like what we saw in Jesse Jackson last year. Jackson's campaign was visionary without self-delusion, rhetorical without meaninglessness, conflictual but hanging loose. Telling it like it is, risking defeat rather than selling a friend down the river for a principle, yet being willing to go down rather than to cave in on what seems "only the right thing to do"—and bouncing back to try it one more time. Underneath all the glamor and all the contradictions was the apparently inexhaustible patience of the black folk and their faith that God will make a way somehow for the poor and the downtrodden, that "God may not come when we want him to, but he always on time," that all you have to do is trust God and, as Fannie Lou Hamer used to say, "keep on keeping on."

I think that the black politicians who were committed to Mondale during the primaries understood that this peculiar relationship between black religion and politics was what they were up against in the Jackson campaign. They held their peace as much as they could. We are not mad with them. They too were committed to bread-and-butter issues like jobs, housing, health care, better schools, majority rule in South Africa, and cutbacks in defense spending. But the way they read it means that one must work through white-dominated systems because movement-oriented politics cannot produce in the 1980s. But that's not all that must be said.

Many of us who were disappointed with their weak support, if not outright rejection, of Jackson understood where they were coming from, and we have not yet abandoned them—not yet. But the handwriting is on the wall. Black churchpeople mistrust conventional party politics and cigar-smoking, back-slapping politicians. They also know that their preachers are not angels, but they have more confidence in them and in the church when it comes to accountability to the black community. Unless black office-holders make themselves equally accountable they will be thrown out of their jobs.

Note

This article originally appeared in *Christianity & Crisis*, 29 April 1985, and is reprinted with permission. Copyright © 1985 by Christianity & Crisis, 537 West 121 Street, New York, NY 10025.

Notes on the Contributors

Gregory Baum teaches theology and sociology at St. Michael's College in the University of Toronto. He is the editor of *The Ecumenist*, a review designed to foster the social ministry of the churches. He is also a member of the editorial committee of *Concilium*, a progressive Catholic theological review published in seven languages. He has published many books, including a commentary on John Paul II's encyclical on labor, *The Priority of Labor* (1982), and a commentary on the social teaching of the Canadian bishops entitled *Ethics and Economics*.

Phillip Berryman is the author of *The Religious Roots of Rebellion: Christians in Central American Revolutions* (1984) and *Inside Central America* (1985), and is completing a book on liberation theology. His own learning process was stimulated by his years as a Catholic priest in Panama (1965–73) and as American Friends Service Committee Central America representative, living in Guatemala (1976–80). He now works as a writer and translator.

Robert McAfee Brown is Professor Emeritus of Theology and Ethics at the Pacific School of Religion in Berkeley, California. He is the author of numerous books, including *Theology in a New Key: Responding to Liberation Themes* (1978), *Making Peace in a Global Village* (1981), and *Unexpected News: Reading the Bible with Third World Eyes* (1984).

Paul Burks trained as an electrical engineer and worked for General Electric for ten years. He then worked for the American

Friends Service Committee as finance secretary, and for the last six years has been with the Northern California Ecumenical Council as editor of their paper, *Sequoia: The Church at Work.* The paper, which is giving continuing coverage to the sanctuary movement across the United States, can be obtained for $12.00 per year from the Northern California Ecumenical Council, 942 Market Street, Room 707, San Francisco, CA 94102.

Sheila D. Collins has been active in peace and social justice movements for the past twenty years, as an organizer, teacher, writer, and lay theologian. She is the author of *A Different Heaven and Earth: A Feminist Perspective on Religion* (1974), one of the first books on feminist theology. In 1984 she served as field organizer and National Rainbow Coordinator for the Jesse Jackson for President campaign. Her book on the historical implications of that campaign, *From Melting Pot to Rainbow Coalition: The Future of Race in American Politics,* will be published by Monthly Review Press in 1986. She is now on the staff of the National Committee for Independent Political Action.

James H. Cone is the Charles A. Briggs Professor of Systematic Theology at Union Theological Seminary in New York City and the author of many books, including *Black Theology and Black Power* (1969), *A Black Theology of Liberation* (1970), and *For My People.* He is an ordained minister in the African Methodist Episcopal Church and a participant in the Ecumenical Association of Third World Theologians (EATWOT).

Gil Dawes is presently pastor of two small United Methodist churches in Cedar Rapids, Iowa, where he is working to build the same kind of base he describes for Camanche, Iowa, in his article in this volume. One of these two churches has, since late 1984, been a sanctuary church and for the past year has had a Salvadorean refugee in residence. He has written extensively for church and leftist journals, including a number of articles in *The Radical Preacher's Sermon* (1983).

Donald W. Dayton is Professor of Theology and Ethics at Northern Baptist Theological Seminary in Lombard, Illinois, and a member of the Wesleyan church. Much of his research and writing has focused on the history of the social engagement of evangelical and pietistic groups, including *Discovering an Evangelical Heritage* (1976) and *Five Sermons and a Tract by Luther Lee* (1975). He has made a special study of the holiness and pentecostal traditions, and his most recent publication is *Theological Roots of Pentecostalism* (1986).

Marc H. Ellis is an associate professor at the Maryknoll School of Theology, where he directs the Institute for Justice and Peace. He has worked among the poor in New York City, Atlanta, and New Orleans, and has traveled to Europe, Latin America, Asia, and the Middle East. He is the author of *A Year at the Catholic Worker* (1978), *Peter Marin: Prophet in the Twentieth Century* (1981), and *The Struggle to Be Faithful: Meditations in an Age of Holocaust* (1985).

Elizabeth Schüssler Fiorenza's career began in Germany, where she earned advanced degrees in theology from the universities of Würzburg and Münster. She is currently Talbott Professor of New Testament Studies at the Episcopal Divinity School in Cambridge, Massachusetts. Her books include *In Memory of Her: A Feminist Theological Reconstruction of Christian Origins* (1983), *Invitation to the Book of Revelation* (1981), and *Bread Not Stone: The Challenge of Feminist Biblical Interpretation* (1985). She is active in the women's movement in academic and church circles, both in the United States and internationally.

Norman Fong was born in San Francisco's Chinatown, where he now serves as co-pastor of a Presbyterian church and pastor of immigrant/refugee work at Donaldina Cameron House. He is the co-founder of the Chinatown Workers' Center, which was created in response to the harassment of workers in the garment shops, and he directs numerous tutorial and recreational programs for newly arrived youth.

Richard W. Gillett holds a Master of Divinity degree from Harvard University and has been an organizer around economic justice issues for most of his life, working with trade unionists and church congregations affected by economic dislocation and related workplace issues. He now works for the Episcopal Publishing Company in Los Angeles, where he is a contributing editor to *The Witness*.

Norman K. Gottwald is Professor of Biblical Studies at New York Theological Seminary. He is the author of *The Tribes of Yahweh: A Sociology of the Religion of Liberated Israel, 1250–1050 B.C.E.* (1979) and the editor of *The Bible and Liberation: Political and Social Hermeneutics* (1983). He is active in the No Business as Usual movement against government preparations for nuclear war.

Beverly Wildung Harrison is Professor of Christian Ethics at Union Theological Seminary in New York City. She writes and lectures on social ethics, particularly economic justice and issues affecting women's lives. She is past president of the Society of Christian Ethics and the author of *Our Right to Choose: Toward a New Ethic of Abortion* (1983) and a collection of essays, *Making the Connections: Essays in Feminist Social Ethics,* edited by Carol S. Robb (1985).

Joel Kovel is Professor of Psychiatry at the Albert Einstein College of Medicine. His books include *White Racism: A Psychohistory* (1974), *The Complete Guide to Therapy* (1976), *The Age of Desire* (1982), and *Against the State of Nuclear Terror* (1984). His interest in liberation theology derives from an encounter with the struggle between the Catholic hierarchy and base Christian communities in Nicaragua, and he has published a number of articles on the subject. He is currently working on a book about the impact of Liberation Theology on Marxist thought.

Harry Magdoff and **Paul M. Sweezy** are co-editors of *Monthly Review,* an independent socialist magazine founded in 1949, at the height of the Cold War and the beginning of the McCarthy period. **Harry Magdoff** worked for many years in government, both for the War Production Board and the Department of Commerce. He is the author of *The Age of Imperialism* (1969) and *Imperialism: From the Colonial Age to the Present* (1978), and co-author, with Paul M. Sweezy, of *The End of Prosperity* (1977) and *The Deepening Crisis of U.S. Capitalism* (1981). **Paul M. Sweezy** received his Ph.D. from Harvard University, and has taught at Cornell, Stanford, the New School for Social Research, and Yale University, and in 1971 delivered the Marshall Lectures at Cambridge University. He is the author of many books, including *The Theory of Capitalist Development* (1942), *Monopoly Capital* (1966; with Paul A. Baran), and *Cuba: Anatomy of a Revolution* (1960; with Leo Huberman).

Charles W. Rawlings is a Presbyterian minister who works in ecumenical circles on a variety of urban, social, and economic problems. He was the organizer of the Ecumenical Coalition in Youngstown, Ohio, which created one of the first large-scale proposals for worker buyout of a steel mill. He also helped to form the Tri-State Conference on Steel and I/ECON, the Interreligious Economic Crisis Organizing Network. He is currently working on a Ph.D. on the sources of moral legitimation behind economic policies and practice.

Rosemary Radford Ruether is the Georgia Harkness Professor of Applied Theology at Garrett-Evangelical Theological Seminary in Evanston, Illinois, and a member of the graduate faculty of Northwestern University. She is the author of many books and articles on feminism and liberation issues, including *Women-Guides: Texts for Feminist Theology* (1984). She has just completed a work on women's worship communities entitled *Women-Church: Theology and Practice of Women's Liturgical Communities,* to be published in 1986. She is active in the feminist, antiwar, and Central America solidarity movements.

T. Richard Snyder is Dean of Graduate Studies and Professor of Theology and Ethics at New York Theological Seminary. He has recently co-edited (with Lee Cormie) a book entitled *Responses to Oppression,* to be published in 1986. He is a Presbyterian minister who has been involved in urban ministry and theological education in the urban context for over twenty years. He has also lived and traveled in Latin America.

Dorothee Sölle is a leading peace activist in West Germany, and teaches part of the year at Union Theological Seminary in New York City. She has written extensively on theological and political issues, both in German and in English, and among her numerous books are *The Arms Race Kills Even Without War* (1983) and (with Shirley A. Cloyes) *To Work and to Love: A Theology of Creation* (1984).

William K. Tabb is Professor of Economics at Queens College, Professor of Sociology at the Graduate Center, City University of New York, and also teaches in the School for Worker Education. He speaks and consults on issues of global justice and political economy, and has lectured at Maryknoll Seminary, New York Theological Seminary, and Union Theological Seminary in New York City. He has worked with local and national constituency organizations in both the Protestant and Catholic churches. His most recent book is *The Long Default: New York City and the Urban Fiscal Crisis* (1982), published by Monthly Review Press.

Cornel West is Associate Professor of Philosophy of Religion at The Divinity School of Yale University. He is the author of *Prophesy Deliverance! An Afro-American Revolutionary Christianity* (1982), and co-editor of *Theology in the Americas* (1982) and *Post-Analytic Philosophy* (1985). He is on the editorial boards of *Social Text, Boundary 2,* and *Theology Today,* is a contributing editor of *Christianity & Crisis,* and is a member of the national executive committee of the Democratic Socialists of America.

Gayraud S. Wilmore is Dean and Professor of Afro-American Religious Studies at New York Theological Seminary, and has taught social ethics and history at Pittsburgh, Boston, and Colgate Rochester seminaries. He was one of the founders of the Black Theology movement in the 1960s and is presently a member of the executive committee of the Black Theology Project of Theology in the Americas. His best-known work is *Black Religion and Black Radicalism: An Interpretation of the Religious History of Afro-American People* (1983).

Charles Yerkes studied comparative literature at the University of California at Berkeley, theology at Princeton Theological Seminary, and received a Ph.D. in Christian social ethics from Union Theological Seminary in New York City. He served the National Council of Churches for two years in the German Democratic Republic, and has also ministered with street gangs, with young adult dissidents in the 1960s, with high-school dropouts, and in New York City's criminal justice system, as well as for national church boards and in inner-city congregations of the Presbyterian church.